# NONE
# BRAVER

# NONE BRAVER

## U.S. AIR FORCE PARARESCUEMEN
## IN THE WAR ON TERRORISM

# MICHAEL HIRSH

NEW AMERICAN LIBRARY

New American Library
Published by New American Library, a division of
Penguin Group (USA) Inc., 375 Hudson Street,
New York, New York 10014, U.S.A.
Penguin Books Ltd, 80 Strand,
London WC2R 0RL, England
Penguin Books Australia Ltd, 250 Camberwell Road,
Camberwell, Victoria 3124, Australia
Penguin Books Canada Ltd, 10 Alcorn Avenue,
Toronto, Ontario, Canada M4V 3B2
Penguin Books (N.Z.) Ltd, Cnr Rosedale and Airborne Roads,
Albany, Auckland 1310, New Zealand

Penguin Books Ltd, Registered Offices:
80 Strand, London WC2R 0RL, England

First published by New American Library,
a division of Penguin Group (USA) Inc.

First Printing, September 2003
10   9   8   7   6   5   4   3   2   1

Photos courtesy of Michael Hirsh, unless otherwise credited

Map courtesy of Central Intelligence Agency

 REGISTERED TRADEMARK—MARCA REGISTRADA

LIBRARY OF CONGRESS CATALOGING-IN-PUBLICATION DATA

Hirsh, Michael.
    None braver : U.S. Air Force pararescuemen in the War on Terrorism / by Michael Hirsh.
        p.   cm.
    Includes index.
    ISBN 0-451-20983-4
    1. Afghanistan—History—2001–   2. Afghanistan—History, Military—21st century.   3. War
on Terrorism, 2001–   4. United States. Air Force—Search and rescue operations—Afghanistan.
I. Title.

    DS371.4.H57 2003        2003048710

Set in Minion
Designed by Ginger Legato
Printed in the United States of America

For My Children


Bill
Who's always been there for me, and who insists that I shouldn't
worry, because he'll come visit in the home he puts me in.


Jennifer
Every father should have a daughter just like Foof.
Her special smile makes my heart soar.

## ACKNOWLEDGMENTS

While writing *None Braver* has been a solitary endeavor, a project like this could not have happened without encouragement, cooperation, assistance, and occasionally aggravation from a disparate group of people, most of whom profess to like me. Aside from the free autographed copy that many of them demanded in exchange for their input, it's important to me that I include a roll call in the book itself.

The "godfather" of the project is Maj. Mike Paoli, who runs the Air Force National Media Outreach office in New York City. When I called Mike and said I wanted to do a book about PJs in combat, his immediate response was, "When do we start?" Almost a year later, he's still taking my calls and has not once said, "It's you again?" Mike is the man who shouldered the responsibility for making sure that my trip to meet pararescuemen and Combat Search and Rescue (CSAR) crews at their deployed locations in Pakistan, Afghanistan, and Uzbekistan didn't get stuck on double-sided military red tape. I can't thank him enough for his support. Without him, there's no book. But that said, a disclaimer: No assumption should be made that either he or his superiors endorse the contents of *None Braver*.

Two people read the early drafts of each chapter, making sure that I didn't embarrass myself by sending—how shall I put this?—unwieldy prose to my editor. The first is my daughter, Jennifer Weisberger. She has an eye for spotting unnecessary assaults on the language, and takes great pleasure in doing to me what I did to her when she was writing all those college essays. I thank her—and forgive her.

The second ad hoc editor is my friend and colleague Ira J. Furman, a Long Island attorney whose lawyerly mind kept my writing honest, and whose sense of humor made his criticisms simultaneously useful and tolerable. A writer himself, Furman recognizes that no one who types words onto a blank screen enjoys having the folly of his sentences pointed out to him. But who can take umbrage at a comment following a sixty-three-word sentence when it pleads, "Pat—can I buy a period? Please?" It was Ira who called one day and said, "I've got the title for your book. *None Braver.*"

Without the encouragement of my agent, Matt Bialer of Sanford J. Greenburger Associates, and his ability to simultaneously assist his wife, Lenora, with the birth of their first child, Isabel, while negotiating a contract for this book, *None Braver* might never have happened. His assistant, Cheryl Capitani, is solely responsible for risking Matt's reputation as an agent by making sure that he returns phone calls in the same month as they were received, for which I thank her.

My editor at New American Library, Doug Grad, has supported this project beyond my wildest dreams. Although he refused to order a custom-tailored desert camouflage uniform to wear at sales meetings, he did show up at an editorial conference with his bosses wearing the official Jacobabad boonie hat, knowing that doing so violated several national security regulations and could get him in trouble with Colonel Hot Lips. His assistant, Ron Martirano, is to be commended for ignoring his boss's instructions and putting me through whenever I called with a bad case of author angst.

Once again, Kathy Kirkland transcribed hours of interview tapes, and then went the extra mile with significant research on the Web that elaborated on or explained concepts that she discovered in the tapes.

Many people allowed me to prevail upon them for technical advice. They read early drafts to make sure that my own confusion didn't result in factual errors. Air Force Lt. Col. Graham Buschor, a CSAR helicopter pilot with the 106th Rescue Wing at Westhampton Beach, Long Island, who, as a safety officer, has investigated numerous helicopter accidents (and whose own flying skills are detailed in my first book, *Pararescue*), explained the intricacies of high-altitude rotary-winged flight until he was certain I got it right.

Sr.M.Sgt. Bill Sine, a twenty-eight-year pararescueman, took the time to make sure that I not only got the facts straight, but also didn't commit or fall victim to an occasional factual embellishment. Two of the PJs I met in Operation Enduring Freedom (OEF), S.Sgts. Justin "Soup" Campbell and Robert Disney, were quite helpful filling in missing details about several of the missions reported in this book, and did so in a timely fashion by e-mail from the war zone.

I'm grateful to all the pararescuemen, aircrew members, and special-ops types who allowed me into their lives so that I could tell their stories. I especially wish to thank Jackie and Red Cunningham and Theresa Cunningham, who spoke with me at length about Jason Cunningham, son and husband, respectively.

My escort officer on the trip, 2d Lt. Alysia Harvey, was handed a difficult assignment for someone relatively new to the Air Force. She had to strike a balance between doing what it took to get me the access I needed, and maintaining her allegiance to the Air Force's core values, not the least of which, she insisted, is "Integrity First." That had to be a balancing act worthy of the Flying Wallendas. I thank her for her good work, and apologize for ever calling her "the Leash." Her boss, Capt. Jill Whitesell—the public affairs officer at Moody AFB, with the support of the commander of the 347th Rescue Wing, Brig. Gen. John H. Folkerts—worked closely with Mike Paoli to make our trip possible. Without all of their efforts I'd never have been able to board the 71st Rescue Squadron's HC-130 that took us to OEF. I'm also grateful to the pilot of that plane, the commander of the 71st, Lt. Col. Tom Bianco, and to the director of operations of the unit in Jacobabad, Maj. Steve "Cato" Caton, who hooked us up once we arrived in country.

Lt. Col. Vinnie Savino, commanding officer of the 38th Rescue Squadron, and the unit's chief master sergeant, Bob Holler, created an environment into which I was welcomed, as did Lt. Col. Lee dePalo, CO of the 41st RQS, and their acting first sergeant at Kandahar, M.Sgt. Mike Pearce.

My fellow passengers and crew on that deluxe flight from Valdosta to Jacobabad cheerfully put up with dozens of my questions on a daily basis and occasionally let me sleep on a litter or bunk when the floor got too cold. They were Capts. Ted White, Steven "Sponge" Kline, Dave McElwee, and Carrie Worth. Also M.Sgt. Brian Williams, S.Sgts. Dave Smith, James Boylan, and Marshal Todman, as well as SrA Jason Fitzpatrick and A1Cs Richard "Brian" Keith and Sarah Jeffers.

Others who gave freely of their time, providing information, assistance, advice, or moral support, include John Corcoran, Sam Hirsh, Sam Sola, Lt. Col. Bruce Gillman, Lt. Col. Jim Finkle, Adrian "Red" Wecer, Kaki-Kate Lundy, Doug Kearney, Lynn Pierce, Capt. Mariano Wecer, Sr.M.Sgt. Pat

Malone, Capt. Tim "Doc" Ozburn, Lt. Brandon Pollachek, SrA Tan Sirisak, Adam Hirsh, Jodi Epstein, Paul Brownstein, Joel Weisberger, Debbie Patire, Roger Akins, Dan Walsh, Jean-Marc Grazzini, and John Dunagan of Tampa's Eagle Photographics. Retired PJ Robert LaPointe and his pjsinnam.com Web site were invaluable resources for historical information about pararescue.

My son, Bill, who was anxious to get me out of the combat zone even before I got in, handled the task of getting me home in an expeditious manner from Frankfurt, no mean accomplishment considering that the date and time of our arrival from Afghanistan seemed to change by the minute.

At least once in their life, every parent should feel the joy I felt when I cleared customs at Newark's Liberty International Airport and saw both my smiling kids waiting to welcome their dad back home from the war.

Finally, my thanks and my love go to my wife, Karen, who, much to the consternation of our children, didn't object when I said I wanted to go to Afghanistan to write this book. After thirty-five years of marriage, she understands me.

Michael Hirsh
Punta Gorda, FL
April 13, 2002
nonebraver@hirshmedia.us

# CONTENTS

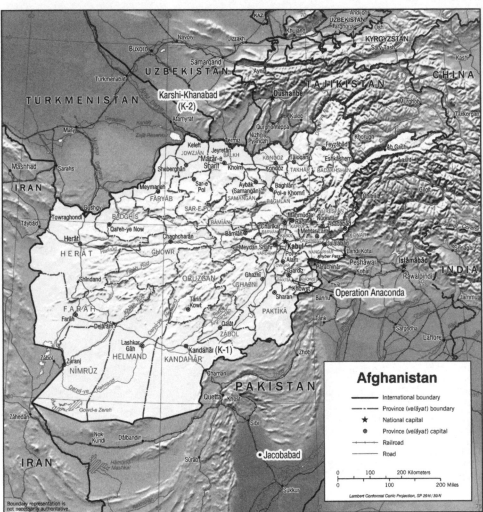

### Afghanistan

- International boundary
- Province (*velāyat*) boundary
- ★ National capital
- ⊛ Province (*velāyat*) capital
- ┼┼┼ Railroad
- ──── Road

| 0 | 100 | 200 Kilometers |
| 0 | 100 | 200 Miles |

*Lambert Conformal Conic Projection, SP 29 N / 39 N*

Base 802867AI (C00362) 6-02

## INTRODUCTION

At 0630 on the morning after Thanksgiving 2002, I was inside a briefing room at the headquarters of the 71st Rescue Squadron at Moody Air Force Base, near Valdosta, Georgia, being told which way I was supposed to run in the event the plane I was about to board crashed on takeoff or landing. Any untoward return from the sky in between those two events would require not running, but swimming, as this particular HC-130 Hercules was headed east, across the Atlantic, ultimately to Operation Enduring Freedom (OEF) in Jacobabad, Pakistan.

I'd dropped off two large duffel bags at Moody a week earlier, and they were already palletized with the rest of the cargo aboard the plane. Now, dragging a carry-on with the clothing I'd need for what would turn out to be a five-day trip, I was watching my fellow passengers say good-bye to their wives and babies. While I would be back home in five weeks, their stay would be as long as three months.

As I was doing my own version of the PJ bag drag out to the plane, I realized that I was fortunate that the Air Force didn't levy charges for excess baggage. In addition to the carry-on, I had a huge rolling backpack filled with cameras, lenses, tape recorders, and enough batteries to keep the Energizer Bunny coming and going for years, plus a sleeping bag, an inflatable mattress,

Author in front of the Ice Cave tent he lived in at Jbad (*Michael Hirsh*)

a CamelBak water supply, and several tubes of peanut butter. While not quite an army of one, I had done my best to be self-sufficient on the trip.

Before being allowed to board the plane, my escort officer, 2d Lt. Alysia Harvey, and I had to undergo a security check. The examination was conducted on the tarmac not far from the plane. "Are you carrying any weapons, handguns, rifles, shotguns, knives, or bayonets?" Nope. "Are you planning to hijack the aircraft?" Nope. I was voluntarily getting on this plane headed to the war zone after more than five months of excruciating negotiations with the military powers that be. Hijack a plane *to* the war? I don't think so. "Do you understand that if you did hijack this plane, the Air Force would be really, really upset?" Absolutely. The last thing I'd want is to have the Air Force really, really upset with me when they needed to be worrying about Osama. With that, we were declared good to go, and climbed aboard a plane that was almost twice as old as everyone on the crew but the pilot, who happened to be the commanding officer of the 71st.

The entire right side of the cargo compartment was filled with baggage belonging to the twenty-three passengers and crew, cartons of morale items donated by various groups in Valdosta, office furniture, and essential war matériel needed by the troops including a foosball table. Eliminating seating on the right side of the plane meant that all the passengers were going to be sitting cheek-to-cheek on the red webbed paratrooper seats, with minimal legroom, for a very long, very uncomfortable flight. Think Southwest Airlines without the frills.

An HC-130 is a four-engine propeller plane that cruises at around three hundred miles per hour. Pakistan is roughly nine thousand miles away. You do the math. Clearly we would be making some stops along the way at locations I'm not permitted to divulge.

I'd been told to dress in layers for the flight, because depending on where I'd be sitting, and what was or wasn't working on the aircraft, the temperature could range from freezing cold to uncomfortably hot. I was layered, from polypropylene long johns through fleece shirts to my Gore-Tex parka, not to mention the Windstopper hat and gloves, which I just mentioned.

I was advised to bring along an air mattress and a sleeping bag, because once we'd taken off it would be okay to claim a chunk of floor space near the back of the plane. I'd also followed instructions about bringing a headlamp if I wanted to read, since the inside of the plane is very dark, and to bring my own food in the event that the crew didn't have enough MREs (meals ready to eat) for all the passengers. My solution was to buy food tubes at a camping store, fill them with peanut butter, and whenever the need arose, squeeze off a shot of Skippy.

Speaking of needs, there is no enclosed lavatory on an HC-130. At the rear of the plane, just beyond the hinge of the loading ramp, is a funnel mounted to the bulkhead, which leads to a tube, which leads outside the plane. If all one needs to do is urinate, and one is a male, the low-tech solution is to climb onto a bar in the sidewall, hang on, and aim well. This trip, after all, is a prelude to combat, and privacy is a luxury. If one happens to be a female, or has a need for more extensive relief, the accommodations are even less accommodating.

The first leg of the journey lasted about eight hours. It was long; it was loud. Even wearing earplugs underneath the headphones for my CD player didn't keep the drone of the engines away. Conversation is virtually impossible; all interpersonal communication is done at a shout, except for those on the crew who are wearing headsets hooked up to the intercom system. In order to kill time, nearly everyone tried to sleep. Perhaps because I was a guest, I was offered the opportunity to stretch out on one of the two crew bunks overhead, which I wasn't shy about accepting. The steel floor would be there another day.

A flight like this gives one a lot of time to think. What was I doing there? Why did I press hard to get the Air Force to embed me with an Air Combat Command unit—something they hadn't yet done in Operation Enduring Freedom—to take me to where I could live with, talk to, and observe the pararescuemen who were flying missions out of Karshi-Khanabad, Uzbekistan; Jacobabad, Pakistan; and Kandahar, Afghanistan?

I'd learned about the PJs when I wrote my first book, *Pararescue—The True Story of an Incredible Rescue at Sea and the Heroes Who Pulled It Off*. I'd been impressed with their credo, "That Others May Live," as it applied to that particular civilian rescue during which they put their lives at risk for complete strangers. Now they were in combat and the credo was that much more significant.

The PJs, and the guys who fly them to where they have to go, define "selfless." While each may have his personal motivation for what he does—don't we all?—the result is that coalition forces who go out on combat operations know that there are Americans standing by who are ready to come get them if bad things happen. Theirs is clearly a story worth telling.

I want to be perfectly clear here, as I was in my letter to the Air Force seeking permission for the trip: Even if it were physically possible, which it isn't in the back of the already crowded Pave Hawk helicopters, I had no intention of going out on combat operations. I'd had my turn doing that as an Army combat correspondent with the 25th Infantry Division at Cu Chi, Vietnam, during most of 1966, where I covered the 1/27th and 2/27th Wolfhounds. Besides, I was writing a book, not reporting for the nightly news. Debriefing the guys when they returned from a mission would yield great stories.

That said, I was prepared for whatever the conditions on the ground turned out to be. I'd brought four large jars of peanut butter, sleeping gear, boots, and clothing for temperatures ranging from zero in the north to one hundred in the south. I'd promised my wife and kids that I wouldn't do anything stupid. My son said it was too late; I'd already broken that promise by making the trip. Or as he put it, "You're Jewish. You're going to Pakistan. Does the name Daniel Pearl ring a bell?"

No amount of explaining could convince them that my plan was to stay with the Air Force, on bases I had access to, access that no other reporter had been given to that point. I was quite clear that the odds of being wounded or killed in combat were minuscule; if something bad were going to happen to me, odds were it would be in an aircraft accident. The chances of that happening were only slightly better than the chance of getting knocked off by a wrong-way senior-citizen driver on the interstate in southwest Florida, where I now live. (I didn't know at the time that the base I'd be going to had a ten-hour bug-out plan in the event it looked like Pakistan and India were going to duke it out with nukes.)

It was on the second leg of the journey that I discovered the joys of stretching out on my air mattress, basking in the warmth generated by the below-floor heaters. For about two hours. Then suddenly I was in the Arctic. The heaters had switched off, and for some unfathomable reason a gale was blowing from front to rear, about a foot above the floor. That's when I knew why I'd been advised not to pack my sleeping bag, but to keep it handy. That day we were in the air almost twelve hours, and I'm firmly convinced that we landed with little more than fumes in the gas tank. The copilot, known by the self-chosen nom de guerre Anita Schpanken, had just switched from flying Air Force VIP Lear jets to the lumbering HC-130, and she bounced the landing. Someone on the intercom said, "Yep, we're down," and the master sergeant seated next to me said, "If she'd bounced it one more time, she could have logged two landings."

We were supposed to go into billeting for the night, and depart bright and early for Jbad, but, in Air Force parlance, "the plane broke." Getting a replacement part took a couple of days, during most of which I was restricted to the base by our not-so-friendly allies, even though they'd already made me pay a hundred bucks for the privilege of entering their country.

Since everyone on our plane knew that this was the last opportunity for a cold beer or a legal drink for some time, no one seemed especially upset by the delay. A few days later, at eight in the morning, we took off, heading east to Afghanistan, then turning south, flying over the war zone, and crossing the border into Pakistan. We were in the midst of a blacked-out tactical approach to Shahbaz Air Base when an unfamiliar, pungent odor permeated the aircraft. The master sergeant seated next to me said, "Smell that? Welcome to Pakistan." At about ten-thirty P.M. local time, we touched down.

We were taken by bus to the headquarters building and given the "Welcome to Jacobabad" briefing. Everyone was cordial, until a tall, slender, mature female in a civilian dress stepped into the room, and was introduced to us as the base mission support commander, Colonel S. (We actually were given her full name, but I've chosen not to use it.) She made it clear that one of her jobs was to monitor water usage on the base, because the Pakistanis were supplying us through a water pipe that she said was no more than two inches in diameter. We were to take "Navy showers. Thirty seconds on. Turn off the water. Wash. Then no more than thirty seconds to rinse off." The colonel seemed smugly pleased when she told us how she'd ordered all the hot water for showers turned off on the entire base because one individual had been timed taking a seventeen-minute shower. My immediate reaction was that she had all the personnel management skills of Hot Lips Houlihan, with none of her charm. No one dared to ask her why 780 people were punished because one person with a stopwatch decided it would be better to snitch than intervene.

After her departure, we were led across the way to the housing supply tent, and got our first pleasant surprise of the trip. The Air Force provided everyone with sheets, a pillow and pillowcase, and a comforter—mine had cute little blue soccer balls on it. I was then assigned to a tent adjacent to the CSAR aircrews. The sign on the door (the tents had real doors because they did a better job of keeping the heat and bugs out) read, *Welcome to the Ice Cave.* It didn't take long to figure out what that meant. With the powerful air-conditioning/heating unit out back, the tent could have done double duty as a meat locker. It was designed for twenty people, but there were only two airmen in it. I had a cot, a homemade table and desk, and shared a small refrigerator. So much for expectations of rugged camping out.

But there were more pleasant surprises to come. Latrines and shower facilities in combat zones often range from nonexistent to primitive (later in the month, at Kandahar, we'd find the latter). Who would've thought that we'd have access to what they called "Cadillac shower units"? These are essentially an RV shell with real flush toilets, sinks with hot and cold running water, mirrors on the walls above them, and individual shower stalls, each one featuring a photo of Colonel Hot Lips with the caption, *She's Watching You.* Okay, so there weren't any photos. Just my imagination working overtime.

It was moments after discovering the high-class bathrooms that I heard a phrase that didn't bode well for one planned aspect of my trip: "Midnight chow is in ten minutes."

A bit of explanation. As you can see from my author photo, I can afford to shed a few pounds. I'd been warned by a couple of journalists who'd been to OEF that I should bring plenty of Imodium, since I would definitely get sick. And a combat surgeon who'd done a tour there suggested bringing antibiotics to cope with the gastrointestinal bugs he said I'd be certain to acquire. Far from finding this news dismaying, I looked on it as a good thing. In Vietnam, I'd come down with what I'm wont to say was dysentery, six weeks running, and lost sixty-five pounds. Preparing for the trip to OEF, I declared that I was going on the "Afghan Diet Plan." By eating only peanut butter, occasional MREs, and being sick, I would come home a slimmer, trimmer me.

But then they brought us to midnight chow. It's when I discovered that to accommodate crews who fly 'round the clock, the Air Force serves four hot meals a day, and at midnight one can get either breakfast or dinner. I love breakfast. Pancakes. Scrambled eggs. Cereal. Bacon. Sausage. Potatoes or grits. And believe it or not, bagels with cream cheese. The Afghan Diet Plan was doomed to failure.

On our first morning at Jbad, as Lieutenant Harvey and I were walking from tent city to the hangar where the CSAR operations center was located, we ran smack into Colonel Hot Lips, this time looking very intimidating in her crisply pressed desert camouflage uniform (DCU) with a cap bearing the eagle insignia of her rank. Without provocation she braced the young lieutenant. "Why didn't we know that you were coming here with a civilian?" she demanded. The LT proffered our official orders, but Hot Lips wasn't interested. The lieutenant informed her that everyone in the Air Force public affairs chain, all the way up to the brigadier general in the Pentagon, knew and supported the trip. She told her that my presence in the AOR (area of responsibility) had been cleared through CENTCOM public affairs headquarters at both Tampa and Bagram, Afghanistan. The paperwork for my trip had passed through more hands than the collection basket at a revival meeting. It didn't seem to matter. Even though the 71st and 38th Expeditionary Rescue Squadrons at Jbad had been informed of and agreed to my stay with them, no one higher up the food chain had notified the management of the base, the 438th Air Expeditionary Wing. And Hot Lips was determined to make the young lieutenant pay for the perceived slight.

Finished, for the moment, with the lieutenant, she turned to me, and with a snarl asked, "What security clearance do you have?"

I responded, "I don't have one."

Hot Lips' eyes burned. "Then how did you get onto this secret base?"

Now I was really annoyed. Her unnecessary nastiness to a defenseless second lieutenant was bad enough; but that question to me deserved nothing more than a Hawkeye-type insouciant response. I spoke it as a question. "The U.S. Air Force flew me here?"

Later in the day, the LT and I went to the headquarters building to see about setting up e-mail accounts. Everybody on the base has one that lets them communicate with the folks back home. The lieutenant's husband, Brian, was anxious to hear from her, and my wife and kids wanted to know that I'd arrived safely. But in life, as in comedy, timing is everything.

Colonel Hot Lips spotted us in the hallway and demanded to know what we were doing. The lieutenant's explanation drew another winning response from Hot Lips. "You don't get anything here unless I say so."

And then she clapped us in irons.

Okay, I exaggerate—but only slightly. It was more like house arrest. She ordered us into the conference room and we had to sit for the next three hours while she purported to contact higher headquarters. You know you're being treated badly when the wing's chief master sergeant drops by and rolls his eyes when told why we're in the penalty box. Finally, with no resolution in sight— my best guess is that the powers that be at CENTCOM in Bagram had more important things to worry about than an indignant bird colonel paper shuffler with, as rumor had it, a star in her eyes—we were released from custody.

Later that same day, we were summoned to the office of the base commander, Col. James Robinson, an Alaska Airlines pilot called up by the Alaska Air National Guard, and then assigned to run Jbad. After our experiences with Hot Lips, his cordiality was a relief. The colonel invited us in to talk about how they could deal with the lack of appropriate paperwork on us, and then get on to helping me accomplish what I came over there to accomplish. From that point on, we never had another unpleasant moment. In fact, after venturing up north to K-2 and spending a few days on that Army-run facility, the LT began referring to our home base as Jacobagood.

Even after my return to the United States, there's been ongoing discussion about the notion that the base at Jacobabad was "secret" and that I should not reveal the American presence there. My response has been based on logic. I know. How silly can I be? But nevertheless, here's what I said.

The fact that American forces were there had been reported in the press, including a *Los Angeles Times* article that spelled out what special-ops units had been there and what they were doing. The roughly two hundred thousand Pakistanis who lived in the city of Jacobabad, many of whom, we were told, would kill us if we were to somehow wander off base, certainly knew we were there. The two hundred or so Pakistanis who worked on the American side of the base, cleaning latrines and doing other menial tasks, knew we were there. The Pakistani base commander, who rumor had it was pocketing more than half the money we were paying the laborers, knew we were there. The Pakistani government, which leased us the base and levied a fee every time one of our aircraft landed, knew we were there. The Al Qaeda sympathizers who had welcomed Americans to Jbad by randomly shooting at arriving aircraft and into the base knew we were there. And two weeks before I got there, the entire Jacksonville Jaguars cheerleading squad had been given the run of the base, including a tour of the supersecret Predator drone operation. When I asked for the same tour, it was denied because I didn't have a security clearance. Or legs like a cheerleader.

The question remained, "From whom are we keeping our presence a secret?"

Months later, I was informally told that it wasn't so much a "secret" as it was "politically sensitive" for the government of Pakistan, which was getting criticized internally for cooperating with the Americans. I understood the problem, and to resolve it, promised that my publisher would not attempt to distribute copies of *None Braver* in Karachi.

During my time with the Air Force, we spent a lot of time with the PJs at Jacobabad, where they fly missions on the HC-130s, and made two trips up to visit the PJs at Kandahar and Karshi-Khanabad, where they fly rescue missions on the HH-60G helicopters. The personal highlight of the trip was on a flight up north, where I got to sit on the open ramp of a Herc at night, watch four PJs do a high-altitude parachute jump to the drop zone at K-2, and then go down to about twelve hundred feet and race across Uzbekistan, Afghanistan, and Tajikistan refueling helicopters. Sitting there (wearing a harness and tether, of course) and looking out through night-vision goggles was a huge rush. Without the NVGs, you see nothing. Put them on and the helicopters seem close enough to reach out and touch.

In mid-December, it looked as though world events might be catching up with us. The LT was told that the plane we were supposed to ride home in early January "may be going in another direction." Making alternative arrangements to get home proved to be almost as complicated as getting to OEF. Getting home directly from Jbad was not possible, so we went up to K-2 to hitch a ride. But after a couple of weather-related false starts there, we caught a Christmas Day ride on a Herc going in the wrong direction, to Kandahar, with a crew that had decorated their cockpit with a two-foot-high tree, tinsel, lights, and Santa hats on top of their helmets. We ended up spending several days with the PJs at Kandahar, or K-1, and early on the night of the twenty-eighth, got a ride on a C-17 headed to points west. After twenty hours of travel time, including two unscheduled stops and a change of planes, we arrived at the U.S.-run Ramstein Air Base in Germany. That's where I parted company with the LT, and headed for Frankfurt International Airport and a commercial flight home to begin writing.

I've gone into detail about my trip to Operation Enduring Freedom because when civilians I meet find out I've been there, they invariably want to know "what it was really like." But there should be no confusion: *None Braver* is not about Michael's Excellent Afghan Adventure. It is about a group of men who have volunteered to undertake in combat a mission that is near the top of the "Most Dangerous" list even in peacetime. As one senior noncom said to me, "Back in the late eighties, I quit counting—because I'd counted twenty friends who had died—not just PJs but people involved in the rescue community. I just quit counting. And that was fourteen years ago."

Why do they do what they do? Most of the younger PJs can't articulate it, and the older ones seem to be long past thinking about it. Early on in their PJ careers, after they get past the notion that they can jump from airplanes, scuba dive, mountain climb, and travel the world, all on Uncle Sam's tab, there is ultimately just a quiet, unspoken acknowledgment that somewhere during the fifteen-month-long training pipeline, they bought into the concept of offering up their own life, if need be, to save another. Clearly they are very special people who possess a selfless dedication to their mission, to their fellow servicemen and -women, and to the United States of America. If there is nobility to be found in war, it can be found with the PJs.

"Perish yourself but rescue your comrade!"

—Field Marshal Alexdandr V. Suvorov (1729–1800)

# THE WORST DAY OF HIS LIFE
## MARCH 5, 2002

It was barely six-thirty in the morning and it was already the worst day of Maj. Vincent Savino's life.

An hour earlier, the Brooklyn-born commander of the Air Force's relatively new, all-PJ 38th Rescue Squadron had reported to the wing commander's office at Moody Air Force Base near Valdosta, Georgia, wearing his dress blue uniform for the first time in months.

The Casualty Assistance Team was already there, ready to brief Savino; Brig. Gen. John H. Folkerts, commanding general of the 347th Rescue Wing; Protestant chaplain (Lt. Col.) Jerry Pitts; and flight surgeon Maj. Mary Brueggemeyer on the protocol for notifying an airman's wife that her husband would not be coming home alive from the war on terrorism.

It was still dark when they left the base on the twenty-minute drive to the apartment complex where the young pararescueman had lived with his family. The general had unexpectedly chosen not only to make the onerous trip with the major, but had also chosen to drive. That was just as well, because Savino couldn't keep his mind from racing. Yesterday morning he'd been down at the headquarters of AFSOC, the Air Force Special Operations Command, at Hurlburt Field, Florida, when word came that a combat controller (CCT) and a pararescueman (PJ) had been killed in Operation Anaconda. By early afternoon, one of his

Lt. Col. Vincent Savino at Arlington National Cemetery (*USAF photo by T.Sgt. Mark D. Smith*)

lieutenants had called from the Rescue Coordination Center in Uzbekistan with word that one of the dead was a PJ from the 38th. Savino immediately returned to Moody to await official word, and General Folkerts had received a confirming call from the commanding general of joint special operations forces at Bagram.

The 38th had been lending pararescuemen to AFSOC since December. The career field has always been undermanned; with a war being fought, that shortage had become acute, and AFSOC was begging, borrowing, and stealing PJs from the Air Force Reserve, the Air National Guard, as well as from active-duty rescue units like the 38th that technically weren't "special tactics" outfits.

Savino recalled that months earlier he'd sat down in the unit's conference room with the PJs chosen to go on the next deployment to Afghanistan. Their wives sat at their sides, listening intently.

"Okay, this is for real," he remembers telling them. "This isn't the Northern Watch or the Southern Watch." Many of his guys had been detailed to units based in Kuwait or at Incirlik Air Base in Turkey, ready to rescue the jet pilots who were patrolling the northern and southern no-fly zones in Iraq. It was stultifying, mind-numbing duty. In a dozen years of standing watch, no pilot had ever gone down and required rescuing.

"This is combat," Savino had lectured. "There's stuff going on right now. Make sure your wills are up-to-date. Make sure we know who to notify if something happens." He knew that when husbands get sent overseas, wives often pack up the kids and go home to their parents or in-laws. He wanted to make sure the unit knew how to find the families if something untoward should happen. Savino wasn't being dramatic; he wasn't being an alarmist. He was merely acknowledging that he knew his men would do their jobs, would uphold their credo, and that the consequences of that level of dedication to duty could be dire.

Even as Savino and the general had been working the phones to try to confirm the reports, wives of unit PJs in Operation Enduring Freedom were calling the base. They'd seen news of the battle on CNN, knew that Americans had died, and wanted to be sure their husbands were still alive. They were told that there was no information available yet. Until the name came through channels, no one was about to tell a wife that her husband was dead. Mistakes happen in combat. Messages get garbled in transmission. It's a mistake Savino wasn't ready to risk. Besides, he was still in a state of personal disbelief. It couldn't be one of his guys. In the past, he had lost men in training accidents and during civilian rescues. Theirs was a dangerous business and risks were routinely accepted. But it never got any easier. The PJ community is a small one where every loss is personal. But this was more so.

He remembered the session he'd had the day before six of his PJs were to leave for Afghanistan. It was just with their wives. "She was sitting right there in that chair and she looked at me and said, 'Everything's going to be okay, right?' And I said, 'They'll be fine. We'll take care of the guys.' And that just kept playing through my mind, y'know, here I am, sitting here telling everybody that everything's going to be all right, and then you got to go back and knock on their door the next morning and tell her, 'Hey, your husband's not coming home.'"

By early evening, they knew unofficially who had been killed. Still, it was not good enough to make a formal notification. General Folkerts's concern was that someone in the unit would hear through the grapevine who had died and, unaware that formal notification had not been made, would with the best of intentions call the widow. By midnight they'd received official word, including details about the circumstances of the young man's death, and had been given authorization to make the notification, but Savino and Folkerts agreed that it would be best not to awaken the young woman now. Both agreed that they'd have to do it very early in the morning. They couldn't risk having the wife wake up and learn about it from CNN.

That's why the phone rang in Dr. Brueggemeyer's home at three in the morning, ordering her to report at 0400, wearing dress blues, to the base per sonnel center for a briefing, and then to go to the commanding general's office. During the phone call, all they told her was that there was a casualty on base. At personnel, she learned a bit more from the chaplain and the mortuary affairs officer. The casualty had occurred in the war overseas, but no details were available about what had actually caused the death.

The doctor was given information about the family of the deceased, his wife and children, and since she had never done this before, was told that the reason for taking a flight surgeon along as part of the notification team was to be ready in the event any urgent situation might arise, such as a complete hysteria-type reaction where sedatives or some type of resuscitation might be needed.

An hour later, when the entire team, including Major Savino, assembled in General Folkerts's office, they double-checked their information about the family, where they lived, how to get there, and most important of all, made sure everybody knew what their role was going to be when they got there. Emotions were to be kept in check; only limited information could be passed along, such as where the airman's body was at that time, when his body would be coming home, where he would be taken.

The mood, as would be expected, was somber. But it was also tense. This was not an everyday occurrence, and everyone wanted to do it right. The general made it clear that he would lead the team, that he would do the talking. He'd made his first casualty notification as a young captain; he'd watched a video the Air Force provided on how to do it, what to say, and, more important, what not to say. But neither experience nor training drains the emotion from a moment like this.

At about 0610 they left in the general's official car, out the main gate, made a left turn onto Bemis Highway for several miles, then made a right turn down a two-lane road past a series of apartment complexes. In the backseat, watching the sun begin to rise on this clear late-winter morning, sat Vinnie Savino, Air Force Academy graduate, special tactics officer, combat control officer, and now a pioneering combat rescue officer in command of his own rescue squadron, embarked on the most painful duty of his career.

Seated next to him, the chaplain quietly voiced a prayer, beseeching the Lord to help this woman and her two young children, and an added plea on their own behalf, that the kids would still be asleep when they arrived at their apartment.

Savino never felt the chill in the still, subfreezing air as he walked with the others from the car, casting a brief backward glance at the second vehicle in this poignant procession, where his own wife, Maria, the wife of the unit's chief master sergeant, as well as the wife of another PJ, waited to take over the job of providing comfort and support once the official notification team departed. In the Air Force, dealing with life and death is a family affair.

As they got out of the car at 0630, the four high-ranking officers in dress blues shocked a young airman who lived upstairs—above the PJ's family—and who was just leaving for work.

Up the concrete walkway they strode, Brigadier General Folkerts in the lead, each of them struggling to find the impossible—words capable of cushioning the blow. How do you tell a thirty-year-old mother of two preschoolers, even one who happens to be a Navy veteran, and is, herself, in the Air Force ROTC program at Valdosta State University, that her husband has the distinction of becoming the first pararescueman to die in combat since Vietnam?

As the general knocked on the apartment door, running through his mind was the thought that his country was truly at war, his men were at war, and he had the prescient notion that this death might just be number one in a series. At that moment, they all knew that the pararescue credo, "That Others May Live," would be tested time and again before the war was won.

# CHAPTER 1

# "HEY, WE GOT COMPANY"
## NOVEMBER 2–3, 2001

If you could ask Genghis Khan, Queen Victoria, or Leonid Brezhnev, they'd all tell you the same thing: Afghanistan is an especially rotten place to fight a war. The climate is inhospitable, the topography brutal, and the indigenous tribes won't run from a good fight.

Just consider the terrain. The southern third of the country is an unforgiving, desertlike plateau. Nomads and the occasional gaggle of Taliban flowing unhampered across the Pakistani border in both directions populate it. In the central two-thirds of the country are the Hindu Kush mountains, a chain nearly a thousand miles long and two hundred miles wide, running from the northeast out of northern Pakistan to the southwest into Iran. The range has more than two dozen peaks above twenty-three thousand feet and alternates between high ridges and deep valleys. That pretty much explains why the entire country, which is about the size of Texas, has only sixteen miles of railroad track and the roads aren't good enough to be considered deplorable. And then there are the millions of land mines strewn across the countryside to think about, a capricious reminder of what's been going on since the late seventies.

Flying over the Hindu Kush in daylight, the mountains appear bare, rocky, and devoid of life—either plant or human, which is why it's a shock to aircrews crossing the Kush at night when they see campfires burning above the

Crews and STS teams of MH-53 helos Razor 03 and Razor 04. Capt. Keith Nicholas is standing, eighth from left; Maj. Peter Forrest is twelfth from left. (*USAF photo*)

ten-thousand-foot level. Living at that altitude is difficult to contemplate; fighting at that altitude is beyond difficult, but routinely contemplated. Altitude sickness can strike even the fittest warrior who is unaccustomed to the elevation, and the only cure is to descend to lower levels.

In the opening of the war, American air support for special operations, both rotary and fixed-wing, flew primarily from Karshi-Khanabad, Uzbekistan, in the north, and from Jacobabad, Pakistan, in the south. It was one of the northern-based helicopter units, flying MH-47 Chinooks, that got the call to evacuate an American special operation forces (SOF) soldier whose high-altitude sickness had apparently advanced to the potentially fatal condition known as High-Altitude Cerebral Edema (HACE).

The onset of HACE usually doesn't occur until the individual has been at high altitude for more than half a day, which is why it wouldn't be expected to affect helicopter crews on relatively short missions. And HACE doesn't strike everyone; some people get it, others don't, irrespective of their physical conditioning.

The symptoms of HACE include loss of coordination, weakness, decreasing levels of consciousness including disorientation, loss of memory, hallucinations, psychotic behavior, and ultimately coma. What happens in HACE is that fluid leaks out of capillaries, resulting in swelling of brain tissue. According to Princeton University's Outdoor Action Center, *immediate* descent of two thousand to four thousand feet is a necessary lifesaving measure, followed by evacuation to a medical facility for proper follow-up treatment.

Very little in Operation Enduring Freedom happens in a communications vacuum. Between SATCOM (satellite communications), assorted radio channels, the classified version of mIRC (Military Internet Relay Chat), CIPRNet (Classified IP Router Network, which is the command and control version of the Internet), and NIPRNet (Nonclassified IP Router Network, the unclassified e-mail system that gives deployed military forces Internet access), it's difficult for the duty officer in any operations center in the theater of operations not to know what's going on.

This is why folks at the Air Force's 20th Special Operations Squadron, based at Jacobabad, were aware of the drama some 350 to 400 miles to the north. They were ready to help when the Army rescue helicopters from the north had to turn back after devoting a couple of hours trying to pierce impenetrable weather in order to reach the soldier.

The word was that it was a life-or-death situation. A special operator with Northern Alliance forces, who were in the middle of the heaviest fighting in

Afghanistan, had developed acute mountain sickness, which over the course of a few days had led to his being diagnosed with HACE. He had now become a burden to his small unit which was actively involved in combat operations. There was also fear that if he wasn't evacuated soon, should he manage to survive the ordeal, he'd suffer permanent brain damage. This was before the fall of Kandahar, before the fall of Kabul, even before the Mazar-i-Sharif bombing incident. There were fewer than a hundred American soldiers in Afghanistan at the time, all of them special-operations types whose principal task was spotting targets for coalition bombers. The Taliban and Al Qaeda still owned the country, except where the Northern Alliance had pockets of control, high up in the mountains.

Capt. Keith Nicholas, a copilot with the 20th, and Maj. Peter Forrest*, a mission commander, say that their analysis indicated they could probably make it coming from the south. The reason the Army helicopter couldn't get through was that the entire northern half of Afghanistan was socked in with fog, rain, or snow, but the victim was actually south of the bad weather. They believed that weather wouldn't be a factor for them, and if it became a factor, they could maneuver around it.

About fifteen minutes after sunset on what would become a bright, moonlit night, they took off as Chalk Lead on a two-ship mission, call signs Razor 03 and Razor 04, in MH-53 Pave Lows, the largest helicopter in the Air Force inventory, and the only model that's outfitted with the most advanced terrain-following, terrain-avoidance radar. ("Chalk" is an identifying term for a load of troops and their transport. "Chalk Lead" would be the helicopter carrying the mission commander and a number of troops.) For flying into the twisting valleys and rising terrain they were going to encounter, it was the perfect aircraft. Just over an hour later they crossed the border into Afghanistan and were setting up to do the first of several aerial refuelings (AR) when their high-tech radar failed. Since the moon was bright and visibility—viz—was "forever," they elected to press on.

Forrest explains that the radar is designed to help them in bad weather

---

*At the insistence of the Air Force Special Operations Command public affairs officer monitoring the interview, and contrary to the wishes of these flyers, pseudonyms are being used for the copilot and mission commander. When the major attempted to provide his full name and was stopped by the PAO and told he must use only his rank and first name, the major said, "Good thing my name isn't Dick." Nothing in the Privacy Act or SOCOM policy later cited by the AFSOC PAO forbids an individual from disclosing his/her full name, and official Air Force policy encourages them to do so.

and low-visibility situations. If the weather and viz weren't going to be a problem, then proceeding without it would be safe. They'd also prepared a backup plan. "We knew Chalk Two had good radar, so if we had any problem along our route, we'd let Two go ahead and take a look into the weather, see how it was."

Clearly, weather problems were not foremost in their minds at this point. They'd spent time on the ground getting intel on where the soldier had to be picked up. What was preeminent at this point was coordination for getting the refuelers in place, getting fast-movers in place should they need fire support, and making sure that when they finally did pick him up that they could take care of him medically. When they were launched, higher headquarters basically told them, "We don't think this guy's gonna make it."

They were also worried about the altitude at which they'd be operating. The Pave Low's manufacturer, Sikorsky Aircraft, says the operating ceiling of the $40 million helicopter is sixteen thousand feet. Listening to the men who fly it talk, one has to presume that the Sikorsky specification writer is the ultimate optimist. With eleven people on board, including a Special Tactics Squadron (STS) team consisting of PJs Jamie Clark and Kenny Curtis, and Combat Controller Jason Brooks, plus all their gear, a pair of miniguns poking out the side windows, plus a .50-caliber machine gun on the ramp, thousands of rounds of ammunition, and enough fuel in the tanks to get it to its next AR, the only way the 53 could get up to sixteen thousand feet would be in the belly of the transport plane that brought it to the war zone. Major Forrest is clear that once they reached the mountains, this mission was flown with no power to spare. "Throughout this whole sortie we were operating at the helo's max capabilities. If you want to say 'the edge of the flight envelope,' we were on it and beyond it."

The second AR took place just prior to the helicopters' beginning their climb into the mountains, and it went perfectly. The artistry here was not so much making the AR work, but deciding how much gas they should be carrying. Forrest says, "You kind of have to do a trade-off: the more gas you put on, the more you weigh; the heavier you are, the less altitude you can get. So you kind of balance it. Before we took off, we worked out what's our minimum fuel, what's our maximum fuel. And by the way, let's take on a few pounds for Mom and the kids. That's the fuel you dump later on when you say, 'Oh, hell, I need to get out of here.' "

As soon as they finished the AR, they started penetrating the mountains, "alone and stupid," as the mission commander puts it, without a Herc tanker playing the role of mother hen. The helicopters can fly low to the ground, hugging the terrain and staying invisible. While a Herc can fly blacked out, it's not as nimble and, as will be demonstrated later in the war, it's less capable of staying out of trouble down in the valleys. When they need gas, they'll pick a meeting point, and the 130 will do a tail chase, catch up and then move ahead of them, and then head back to base to refuel.

By now it's around ten P.M., and the two helicopters are flying at well in excess of ten thousand feet, as close to terrain as practical. They're over a big plateau, a dry lake bed, when they get the first indication that this mission might be more of an adventure than they bargained for. Razor 03's copilot, Capt. Keith Nicholas, says, "This is when we start seeing the first onset of clouds, a scattered deck, and then it becomes pretty much socked in, but we've got about a thousand feet or so between the terrain and the top of the clouds, and it's clear underneath."

The clouds above them blocked the moonlight, making it a bit more of a strain to see wearing their night-vision goggles, but as long as the two helicopters can keep each other in sight, they decided to continue. "We're continuing for a good hour or so, and the cloud deck is creeping down, getting lower, and we're looking at a point where we need to make a turn to get toward the survivor. But the valley where we'd done our route study and are intending to fly through is socked in."

Nicholas was flying the helicopter, and Forrest was sitting on the floor behind the pilots, watching a console with a moving map display and handling radio communications with fire support, tankers, and command and control. On the 53s, the mission commander does all the coordinating; the pilots do the flying. And at this point, they were all worrying.

"I'm flying the helicopter, leading the two-ship in, and I stick my nose into weather, just to see how bad the viz is going to get. Hopefully we'll break out and it shouldn't be too bad. But we weren't lucky enough. Viz really was poor at that point, so we turned around back to where we started in that flat lake bed area."

Fortunately, when they got back to the lake bed, the visibility there was still acceptable, although the cloud deck had dropped down to between three hundred and four hundred feet above terrain. That limited the flying space for the helicopters.

With the pair of helicopters flying no more than one to two rotor diameters apart, they circled around the lake bed area while discussing their options. At that point, the decision was made to give Razor 04 the lead, letting him take the role of pathfinder. Nicholas says, "We'd tuck in close to him if the weather got too bad. Hopefully, we'd have viz on him, and he'd use the systems to get us through this valley and onto the next one, where the survivor was."

Before they tried it, however, they sent Two into the valley to actually fly the route to see how it was. When he came back, the report was good. "The [clouds] are actually pretty thin; we can proceed on."

Pathfinder missions are basic technique for the MH-53. Part of what the helicopter was designed to do is lead other aircraft into areas where their own navigation aids can't take them. They did it in Desert Storm, although leading another 53 into the weather was a unique event.

With Lieutenant Mike flying Razor 04 in the lead, and only about thirty more minutes of flying time to the survivor, the crews are feeling optimistic. All they have to do is go through a few more miles of bad weather, and then if it breaks clear, they get the guy, get out of bad-guy land, and head home. While they don't have direct communication with his special-ops unit, they're getting messages via SATCOM from the Joint Special Operations Air Center (JSOAC), which is in contact with the SOF team, that he's still alive, he's stable, and they're at the LZ waiting for the rescue choppers to come in.

About a mile into the weather, they're two rotor diameters behind Razor 04 when the leading helicopter completely disappeared from sight. Nicholas got a mental image of two pieces of machinery trying to occupy the same space at the same time. "Hey, guys," he says on comm, "I'm breaking off, left turn." His expectation is that the crewmembers scanning out the side windows will watch for terrain and clear him around. Since they'd been on the left side of the lead helo, he put his ship into a left 180-degree turn and went back to where the weather was clear, while Forrest called the other helicopter to say they've lost sight of him and are going back to their hold point.

Hearing that Razor 03 has elected to bail out, Razor 04 now moves to join them in clear airspace, and comes close to crashing. Nicholas recalls that 04 almost crashed during that turn, "because he went completely blind as well. Couldn't see anything. I know 04's VVI—his Vertical Velocity Indicator—had a pretty good sink rate, but he was able to salvage the aircraft and turn it around and recover."

Forrest elaborated on what happened up there, in the dark, in the clouds. "You got a tight valley, so when we called and said, 'Hey, we've got to do a one-eighty,' he has to give us a few seconds to get separation from him, so that he can make his turn and not worry about turning into us. Now, the valley's a little bit narrower there, so he had to make a real tight turn at a real high altitude, and when you do that . . . the helicopter's only got a certain speed, a window it can operate in, and he almost got bit by what will bite us about twenty minutes from this point."

Once both helicopters were back over the plateau, they began flying a "wagon wheel," a large circle with the birds on opposite sides of the wheel. Even there, however, the weather was rapidly deteriorating. The cloud deck was down to two hundred feet and what had been clear air was getting foggy. While flying the wheel, the pilots talk with each other. "Are we going to stay here and orbit and wait the weather out; are we going to land; or are we going to get out of these mountains and go to where the weather is better?"

Major Forrest recalls how difficult a moment that was. "I remember asking, 'Give me some ideas here. What options have we got?' One was 'land here,' one was 'fly here, get out of the weather,' or 'let's go where we know that we're not as exposed to the front as we are here.' And not just the weather front but also the combat front."

But the duty roster said "Mission Commander" next to his name, and it was his job to make the decision. He told his men, "Okay, I can't think of any better option we've got right now except to go land in friendly territory, wait out the weather, and hopefully make a rescue attempt in maybe six more hours, when we think the weather will be clear through [to the area].

"In all honesty, the hardest decision in my life was made at that point, which was, 'I know this guy is life or death, but I've got to leave him in the field. We're talking about our options, and Keith mentioned landing. Well, to do that I'm going to have to dump a bunch of gas, which means I've got no range. That doesn't make sense 'cause now I can't go anywhere. So at that point I made the hardest call I've ever made in my life. 'Abort. We're abort, guys.' In my mind, I'm thinking that I've just, in essence, killed this guy, 'cause I can't rescue him."

The issue is not one of personal bravery, not a matter of willingness to fight the elements. It's a sensible conclusion based on the capabilities of the equipment they've been given to prosecute the mission. Copilot Nicholas says, "The problem with the weather is that we won't be able to see any of the terrain around us, and being power-limited at those extreme altitudes, even with all the training and everything that we have, that helicopter just didn't have enough power to make it over. So if we lost viz on the mountains, it increased our potential for running into terrain, and that's what we did not want to happen."

By this time, in the face of diminishing visibility, 03 and 04 had waited a bit too long to join up and head for safer territory. The problem with orbiting in a wagon wheel is that when you're on opposite sides of the wheel, one ship is flying is one direction and the other is heading the other way. Now, 03 asks the pilot of 04 to take the lead and guide them south, out of the mountains. So 03 breaks out of the circle and attempts to rejoin 04, but they're tail-chasing him from about a mile behind, trying to catch up. It isn't going to happen. They lose sight of him. Forrest recalls the moment. "Our biggest fear is you can't see the mountains but you know they're above you. You don't go into the heavy weather. You've got to stay where you can see the terrain and hope you can push your way through it."

What they do is call the other ship. "Hey, we need you to come back. We need to rejoin up, get tighter with you, and then you lead us out of here."

Unfortunately, while they were heading north into the valley that would take them to the survivor, the bad weather was creeping in behind them. Now, as they head south, they are trapped. Nicholas says, "We're in a little sucker hole, so to speak, a pocket, and all the valleys that leave that area are totally socked in with weather." And they can't climb, and they can't land.

The decision they make is just to stay airborne and let Razor 04 rejoin them, then use that ship as a pathfinder to lead them out, with the hope that the weather to the south was not as impenetrable as it was to the north.

The problem is that Razor 04 now can't find them in the clouds. Nicholas attempted to provide 04 with GPS coordinates, but as he was transmitting, someone in another aircraft keyed in on the same frequency. "The radio call got stepped on, so he didn't get to hear the coordinates. The last words Lieutenant Mike heard from us is, 'Stand by.' "

Not knowing that 04 didn't get the coordinates, the cockpit crew of Razor 03 has moved into survival mode. They're taught to prioritize their tasks when stressed. Aviate. Navigate. Communicate. Forrest explains: "The first thing to do is fly the helicopter. Second thing is to make sure you're flying in the right place you want to go, and the third thing is to talk to somebody."

The pilot, Captain Frank, is now flying the aircraft, the center engineer and the copilot are navigating, and both the copilot and MC are on the radios. Forrest remembers that they're literally flying from valley to valley, ridge to ridge, just trying to keep flying. On the moving map display they spot a valley that looks like it may take them out of trouble, but in order to get to it, they have to go over a small village and two ridgelines.

An MH-53 only three hundred feet above the ground, with clouds immediately overhead reflecting the sound back to earth, can wake up the neighborhood. But whether the locals know they're overhead is not their biggest concern at that moment. Staying in the air is, and they're still pushing the helicopter beyond its limits to accomplish that task.

They pass the village and have enough power to get over the first ridgeline. Right behind it is a second ridge that's a little bit higher. The helicopter doesn't have the muscle to get over it, forcing Frank to turn away from the high terrain.

Forrest says, "What happens is, we've got very few knots of speed to work with. You go too slow, you're going to fall out of the sky. And what happens at this point was, he's got to turn, and you either hit the terrain in front of you or you make the turn. And we're probably only—what?—about seven degrees into the turn, banked, and we literally fall out of the sky at that point. I mean, once we started the turn to avoid the terrain, we departed controlled flight and started about a three-hundred-foot fall, right into the ground."

Why would a turn cause the helicopter to fall from the sky? New York Air National Guard Lt. Col. Graham Buschor has flown military helicopters for years. He's a safety officer who has conducted crash investigations all over the country, and he was the copilot of the HH-60G helicopter that was forced to ditch in the Atlantic in the so-called "perfect storm." Here's his explanation in layman's terms of why Razor 03 crashed—and why it was almost impossible not to in those circumstances and at that altitude.

"He turned to avoid terrain. Turning involves tilting the rotor. When you tilt the rotor you dump some of your lift. You add collective—power—to compensate for the lost lift, but the helicopter has no more power to give, so you start descending. The descent normally increases exponentially, faster and faster.

"The only way to recover from this situation is to get back to level flight and get the helo flying again. This requires altitude, of which he does not have enough."

Buschor uses the analogy of an electric fan blowing directly on your face. If you turn the fan on an angle, the breeze hitting you isn't as strong. In order to make it stronger, you either have to turn it back so it's once again blowing in your face, or you need to increase the power—switch it from low to high. The problems were multiple: He had to make the turn or crash into the mountain; he already had the power set on high. There was no more power. Falling from the sky was, unfortunately, inevitable.

Instinctively, the pilot moves to the next problem: trying to get the helicopter level. Buschor explains, "When crashing, you want to try to crash level, and let the landing gear do what it was designed to do, absorb the impact. The engineers design aircraft to crash in a level attitude. No one wants to crash on their side or upside down, as the likelihood of fire, injury, damage, and death is greater. At such a high altitude, the helicopter is very sluggish to respond because of the thin air. It flies like a pig. What Frank did was level the airframe for impact, and prior to impact you pull the collective up to your armpit and use whatever energy you have left in the rotor to cushion the impact.

"It's every helo pilot's worst nightmare. You've got one chance to get it right. This all happens very, very quickly," notes Buschor. "You have a highly skilled pilot in this situation."

What does a three-hundred-foot fall feel like? "Like an elevator coming down," recalls the copilot, Capt. Keith Nicholas. "But Frank did a fantastic job of leveling the aircraft and pulling the guts out of that bird, getting every last bit of energy he could out of that rotor system to cushion our fall. We were committed, we were going in, but he did a phenomenal job of airmanship."

What the pilot was able to do was take the ship from about sixty degrees of bank angle to almost level by the time they hit the ground. It took somewhere between five and eight seconds to crash, but in that time, Nicholas was able to get off a call. "It's one of those things where you're probably already in the crash or going down; takes your brain a second or two to recognize that. Took me another second, probably, to punch the mike, and then another second to get my Mayday call out before we hit."

The Mayday call didn't include a location; there was no time for that. It was just a last-ditch effort to let whomever was monitoring radios know that they were going down. Because Nicholas was actively working, he didn't have time to contemplate the consequences of what was happening to them. He could only register disbelief, or as he recalls the moment, "Can't believe this is happening, but here we go."

Forrest, on the other hand, could observe what was going on, and had a few moments to plan for impact. "I had enough time to look and to realize, just listening. They're flying, so I'm just shutting up and listening, but once you realize what's going to happen—my idea was to lay as flat as possible, 'cause I'm actually sitting on the floor of the helicopter in the back. My idea is to just lay down and hopefully take the impact."

He was on the floor, about five feet forward of the tail gunner. "One of the things that kind of went through my mind is, when helicopters crash, pieces go all over the place, so I'm going to get as small and as low as I can, so hopefully I don't have pieces going through me."

The last thing he remembers seeing out the ramp is the ridge they just crossed, watching it go to a sixty-degree bank and shouting, "What the hell?" He saw the tail gunner turn around and look, and then they hit.

"And you literally get the elevator ride. You can feel the G kind of give out from underneath you, and you're just waiting for the moment. And I can remember literally watching the tail strike, and then, boom! Everything's kind of getting bounced around from the back end there.

"About two seconds before the crash, I can still remember my thoughts, verbatim: 'Holy shit, I'm about to crash. Holy shit, I am crashing. Holy shit, I'm alive.'"

One thing that kept him alive is that not one of the helicopter's five rotor blades—each one thirty-four feet long—hit the ground. That was due to incredible airmanship on the part of the pilot, since he was able to maintain enough control to level the helo, keeping it upright on impact. The other element that worked to minimize the damage was that even though the cockpit flight engineer's seat broke on impact, Tech Sergeant Abe was able to reach up from the floor to the overhead switches and chop the throttles off, then get the emergency rotor brake on. Otherwise, Nicholas says they would have acted "like a Weed Eater gone crazy." The blades would have hit the ground, and with all the torque from the pair of 4,330-horsepower engines at full power, the helicopter would have flipped and been chewed apart.

Even if the blades hadn't touched, but one wheel had hit first, they would have flipped, and the whole aircraft would have twisted over and torn itself to bits.

Forrest explains, "She has so much torque that the tail twisted a full ninety degrees. When it hit, the back end crushed, the tail had bent forty-five, forty-five, and forty-five if you're looking at it in a three-dimensional axis. It looked like a crushed beer can in the back. Objects were flinging all over the place. I can remember hearing the transmission shaft go under the back, just bumping on the top of the helicopter as it was slowly winding down when Abe shut things down."

Now, each of the eleven men on Razor 03 had come to a rational understanding that he'd survived the impact. There was a lot of yelling and screaming at each other at the time, but that was because most of the crew didn't realize they still had their earplugs in and their helmets on. Forrest says, "My realization was all of a sudden, I think it was the pilot, Frank, yelling at me, saying, 'Take off your helmet, you idiot.'"

Up front, the two pilots, Frank and Captain Nicholas, are both in good shape. Nicholas says, "I guess those crashworthy seats the Air Force invested in worked out pretty well. I'm in good shape up front. Frank's in good shape." All they can see on each other are some relatively minor bumps and bruises.

While the cockpit crew is checking each other and coming to the realization that they're alive, the mission commander has discovered that the tail gunner is missing. One second he sees him—they call him Daisy—on the ramp behind his gun; the next second he was gone. Forrest says, "It's one of those funny things—time stands still. As we're hitting, getting thrown around, the back end of the helicopter went from about six feet high to about a foot high on the back right. I thought Daisy was crushed underneath the tail, 'cause the tail was now resting on his fifty-cal."

After taking mere seconds to realize that he's alive and lucky to be so, the copilot starts trying to make more Mayday calls, but when the generators aren't running, that particular radio doesn't work. He begins shouting at Abe to get his transmitter working on the UHF "guard" frequency—the one that's monitored by all military aircraft in the area for just such an event.

What they have no way of knowing at that moment is that the original Mayday call had been heard, but not by the other helicopter. The fighters they had asked for at the beginning of the sortie, Navy F/A-18 Hornets, were to come on station thirty minutes prior to their landing to pick up the survivor, and then escort them out. The jets had arrived just in time to hear the Mayday.

Nicholas's instructions about the radio are interrupted on the intercom by the pilot, who tells everybody to check in. Quickly, the two pilots and Abe check in, followed by the left and right gunners. Forrest's comm box had been destroyed in the crash, but they knew he was alive. They don't, however, hear from Daisy or any of the STS guys, the two PJs, the combat controller, or their interpreter. What immediately goes through Nicholas's mind is a crash a few years earlier at Pope Air Force Base, North Carolina, in which a tail gunner perished. Everyone knows that he's the most vulnerable person on the crew, sitting way back out on the tail ramp.

That's when the other flight engineer tells the pilot, "Hold on, boss; I'm going to go off comm and run to the back and get accountability for you." Seconds later he's back up on comm, saying, "Hey, I got accountability for everybody. We've got some injuries, but everyone's alive and everyone's still here." He doesn't mention the five-foot hole that's been torn in one side of the aircraft.

Forrest, who's in pain from "wrapping his back around a crate" on the floor during the crash, still doesn't see the tail gunner. He's yelling, "Where's Daisy? Where's Daisy?" "My mind told me, 'he's dead,' and he's standing right beside me. Finally, he hit me and told me, 'Oh, yeah, by the way, I'm here!' He had been thrown forward when we hit and the tail came down. He went past me, so that's why, when I hit and looked right back at him, he wasn't there, because he's now on my opposite side. His gunner's restraint was the only thing that wound up keeping him from getting tossed all the way forward in the helicopter. He wound up hitting our linguist."

The linguist, T.Sgt. Navid Garshasb, or "Gee," got hurt because he hadn't caught on that they were about to crash. When Daisy came flying forward, he slammed into Gee, who was sitting sideways. The impact broke several vertebrae in Gee's back, and when everything settled, he had the tail gunner in his lap.

With everyone accounted for, the pilot continues making Mayday calls on the guard frequency, trying to get the message out that they're down, provide a status report, and make contact with friendlies so they can begin to work their own rescue. As the mission commander says, "Now the rescuers have become the rescuees."

Only moments before the crash they'd flown over a village, and then over a small ridge. It had been all but forgotten in the crash. The people in back are still attempting to figure out how bad their injuries are, the PJs have crawled out of the new five-foot-wide hole in the side of the helicopter and have taken the linguist outside to check his injuries, when the left gunner calls out, "Hey, we got company." And as they turn to see whom he's talking about, Gee says, "What's that smell?"

The smell is fuel, leaking all over the place, pooling on the floor of the helicopter. The tanks had ruptured in the crash. Once more, the fact that the flight engineer had been able to shut down the engines quickly comes into play. Any source of flame was gone; moving parts that could generate sparks had been stopped.

That's when most of the rest of the crew crawls through the hole. Forrest remembers the scene vividly: "We could see the guys coming, like eleven guys coming over the hill. And at that point, it's, 'Gather your gear, 'cause things are going to get interesting around here.'"

While Major Forrest is the mission commander, he clearly recognizes that the need for his expertise in flight operations had effectively ended when Razor 03 went from being a high-tech weapons system that cost $40 million, to a pile of scrap metal worth perhaps 2.2 million afghanis—about fifty bucks. The guys with the know-how to get them out of this mess are the STS team, and team leader Jamie Clark.

Seeing that the villagers—or worse—were still a couple hundred yards away, Clark begins to put his Survival, Escape, Resistance, and Evasion (SERE) training to work and calls for the crew to break contact by leaving the helicopter and seeking shelter elsewhere. His first move is to motion the entire crew over a hill, down the other side, across a creek or two, into a stand of trees. Unfortunately, the back side of the hill would make a good black diamond ski run at Park City. It's steep. Everyone falls down at least once, if not twice, twisting ankles in the process.

The move to the trees seemed to work. "Fortunately," says Nicholas, "the villagers were more interested in the helicopter at that point than a foot chase, which they were going to get into if they started coming after us. Or they were going to eat some lead."

At that point, the PJ team leader calls for them to take inventory of everything they took with them when they left the helicopter. At the same time, he wants a self-assessment of their injuries. What is it they need to worry about? What equipment do they have?

That was the moment when Forrest discovered how badly he was hurt. "When I sat down, that's when the adrenaline kicked off, and that's when I first realized I'd busted my back and my head. We noticed that Jamie had a pretty good cut above his eye. It was kind of funny, 'cause it looked like camouflage in the dark, but it was actually blood going down the side of his face. We knew that Gee was the most seriously injured. That we could tell right off the bat. We also find out at that point that we have one foot injury with our tail gunner.

"All of us can move, we're mobile, but we're not comfortable by any means, especially Gee. We knew we were going to have to work and help him out. He was in pretty severe pain."

The next step was to deal with security. Clark had the trio who were most seriously injured remain in the center of a circle that was roughly thirty or forty yards in diameter. They had the radios. Then he began positioning each of the other survivors around the circle, sending the other PJ, Ken Curtis, and the combat controller around to make sure that each understood the field of fire he was responsible for, should they come under attack. The instructions were very precise, recalls Forrest: "All right, this is your responsibility. I want you to look from here to here; you've got that. And he'd walk off to the next guy and go through it again. It was quick, down and dirty. The main thing at that point is that it's allowing you to keep your mind in the game. One of the factors was if you start worrying, and everybody starts talking, we start forgetting that we've still got guys that are around here who don't like us. He did an awesome job of being able to maintain the calm, being able to give everybody a job to do."

Nicholas concurs that Clark was very effective at keeping everyone focused on solving problems, not lamenting their situation. "It was important, because at that point the adrenaline has worn off and the pain's starting to set in. Guys are starting to realize things, the doom-and-gloom picture, like, 'Great, I just crashed. I'm being followed. And now I'm freezing and it's snowing all over the place.' By being able to say, 'Hey, this is your job, do it,' it got us thinking, 'Hell, screw it. I can stay cold for a while.' There was definitely a distribution of duties, including designated radio duty instead of eleven guys all trying to talk at the same time."

Then Jamie Clark says, "Okay, guys, what's our plan?"

There were very basic questions that needed answering. Where were they? They set about figuring it out on the map. Forrest says, "I remember Jamie making a comment; 'We're not in a good location, 'cause if I want to go look for a bunch of people hiding, I'm gonna look at the only cluster of trees around, and guess what? That's the one we're in.'"

The good news, of sorts, is that it is now snowing heavily, with visibility down to fifteen, maybe only ten feet. So even if the locals could have seen the trees, it's not likely they will discover the crew unless they stumble into them. The temperature is obviously below freezing, which is causing a problem for several of the survivors. When they took off from Jacobabad, it was above ninety degrees, and the aircrew wasn't wearing heavy thermal underwear beneath their Nomex fire-resistant flight suits. The STS team was dressed in the standard DCUs and was probably better prepared for the weather they now found themselves in.

Some of the aircrew had cold-weather gear in their hit-and-run bags, but weren't able to find them when they had to quickly abandon the wreckage. Nicholas is fortunate that he does have his bag, and in it he'd packed a full set of DCUs, plus a turtleneck sweatshirt, watch cap, and Gore-Tex winter-weight gloves, all of which he put on. He gives his Gore-Tex camouflage jacket to Abe, since the flight engineer is one of those who didn't have any extra clothing. By the time he's re-dressed himself, two or three inches of snow have accumulated on his gear. He settles into his post with his bag in front of him, his weapon on top of that.

An early concern is making sure that the information they were transmitting about their location was accurate. They'd all heard horror stories from downed crewmen in Bosnia who transmitted the coordinates on their hand-held GPS devices, only to learn later on that the instrument was wrong. Almost as soon as they left the helicopter, Nicholas fired up one of the two he'd brought with him—one personal, one squadron-issued. Moments later Clark came along and grabbed the GPS device that had been turned on so that he'd have his own and a backup when the time came to figure out where they were.

While they are unable to directly contact Razor 04, they are able to relay information to their sister ship through the Hornets orbiting high overhead. Unfortunately, the weather has gotten so bad that three times they can hear Razor 04 trying to penetrate past the ridgeline near the village, and three times he has to turn around and leave the area.

Soon after the third try, they get word on the radio from the jets that they will have to move seven miles to a suitable pickup zone. The actual message had gotten screwed up when it was relayed from Razor 04 to the jets, and then passed on to the survivors, but they don't know that. The result is that the tiny command group sucks it up and says, "Well, if we've got seven miles to go, we'd better get going now." They know they aren't in a good place to defend themselves, especially with the weather beginning to clear up.

At that point, Clark goes out and has everyone collapse into the center of the circle to be briefed. The plan is to hike down the valley they were originally going to try to fly into before the crash. They have a healthy group of survivors and an injured group. By mixing and matching, they put together groups of twos and threes that can help each other and avoid spreading out too much. And then, somewhere between one and two in the morning, they start walking. As they move out, Clark has the guys with extra clothing take some of the layers off. He knows they'll be working up a sweat, and if they are all zipped up with no way for it to evaporate, they run a greater risk of hypothermia.

It doesn't take too long before the PJ team leader, the pilot, and the mission commander all come to the same realization: With the injuries their people have, they're not going to be able to go seven miles very easily. Forrest says, "I think we realized that we're over ten thousand feet, you're in freezing cold temperatures, you've got the stress of just going through a crash, and you've got injuries. I don't know many healthy people out there who can go and do a nice hike at over ten thousand feet. Fatigue was setting in. In fact, I kind of got paranoid, 'cause I'm sitting there going, 'My God, I can barely get my breath. Hell, I can't be that far out of shape.' Now I'm seeing the PJs, who are in awesome shape, and they're huffing and puffing just as much, so I felt a little bit better at that point."

The upshot is that they realize that the valley they are in at the moment is actually a pretty good pickup point. So they find another hole-up site, mainly to take care of the badly injured guys. That's when Gee begins going into shock, and they start seeing hypothermia setting in on a few of the crew. Forrest says he was seeing "confusion, frostbite in the toes. You see a lot of the shaking going on. The cold was getting so extreme, when you say 'bone-chilling-cold,' this was it."

On top of that, hypoxia is beginning to set in. Hypoxia occurs most often above ten thousand feet in people who haven't been acclimatized. It's a state of oxygen deficiency in the body's tissues that causes impairment of function. The symptoms vary from person to person, are slow to develop but are progressive, and worst of all, are insidious. Intellectual impairment is an early sign, making it improbable that an individual can comprehend his own disability. According to the *Mountain Flying Bible*, "in later stages of hypoxia, thinking is slow, calculations are unreliable, memory is faulty, judgment is poor and reaction time is delayed." It's not a condition that bodes well for assisting with their own rescue, and fighting off the enemy if it should come to that.

While the PJs weren't immune to the effects of the high altitude, Nicholas feels they tolerated it better than the aircrew. "I was paired up with Ken [Curtis] for the movement south for that seven miles. He was leading and I was navigating right behind. We were the first two people out. At that hole-up site, I was sitting next to him. We had a long discussion about where he's from. I can't remember exactly, but it was up north where there's snow, so he felt like he was at home. He seemed like he was enjoying himself, to be honest with you. The PJs were very professional and did an outstanding job."

The condition of Gee, the interpreter, was the greatest cause for concern. He was in significant pain, but they didn't dare give him morphine or any other drugs the PJs carry to battle pain. Forrest says, "The main thing is you don't want to knock this guy out. We've got to hike seven miles, and we're kind of looking at him for his input on what he thinks and what he needs. You don't want to do morphine or some other type of drug because it's more designed for someone in a controlled atmosphere where, 'All right, I can put you on the litter and I'm going to carry you.' Well, sorry, I don't have a litter, and we're going to be having arms over shoulders, and that's how we were actually walking that last quarter or half mile before we said we need to take a break and regroup—Gee was in the middle, hanging on to the shoulders of two of the healthy guys, trying to walk."

It is becoming increasingly apparent to the mission commander that with their physical conditions deteriorating, a seven-mile hike is out of the question. That's when he sends a radio message to the pilot of Razor 04, telling him their GPS coordinates, their altitude, and that this is going to have to be the spot.

The response is encouraging: "Looks like we can probably try to do the rescue, but we're waiting for the weather to clear a little bit more before we come in."

At this point, the guys who aren't injured are given security assignments, and everyone prepares to sit it out for an hour or so. Optimism returns. Help is on the way.

But so are the locals.

Nicholas says, "We got compromised again. The weather getting better was negative, so to speak. They acquired us again and they started yelling and screaming and shining flashlights at us when they were still several hundred yards away."

The last thing this crew wanted was a firefight. In fact, earlier they'd been asked by pilots in the F/A-18s about blowing up the wrecked helicopter, and Forrest said absolutely not. "We don't start the fight. We don't want to start a fight. And whether it's a bomb dropping or us taking a shot, once the fight starts, all bets are off. So we didn't want to have any of that."

As far as they knew, only residents of the small village nearby were aware of the crash. But there were several other villages on other ridgelines, a mile or two away. If the jets had bombed the wreckage, everyone would know that something was going on, and in Nicholas's opinion, they would have been compromised and it would have jeopardized any rescue attempt.

His concern wasn't that they weren't able to defend themselves. Unlike a fighter pilot who bails out with a 9mm pistol and nothing more, the crew had their rifles and sidearms, and were lugging a significant amount of ammunition. "We're eleven quite well-armed guys roaming on the ground here, and they don't know who we are. And it took them by as much surprise as it took us. So when these guys show up, our main thing is we just want to keep it nice and calm."

This is when the decision not to give their interpreter, Gee, any morphine begins to make a whole lot of sense.

"We're talking to Gee, and he's trying to figure out what they're saying. He says, 'They want to come talk,' and we're basically telling him, 'No! Just tell them to go away. We mean them no harm. Go away!' "

Then things begin to get dicey. Two of the Afghans move down from the ridge they'd been on and start coming toward the crash survivors. They make it to the bottom of the hill, and then a third man comes down. Nicholas recalls it in vivid detail. "The third guy kept his distance. It looked like a bad drug deal, y'know? The guy stands off in the back, guarding everything, while his other guys go up to do the talking and negotiations."

Tension rises as the first two men come within shouting distance. The Americans don't want to shoot, and they know that talking is going to be difficult for Gee, since he is still in extreme pain from the injury to his back. Nevertheless, he puts down his weapon and struggles to his feet, then climbs on top of the bunker-type hill they've been hiding behind, and begins talking.

Captain Nicholas had high praise for what he did. "The professionalism he displayed that day was immense. He worked it to where there wasn't a firefight, and no lives were lost."

Forrest concurs. "Without [Gee's language] capability, about the only thing we would've been able to do is fire a shot to say, 'Go away.' Are they going to take that as a warning shot, or are they going to take that as a missed shot, and the fight's on? The shooting would have had to start just to be able to say, 'Oh, by the way, you're just too close. You gotta go away.' 'Cause we can't let those guys approach us."

While the talking is going on, eight gun barrels are pointed at the interlopers, but Jamie Clark is moving from man to man, urging them not to shoot, to wait and see if they're armed and what they want. Nicholas had a set of binoculars in his hit-and-run bag that he gave to the other PJ, but he can't tell if the men have weapons. A couple of the survivors still have their night-vision goggles, and they, too, can't tell if the men Gee was talking with are armed. It was an uncertainty that would continue to concern them as the night wore on.

Forrest feels that when Gee began speaking the local language, it confused the two men. They couldn't figure out just who it was they were talking to. "Anything we can do to keep a low profile, keep these guys guessing, where are we? Who are we? What are we? Is it a bad guy? Maybe it's one of their local helicopters that crashed? Who knows what? The idea is to keep as low a signature as possible, no lights, nothing. We just want to let them think it's a normal night, they heard a lot of banging and go back to sleep." Whatever it was that Gee said, it worked. The locals, apparently friendlies, walked away.

Then the crew is given another reason for optimism: the weather is clearing up. From total cloud cover and low light, it would go to 100 percent illumination as the moon broke through the clouds, lighting up the valley. Forrest, who was dealing with a lot of pain and an early stage of hypoxia, says he remembers that while they were walking, they suddenly thought they saw automobile headlights in front of them. The headlights turned out to be the moon shining across the valley.

It is while they are waiting to get word when Razor 04 will be ready to try to pick them up that they begin pondering whether or not the helicopter will have enough power to evacuate all eleven men. That helicopter already has nine people on board, and everyone knows how power-limited the MH-53s are at that altitude.

Nicholas says, "Major Forrest and Jamie had a talk about who would go, who would stay, and that's a sickening feeling when you know two guys are sitting on the side, talking about the fate of your life. Are you going to be a chosen one, or are you going to stay behind? I tell you the truth, I wasn't injured, and I'm thinking, 'Shit, this sucks. How can I break my leg? I can get out of here.'

"They came back and said, 'aircrew's going and the team's going to stay,' which sucks for them." The team is the trio of special tactics operators—the two PJs and the combat controller.

"We were trying to get a message back to Lieutenant Mike in the other helicopter," says Forrest. "We were trying to get the answer to 'What can you pick up? What's realistic?' And the unfortunate problem was, we had to go through the fighter guys, who then went over another relay net, trying to talk back to our helicopter. So the translation didn't go through too well.

"But our main thing was, if he comes in and he's power-limited—the first thing was if you can only get one or two guys out, what do we do? If you can only get a few more guys out, what do you do? And Jamie was the first one to say, 'I'll tell you what, boss, there ain't no way I'm going out of here. I'm trained for this. I know how to do this stuff. If anybody's going to have to walk their way out, that's what we're going to do.' "

The credo "That Others May Live" had just kicked in, and Forrest recognized it. "From the days when I was in rescue, I had a PJ that I knew from Vietnam who jumped off a helicopter because they were so power-limited they couldn't get out of an LZ. He jumped out and wound up walking out of Vietnam. It took him six days to get out. These guys realize that they're the best-trained, best-equipped person in the world to do their job.

"And then it was, 'Okay, who are the first guys out?' You get the injuries out, 'cause you're our gimps. You're the guys who're going to slow the rest of us down. The hard part was, me being one of the injured, I didn't like having to say that, yeah, I'm gonna be one of the guys out. I'm also going to be the guy who's going to get these guys killed if I try to stay with them. And Gee, he was our number one, we gotta get him out of here. We'd love to have the language skill, but he's just too injured, he's too hurt."

One way to make it possible to get another one or two bodies on the helicopter was to dump gear. At the same time, it allowed them to make sure that any supplies that might be of use to the men left on the ground were given to them. The stay-behind bag held food, ammo, water, radio batteries, and warm clothing.

The PJ team leader had spotted Nicholas's backpack and claimed it to carry the supplies. But first, the copilot had to empty it, which was a bit like emptying a magic Christmas bag—the more you take out of it, the more it seems to hold. "I had everything from snakebite kits, aspirin, bandages, flashlights, fire starters, lighters, matches, candles, extra signaling mirrors, an extra GPS."

To each item that he pulls out, the PJ team leader is saying, "No, no, no." Then Nicholas says, "Well, I got an ax. You want an ax? He's like, 'You ain't got no fuckin' ax.' And I said, 'Yeah, I got an ax.' He says, 'Good, then dig a hole with that ax and bury everything.' "

This is all taking place only about thirty minutes prior to the scheduled pickup by Razor 04. Except for concern that the STS team is going to be left on the ground, things are looking up. They're hearing on one of the radios that the helicopter is heading off to get some gas before coming in to try the rescue. It's in the midst of this rising euphoria that Gee goes into shock and collapses.

Meantime, the combat controller has left their hiding place and gone out in the middle of the nearby field to mark the landing site. Realizing that they're all going to have to cross a little ridge and a stream to get there, the rest of the group follows, with Abe and Nicholas helping Gee walk between them, very slowly and gingerly. The object is to get Gee as close as possible to where the helicopter would be directed to land by the CCT, and they have nearly completed the journey when someone asks, "What if the helicopter balls it in?" That's Air Force jargon for crashing on landing, as in "going down in a fireball."

The thrust of the question is that they all realize the helicopter has one shot at making the landing. An acceptable batting average in this game is not .300. Only perfect will do. That's because landing a helicopter at this altitude requires a gradual reduction in speed; once the aircraft is below a certain speed, it's committed to the landing. There's no way to ramp up power and fly out of it. It truly is a controlled crash.

Making the landing even dicier is that it will be done in full whiteout conditions. That means that as the helo gets between roughly 100 and 150 feet off the ground—one and a half to two rotor diameters—the downward thrust of air beneath it will hit the ground, causing the snow to billow up, completely obscuring the ground, eliminating any chance of maintaining a visual on a horizon, and filling the entire aircraft cabin, including the cockpit. Under those conditions, anything can happen, including an extreme bank angle resulting in a total loss of lift and that rapid elevator ride down to the ground.

Once the vision of that possibility made the rounds, the wisdom of moving well back from the intended landing site becomes apparent. It is at that moment that Clark notices that Gee still has his Helicopter Emergency Egress Device attached to his flight suit. The HEEDS bottle is sort of a miniature scuba tank, filled with enough air to give an aviator a minute or two to escape from a ditched helicopter and swim up to the surface. While it doesn't contain pure oxygen, the gas within it is certainly richer than the air they were breathing. Sure enough, after the PJ has Gee take a couple of puffs, some color comes back into his face. That's when Forrest realizes that he, too, still has his HEEDS bottle. He pulls it out and hands it off to Nicholas, who at that point is quite literally falling to the ground with what was probably hypoxia-related exhaustion. After a few puffs, Forrest says the copilot seemed to just snap awake. "It was, like, 'Hi, guys, where you been?' "

Once again, a momentary euphoric high was crushed by reality. Razor 04 came in, flew over them, and left. "The worst feeling in the world," says Forrest, "is you've been waiting and waiting for somebody to come in and save you, and the guy comes, he flies over, and he flies away. And you feel very lonely at that point."

Had they still had their wits about them, they would have understood what Lieutenant Mike was doing. But all the guys on the ground can think is,

"Where is he? What's happening?" During what had to be the longest five minutes of their lives, they can barely hear Razor 04 and certainly can't see him. Everyone at that point has the same wish: They just want him to come in and get their asses out of Dodge. They're tired, they're cold, and they're ready to go home.

Finally, Razor 04 comes back. Forrest has vivid memories of the scene. "It's kind of weird when you watch it landing, 'cause all of a sudden you see him come in, and then the whiteout cloud comes over him. It was kind of like back before the crash, where we're flying and the one second he's there, and the next second he's not. The snow envelops him, and your best sense at this point is your ears. You're just waiting to hear the sounds you want to hear, and that was the engines winding down as he lets out the power, sounds that meant he didn't crash."

Not only didn't Razor 04 crash, the landing was so perfect that when the helicopter came to a stop, the combat controller who'd marked the LZ was sitting on the ground, just outside the rotor path. It was so close that Forrest says it scared the hell out of Jamie Clark, who saw his CCT suddenly disappear in a snow cloud, and thought that he was about to be landed on.

Air Force PJs have certain, secret authentication procedures they're supposed to go through when approaching downed aircrew. The purpose is to prevent the enemy from pretending to be the downed pilot they've homed in on, and then attacking the rescuers. At a minimum the procedures require that the survivor know the correct password and display some form of official identification. Rules are rules, and this is one that's important to the very survival of rescue personnel.

Nevertheless, with eleven survivors to authenticate and uncertainty as to the whereabouts of the curious locals, the PJs on the incoming aircraft came running off the tail ramp, took one look at the group of guys they'd been living with at Jacobabad, and dispensed with a request for identification authenticator code words, saying instead, "Get your asses on the helicopter; we're leaving."

It turned out that when they'd flown over the site they were able to measure its precise altitude with both barometric and radar altimeters, and to record the ambient temperature. With those numbers plugged into the flight engineer's computer, along with their weight, they were able to calculate how much fuel they'd have to dump in order to land, take everyone on board, and have enough power to take off. They had also matched up the LZ they could see through their NVGs with information the PJs on the ground had passed along as far as precise GPS coordinates, size, suitability, and shape of the pickup site.

With two of the rescuees carrying Gee, all eleven begin climbing aboard, most of them moving as far forward as possible, finding space on the floor to settle in for takeoff. The last to board are their PJs, Staff Sergeants Jamie Clark and Ken Curtis.

Now comes what Maj. Peter Forrest describes as the second scariest moment of his life. "Mike pulls into the hover, and in all honesty we're doing some high-fives there, and then as he pulls in, trying to get the power, you could hear the helicopter groaning."

The survivors who were celebrating didn't hear the grinding, but those crewmembers who heard it could tell that the pilot was pulling every ounce of energy he could out of that helicopter and wound up getting only about five feet of altitude.

But the situation gets worse. As they gain height above the ground, the pilots slowly start to pick up some forward airspeed, but then the rotors start to droop. If they can gain forward airspeed, they should eventually be able to climb. But at this point the helicopter is so stressed that it never got above ten feet while traveling roughly half a mile along the ground. It's a potentially terminal situation.

Here's Lt. Col. Graham Buschor's explanation of what was happening, and what the pilots were trying to do to get them off the ground:

"He's in a hover, demanding maximum power from the helicopter due to its high gross weight and altitude. The pilot pushes the cyclic to move forward, which tilts the rotor forward, dumping some lift. In order to compensate for the lost lift, you would normally add power, but the helo has no more to give and the rotor starts to slow down, or 'droop.'

"If they could keep their acceleration going through what's called 'translation lift' (ten to twenty knots airspeed), the rotor will start to become more efficient, and they'll require less power to stay airborne. The helicopter will then start climbing, however slowly.

"Because they were at their maximum limit and could not get the helicopter going fast enough to get through translational lift, they couldn't stay airborne and accelerate. That's why they kept moving forward, barely above the ground for a half mile, with the rotor still drooping."

They need an ingenious solution to the dilemma, and it is the copilot, Lieutenant Jay, who comes up with it. He suggests a maneuver that allows the pilot to take the strain off the rotors, let them spin up quickly, then pull power.

He thinks the technique might give him enough muscle to gain sufficient altitude to get out of the ground effect and actually fly away from the terrain.

Buschor explains, "What he did was let the collective out briefly, giving the rotors a chance to come back up to speed. At the same time he lowered the nose, which will help him gain airspeed, getting closer to translational lift. Ultimately, he was able to pull back on the collective and fly out of it. Fortunately, he had ten feet of altitude to work with. When you lower the collective in this situation, you descend, so this had to be a very well timed maneuver. Actually, it was pretty slick."

The crew of the late Razor 03 had dodged four big bullets in the space of a few hours: They'd all survived the crash; they'd successfully evaded potential enemy forces; the helicopter coming in to rescue them had managed to land safely in full whiteout conditions; and now, despite a severe shortage of power, the rescue helicopter was flying home.

There is only one little obstacle between where they were and a hot shower back at the base: The helicopter that has just rescued them has no gas. They'd dumped just about everything they had in the tanks, including the few extra pounds they'd loaded for Mom and the kids, in order to be able to get all eleven survivors out of bad-guy land. Now they urgently need to refuel.

The good news is that the tanker that was supposed to meet up with them is right on time, hoses out and ready. The bad news is that with the helicopter overloaded and underpowered at that altitude, as it took on the weight of the gasoline flowing into its tanks, it couldn't keep up with the tanker that was already flying as slowly as it could.

What would happen was that the pilots would maneuver into position and score a bull's-eye in the refueling drogue with their probe, begin taking on gas, and then fall off the hose and not be able to climb back up to make contact again. The only solution was one that required incredible patience and skill, especially for a crew that had already been in the seats for more than nine hours. What they had to do was make contact and take a small sip of gas, and wait. Then take a little bit more gas, and wait. If they tried to rush things and take a gulp instead of a sip, the weight would cause the helicopter to fall off the hose.

While the pilots are going through hell up front trying to make sure that they'd be able to make it to the small airfield that had been designated as a transload point, where they could transfer the injured to a C-130 equipped to transport and care for seriously injured patients, all four PJs in the back are starting to assess the injuries.

Gee was the most seriously hurt in the crash, and now is suffering from shock and hypothermia. The PJs put him in a sleeping bag, then strap him to a backboard to immobilize his spine. Next they turn to Peter Forrest, the mission commander, strapping him to a backboard as well, trying to ensure that he doesn't complicate his back injury any more than he's already done with the hike from crash site to pickup zone.

The flight to the small field where the transload of Gee, Forrest, and the STS team was to take place took two and a half hours. The last thing Forrest remembers after the PJs strapped him down was yelling at the right gunner, "My last command as mission commander: Take me home!"

The remaining six crewmembers from Razor 03 flew back to Jacobabad to rejoin their unit. A day later, it was discovered that Daisy, the tail gunner, had not only injured his back in the crash, he'd broken his foot. He, too, was hospitalized.

F-14 Tomcat fighters from the aircraft carrier USS *Theodore Roosevelt* came in hours later and destroyed the damaged helicopter. Later that same day, U.S. special forces were able to evacuate the soldier whose illness had prompted the rescue mission. Luckily, his condition was not as bad as had been originally reported.

Nine days later, the injured crewmen were medevacked from the U.S. Army's Landstuhl Regional Medical Center in Germany to the States. What should have been an uneventful trip turned interesting when they were ordered to hold over the ocean for about two hours. An American Airlines jet taking off from JFK International Airport had lost its tail section and crashed into a Queens, New York, neighborhood. Fear that it might have been a terrorist act caused the FAA to close all New York–area airports. Their homecoming flight was diverted to Canada, and when U.S. airspace was reopened, they resumed their journey back to Hurlburt Field, Florida.

The mission marked the first time since Vietnam that eleven survivors were rescued in a single operation. The crew of Razor 04 won the Mackay Trophy, presented annually by the National Aeronautic Association to the Air Force aviators deemed to have made the most meritorious flight of the year. The three-foot-tall silver trophy is on permanent display at the National Air and Space Museum in Washington, D.C. Each recipient received an engraved gold medal to commemorate the achievement.

Two of the pararescuemen involved in the mission were honored as PJs of the Year in ceremonies that took place several months later at the PJ Schoolhouse at Kirtland Air Force Base, New Mexico. S.Sgt. James E. Clark was recognized as NCO PJ of the Year, and SrA Jason D. Andrews, who had been aboard Razor 04, received the honor of Outstanding Airman.

T.Sgt. Navid Garshasb—Gee—received the William H. Pitsenbarger Award for Heroism, presented annually by the Air Force Sergeant's Association to an enlisted member of the service for heroic acts on or off duty that save a life or prevent a serious injury. The award is named for the only PJ ever to win the Medal of Honor.

And finally, in the "truth is the first casualty of war" category, consider these news reports about the Razor 03 crash. This version of the story is from the Web site of the English-language version of the *China People's Daily* on Sunday, November 4, 2001:

## 40–50 U.S. Troops Killed While Helicopter Crashes in Afghanistan: AIP

A spokesman for the Afghan Taliban claimed Saturday that 40 to 50 U.S. troops were killed while their helicopter was shot down by the Taliban anti-aircraft gunfire, according to the Afghan Islamic Press (AIP).

The spokesman, Mullah Amir Khan Muttaqi, told AIP that a U.S. helicopter crashed for unknown reasons in Nawur district of Ghazni province and a second gunship was shot down by the Taliban soldiers as it came to rescue the crew of the first. "Pieces of 40 to 50 dead bodies were spread everywhere," he said.

According to the spokesman, the helicopter with 40 to 50 U.S. troops on board entered Afghanistan from the Pakistan side and was heading toward Dara-e-Souf, the key frontline between the Taliban militia and its opposition Northern Alliance in Samangan province. Early Saturday, a Taliban diplomat claimed that two U.S. aircraft were shot down by Taliban anti-aircraft gunfire in southern Afghan province of Ghazni during the U.S. air strikes Friday night.

Najibullah, a senior Taliban diplomat, told AIP that the two U.S. aircraft took part in a round of air attacks on Nawar district in Ghazni. One crashed near Hokack village and the other crashed near Hasrat village.

In Washington, the U.S. Defense Department announced on Friday that a U.S. military helicopter crash-landed in Afghanistan due to bad weather, injuring four crew members. It said the crash landing, was the first reported loss of a U.S. aircraft within Afghanistan since the U.S. and its allies launched military strikes against the Taliban four weeks ago.

A Reuters report with a Kabul dateline embellished the story:

The Taliban said they had shot down the helicopter on Friday night in an operation south of the capital, Kabul, killing up to 50 U.S. soldiers. The helicopter was brought down after the Taliban opened fire on it in the Nawoor district of Ghazni province while it was trying to rescue another aircraft that had crashed in the area, said Qari Fazil Rabi, an Information Ministry official.

"Altogether between 40 to 50 Americans have died in both these incidents," he said. "You can see the bodies of the Americans on board the helicopters with their uniforms."

And on Wednesday, November 7, the *Guardian Unlimited*, on-line affiliate of the *Manchester Guardian*, added additional details about the alleged Taliban triumph:

## Conflicting Reports as Helicopter Wreckage Paraded Through Kabul

The Taliban triumphantly paraded the remains of an American helicopter through Kabul yesterday, amid conflicting reports that a second U.S. helicopter had crash-landed in Pakistan's remote western desert.

Thousands of Kabul residents came onto the streets to watch Taliban fighters show off the wreckage, which was driven through the war-shattered city on the back of a lorry. Two tyres and several twisted metal helicopter parts were clearly visible.

"Their attack here will soon share the fate of this aircraft," a Taliban fighter shouted through a loud-speaker, as U.S. warplanes continued their bombardment yesterday of the Taliban front line north of Kabul. "Don't worry, we will defeat the Americans and their allies," he added.

**CHAPTER 2**

# JDAMned
## DECEMBER 5, 2001

Sr.M.Sgt. Patrick Malone was living in shit. Well, perhaps not exactly *in* shit, but definitely surrounded by it. And since he wasn't alone, he didn't take it personally. *Alone* would have actually been an improvement. He was sharing the inside of a spacious, mosquito- and exotic-bug-infested hangar on the Pakistani Air Force's Shahbaz Air Base with a couple of hundred American special-operations types—Navy SEALs, Army Special Forces and Rangers, Malone's unit of Air Force pararescuemen, Marine security guards, and the Army, Air Force, and Marine aviators whose job it was to get them where they were needed.

For the Americans, the hangar on the base at Jacobabad, Pakistan, was the only secure building there. They slept, worked, ate, and, in their off hours, watched DVDs in it. They also used its woefully inadequate toilet facilities and suffered the consequences when the effluent came bubbling up in a lagoon of excrement, sort of a moat of crap across the eastern end of the building. In the morning, when the sun was shining and the air was relatively clear, kinder souls referred to it as Lake Jacobabad. But as the heat of the day built up and the men and women who worked nights began to wake up and use the facilities, the name given it by some of the world travelers within the building seemed more appropriate. They called it Lake Shittycaca.

Two-thousand-pound JDAM bomb (*USAF photo*)

Eventually, the U.S. Air Force civil engineers would bring in canvas portable toilet and shower units, ultimately upgrading them to what the troops called Cadillac showers. Could orders to shave regularly and wear uniforms properly be far behind?

What wouldn't change was the water supply. There was never enough to permit more than Navy-type showers, and the warnings of its nonpotability were everywhere. While an Army may move on its stomach, this Air Force–run base was lubricated with planeloads of cases of bottled water, most of it brought in from Saudi Arabia, which, as everyone knows, is a desert. Go figure.

Malone recalls that in those early days just coming in contact with the local water supply was enough to cause guys to break out in rashes. Whoever coined that phrase about war not being healthy for children and other living things wasn't only talking about the consequences of gunfire. While the rashes may not kill you—or worse, take you off of flying status (the Air Force calls it "going DNIF," for "duties not including flying")—mosquito-borne malaria remained a constant concern, and they conscientiously used mosquito netting around their cots.

Adding to Jbad's reputation as an airman's R&R paradise was the local fauna. One soldier patrolling the perimeter had already been bitten by a cobra and was lucky to be alive. The venom stopped the man's heart. There were warnings posted everywhere to avoid contact with the monitor lizards wandering the base, occasionally even inside buildings. One bite from these two- to five-foot-long creatures is enough to cause a fatal infection. And then there are the nighttime visitors, like the jackals that provide a serenade that's really annoying to anyone actually trying to do something outlandish like sleep when it's dark out. The security forces took to organizing jackal hunts on a regular basis.

Malone had been accompanied on the journey to Jacobabad from the headquarters of the 123rd Special Tactics Squadron of the Kentucky Air National Guard in Louisville by another PJ, T.Sgt. Ryan Schultz. They were sent to replace two pararescuemen who had to go home on emergency leave. The duo got word on October 29, 2001; Schultz was federalized and mobilized, and in less than twenty-four hours both were on their way, doing the PJ bag drag to Baltimore where they boarded the Rotator—the sardine can impersonating a DC-10 that the Defense Department charters from commercial airlines to deliver individual replacement troops overseas—that would take thirty hours to get them to Oman, stopping along the way to pick up and drop off individuals and small units. Each of them had at least a dozen bags with equipment that would make it possible for them to climb a mountain, dive in an ocean, or tackle just about any environment in between. Paying exorbitant excess baggage charges—reimbursable—is a way of life for traveling PJs.

It took them two days in Oman before they could hop a flight on a C-17 cargo plane bound for Jbad. And it was on that flight that they found themselves in war.

"It was hilarious, in a kind of weird way," recalls Malone. "When are you really in a war? 'Cause you're not in war in Oman; you're not in war in Baltimore. You know you're in a *state* of war, but when are you truly *in* a war?" he asks.

"Well, when we landed in Jacobabad, we were in a war."

The crew of the C-17 was brand-new in theater, "spooled up and nerved up," according to Malone. They knew that the locals were taking potshots with rifles at incoming aircraft, and feared that someone might try it with a shoulder-fired missile or a rocket-propelled grenade. They also knew that Air Force combat controllers were handling airfield operations, and the pilots had been told that there were guns going off outside the gate and snipers on rooftops, watching. (Remember, in this war, Pakistan is theoretically our ally.) Because of the threat, all operations into Jbad took place at night, and the aircraft were blacked out. The theory was that they could be heard, but not seen, and by the time a bad guy fired at the sound the plane would be long gone.

Inside the cavernous plane, you're strapped in and helpless as the pilots fly a tactical approach to the field. That means it's not a predictable, straight-in shot, but a sequence of sudden left and right turns that makes the ride reminiscent of Disneyland's Space Mountain—a roller coaster in the dark. As a passenger, you sit there in blacked-out conditions, hanging on, knowing that sooner or later you'll hit the ground—it could be ten seconds or ten minutes.

When Malone and Schultz made their first landing at Jbad, it was, as the aircrews are wont to say, "a bit sporty."

"We're going in. *Boom!* Chaffs and flares firing." Malone acknowledges that firing flares does tend to reveal the position of the aircraft, and they offer no protection against anything other than heat-seeking missiles. It was, he says, "inexperience of some of the younger pilots, getting used to it. As time went on, those guys were whipping in and out of those runways. They learned the gig quick, and they adapted and overcame."

The local indigenous population of two hundred thousand, most of them

Muslim, was not especially thrilled to have Americans in their midst. In addition to the now de rigueur custom of burning the Stars and Stripes to express their displeasure shortly after Americans arrived at the base, at least one person had been shot and killed protesting the Pakistani government's leasing more than half of their third-largest air base to the United States. Massed attacks on the facility were not a concern, according to one Air Force officer expressing an unofficial opinion, only because the locals were split into twenty or so political parties—from the control tower their flags could be seen flying in the city—that couldn't agree on anything. Nevertheless, off-base excursions by American troops were forbidden, a precaution proved sensible less than three months later when *Wall Street Journal* reporter Daniel Pearl was kidnapped and murdered in Karachi.

As time went by, security at Jbad was expanded beyond the immediate area of the hangar, and either the locals stopped shooting over the fence every night, or the Americans just got used to it. Since no one had been hit, it was deemed more an annoyance than a threat. Ultimately, Army infantrymen and -women from the 10th Mountain Division relieved the Marines pulling security. The grunts assumed the unenviable task of climbing into sandbagged bunkers on top of hardened aircraft shelters (HAS) and along the perimeter every night, to remain vigilant behind .50-caliber machine guns in near-freezing temperatures while under relentless attack by a strain of mosquitoes that hadn't gotten the word about cold weather making them sluggish.

Early in Operation Enduring Freedom, American authorities had divided areas of responsibility at the thirty-fourth parallel, which essentially sliced across Afghanistan at the southern edge of Kabul. All rescue and refueling activities north of the line were flown out of K-2, the former Soviet airfield at Karshi-Khanabad, Uzbekistan. And everything south of the thirty-fourth was the responsibility of units based at Jbad. No tanker aircraft were based in Afghanistan itself. The huge field at Bagram, with its ten-thousand-foot runway, was overtaxed with helicopter and cargo plane activity, and the presence of millions of land mines and pieces of unexploded ordnance just off the tarmac made tanker operations there especially dicey. What's more, unlike the airfields at K-2 and Jbad, Bagram was subjected to intermittent rocket attacks; using the place as a storage dump for hundreds of thousands of gallons of jet fuel was probably not a good idea.

The CSAR mission was assigned to the special-tactics squadrons of AFSOC. They had their own MH-53 Pave Low helicopters, eighty-eight-foot-long behemoths that are the largest rotary-wing aircraft in the Air Force inventory, and the special-tactics teams that included PJs and combat controllers and were trained in commando operations. They also had their own refuelers, the MC-130P Combat Shadow version of the C-130. It was just coincidence that the NCO in charge of the operation in Jbad, Sr.M.Sgt. Pat Malone, and the NCO in charge at K-2, T.Sgt. Keary Miller, were both from the Guard unit at Louisville.

On December 5, the division of labor for PJs in Operation Enduring Freedom got a bit more complicated. It happened with the entry of the Air Force's Air Combat Command (ACC) Combat Search and Rescue units into the war. ACC CSAR units, such as the 347th Rescue Wing out of Moody Air Force Base, Georgia, flew HC-130 refueling planes and HH-60G Pave Hawk helicopters, and carried PJs on both airframes. Their assignment was traditional CSAR: If a plane went down, it was their mission. The AFSOC PJs were now assigned solely to missions that were related to special operations, primarily infiltrating and exfiltrating ground teams for purposes of reconnaissance or combat. The PJs' purpose in this configuration was to provide a rescue force that would already be on scene if needed.

In the south, the plan worked well after Malone used his rank and twenty years of rescue experience to keep his guys flying when others were arguing that they could be eliminated from helicopter missions. "Because of the altitudes that flights were going in on, and sometimes the equipment that was being carried in or personnel being carried in or out, weight limitations were becoming a concern. We were starting to run into, 'What can we do without? In order to make a mission successful, what can we do without?' "

Because PJs in AFSOC were not considered part of the flight crews (as opposed to ACC, where PJs are as integral to the mission as a loadmaster might be), Malone feels it was relatively easy for commanders to say, "Okay, we'll cut the PJs, cut the rescue team off." That's where he was able to speak to the flying commanders, and say, "Colonels, let's look at the bigger picture here. You have a job to do within the job: whatever your mission is for the night, but you also have a rescue force to provide. If you start dropping your PJs, or their equipment, then you're not providing the service you should be providing."

The Air Force officers who were running the show in the south understood Malone's argument. But up north, where Keary Miller was dealing with an Army-run operation, there were problems trying to keep PJs on aircraft.

Malone says of the younger pararescueman, "He had a fight. The Army didn't understand that. Army aviation didn't always understand that. They're Army. They have their missions, haul Army guys around and do Army stuff. 'Rescue? Where does that register in this game?' The answer was, it didn't." Malone says Miller was told to sit on the sidelines while the Army flew their mission. If something happened, they'd come back and get the PJs. "Well, in that 'I'll come back and get you,' a lot of people can die, a lot of bad stuff can happen." It's a battle that the PJs up north continued to fight, and as would be demonstrated a couple of months later, Malone's words were prophetic.

December 5, 2001, dawned clear and sunny. This was to be ACC's first day standing up, pulling CSAR alert for the theater. Since they were shorthanded, Malone was planning on filling in as a jumpmaster team leader on their Herc crew. He briefed the team, and then joined them on the taxiway, checking out the alert aircraft. It was around ten A.M. local time, while he was on the plane, that Ryan Schultz came out to get him.

"Hey, got something going on. You need to come back and start coordinating."

The original call was mortar fire, with three injured. Then it quickly jumped to seven or eight injured. Not knowing the details, Malone opted to plan big, especially once the decision was made to get the survivors in daylight, which he says was thinking way outside the box.

"I wanted to beef the crews up, rescue-guys-wise, PJs-wise, because I had a funny feeling; you just never know. I'd been on enough missions where one is twenty, or one is fifty, and it's not eight. If you get out there and it is truly seven, no big deal. We got extra PJs; we can really tend to their needs."

Two of his crews had flown the night before, till three or four in the morning, and were still in the mandatory twelve-hour crew rest. Ryan would fly as team leader on one of the MH-53 helicopters; Malone would fill in, joining him as a team member, along with two more pararescuemen, S.Sgt. Ryan Hall and Ken Curtis, and CCT Jason Brooks. Two PJs were assigned to the other helicopter, along with an Army doctor and one Army medic.

Malone acknowledges that "everybody's pucker factor was pretty high; first daylight combat search and rescue mission for the south, with a firefight within half a klick." This was going to be no ordinary mission.

Just before taking off, Schultz throws an extra accessory kit on his helicopter. It's got extra medical supplies, bandages, IVs, extra oxygen containers.

They also toss on extra litters; the latest report had three dead, eight injured. Malone's idea of planning for the worst is beginning to make sense.

The flight is going to take about two and a half hours; their destination is near the village of Shawali Kowt, about twenty-one miles north of Kandahar. It is hotly contested territory, with the forces of then warlord Hamid Karzai moving down from the north, accompanied by an American Special Forces team, and the forces of Gul Agha Sherzai, having crossed into southern Afghanistan from Pakistan, moving up from the south. The object of both leaders is to assault and capture Kandahar, the Taliban stronghold of Mullah Omar.

Halfway to their objective, the PJs get another update: eighteen injured and three dead. An hour later, another update. It's now up to twenty-five injured, and word comes that it wasn't a mortar attack; it was friendly fire, or what they now call "blue on blue" or even "fratricide." Pat and Ryan hear the latest report on the radio and look at each other, eyebrows raised. This is going to be a mission to be remembered. To get ready, Schultz sits down on the floor and eats a cold cheese tortellini MRE.

What neither Schultz nor Malone could know at that point is that there may be as many as fifty or sixty wounded and close to thirty dead, among them three American Special Forces soldiers. They'd been hit by one of our own two thousand-pound bombs, outfitted with a Joint Direct Attack Munition (JDAM) guidance tail kit. It converts a dumb gravity bomb into what manufacturer Boeing, the Air Force, and the Navy call "accurate, adverse weathersmart munitions."

The twenty-thousand-dollar kit puts a new tail section on the two-thousand-pound BLU-109/MK 84 warhead. It contains an inertial navigational system and a global positioning system guidance control unit. Once released from the aircraft, the JDAM autonomously navigates to the designated target coordinates that were either loaded into the JDAM's guidance unit before takeoff, or manually altered by the aircrew before the weapon is released. When GPS data is available, the bomb will nearly always hit within forty feet of its target, even when released from a B-52 flying at forty-five thousand feet, up to fifteen miles away.

In 1996, after testing demonstrated the weapon performed as advertised by Boeing, the U.S. Air Force ordered 62,000 and the Navy another 25,496 JDAM bomb kits.

So what had happened?

According to Lt. Col. David Fox—the U.S. Special Forces battalion commander whose mission included advising Hamid Karzai as he negotiated with the Taliban for the surrender of Kandahar—his units had been taking intermittent fire from across a nearby bridge over the Arghandab River. At about nine in the morning, they spotted a cave entrance about two and a half kilometers to their south. Air Force controllers brought in a flight of F-18s, and once the controllers put lasers on the target, the jets dropped laser-guided munitions.

Fox says he watched two munitions fall a little short of the cave entrance, and it didn't look like much damage had been caused. The controllers, in the meantime, were talking to a B-52 overhead about dropping the JDAM.

About nine-thirty in the morning, as Lieutenant Colonel Fox reached down to grab his binoculars, he was knocked to the ground. "I can't figure out exactly what had happened. I look around and once I see the devastation, I knew that we had been hit by a very large munition."

Initially he thought it was enemy artillery; but there was no such artillery reported in the south. It took about three or four hours before it was officially determined that they'd been hit by friendly fire. The two-thousand-pound JDAM had fallen approximately two kilometers short of its intended target, and had impacted directly on the Special Forces position. Karzai suffered a minor face wound, either from shrapnel or a piece of glass from blown-out windows. An Afghan fighter standing near the soon-to-be head of government was decapitated.

None of this information, of course, is conveyed to the two inbound helicopters, rocketing toward the area as low as twenty-five feet above the ground. The only advantage they have going into an unknown situation is that before departing Jbad, they found a soldier who had actually been exfilled from the area the night before, and brought him with them. The hope is that his familiarity with the ground situation will keep them from becoming an easy target for enemy fighters armed with RPGs.

As the pair of Pave Lows approach the objective, their impromptu adviser says to Malone, "Hey, whatever you do, don't let 'em fly over the river. That's right where the firefight is." And until he spoke up, that's just what the helicopters were planning on doing, circling over the river and landing on the far side, near the village where the accidental bombing took place.

Malone immediately keys the intercom, warning the pilots, who adjust their approach. Standing on the open ramp at the rear of the helicopter, Schultz is getting ready to unhook and exit the aircraft as soon as it touches down. As they come in he sees the river, then rolling hills with people on top of them watching the big helicopter approach. That's a brain-jarring moment. He's already dealing with what it's going to take to treat a couple dozen casualties, up from a mere handful when they first got the mission. Now he's wondering whether or not he's going to have to defend himself in a firefight before he can begin treating the injured. And if there is a firefight, are the helicopters going to sit there, or are they going to insert the PJs and get out of the way, allowing the CCT to bring in close air support to deal with the folks on the hilltops?

Even though the PJs' expectation was that they'd hop off the helicopters, triage, treat and load patients, get back on, and leave, their training prevents them from assuming anything—including the fact that the helicopter is going to wait for them. Malone explains: "A PJ's perspective on a rescue mission is, 'Once I step off that helicopter, until I step back on, it's never coming back.' They have to be prepared to stay in the field, stay in the environment, whatever that environment is.

"Everybody's got enough gear to stay out there. Some water [in a Camel-Bak], an MRE or two. All your ammo, your guns, your medical gear."

Despite the fact that you're coming in on a large helicopter with Kevlar armor on its belly that should be able to stop small-arms fire, the factors you can't control are what cause a knot in the pit of the stomach and the involuntary clenching of sphincter muscles—the legendary but very real pucker factor. You don't think you're going to get hit, you don't believe you're going to get hit, but like a fighter in the ring you brace for the punch. It would have to be a lucky rifle bullet that finds you inside the Pave Low. But the windows are open for the gunners; the ramp is wide open. The odds are not infinitesimal, especially since they're doing what American special-ops helicopters almost never do: they're landing in bad-guy territory in broad daylight.

The lucky rifle shot is not their only worry. The pièce de résistance for rebel armies is the rocket-propelled grenade, or RPG. It's a grenade with a small motor, fired from a bazookalike tube. The Russians invented it in the 1960s as an antitank weapon, but skilled Afghan mujahideen gunners used them successfully against Soviet helicopters, and in 1993, Somalis firing RPGs brought down a pair of U.S. Black Hawk assault helicopters. Schultz and Malone know that an RPG aimed at their helicopter can easily ruin their day. A skilled shooter can hit moving targets from a distance of three hundred yards, and as the helicopters flare to a landing, there's plenty of time for more than one shot.

What doesn't seem to be bothering the PJs is the total brownout on landing. This part of Afghanistan is a moonscape of cocoa-colored dust that has the consistency of talcum powder. The instant the helicopter's downdraft hits the ground, the aircraft is enveloped in a cloud of choking dust that fills the interior, blinding its occupants. Goggles and bandanas keep it from disabling the crew, but it still takes many heart-pounding seconds for the dust to settle enough so that safe movement off the ramp is even possible. Even then, visibility remains impaired for more than a minute. Schultz has done a lot of landings like this, so he just rides it out, listening on comm. "I listen to what the pilots are doing, but their voices aren't raised. They're not high-pitched, they're not all over the place, so I'm not that worried."

Schultz and Malone's helo settles in about thirty seconds after the other helicopter lands. When the dust clears, they can see that the two 53s are about three hundred yards apart, with their ship closer to the dirt road that ran perpendicular to the river, and the other helo southwest of them, closer to the village. Telling PJs Hall and Curtis to grab two extra litters, they step off the ramp. True to Malone's word, they are all prepared to be there for a while if necessary. The rucks they're carrying weigh roughly forty pounds. Body armor adds another twenty-five pounds. The LBE—the load-bearing vest—is carrying at least seven thirty-round magazines for each man's rifle, plus extra clips for the 9mm pistol strapped to his thigh, plus additional medical and survival gear, and weighs another twenty-five pounds. Add the weight of the M4, the cut-down version of the standard M16 rifle, and each man is hauling more than a hundred pounds.

With that burden, it doesn't take long for the altitude to get to them. Even for men in great physical shape, sudden exertion at six thousand feet is enough to wind them. And then there is the emotional wallop of what they see.

Pat Malone says, "The minute we stepped off that plane and the dust started to settle, you got that vision of the chaos of war. It was so evident. The guy that approached us was completely shell-shocked, almost to the point of incoherency."

The man is one of the American Special Forces troops, apparently sent from where the bomb hit to guide the PJs in. But he can barely talk. Malone recalls that they couldn't communicate enough to get the information they needed to know about where the patients were, where the PJs needed to be.

Schultz says when he asked the soldier where everyone was and what was going on, he said, "Don't really know. They should be coming." That's when he spots the man's interteam radio, grabs it, and hooks his comm system to it, and tries in vain to contact the ground team. At this point, the assumption is that they are still at least half a mile from the patients who are near the river to the south, where the firefight had taken place. Then he sees people starting to line the hills on the other side of the helicopter.

Bad guys or good guys? The combat controller begins setting up his radios to be ready to call in close air support (CAS). But it quickly becomes apparent that the people on the hill aren't shooting at them. (Later, they figured out that what the locals had done was set up a perimeter between the helicopters and the firefight that was going on.) He tries once more to get information from the barely coherent SF operator. "Are the casualties on litters?"

"Yeah, they're all on litters," he responds. With that, the PJs put their litters back on the helicopter, and begin moving down the road to the south.

Then they see the trucks: five, ten, as many as fifteen trucks ranging from tiny Toyota pickups to full-size SUVs. The windows are either shot out or blasted out. Tires are flattened and they're driving on the rims. Many of them are bristling with RPGs, and people are hanging on to them wherever and however they can. And they are coming up the road toward the PJs.

Are they about to be attacked? Are these hostiles or friendlies? For a second, no one knows. Then Malone takes a cue from the shell-shocked SF troop, who doesn't appear to be alarmed at the sight of the trucks. "I think about the training and the caliber of people that're on the ground. He would've keyed back up into his war-fighting mode if these people were a threat, and he didn't."

Malone asks himself, "Okay, what're we into now?" And very quickly he answers his own question. "As the trucks roll up, now we start to see every type of blast injury you could ever imagine. So we got our guys huddled together, and say, 'How are we going to do this? Where's the Americans?'"

And then they see the numbers are growing. There are a lot more than eight people. There are more than twenty. And still they keep coming.

The original game plan had been for the Army doctor on the other helicopter to triage, and the PJs would take it from there. That scheme quickly went on the scrap heap of plans confounded by reality. The American victims of the bombing are on the lead trucks in the convoy, on litters. But since the helicopter had landed a couple of hundred meters off the road on a rock outcropping, the trucks can't be driven right up to the ramp. So the PJs begin humping the casualties from the road to the helicopter, where the physician, his medic, and the two PJs on that bird begin to care for them. Schultz recalls,

"Some guys were on litters; some weren't. Some were on blankets, bed pads, whatever they could find to put them on. And we just started carrying, two-man carries to get them on the helicopter.

"The first ones, all in the first vehicles, were all pretty much critical, but they had been treated. They were stable, so there really wasn't a lot to do." All the casualties loaded on that helicopter were Americans.

After Schultz's third carry, he ran back to the helicopter he'd come in on. Since it had landed near the road, the trucks with the remaining casualties had driven right up to it. It's there that he encountered one of the Special Forces soldiers who had survived the attack apparently unhurt. "I had asked him what happened. He told me he thought they took a two-thousand-pounder, and I said, 'Take care. Is there anything you need?' He goes, 'No.' I said, 'There's a bag of body bags; do you think you're going to need 'em?' He goes, 'Yeah.' So I shook his hand and grabbed the rest of my gear and began helping with the other casualties."

Both Schultz and Malone were struck by how shell-shocked everyone was, including the SF guys. Schultz says, "I wouldn't quite call everybody zombies, but they were kind of in a catatonic state. Most of them were white, their faces were white, and they would do things if you told them to do it, like a tunnel vision kind of thing. I'd seen most of these people before because they'd come through Jacobabad. I recognized them, talked to quite a few of them. It was a surprise for me to see their condition. It's things you've heard about before in books."

Both PJs agree that there were SF troops around who still had their wits about them and were focused. The others were relegated to carrying litters under the watchful eye of the pararescuemen. The emotional damage done by the bomb was brought home when they saw one of the Green Berets standing underneath the tail rotor of the MH-53 helicopter. The rotor is only six feet, six inches above the ground, and he was standing on an incline. Schultz says, "An inch either way and his head would've been cut off."

The Afghan victims hadn't been triaged as well as the Americans had been. Malone instantly could see that the sheer number of severe casualties had overwhelmed the medic with the ground unit. "He's got twenty-plus people on the ground injured, and some pretty seriously injured; then you've got a mess on your hands. I mean, no litters. They're on blankets and sleeping bags and whatever. So we bring 'em up to our helicopter."

The plan is to sort out the casualties, loading from forward to aft, least critical to most critical. That way, when they get to their transload point, the most seriously injured will be first off the helicopter, and first onto the waiting HC-130 with its high-tech casualty team and airborne operating facility. Five or six trucks filled with casualties are lined up at the ramp. Four Americans are among them. One goes all the way forward, two are on litters that are suspended on stanchions on the left side of the bird, and one critical case is put on the floor.

Then they begin loading the Afghans, many of whom are critical and have not been treated; some are still bleeding from their wounds. There are no litters left for these patients, so they are put on the floor, on blankets where they are available. It reaches the point where there is no method to the process; it is just a matter of cramming people in, some sitting up, some lying down. Then the walking wounded are moved all the way forward in the aircraft. Schultz recalls, "I think we took four or five of them, and they just had shrapnel wounds and head lacerations. And we just kept loading, and we crammed—we couldn't have put anybody else on the aircraft. There was one person that they wanted to load but we couldn't. There just wasn't any room to put him any place. He would've been on top of somebody. And we already had people on top of each other."

One of the last Toyotas that pulls up to their aircraft is a pickup truck. In it, they are told, is the last American to be evacuated from the site, one of the two who were killed when the bomb hit. Malone says, "When we looked down, he was in a bivvy sack, zipped up, with an American flag pinned on it." They placed him under the last set of litters hanging in the rear of the helo, which meant that every time the PJs turned around, he was right there, under the Stars and Stripes. Though their training prepares them to deal clinically with blood, gore, and even death, that three-by-five-foot American flag gave them an unexpected and disturbing jolt. Some soldier had deliberately carried it with him into battle, and now had used it to honor his buddy. It meant something. For the next couple of hours the flag would rarely be out of their sight. Even a glimpse out of the corner of an eye was enough to stir a conscious thought. It was a fellow American soldier in that bivvy sack, under that flag. Did he have a wife? Kids? How old was he? Who would tell his parents? How would they deal with it? And ultimately, That could be me.

The thoughts process quickly. There's no time to stop and think, to dwell on the personal tragedy, to utter a prayer, even to recognize, much less respond to, the icy blade of fear that cuts through your gut with laserlike speed, and then is gone. Because the war hasn't gone away.

In fact, it's gotten louder. While it should be apparent that the entire cargo compartment of the eighty-eight-foot-long helicopter is filled beyond capacity, Afghans who were not injured are trying to force themselves onto the aircraft. The PJs presume they're relatives of the wounded, or elders from the village. But the harsh reality is there is no room for them, so amidst what Malone describes as a lot of "hooting, hollering and yelling" over the roar of the engines, they had to take four or five minutes to get them off. It was a nervous moment, acknowledges the senior PJ, who was thankful that with all the weapons available in the nearby trucks, there was no serious trouble. "That's all we needed was a firefight in the back of the helicopter, while we're just trying to get off the ground to help people."

Ryan Schultz was the last person to jump onto the ramp as the helicopter lifted off. The fact of the matter was, he never really did make it *inside* the 53. "I'm literally standing bent over the whole time with my ass sticking out the back of the helicopter, trying to move around the gunner and treat patients." All he had time to do before beginning to work on patients was shed his med ruck; the body armor stayed on. It was his second skin.

In the back of Schultz's mind is the knowledge that they're going to have to refuel in order to make it back to Camp Rhino, the only secure location for Americans fighting in the southern half of Afghanistan. Listening on the intercom as he works on his patients, he hears the details. "We were critical on gas when we took off, 'cause we'd dumped fuel to get in to make sure we could take out as many as we could. And as we were coming out, we hit the west side of Kandahar, and we had to refuel quickly. We were critical gas. We didn't have enough to get to anywhere. If we couldn't get gas, we were going to have to land."

Did it bother him? No.

"That's the pilots' issue. My job is working in the back. I'm aware of it. I mean I hear it, but I don't hear it, if you know what I mean."

Pat Malone was not nearly as blasé about having to refuel. The issue wasn't the refueling itself, a process PJs are notorious for disliking. It was *where* they had to refuel. "It's never done under five hundred feet," Malone says. "But if we were at two hundred feet, we'd be lucky. We were down low. We were afraid we were going to get lit up, and rightly so. We know, map-wise, where we are, but you don't know who else is around there. We're crossing Highway 1, which is the major communications line; we've got patients with varying degrees of blast injuries; they can't go above altitude, so it's like, 'Hey, this is the place to be, in the dirt.'"

Even when a sidelong glance off the ramp revealed the shadow of their helicopter snuggled up to the 130 refueler rippling across the terrain at 115 miles an hour, Ryan Schultz insists he didn't have time to worry about it. "Guys were throwing up all over the back of the helicopter. The two guys on the ramp were bleeding out. One guy had half his hand blown off, most of his arm blown off here on his right side. The other guy was bleeding out his leg. And I'm just going back and forth between these two guys, treating the injuries as I find them.

"The first guy I bandage up. I do a sweep and find that he's bleeding out his hand, and I bandaged up his hand real quick. Then I roll him over and find that most of his arm's blown off. Then I just went ahead and amputated the rest of it with a scissors." Then he rolled the patient over and stuffed the arm underneath him.

The decision to take off the man's arm is made quickly and clinically. "There was not much left. He had basically mid-forearm down, and then a lot of mush, and then from about mid-humerus up was viable."

All the while Schultz is working, his patient is rolling around and is in shock. Schultz administers no morphine, no painkillers. "There wasn't time. Pain never killed anybody. So if he's in pain, there's not much I can do about it, plus it's been four or so hours; he's still bleeding, which is a greater concern to me."

Schultz's attitude toward the administration of painkillers should not be taken to mean he's uncaring or unfeeling; it would be very difficult to be uncaring about your fellow human being and sign up for a job that posits "That Others May Live" as its credo. He's applying his training, evaluating patients, considering the circumstances, and doing what he can do to preserve life. Does he consider getting on the radio to consult with a physician at one of the Forward Surgical Teams (FST) before he amputates? Not even for a second. The decision is his to make, and his training and experience dictate that the way to save the man's life, to stop the bleeding that will surely kill him, is to remove the arm. "A doctor may see it differently, 'cause a doctor is a higher medical authority. But they're not in the back of the helicopter, and they shouldn't be."

Before he turns to the patient with the bleeding leg, he does start an IV in the amputee's good arm. With Pat Malone holding the patient down, Schultz recalls, it was probably the best stick he's ever gotten: an off angle, reaching across the man's body, with the patient moving around. In this situation, satisfaction comes in small victories.

Finished for the moment with his first patient, he moves around the gunner—who has been watching the action wide-eyed—to the other patient on the ramp. This casualty has a bleeder out his leg, which Schultz initially dealt with by putting on a tourniquet. Just as he is starting to bandage the wound, his first patient unexpectedly sits up. Schultz tethered himself to a ring on the right side of the helo, but the patients weren't restrained. A sudden lurch of the helicopter and either or both of them could be tossed from the ramp. Disaster is only inches away.

He jumps back, steps around the gunner, and grabs the patient, laying him back down. Then he calls for a cargo strap, runs it across the two patients, and ties it off on both sides of the ramp. Finally he unhooks his tether from the ring and attachs it to the cargo strap, allowing him to move back and forth across the blood-slicked ramp in relative safety. That's when the amputee catches his eye.

"He looked at me and he started pointing to his mouth. And a guy threw me a jug of water, and I gave him a little sip, just to get his mouth wet, and that was it. He was the most critical on the plane. He looked bad. He was in shock. I didn't know how much blood he had lost. I didn't know what was going on internally. 'Cause he obviously took the brunt of the bomb."

Minutes later he looks back at this patient and sees that his eyes have glazed over. He's died of his injuries. All Schultz can do is move on with his work. He and Malone have done their best in an impossible situation. There's nothing to dwell on.

Looking into the helo, he can see the other casualties rolling around— "writhing" is how he describes it. "But not chaotic screams. Remember, these are warriors, too. They're soldiers." He can also see his PJ team at work. Pat Malone is moving from the middle of the helicopter, where he's been helping Ryan Hall treat the American soldier who'd taken a blast to his upper body and had an open chest wound, back to the ramp. Schultz, seeing that Hall has apparently done all he can for the GI, tells him to move to the front of the aircraft and help Ken Curtis with a number of Afghans whose wounds need tending. And in the middle of it all is Jason Brooks, their combat controller, acting as the pivot man, taking supplies from the medical accessory kit and feeding them to whichever of the four pararescuemen on the team need them.

Nearly an hour after taking off, they come in for a landing at Camp Rhino, a desolate place with a dirt runway that is mid-shin-deep in nothing but fine dust. Malone recalls, "When we hit that, the place went black. Right up through the cabin, right to the front, out the cockpit windows. And the patients are laying in this mess. There's nothing you can do but try and get 'em out of the environment as quickly as you can."

"It was the most desolate place you'd ever think of," concurs Schultz. "It was horrible. It was the dustiest landing going into that place that I've ever had. I put a muslin bandage over my face, and I had goggles on, but the patients . . . The only emotion I felt was feeling sorry for them as we went in to land, 'cause the whole cabin filled up with dust. You couldn't even see two feet in front of you and it took probably two minutes for the dust to clear out."

Even though the Special Tactics Squadron guys who were running the field were expecting two helicopters filled with casualties, there was still a measure of chaos when they landed. Navy SEALs who had responsibility for perimeter security managed to have litters lined up for the PJs, and then helped them transfer the patients to a staging area. From there they were loaded onto a waiting J-MAU Herc, a Joint Medical Augmentation Unit HC-130, staffed with an emergency surgery team ready to work on those casualties who might not make it to the nearest hospital in time.

With their patients handed off to a higher level of medical care, the PJs were finally able to let down, physically and emotionally. Schultz remembers them just sitting down, exhausted. Before they cleaned up, they all just went into the helicopter and sat down and ate an MRE amid all the blood and the bandages and alongside their comrade in arms in the bivvy sack covered with the American flag.

"And then after we ate, that's when we cleaned up the back of the helicopter as best we could," says Schultz. "Grabbed a big body bag and threw all the stuff in there, the bloody blankets. We were loading up, picking up a blanket, and the arm fell out."

Is it comedy? Tragedy? Or just another demonstration that even in war, they're opposite sides of the same coin? If you haven't been there, it might be hard to laugh at the situation. But those who read this, who have been there, will understand why Pat Malone was able to say what he did to Ryan Schultz about five minutes before their helicopter was to land at Rhino. The forty-year-old senior master sergeant and the thirty-one-year-old tech sergeant were standing on the open ramp thinking about what they'd been doing together for the past several hours, and probably for the past few years. Malone looked at his protégé. He knew the younger man had to be feeling the effects of losing a patient he'd done his best to save. Console him? Hell, no. What he said was, "You're never stickin' me with an IV."

It's difficult in the midst of this kind of organized chaos for the PJs to step back and see what it is that the training they've received has equipped them to deal with. But the four PJs treated eighteen casualties who were brought on board more than four hours after a two-thousand-pound bomb dropped right on top of them. Seventeen of them were delivered alive to a surgical team equipped to give them their best shot at survival. By the time they got back to Jacobabad, they would have been on duty for seventeen hours.

Malone says, "You train and you live and you breathe to do that, and the young guys that got to do that will have that with them for the rest of their lives. Pretty good stuff."

# CHAPTER 3

# BOYZ 'N THE HAS

"You gonna finish that?" asks one PJ of another, who has a half-eaten Three Musketeers bar on the table in front of him.

"No," replies PJ Kip Wise, the owner of the candy bar.

"You mind if I have it?" queries the first PJ politely.

"No," says Kip.

"Did you spit on it?" asks the first PJ.

"No," responds Kip.

"You wanna?"

Who are the PJs deployed to Operation Enduring Freedom? They range in age from twenty-two to forty-six, their time in the Air Force from less than three years to twenty-eight. They're white, black, Hispanic, and Asian-American. There are PJs who are single, married, and divorced—some, multiple times. Some are garrulous, a few taciturn. All of them are religious about staying in shape—just watching them killing flight time in the back of a C-130 by doing pull-ups from one of the plane's structural crossbeams, or sit-ups and crunches on the angled ramp, can tire ordinary people out.

One of the newest PJs—he's been in the Air Force less than three years—

HAS with snow at K-2 (*Michael Hirsh*)

Senior Airman Adrian Durham—observes that all of them are variations on a theme: type A.

"See, that's the cool thing about it. We're all ourselves. We're all type A personalities. But you got type A, type A small, type A big, type A bigger, all the way up, y'know? And type A small listens to type A bigger." Durham is twenty-five years old, divorced, and the father of two-year-old Seth, upon whom he dotes. While the other PJs at K-2 wander off to bed by three in the morning, Durham is sitting in their day room drinking canned orange juice—the PJs refer to OJ as "free radical reducer"—and watching a financial news program on Fox News. He makes no comment on the fact that while he's sitting in relatively crude quarters in a HAS in Uzbekistan, the conversation being fed to the war zone by Armed Forces Television is all about stock prices and what companies to buy and sell, as the graphic on the bottom of the screen says, *The Cost of Freedom.*

Durham isn't certain whether or not he's going to make the Air Force a career, or if he does, whether he'd remain a PJ. He knows he's got an aptitude for medical work, and the notion of going to medical school pops into his head on a regular basis. But in the small hours of the morning, he broods over what life would be like if he weren't a pararescueman.

"I know life won't be as exciting as it is now. Our everyday life is jumping out of planes and doing high-adrenaline-rush stuff. It'll never be the same. When I look at life now, what makes it great is the guys I hang with, no matter who they are. We can go anywhere and make a shithole seem like heaven, and that's just 'cause you want the best for yourself. Life in the war zone is already fucked up, so why make it any worse? Try and make it better."

Adrian's biggest fear is that if he makes the leap to the outside, he'll be someplace where people don't understand him. "Everyone understands me here. They think I'm weird, y'know, but out there, it's all different. It worries me in a way. How do you let it go? It's hard to let go. And I know I'll never find it anywhere else."

S.Sgt. Kip Wise, a twenty-eight-year-old from Pasadena, California, who stands six-three, 215 pounds, is on the same wavelength as Durham. "There have been times where I've thought, 'This really sucks today,' but I think this is, by far, the best job in the Air Force, for enlisted, at least. We do just about everything. We parachute, we scuba dive, land, air, sea. I think we've got the best mission, to go out there and save lives. It's so much harder to save lives. It's easy to just kill somebody and pull the trigger and that's it. But to plug that hole and make a difference, that's the ultimate rush right there for me.

"PJs have this commonality, 'cause we all went through the same training. It's probably the toughest in the military. And you form that camaraderie, even if it's a person you don't really care for; no matter what, you know that he's got your back and you've got his back. It's the same thing with the aircrew. We're all one big team. We've got to look out for each other."

What Kip Wise and Adrian Durham have found is a community into which they fit, into which they're accepted for who they are and for the job they can do, a community where their race—African-American—is absolutely irrelevant.

It is surely hyperbole to say the PJs turned their Jacobabad dump into "heaven." But when one considers that the Army troops at K-2 and most Air Force personnel at Jbad are living in tents while the PJs at both bases are living in relative comfort, indoors, enjoying life in the HAS, there's a modicum of truth to what Durham says.

So what is a HAS?

A HAS is a hardened aircraft shelter. They can be found on military airfields around the world. Imagine a gigantic, concrete bandshell, the rear of which might be burrowed into an earthen embankment. The opening is covered with huge doors, as much as three feet thick, which are meant to be moved by powerful motors. Behind these doors is where an air force protects its fighter planes from enemy bombardment. The airfields that the United States is leasing at Karshi-Khanabad, Uzbekistan (K-2), and Jacobabad, Pakistan, are sprinkled with these shelters. Now the doors are permanently open, the motors that move them in various states of decay.

While the structures are no longer needed to protect aircraft, they offer a unique opportunity for upscale housing on these bases. And at their earliest opportunity, the PJs moved out of tents and into the HAS where they put their talents to work making life, if not good, then certainly less awful than it could be if they just had to make do with the basics. At Jacobabad, the PJs moved out of the hangar and away from its surrounding moat into one HAS, then moved a second time, into what they believed to be a more suitable HAS.

At both Jbad and K-2, in order to keep out the elements, especially blowing sand and dust, the PJs put up wooden framing in the open doorway, and built a huge wall of plywood. Inside the K-2 HAS, in addition to their combination day room/office/locked supply room, they have a two-story structure of eight-by-eight cubicles allowing each of the guys to have his own private room. Somehow the PJs convinced an Army Reserve engineering battalion to do the basic construction work, which included wiring each of the rooms with

AC power. The accommodations were so nice that the Army command that runs the base at Karshi-Khanabad tried to evict the pararescuemen and claim it for their own. At first, according to the guys, they were told that the reason they needed to vacate the HAS was that it was sitting on radioactive waste. There is an area of the base that is, indeed, contaminated with radioactive material, but it's nowhere near the HAS and the PJs weren't buying the Army's act.

Finally, when the effort to evict the PJs reached critical mass, so to speak, the guys pulled off their own little power play. They invited the Air Force commanders who were living in tents to move in and share the facility, recognizing that if the Army now tried to force them out of their HAS, they'd be in a battle with at least one full colonel, four other field-grade officers, and a chief master sergeant. Problem solved.

One room on the second floor at K-2 has been made available for visitors, and the sign on the door identifies it as *K-2 Bed-and-Breakfast*, while the adjacent cubicle is designated the Lt. John Shoemaker Suite. Shoe was the first combat rescue officer assigned to K-2 and supervised construction. Guests at the B-and-B find their room furnished with a cot, sleeping bag, electrical outlet, and various toiletries donated by good-hearted American citizens who want to support their troops overseas. The room also comes with a printed "History of the K-2 Bed-and-Breakfast."

It was a cool fall evening in 2002 when the idea for the bed-and-breakfast occurred to John Shoemaker. Inspired by the rolling hills covered by lush foliage and the expansive, silky beaches, he saw the potential for a virtual paradise here on earth. With a keen eye for traditional décor, a taste for the finest in gourmet cuisine, and a desire for fine slumber on only the best bedding, he set in motion the blueprints that would become the world-renowned K-2 Bed-and-Breakfast. Please feel free to relax on our tranquil beaches, take in a breath of fresh dirt, and enjoy the gourmet meals while taking in the magic that is Uzbekistan.

### THE MENU

**Breakfast:** Quaker oatmeal, Pop-Tarts, Grape-Nuts, Frosted Mini-Wheats, fresh fruit, assorted juices, coffee or Pork Chop MRE #12.

**Lunch:** Your choice of MRE. We're currently out of MREs 2, 19, 6, 13, 4, and 7.

**Dinner:** Our chefs scour the countryside for the freshest ingredients each day to bring you something delicious and exotic each night at the following hours: 1600 to 1900 local. Please, no hats in the dining facility, and with regard to breakfast, our senior airman will deliver to your door.

You'll note that neither aperitifs nor other alcoholic beverages are offered on the menu. That is definitely not an oversight, for as anyone who has met them knows, the PJs are a cultured group and have a deep appreciation of fine spirits, wines, and cigars. (S.Sgt. Rob Disney personally recommends the Rosemount Shiraz from southeastern Australia, which, he says, at twelve dollars is a very good value.) The reason there's no liquor served is the notorious General Order Number One, which also prohibits materials that are pornographic or sexually explicit, as well as gambling throughout the entire war zone. It's been expanded upon by the Army commander at K-2 to forbid sunbathing by female service personnel wearing bikinis. As one PJ observed, "General Order Number One takes away everything good about being an American."

Some elaboration is required on the prohibition of pornography. By definition handed down from commanders who feel the need to be deferential to the religious beliefs of some of the host countries, anything that shows completely exposed erogenous zones is considered pornographic. Thus, *Playboy* is verboten, but *Maxim* is not. Mullah Omar has probably not divined that distinction, but this is the military, and what the commanding general says, goes. Throughout the troop living areas at K-2, the CG has thoughtfully placed "amnesty boxes" into which conscience-stricken troops can conveniently deposit anything that might cross the panty line into contraband.

Newly arrived Air Force personnel at Jacobabad are informed by old hands that the local interpretation of General Order Number One is that not only is porn prohibited, but sex is also disallowed. Leaving no investigative stone unturned, the details of that interpretation were sought, resulting in several interesting discoveries. One point of view expressed by certain pararescuemen holds that General Order Number One was intended to say, "Don't get caught" with booze, porn, or having sex. Some aircrew officers, who try to use the fact that they're not PJs as ipso facto proof that whatever they have to say on the subject is credible, declare that there is, indeed, a prohibition on sex in the AOR, but add that the rule has a corollary which states, "If sex is unavoidable, use a condom." (Condoms are available at the BX.) Further investigation determined that the corollary was not actually part of the general order, but was promulgated at a medical orientation lecture that included warnings about insect-borne diseases, heatstroke, and the need to avoid coming into close personal contact with the monitor lizards and cobras that also live on the base.

At K-2, the Army forbids visits by the opposite sex in tents between the hours of 2200 and 0800. The Air Force, however, has no such rule. Tents are assigned to entire flight crews, irrespective not only of gender, but rank. The reason is simple: "hard-crewing" as it's called, keeps the same group of cockpit and backenders together under the theory that people who fly together regularly make better, safer aircrews. Also, because of crew-rest requirements, it makes sense to have a crew that's flown together sleep in the same tent, undisturbed by the comings and goings of extraneous personnel who may be working different hours.

But enough about sex. Back to the Boyz 'N the HAS.

At Jbad as at K-2, the pararescue detachment used as its raison d'être to claim a HAS the legitimate need to have a place to lock up narcotics and other medications, as well as an array of weaponry. Rather than a bilevel cubicle complex, however, they constructed a one-story apartment complex, then turned design and construction of improvements over to S.Sgt. Terra Barrington. A millwright before joining the Air Force five years earlier, Terra got the nickname "Bob Vila" after proving himself adept at turning two-by-fours and plywood into all sorts of creature comforts for what they describe as "This Old HAS."

Terra enlisted when he was twenty-two after growing up in California's wine country, the son of an impoverished hippie mom. He'd decided he wanted to travel and see the world, and felt a compulsion to give something back to his country, which still surprises him, considering that the community in which he grew up was pretty much post-Vietnam hard-core antimilitary.

The Navy recruiter was his first stop, but after taking the required test, he decided he didn't like the Navy vibe. So he wandered down the hall to the Air Force office and told the sergeant that he wanted to fly planes. Not having a college degree made that a nonstarter—Terra didn't even understand the concept of officers and enlisted ranks—but the sergeant picked up his test results from the Navy office, came back, and said, "You can do anything you want to do that's enlisted. You scored a ninety-nine."

Barrington asked if that was good. The recruiter said, "That's ninety-nine out of ninety-nine." That's when Terra discussed the kind of life he wanted with a visiting TACP, who described himself as a radio operator attached to infantry or special-ops units. "And he said, 'Well, y'know what? If you really want to do something hard-core, don't be a TACP. You gotta go PJ.'"

Despite the fact that he's only five feet, six inches tall and weighs 145 if his hair is wet, the physical demands of becoming a PJ weren't daunting. He wasn't a jock in high school, "just an all-around stud" whose lifestyle included a variety of outdoor sports. "Mountain biking, hang gliding. I hang glide right now. That's kind of my dangerous pastime. And just being out in the woods. Hiking. I've done a few peaks—Shasta, Whitney. I don't do any technical stuff. Mount Whitney's the tallest peak in the U.S. I actually didn't summit Whitney. I got to about eleven thousand feet and got altitude sick, but I've done Shasta twice, which is six hundred feet lower."

Swimming was a problem for him during indoc. He claims to have barely passed the distance test in the time allotted. He also had a problem with sit-ups that caused him to get sent back to start the indoc cycle over with the next group of candidates. He says he missed the minimum sit-up requirement by only one, and fully expected the NCO to cut him some slack and click the counter an extra time or two because he was a good guy. No such luck. Ultimately, it took Barrington nearly two years to get through what is typically a ten-week indoc followed by fifteen months of the PJ pipeline. But he made it.

Now he's the pull-up champ of the HAS, capable of doing twenty-six, with his nearest competition, Lt. Rob Taylor and S.Sgt. Rob Disney, reaching only the low twenties.

Barrington is one of the guys who figured out the way to do an entire exercise routine in the back of a Herc. After realizing that they might spend fifteen hours a day inside the aircraft, and that it was cutting into their workout time, they began developing the midair routine. "You can do back and bi, you can do chest and tri, and legs all on the airplane. We go up into the back, right into where the tail is in a V, and there's a couple of bars right there. You can do incline on the ramp, decline. You can jack your feet up on the benches, wide grip, narrow grip. That gives you a well-rounded chest exercise. And then the same thing with pull-ups, narrow grip, wide grip."

To say he's smart understates the obvious, which makes one wonder why he didn't go to college. The short answer—he's an iconoclast who graduated at the bottom of his high school class. That compels the longer answer.

"I don't like homework. It's the whole rule thing. They want you to know that A plus B equals C; then you're going to go home and you're going to write down, 'A plus B equals C. B plus A equals C. C minus B equals A,' and you're going to do that for forty problems, a couple pages' worth. You got an engine in your car that needs working on, a new exhaust system to put on, and the lawn mower to fix. You've got countless other projects going on in the mean-time, and you know very well that A plus B equals C. You got that figured out, so why are you going to waste two hours out of your life to write it down a bunch of times?

"I was the top student in my classes in tests, but I wouldn't do my home-work for a month. I have a fundamental belief, if it was a waste of time, I wasn't going to waste my time on it. So my grades suffered. That's just the way I am."

This exposition on Barrington's attitude toward the regimentation of public school education in America comes on the heels of his elaborating on "the rule thing" as viewed by pararescuemen. "We kind of don't belong in the military. My rule for being pararescue is, break at least one rule a day. Never be in a uniform. If you are in a uniform, take it off at your earliest convenience. And make sure you're not wearing a perfect, proper uniform. Those are my rules."

Is it braggadocio? Or does he mean it? Either way, his elucidation on the subject caused a severe case of twitching in the Air Force PAO who was moni-toring the conversation, ostensibly to protect the airman from exploitation by the media person asking the questions. The PAO warned Barrington that his answers were being recorded, implying that perhaps he didn't want to be so forthcoming. He thanked her for her concern, and indicated that the ques-tioning should continue.

"What rule did you break today?" It was already nearing midnight, and presumably he'd had an opportunity to fill his daily quota. He laughed.

"You want the whole list or just one? Well, let's see, starting out, didn't blouse my pants, didn't wear a hat from the vehicle to the hangar, didn't wear a seat belt when I was driving, exceeded the speed limit in the Humvee. Hmm, I know I could think of some more. I probably broke a bunch on the quads [four-wheel ATVs the PJs have rigged for parachute deployment], considering I crashed that one. Not wearing a helmet or shoes or gloves. No, I was wearing a helmet but no eye protection, no gloves, and no shoes. Yeah, I broke a bunch of rules today. But it's stupid. . . .

"We don't get in trouble. I hear a lot of people say that in other shops. I'm sort of like a liaison between PJs and the rest of the Air Force. That's my own personal thing, 'cause I'm not the typical PJ. They all confide in me that if they did the same thing, they'd get in trouble. It's not that we're intentionally mis-fits. It's that we've got much more important things to think about, to worry about than whether or not your boots are bloused or your hat is on. It's like, if somebody comes up to me and tells me, 'Hey, where's your reflective belt?' I'm thinking, 'All right, the war must be over here, 'cause you're worried about me having a reflective belt on.' There's many more things you could worry about than me having a reflective belt on, or something stupid like standing up in the back of the truck when you're driving to a brief or whatever. To me, my job is dangerous. Riding around in the back of a truck at fifteen miles an hour is not dangerous. Even if I fell out at fifteen miles an hour, it would be less dan-gerous than my job on a day-to-day basis."

And then he sums it up with the essence of the situation. "I don't really belong in the military, but I kind of fit in pararescue. I didn't know what we'd be doing when I was back as a civilian, obviously, but I read the little brochure and I watched a little clip. And I was thinking, 'Oooh, mountain climbing.' And in my mind's eye, I pictured a pilot in a foreign country, hanging from his parachute by a root on the side of a mountain. That's what I was picturing. He's stuck hanging on the side of the mountain, no way for him to do any-thing, and then what he sees is my hand reaching in and me saying, 'Hi, my name's Terra. I'm gonna save your life now. Are you ready?' That's what at-tracted me, because that's the essence of good. It doesn't get any more real than one man to another man, 'I will save your life now.'

"It's just an old idea of nobility. Yes, firefighter's also another very noble job. The stuff that little kids make into heroes. When I was going through the school, what we were supposed to carry with us is 'silent professional.' Not the Navy SEAL image where you tell everybody that you're a Navy SEAL and then you prove it by getting in a bar fight. We're supposed to sneak in, do our thing, and go out. So we'll go into the burning building and then not try to get on the news about it. But we're changing our image from 'silent professional' to 'how come nobody knows who we are?'"

The "nobody knows who we are" complaint has nothing to do with get-ting his picture in the paper for a spectacular rescue. What he's leading up to is a plug to expand the pararescue corps so that there's less burnout, fewer de-stroyed marriages, and more time for additional training. Until recently, the Air Force never mounted a recruiting effort for PJs. But Barrington and others say it desperately needs to be done.

"We need to get the word out, because this is my fifth month over here in this little dwelling. Got two more to go. And that's this year. I was home for about two months, half of which I was at emergency medical service advanced training, which left a month at home between then and now, which is completely the way I like it. However, I would like more freedom to go to other schools. I don't just want to deploy; I'd like to go to jumpmaster school, divemaster school, static line, free fall, structural collapse school, tactical lead climbing schools. It's endless, the places you can go. Having more PJs would allow the flexibility and maybe save some marriages. The deployment schedule is hard on a lot of women and a lot of marriages. That might be the number one reason for the high divorce rate. Just the sheer fact that it's hard to be married to a guy who's gone most of the year, every year, year after year. It just finally falls apart. If we got more PJs, and I would say we need about double what we've got, we could allow the flexibility for married guys to just be asked, 'Hey, would you like to go on these two deployments back-to-back? And they could say, 'Well, I've got a baby coming. I'd like to spend some time with my family.' Having more PJs would allow them to do that. But that's never going to happen; that's just my little pipe dream."

The senior pararescue leadership agrees that they need to do a better job of recruiting. Chief M.Sgt. Bob Holler says, "We just need to get more people in the front door, because I don't want to change standards; I like who we are." Holler's implication is that the PJ school is not unhappy with the 85 percent washout rate at indoc, because they know that 99 percent of the candidates that indoc feeds into the training pipeline will graduate. That's why he says the only way to fix their manpower shortage is to get more guys in the front door.

The pararescuemen are extraordinarily concerned about constantly upgrading their training, and guys like Barrington feel that the excessively heavy deployment schedule—whether or not there's a war on—is problematic.

Medical skills need constant updating as new techniques and new equipment are integrated into their bag of tricks. And it's not the sort of thing that can be learned on the job. Take the complicated medical procedure known as insertion of an interosseous catheter that the PJs learned how to do by practicing on each other during advanced medical training classes. The procedure allows IV fluids to be given to, for example, a burn victim who doesn't have veins suitable for injection. It involves administering a local anesthetic, then using a device to punch a hole in mid-sternum, threading a tube into the bone marrow, locking it in place, and giving the IV injection directly into the bone. Doing it this way, they can give a liter of fluid in thirty seconds. In the training program, they had to perform it on their fellow trainees, and in turn have it done to them.

While preparing couscous on an electric burner in the HAS—Barrington is the unit's only vegan at the moment, and their kitchen is supplied with four different kinds of olive oil and enough seasonings and spices to provision a gourmet restaurant—Terra described another medical procedure the PJs are prepared to perform that has amazed visiting doctors. "We can do superpubic needle cystotomy. Maybe somebody stepped on a land mine and the part of their body that they need to urinate is either blown off or severely damaged, where they can't pee voluntarily, and you can't catheterize them, you still need to drain their bladder or it's going to become a very serious problem, so you just take a big long needle, like you'd give as an IV, and you poke it right in above the pubic symphesis. Boom! Right into the bladder, 'cause the bladder, when it's full, comes right up there. Poke it in, drain the bladder; then you can pull it out. Suddenly they're your best friend, 'cause they had to pee really, really, really bad. Instant success. That's something that these docs don't even do here. I don't know how many of them have training on it. There's a lot of things that we do in the field that has them asking, 'You do *what*? Now, how's that go?' I can do minor surgeries like suturing, for instance. No problem, hands down, no problem."

The problem for Terra and the other Boyz 'N the HAS is that while they're training to deal with medical problems that would cause an urban EMT in a fancy ambulance to just step on the gas a lot harder, they're not getting very many missions. They all salivate at Bill Sine's parachute jump to the minefield, which Barrington is quick to point out was a "jump to an injured patient. The minefield is just a bonus."

And that's the pararescue dilemma. "We're waiting for somebody to have a really bad day. If we come away from this and that somebody didn't have that really bad day, I don't know, it's kind of mixed feelings. We didn't get to do what we do best, but then again, that guy's probably all the happier for it, so that might be the only thing that keeps this from being a total disappointment. We got to do some minor stuff, like transloads, but there's nothing cool about that. 'Hey, you want some Skittles? Sure, all right. Thirsty? All right.' I mean, the guy was sick with dengue fever, but what am I gonna do? Give him some Skittles. He was happy for them. He hadn't had food in a couple of days."

What Barrington and the others fail to acknowledge—or refuse to acknowledge—is that the environment in which they're doing these "transload" missions on lumbering HC-130 aircraft is a dangerous one. Even though some of the aircrew refer to themselves as the 71st E-HMO instead of ERQS (expeditionary rescue squadron), they know the most benign mission can turn ugly in less than a second.

Sr.M.Sgt. Bill Sine, who was instrumental in getting the HAS at Jbad built to pararescue specifications, can personally testify to that PJ fact of life. He didn't even need to be out on a mission for things to get ugly. The war on terrorism came to him. It happened six years earlier, on June 25, 1996, in Saudi Arabia. He was leaving his room in the Khobar Tower apartments to work out in the gym when a huge terrorist bomb blew the front off the building at Dharan Air Force Base, killing nineteen Americans and injuring 372, among them, Sine. The bombers struck at ten P.M., a time they chose by observing that most locals would have vacated the area adjacent to the huge apartment complex by then, and most of the American servicemen would be in their rooms. Their plan worked: almost no locals were injured, minimizing any potential political backlash, and maximizing casualties among the U.S. troops stationed there.

Sine had just stepped out the door of the room he shared with another PJ, S.Sgt. Eric Castor, and was waiting to catch the elevator to the gym, when he heard a muffled explosion. "Then it was like I got tackled from behind. I could feel my hand sting when it hit the marble floor, and then it was all dark and you could hear glass tinkling and falling."

He thought he never lost consciousness, but later pieced together the facts and realized he'd been knocked out. When he came to, he freed himself from the debris that covered him and began yelling to see if any other people were around. He knew something bad had happened to one arm and one leg because they hurt, but in the pitch dark of the bombed out fourth-floor hallway, he couldn't see what was causing the pain. Sine was bleeding, but true to PJ form, decided that it was "nothing like copious," so he didn't need to worry about it right away. His plan was to get out of the building, find the other PJs, and begin helping casualties, and he thought he was up to the task. Years later he realizes that he was doing some things that were probably not normal.

"I got halfway down the stairs—they're all broken—from the fourth floor. I thought I should be down at the ground level—I'd been traveling for a long time. And so I stopped and I yelled out, 'Can anyone hear me? Hey, am I on the ground floor or the basement?' Of course no one answers, and I'm thinking, 'I'm in the basement.' I spent probably a year and a half in this place through the rotations, and I [realized] there's no basement in here; I just must not have gone far enough."

Sine continued down until he could see a strange kind of yellow light from the outside. Pushing his way out the front door, he found a surreal scene with people on the ground screaming and PJs and medics already establishing a casualty collection point in the center of the compound. He walked up to a female medic who he knew, working on one of the injured, and said, "Hey, Rachel, what's up?" "That's when I knew I wasn't right. She looked at me kind of funny—I guess I didn't look too good. My arm was compressed and twisted, like the muscle hadn't popped back. Crunched. My calf was like that, too. They thought that both of them were broken, but they weren't."

About this time, his head started to clear a bit and he hooked up with an-other PJ, S.Sgt. Mike Atkins. The two retrieved their med kits from the Humvees in the parking lot, and suddenly it hit Sine that he hadn't seen his roommate, Eric Castor, who had been sitting at his computer in their room when the bomb went off.

The two bloody PJs rushed back to the front door where a cop was guard-ing it. "You can't go in there until the rescue people get here," he said. "So we said, 'We are the rescue people.'" With their shrapnel wounds and dripping blood, they didn't look like it, but the guard lent them his flashlight and they picked their way up to the fourth floor. That's when Sine realized that the front of the building was gone. "When you look in [to his room], just sky." He felt there was no way Eric could have survived the blast. But at that moment, three other PJs coming from the gym arrived and told him they'd seen him. Castor had suffered many injuries, none of them life threatening.

Later, when Sine spoke with Eric, he learned his friend had been sitting in their room, typing on the computer, and it just so happened he was doing something on e-mail and he hit Enter just as the bomb went off. "And of course now he's flying through the air, a giant explosion, and for just a split second, he was, like, 'Okay, this practical joke stuff has gone too far.'"

The five PJs quickly decided to clear all the rooms in the building, looking for people who were still alive. They immediately found a group of about six in the stairwell—pilots that they knew—and started bandaging them and tak-ing them outside. Sine was beginning to have trouble walking, so they set up a picnic table out in front and he did all the medical treatment while the others went back into the building, bringing out more injured and marking where the dead were located. When other members of the rescue squadron arrived, he used them as litter bearers to carry the most serious victims to the casualty collection point.

About an hour—maybe two—after the blast, the PJ he'd first linked up with came over to him with a complaint. He was holding a torn shirt to his head, and said, "This is really annoying, 'cause I'm trying to work on people and the blood keeps getting in my eye. Can you take a look at it?" Sine removed the bloody shirt and discovered that Atkins had a hole in his temple the size of his little finger, and the blood was spurting from it because his temporal artery had been severed. Sine took an entire role of Kerlex gauze, put it on, and then grabbed an Ace wrap and "really cranked it down. You've got to put a lot of pressure on the artery. I did that, and he's waiting for a second to see if the blood starts coming back in his eye. It didn't, so he's like, 'Oh, cool,' and took the other medical kit and went off back to do his thing."

Six hours later, when they took him to the hospital, doctors had to sew Atkins's artery back together. They also discovered he had a piece of a door stuck through his calf. About the same time, Sine also went to the casualty collection point. He was examined and shipped off to the local Saudi hospital, where they determined he had no broken bones but was suffering from the after-effects of a concussion, so they sedated him and put him to bed.

Consider for a moment everything Bill Sine had just been through, all of which he regards as more or less normal for the career field he's chosen. Then, he says, things began to get strange. "Somebody wakes me up at six in the morning and says he's from the Bahrainian Associated Press and wants to ask me some questions. I told him what my name was and that I was in the building, very basic stuff like that. And he left. An hour or so later, the phone rings in my room. It's the *Today* show office in London, and they're waiting to do a phone interview with Bryant Gumbel. I didn't even know where I was. I didn't know the name of the hospital, anything. The base didn't even know where I was." NBC had gotten the AP story off the wire with Sine's name in it, and tracked him down in his room and was all set to put him on the air, live.

Even in his stupor, Sine knew that Air Force Public Affairs would have his ass if he spoke without clearing the interview with them, and that's what he told the NBC News producer on the phone. Within minutes, NBC London had connected him with Air Force Headquarters Public Affairs. He was told that he could talk about his personal experiences, but couldn't comment on questions about security. Formalities aside, he was switched to New York and in seconds was on the air live with Gumbel.

Sine's parents in Ohio saw the interview and that's how they learned their son was all right. As soon as he hung up with NBC, the hospital phone began ringing off the hook. CNN said if he'd do an interview, they'd conference in his mom, and then get him on the line with his twelve-year-old son, Billy (now a nineteen-year-old who wants to be a PJ), and his dad in Melbourne, Florida.

Ultimately, the Air Force evacuated Sine and his roommate, Castor, to Landstuhl Hospital in Germany. It was then that Eric told him that the back of his computer chair had shielded his body from much of the bomb blast, and that he'd crawled out into the hallway and saw someone covered in rubble. Because of Eric's condition, he was unable to stop and help. The person Eric had seen was Sine, who now realizes he'd been unconscious for at least fifteen minutes, although in his mind, there had been no break in time.

It was at Landstuhl that Sine had to lead a mini-insurrection to get himself and his buddies released from the hospital and flown back to the States in order to be present at the memorial service with President Clinton for the nineteen who died.

As can be imagined, managing a group of type A independent thinkers can be a job and a half. During the last four months of 2002, that job fell to M.Sgt. Dan Killough, a thirty-eight-year-old with twenty years in the Air Force. (Decidedly uncomfortable with personal publicity, he agreed to talk on condition that his real name is not used.) Dan saw action during Desert Storm, where he and a PJ only three months out of school medevacked eight coalition fighters whose armored personnel carrier took a round through the side, resulting in burns and shrapnel wounds.

Killough, himself, has suffered six injuries during his career, all of them in parachute mishaps, and all of them he remembers as though they just happened.

"Let's see, I cracked a vertebra in my neck, I compressed a disk, I cracked my back, I broke two ribs, and I busted my ankle. All while jumping. Except for one, they were all under a static line chute. Two of them were because I wasn't paying attention and hit the ground when I wasn't ready for it; landed with my feet apart and straight up and jarred my back. My ankle I broke freefalling. I slipped going out, so my foot was still in the helicopter, and the aircraft hit me. Cracked my ankle on that one." The list is recited as though it's no big deal, just all in a day's work.

Dan's management style is a quiet one, but intense when need be. During a high-altitude parachute-training jump into the drop zone at K-2, one of the PJs sprained his ankle. When Dan saw that Ed Ha, a relatively new pararescueman, had jumped wearing standard suede desert combat boots rather than the expensive, high-tech leather boots that he had not only researched, but fought to get the money allocated so he could buy them for his guys on the civilian market, the fire in the master sergeant's eyes could have burned a hole through concrete. But he never raised his voice; never used profanity.

Questioned as to whether his rebuke had been tempered because an outside observer was there, with a tape recorder running, Dan said no. The reprimand was what was warranted for the situation. And what does it sound like when a less understated response is called for? He demonstrated at half-intensity: "Airman Johnson, sit down and shut up. This is a one-way conversation." He would have easily had the airman's undivided attention.

Killough's big concerns at Jbad are that his airmen stay current with their training, and that the equipment he's bought them is maintained to the highest standards, so it's always ready to go. Unlike regular military units, there's very little that's *uniform* about the PJ's kit. He says, "The only thing you can find that is standard among pararescue gear is that no pararescue gear is standard. The only thing that's consistent is the inconsistency. If I were to pick up that vest, I'd have to get to know it first and find out what's going on about it. I have my stuff configured specially so that nothing's on the front of my body, so if I'm ever on my belly, I don't have to expose myself any more, give myself any kind of a bigger profile."

PJs are forever creating new pockets custom-tailored to the toys they've been given. A standard piece of equipment back at Moody and in their deployed location is a heavy-duty sewing machine, where the men make their own modifications.

The clothing and boots they brought with them for the environmental extremes of OEF generally do not come through the military supply system. Killough says, "With the changes in the military ordering system and unique nature of our job, we're authorized to buy off-shelf stuff. Most of the bosses, especially me, I fight to buy the best stuff. To keep the guys alive. Why make them wear two inches of fleece or down when I can have it down to a half inch of high-tech fabric and be better equipped?"

Dan enlisted in the Air Force to be an F-4 crew chief, but learned about pararescue in basic, deciding to join when he realized that the Air Force was willing to teach him to do everything he would be paying to do in his spare time. "I was lucky. I happened to come straight out of high school, join the military, found a job I love. Sure, there might be something out there I might like more, but I couldn't imagine it. I could've gotten out and made more money if I felt like it. Money's nice, but it definitely isn't my driving motivation in life."

He's a self-declared introvert who tried marriage once before realizing that for him, the job is more important. Now, in an introspective moment, he questions whether he could make it "on the outside." Clearly, with his management skills, his teaching ability, and his physicality, he has skills that transfer to the civilian world. But the sense is that what he'd really miss is the brotherhood that PJs acknowledge, but seem to speak of only at formal occasions or when tragedy occurs.

At Jbad, where the hardest thing to do is wait for a mission, one ear tuned to the radio while ordinary life goes on, Dan is planning for a return to Moody, and ultimately retirement. The only thing that could get him more excited than a rescue mission will be taking delivery on the new pickup truck that he bought while at Jbad, and will be using to haul around the fifth-wheel trailer that he plans to live in, parked somewhere in a piece of Georgia wilderness owned by Moody Air Force Base.

Were it not for the fact that Chief M.Sgt. Bob Holler came to OEF from Moody in order to spend Christmas with his guys, Dan would be the senior NCO in charge of all PJs in the theater. That includes the guys at Karshi-Khanabad and Kandahar, who fly in two-man teams on HH-60G helicopters, and his team at Jacobabad, where three- or four-man teams fly missions on the C-130s. With a shortage of team leaders holding jumpmaster ratings for both free fall and static line chutes, Dan found it necessary to run the PJ mission from Jbad. There, he flies regularly on the Hercs, which is admittedly less exciting duty than on the helos. Of course, flying on the 130s, there's always the chance that a jump mission will come along, and even after more than eight hundred jumps and four serious injuries, that's a thrill he doesn't get enough of.

"Leaving an airplane, it's almost complete sensory overload. Especially when you first start jumping. You get the wind hitting you in the face; you know you're falling. It's hard to explain; it really is. It's one of the best adrenaline rushes out there. Every time you pull the cord, it's, 'Okay, is it gonna work this time?' And as soon as you get a full canopy, then you're looking for the drop zone, your other jump partners and trying to get down. For me, the only reason to use a parachute is to slow your descent so you don't die on landing. The fun part's the free fall. I've been free-falling for seventeen years now, and still every time I leave the airplane, my stomach ends up in my throat. It's a combination of excitement and fear."

Fear? After seventeen years and more than eight hundred jumps?

"Oh, yeah. If you do anything like that, mountaineering, rock climbing, jumping, even some types of diving, when you lose respect for what you're doing, that's when you die. You've got to realize that you're throwing your body out of an airplane high up in the air, and, unlike civilian skydiving, I might have a sixty-pound ruck on me, an O2 bottle, a weapon, and it can be hard to control. That's a lot of things for your parachute to get hung up on when you deploy it."

Dan says he's never had a canopy failure, but that he's about three hundred jumps overdue for one, given the average failure rate of one in every five hundred jumps.

The HAS at Jbad is set up differently than at K-2, with the day room/kitchen/briefing room actually in a double-walled, insulated, heated/air-conditioned tent that one enters from inside the HAS. The tent is carpeted—shoes to be removed upon entering the room—and furnished with an assortment of couches, equipped with computers that hook into both military and civilian Internet, and has as its focal point a fifty-inch plasma television screen that visitors are assured is essential equipment for training purposes. Use of the screen and attached DVD player for a nightly gorefest of Hollywood's bloodiest movies is merely for testing purposes, in order to ensure that the gear will be in working order when needed for official use.

A perusal of the PJ DVD library could lead one to believe that as a group, they have an unhealthy interest in mayhem. The closest thing to a comedy on the shelf is *Dirty Harry*.

On any given evening, four or five of the PJs will be watching a movie, Terra might be cooking, Kip might be in the back doing laundry, Disney is on the Internet or back in his room playing guitar, Dan may be checking training records or watching the film, and Lt. Rob Taylor is doing what young officers in charge do—paperwork.

There are always at least three PJs on alert status, which means that they're either in the HAS, where the op center can reach them by phone, or carrying a radio if they're elsewhere on the base. What they're listening for is the call that tells them there's a potential mission. If it comes over the radio, all they may hear is the code word and a number—"Houdini fifteen, Houdini fifteen, Houdini fifteen."

When that happens, the alert crew immediately goes to the central area of the HAS and gets their rucksacks, which weigh roughly eighty pounds each when packed for a mission. Someone will open the weapons locker, and they'll grab their M-4 rifles and 9mm pistols. One of the nonalert guys will jump into the driver's seat of the truck already backed up to the HAS door, and in less than ten minutes, they'll be on their way out to the alert bird parked at one end of the runway. The truck gets backed up to the open loading ramp, and in another two minutes all the PJ gear is on board, and they're ready to roll. Sometimes the plane will take off immediately; other times they'll sit and wait, perhaps for a couple of hours, while the Joint Search and Rescue Center (JSRC) decides whether or not to launch them.

That's the way it works when an alert occurs. But most often the hours are filled with the routine tasks of life, made more difficult by the fact that they're on an extended camping trip, and everything from eating to bathing is that much more difficult.

Take the prosaic matter of just doing the laundry. At K-2, Brown and Root, the civilian contractor that runs the dining facility, maintains the water supply, and cleans the latrines, provides a laundry service that's free for everyone on the base. No such luck at Jbad, where doing laundry is a do-it-yourself proposition for the 780 Air Force and Army personnel. Laundry facilities are located in a very large tent that holds twenty commercial washers and as many dryers. Detergent is supplied in boxes and barrels—no shortage there. What clogs up the works is the limited water supply to the base, which means the washers take forever to fill, which means there's often a line of people waiting to use them.

Obviously, this use of common facilities is way too much hassle for the PJs. Readers should note that certain details in the following have been omitted to protect operational security and the always-important TT&P (Tactics, Techniques, and Procedures).

Sanitation facilities, as previously noted, improved from basic Porta Pottis, through various types of multiholers, up to the so-called Cadillac shower facility. However, the PJs are still using a tent adjacent to the HAS that has RV-type toilets with a flush pedal. Considering their other rather luxurious amenities, this seemed curious.

Master Sergeant Killough was politely tweaked about the situation, with the notion that it's surprising that a Cadillac shower unit didn't somehow just show up in the middle of the night, replacing the tent and trough setup. His two-word response was telling: "Too obvious."

Only when Terra Barrington conducted a tour of the back of the HAS did Killough's comment make sense. There, to the surprise of the visitor, was a private shower, one of the heavy-duty washing machines, and a double dryer next to a utility sink. How they got there is answered with little more than a shrug. How they got connected with appropriate water and electrical hookups is pure genius. In fact, how the PJs got an armed forces TV connection, phone service, Internet hookup, and extra heating and air-conditioning units, on their timetable, is a tribute to prior planning and an understanding of how the military functions in ways that will never be found in any official manual of policy and procedures. As a very senior NCO said, "We're going to make our lives as comfortable as we can. And through hook or crook, we accomplish that goal. I could tell these guys, 'Hey, I need this,' and they'll go out and find it. And I don't ask how they got it, 'cause I really don't care, as long as we get it."

While the attitude sounds anarchic, it's really a paradigm for the way pararescuemen are taught to think in the field, where they're on their own, charged with saving the lives of wounded who may be hours away from a doctor's care. The mission is saving a life; they're taught methods that have been known to work in the past. But if those methods aren't doing the job, they've got the green light to use their smarts and intuition.

The greatest change that's come to the PJ career field in recent years is the advent of their own officer corps. While the back-door, NCO-to-NCO method worked well for quality-of-life matters, the fact that PJs didn't have their own officers to represent them at higher levels of command adversely impacted larger operational issues. As a small part of a much larger squadron whose main job was flying helicopters or Hercs, the PJs' needs were often neglected.

In 2000, that changed, as the career field known as CRO—combat rescue officer—was set up. The first two officers were virtually hand-selected by the NCO cadre. Maj. (now Lt. Col.) Vinnie Savino had been Director of Operations (DO)—second-in-command—of the elite 24th Special Tactics Squadron at Pope Air Force Base, North Carolina. Much to the chagrin of the STS community, Savino gave up a promising career there to head up the new 38th Rescue Squadron at Moody. Maj. Terry Johnson, who'd been special tactics liaison officer to HQ, U.S. Armed Forces Europe, joined him at Moody to be DO of the 38th, then was asked to stand up the 58th Rescue Squadron at Nellis AFB, Nevada.

One of the first of the newly minted CROs is twenty-four-year-old Robert

Taylor, an Air Force Academy graduate who gave up a guaranteed slot in pilot training to opt for pararescue. Taylor was the first CRO candidate to actually go through the indoc program.

At Jbad, he's being mentored by Master Sergeant Killough. Clearly, there's a mutual respect at work. The LT was the man who had to represent the PJs whenever conflict arose with the 71st ERQS, the unit that owns the HC-130 aircraft on which they fly. Consequently, it was in Killough's best interests to make sure he understood what the issues were and what his men needed in order to do the job. True, Savino made a tour of the theater of operations to stand up the 38th Expeditionary Rescue Squadron, but the day-to-day working relationship must be maintained, massaged, and negotiated by the young lieutenant, often with a lieutenant colonel who didn't necessarily see the PJs as an integral part of a Herc crew. (It's fair to say that the leadership of the 41st ERQS, which flies the Pave Hawk helicopters out of K-1 and K-2, treats the PJs more as fellow crew than back-end passengers.)

Lieutenant Taylor was to have been a third-generation military pilot. His grandfather flew B-24 bombers in World War II, his father flew C-130s in the Navy, and he grew up knowing that he had to apply to at least one military academy. Since Air Force had the best soccer team, that was where he went, doing a semester at West Point in his junior year. His grades were good enough to guarantee pilot training, but he learned about the CRO career field, called his fiancée (an Academy grad who became a pilot), and said, "This is what I want to do." His class at indoc started with fourteen men; only four graduated.

Clearly, making the commitment to sacrifice one's life that others may live is not something a man does lightly. But in Taylor's case, it's a commitment that fills a personal need that he clearly articulates.

"The greatest thing in life, the greatest thing you can do to better yourself or to find happiness, I found, is to be selfless. And there's no more selfless way in life than to give your life for somebody else's life. And it's something I've just always believed and always known that if I were ever in a position, I would be willing to do that. Obviously, there's a great deal of patriotism and loyalty embedded in me.

"I love taking care of my people," says the young LT. "It's a great opportunity to learn and to lead, and to be part of something that's so much bigger than myself. It's not just me being selfless, but it's three hundred men now, and a legacy of one thousand men who have stood up and said, 'Pick me. If someone must go, then send me.' I'm pretty proud of the people I associate with and the people that I call myself a part of."

One of the people he's talking about is T.Sgt. Ken Howk, a thirty-year-old with ten years in the Air Force, some of it as a PJ in a Special Tactics unit stationed at Mildenhall, England. For the action in Bosnia, his unit pulled rotations at Brindisi, Italy, flying airborne alert for scheduled bombing missions. The first "real" mission he got came in June of 1995, when pilot Scott O'Grady was shot down. Ultimately, in a manifestation of turf warfare over CSAR rights that would continue into Operation Enduring Freedom, the Marines made that pickup.

Shortly after the O'Grady mission, a French Mirage jet was downed and the PJs participated in a week-long search to find the crew. The second night of the search remains memorable. Howk recalls, "We got lit up almost every corner we turned. I mean, we had, I think, eight or ten rounds through the helicopter. You could hear them just plinking around on the inside. It was pretty exciting, actually. I remember I was on the tail, and they have a tail gunner there, too, and I was just lying there, searching out with my NVGs. We'd actually come over this road, and there was somebody shooting up at us. And I could see, with my NVGs on, the rounds just shooting past the tail. I don't know how it never hit anything on the tail, but you could just see the rounds coming right by us. And he buried the fifty-cal [machine gun] right on top of him. It was pretty awesome. But as we were coming around that corner, they said that somebody got hit up in the front. We went up to the front of the helicopter, and one of the door gunners had taken some shrapnel in his leg. And I was looking past him out the door, and this house just started lighting up the helicopter with everything it had. We were no more than a hundred feet off the ground—and the door gunner and the tail gunner at the same time just laid a barrage of fire on this house and pretty much quelled the fire that was coming from it. Then the other gunner also took some shrapnel in his knee, which turned out to be nothing big. But we ended up flying back across the Adriatic, and apparently they hadn't relayed exactly what was wrong with our helicopter or how many rounds we'd taken or the status of the personnel, so the head shed was pretty paranoid. They thought the helicopter was going to go in the drink, so they had us covered with all kinds of CSAR assets on the flight back. Then we landed, and they're out there with chalk circling all the holes, and I think there were eight or ten holes in the helicopter and blades. There was actually one right through the middle of the fuselage; that was a pretty good-sized one. But that was about it for that."

In other words, for Howk, it was just a good day's work. "From my perspective, our guys do things that I don't think are that big of a deal." Other people, even those in the Air Force, see it much differently. "I've been out and actually done training missions simulating the pickup of a downed pilot where we've fast-roped off a helicopter and gone and snatched the pilot, and this was a captain in the Air Force who was awestruck by the whole thing. He's standing there, and all of a sudden we're right there, just taking him. And he has no clue that we're even in the area, other than he knew there was a helicopter there. That was it. But he didn't know we came out of the helicopter, he didn't know that we were right there in front of him, and we grabbed him before he even knew it. He knew he was going to be rescued, yes, but he just didn't grasp the concept. Then I go home, and my family, they don't really have a clue about what exactly I do. I mean, they know what my job is, they know basically what I do. But that's about it."

Howk is fairly sanguine that his wife, Heather, whom he's known since 1996, understands both him and the pararescue mission. "She's been around the job, and she knows what we do. I'm sure she worries about it, but she doesn't think that I'm going to do anything that's gonna mess me up. If something's going to happen, it's going to happen." Deployments happen too, but neither Howk nor his wife expected him to be gone as much as he has been since being assigned to the 38th at Moody. In the year before his deployment to Operation Enduring Freedom, he was away from home for 220 days.

On a mid-December night outside the Jbad HAS the temperature is in the forties. At first glance, it looks as though it's snowing. What's actually filling the air is a cloud of smoke and particulate from the burn-pit fires on the base, and from the coal-burning fires in thousands of homes surrounding the base. The pungent air is thick enough to taste, and accounts for the residual cough that many who are stationed there for months will take home with them. If the appearance of snowfall in the Pakistani desert isn't eerie enough, throughout the night the air is pierced with the yelping of jackals, and on an almost hourly basis with the sound of trumpets and the voice of the muezzin in the city, calling the faithful to special worship for the Eid al-Fitr. While it might be politically correct for the Americans inside the surrounding wall and concertina wire to acknowledge that the sounds merely represent the observance of religious customs by the local people, the fact that many of those people are known to be fanatically hostile to the Americans in their midst makes the sounds seem ominous.

On a typical night, after the movie, some of the guys pile into the Humvee and drive the mile to the main base for midnight chow. That's a choice of breakfast items—the pancakes and French toast are actually better at night than they will be rewarmed for breakfast at 0600—or leftover items from dinner. (In the early days at Jbad, the tale is told that the 71st would send a scout to the dining hall to determine what color the scrambled eggs were. If the eggs weren't properly cooked, which was often, they'd range from green to brown. But on those days when they came out yellow, the scout would return with the word, which would quickly spread all over the base, and there'd be a mad dash for breakfast.)

It's a reasonable bet that no matter what he chooses to eat—even if it's just potato chips—Killough will apply a liberal dose of hot sauce. As someone in the dining hall remarked, hot sauce can even make concrete taste good, which is perhaps why miniature bottles of Tabasco are part of the standard amenity kit packed with each MRE.

Sometime after midnight chow, the PJs disperse. Disney opts to go to the gym about the same time that the LT decides to go for a run. Other PJs can be found heading to the gym well after two in the morning.

What becomes apparent after spending more than a week at Jbad, Kandahar, or Karshi-Khanabad is that the day of the week and the time of day hold little meaning for those serving here. Were it not for a "day" indicator on electronic wristwatches, it's likely that most couldn't even tell you what day it is. With the exception of those manning the 71st operations center during daylight hours, the Air Force flies most scheduled missions at night. Crews go to bed at three or four in the morning and sleep until noon or later. It's not unusual to be passing someone on the way to the shower at two in the afternoon and have him or her say, "Good morning."

At Kandahar, the living is not nearly as luxurious as at the other two bases. The PJs have a tent that serves as squad room, day room, supply room, and kitchen. Nominally in charge by virtue of the fact that he is a tech sergeant (select), is Justin "Soup" Campbell. True, the visiting Chief M.Sgt. Bob Holler is the ranking enlisted man for the entire 38th Rescue Squadron, but once the chief goes home, Soup is it.

He joined the Air Force at age eighteen to be a PJ. His father wasn't thrilled with that career choice, but backed off after a recruiter told him that he needn't worry about his son, because there was no way he'd make it in pararescue. Soup says he heard that and said, "Well, we'll see. There's no way in hell I'd ever quit, because ever since I was a little kid, my old man told me, 'You're not quittin' anything. If you start something, you finish it.' So there's no way I could ever call my dad and say, 'Yeah, I quit.' "

At that point he didn't know that part of what the instructors do at indoc is to try to make the candidates quit, and when that realization struck him, he knew he'd just have to mentally "suck it up, because I wasn't about to let them beat me." That doesn't mean there weren't times that he came close to throwing in the towel.

"There's times when you're sitting at the bottom of the pool and you're drowning and going, 'What the hell am I doing here? How did I end up here at the bottom of the pool with weights strapped to me?"

About eighty men started indoc with him. He didn't graduate the first time around because of stress fractures in his foot. That set him back to the beginning, and he had to do the ten-week indoc all over again. The second time around, another eighty started the course. At the end of the pipeline about fifteen months later, seven graduated.

Were they physically stronger than the seventy-three who didn't graduate? Probably not. Were they better swimmers? Not necessarily. Smarter? Maybe, maybe not. What all seven had was the tenacity not to quit. A psychologist could probably have a field day with the graduates. Some, like Soup, make no bones about the fact that they're determined to meet the expectations of a demanding father, no matter how unfair or unrealistic those expectations may be. But no matter the reason, the instructors are looking to find men for whom quitting is not an option.

S.Sgt. Rob Disney is another PJ who may be proving to a demanding father who had been a Marine that he can tough it out. Indoc was hell, but quitting was not an option. "In the first four weeks, the object is, 'Don't quit and don't get hurt.' That's the only way, really, to fail out until after the fourth week, when you start getting tested on your ability. The first four weeks is just train-up. They teach you how to do everything that you're going to get evaluated on for the next six weeks after that. And then as long as you don't get hurt, don't quit, and continue to meet the standards, you graduate the course."

What he's glossing over in his fond remembrance of indoc is the effort the instructors went through to make them quit. Consider buddy breathing. "Buddy breathing is two guys, one snorkel, and both of them wearing their masks. And the object is, don't let go of your buddy, don't let go of the snorkel, and don't come up for air. And it's two men passing the snorkel around, and you have one or two instructors on you. And at a certain point, the instructors can block two breaths from you by putting their hand over the end of the snorkel or pushing the snorkel into the water."

What they're trying to do is induce a sense of panic in the PJ candidates. The ones who succeed are the ones who relax and realize that they can control the sense of panic.

"On any breath of air, when you're passing the snorkel between the two of you, it feels like just an eternity's going by, because you're getting rolled, and you're getting twisted, and you're getting pushed to the bottom. And you push off, and they push you back down. But the reality is that you're in such good shape that you can hold your breath for between two and three minutes at a time if you're just at a good rest. So even while they're harassing you, you can hold your breath easily up to a minute. You've always got a little reserve left over."

The trick is that while the instructors know about the air reserve, in the beginning, Disney and the other PJ candidates didn't. "By the end of it, you start to get the picture. But you get so caught up in the fact that, 'I just tried to breathe, and I can't,' that weighs heavy on your mind when you're down there. You have to think it through. If you try to take a breath and they stop you, the easiest thing to do—not the easiest; the hardest thing to do but the best thing for you to do—is to pass it off. Pass it to your buddy. If he gets a breath blocked, the first thing he needs to do is not freak out and try to pull it to his mouth and take another breath. The best thing for him to do is pass it off to me, because if I get another breath blocked, then I can pass it back to him, and then it's going to come back to me, and I'm going to get the breath, because that's two blocked breaths. They have to give you that third breath. That's the rule and we all know it. So you just stay calm and keep your head in the game, and things pan out."

Clearly, it takes a special breed of guy who can keep his wits about him when most people would be screaming for help. It's not surprising that those who've made it through indoc to the battlefield begin to reflect back on those first days with similar thoughts.

Soup Campbell says, "That's what it comes down to . . . we're a different breed, and that's why there's only so many of us who are ignorant enough to not quit and to say, 'Hey, yeah, I'm drowning here, I'm going to pass out, but I'm not getting out of this pool and quitting.' It's the same mentality you have when you're laying there going, 'Yeah, I'm shot and I'm bleeding to death here, but I'm not going to let these guys die on me.'

"When we got tasked, I was one of the first volunteers. I wanted to come over here and do my job that I've trained to do. That's not saying that I'm some kind of war junkie, 'cause that's not what it is. But the action, the adrenaline, the job satisfaction of saying, 'Yes, I actually went out into a combat situation and saved people and did my job that I trained to do for years.' To save people and to go get people when they needed help and have no other hope. That's what I'm here for; that's what I signed up for."

The kind of motivation and commitment that Soup brings to the job is what the senior pararescue NCOs attempt to instill in the PJ candidates as they go through the hell of indoc and then, if they make it without quitting, on to the specialized training in the pipeline.

Comparisons to other elite special-ops forces, especially the Navy SEALs, are inevitable. The major difference seems to be a much less pronounced need for PJs to swagger. PJ T.Sgt. Ryan Schultz says, "I've worked with SEALs a lot, so I know how to deal with them. Some people, they go with the rivalry kind of thing, and you've just got to realize that their mission's different than our mission. And work around it. SEALs are cocky, so is STS, and so are PJs and controllers. We don't walk around with a broomstick up our ass like SEALs do. We don't think the world revolves around us. Whereas SEALs do. You walk into a room with SEALs, you can tell."

The difference, says Schultz, has to do with the ego buildup he believes SEALs get. "It's brainwashing, basically, is my opinion. They're told over and over and over again how good they are, and there are instances where they are good, and there are instances where they're bad. It's like a fighter pilot. You got to tell a fighter pilot how good he is so he'll go fly over the lines and do the mission. Same thing with a SEAL. You tell him that nobody's going to hurt him.

"As far as capabilities, across the board, we're all fairly equal in ability, athletics. If you want to stop and do push-ups, we're not iron-pushers for the most part, like a lot of SEALs are. They've got to see how much they can bench, but we can go run forever, and we can go swim with them, 'cause I've done it."

A ranking PJ NCO has a more incendiary way of looking at the SEALs' need to let everyone know that they're the baddest dudes on the block. "You know what they say. Big watch, little dick."

Chief M.Sgt. Bob Holler, who at forty-six years old is still psyched about pulling alert and flying missions out of Kandahar, is used to hearing people—including many that they work with—say that PJs are just plain crazy. After spending the afternoon at Kandahar doing snatch and grab exercises on the end of a cable suspended from a hovering helicopter, it's not surprising that the chief would disagree with that assessment.

"When a prospective pararescueman gets through his training, especially what we now call the indoctrination training down at Lackland where the washout rate is eighty-five percent, that individual at that point is reborn. You take somebody who is, if not doubtful, they're not aware of what their true capabilities are as a human, as a team member. And you test them to the point where all of a sudden they wake up, they're reborn. They realize, 'Hey, I can do whatever I set my mind to.' And because of that mentality, that mind-set, and the team cohesiveness that we instill in those schools, you get a group of us together and we can do anything that we put our minds to."

"And because of what we do, the jumping, the diving, the climbing, the modes of transportation that we use to get to a patient or extract him from danger, commonly called adrenaline sports in society, we need that mind-set that says, 'Hey, give me a task and I'll figure out how to do it. I'll go through the wall, over the wall, around the wall, but I'll get it done,'—yeah, we could be called crazy. But it's not crazy; it's calculated, we're going to press until we get it done."

Holler, who is a connoisseur of good cigars and Thai food, and has been skydiving since 1976—he was on the world-record large-formation jump with 281 other jumpers—has developed his own exercise regimen that PJs half his age and twice his height can't do. (Okay, that's an exaggeration—he's five-seven and there are no PJs over eleven feet tall.) Here's his description of the routine.

"It's a calisthenics pyramid set, starting with pull-ups. You do one pull-up, followed by two curls with forty-five pounds of weight, two dips, two push-ups, twenty-five bicycle crunches. Then you do two pull-ups, four curls, four dips, four push-ups, twenty-five bicycle crunches. And then you go to three pull-ups, and then six, six, six, twenty-five; four, eight, eight, eight, twenty-five; five, five, ten, ten, ten, twenty-five, and so on and so forth. You work that pyramid up to however high you can get it. Right now I'm up to nine, and then you work it all the way back down. And the totals come out to whatever number you reach, you square that number. So that workout is eighty-one pull-ups, one hundred and sixty-two curls, one hundred and sixty-two dips, one hundred and sixty-two push-ups, and three hundred and seventy-five bicycle crunches. Now, if you do the math, that doesn't work out, because actually I don't start with one. I start with three; I combine one and two together. So I actually do three, three, four, five, six, seven, eight, nine, eight, seven, six, five, four, three, three."

And he does it all in less than an hour. "So you're busting your ass. It's both an aerobic and anaerobic workout."

Lest one get the impression that the chief is a by-the-rules administrator, hung up on physical fitness and doing the mission, he volunteered to tell a "Charlie" story. "Charlie" is an ugly wooden doll that was brought back in the sixties by two PJs who had a jump mission near Fiji. Somehow, Charlie became the symbol of all things pararescue, and possession of the doll imbues the unit that has him with a level of pride not even attainable in combat. Shortly after Charlie arrived in the United States, one PJ unit stole him from the guys who brought him back. And that began what the Chief describes as "forty years' worth of shenanigans and exchanges of Charlie."

While the liberation of Charlie from the possessing unit is not quite governed by the Geneva Convention, there are rules. But they're PJ rules. "You probably have a flavor for PJs well enough now to know that we don't really abide by rules much. But it's supposed to be a game of stealth, where you use brain and stealth and mission planning to abscond with Charlie, rather than pure numbers and muscle. Although I've seen some pretty good fistfights. One of the most dramatic Charlie stories that I've been witness to was at Kirtland, at a pararescue graduation ceremony.

"Portland had Charlie at the time, and they had built this extravagant thick steel sedan chair. Well, that's what they had built for Charlie, this big, heavy steel cage with carrying poles. And they drove up in a van in the parking lot at the officers' club there at Kirtland, and started bringing him up, and they were immediately attacked by some instructors and a whole shitload of students. And we're talking a service dress affair, blues, ribbons, y'know, everybody's got shiny boots. They had a brawl out in the parking lot. We're talking fists-to-the-face brawl. I was in the bar having a beer—not something I do on a normal basis—and somebody ran in and said, 'Chief, Chief, they're fighting out in the parking lot.' So I ran out to the parking lot, and there's a blue Air Force van hauling ass right in front of the entranceway, and there's a kid hanging off the left rearview mirror, being dragged down the street, and I ran out yelling, 'Stop that motherfuckin' van!' Screeech! I started questioning them,— 'What the hell's going on?'—and it was a madhouse. There were guys with ripped coats, ribbons all over the ground, berets everywhere. Guys were bleeding, ripped ties. And it was a mess. It was, like, wow. I said, 'You guys, you can't be dragging each other down the street on the side of a moving vehicle. What if he fell down and got run over?' I was doing the chief thing. And so every-body gets settled down and everybody's putting their uniforms back together.

"So I come back in, and about thirty seconds later, this kid comes in, and he's proudly pronouncing, 'We got him! We got him! Class So-and-So, we got Charlie!' And I turned around, and I said, 'Excuse me, but' "—the chief is screaming here—" 'last time I checked, only pararescuemen can steal Charlie, and the last time I checked, you are not yet one, and you will not fuckin' be one unless Charlie shows up here tonight!' And he said, 'But, Chief—' and I said, 'I don't wanna hear it. Charlie's here, or you're not going to graduate. I'll fuckin' promise you that right now.' So we have dinner. The kids get up on-stage after dinner, the guest speaker comes out, and right when the guest speaker's speaking, Rick Weaver comes out and he sets Charlie on the stage. And everybody, bless their hearts, maintained until the guest speaker was done. And then it was a huge brawl again. Everybody was on it. The Kirtland O-club used to have a baby grand piano—notice I said 'used to'—that sat there in the dining room. There was a horrendous mass of humans rolling over the floor, and it ended up on that baby grand piano. There were piano keys—phew! phew!—everywhere. And I forget who actually ended up with Charlie after that whole brawl, but it was one of the wildest Charlie stories I've seen."

Charlie was most recently seen with one of the PJ units flying in support of Operation Iraqi Freedom.

**CHAPTER 4**

# MURPHY NEVER RESTS
## FEBRUARY 12–13, 2002

Some days, it just doesn't pay to get out of your sleeping bag.

But when Maj. John Cline rolled out of his on the afternoon of Tuesday, February 12, 2002, the thirty-four-year-old pilot had no idea that this day—or rather, night, since the operations he and his seven crewmembers from the 9th Special Operations Squadron support almost always take place under cover of darkness—was going to be one of those days. In spades.

The briefing held no surprises; the mission was expected to be routine. Cline's MC-130P Combat Shadow, tail number 0213, an aircraft three years older than its pilot, with the call sign Ditka 03, and his wingman, Ditka 04, were going to take off from Shahbaz Air Base at Jacobabad, Pakistan, and fly north into the mountains of Afghanistan. There they'd refuel some MH-53 Air Force special ops helicopters on an administrative repositioning—going from a forward deployed location back to their regular operating base. After that, the two ships were going to split up and, in the parlance of the trade, haul trash. They'd go to a couple of separate forward operating locations, transfer some people, and move some equipment.

The MC-130P Combat Shadow is basically a Vietnam-era HC-130 "King" bird Air Rescue platform modified for special operations missions. Covert helicopter air refueling is their primary mission, but they also train

MH-47E Chinook helicopter refueling from an HC-130P/N. Notice that the rotor blades extend well beyond the end of the refueling probe. (*U.S. Special Operations Command photo*)

extensively for night airdrops, blacked-out landings to austere runways, and in-flight refueling from KC-135 and KC-10 tankers. Typically neglected in the competition for advanced modifications by "shinier toys" in AFSOC's arsenal, Combat Shadow crews take bittersweet pride in operating in the night low-level environment without the terrain-following radars and other advanced avionics common to all other night low-level platforms in AFSOC. "Half the Equipment, Twice the Skill" is their unofficial credo.

Just after sunset they took off, watching the desert flatland of northern Pakistan rise slowly into foothills where, barely an hour later, the nav watching their progress on a moving map display announced that they'd crossed the unmarked border into Afghanistan. They didn't get very far over that border when command and control canceled the plan for Ditka 03, and directed Cline to return to base to replan for an emerging, high-priority mission.

There are many layers of control for the hundreds of aircraft flying in OEF, and headquarters higher up the food chain often exercise their authority to cancel missions that have already launched, and reassign the aircraft based on shifting operational needs. In this case, Cline didn't need a crystal ball to guess that they'd been tapped for an air-refueling mission. What he needed to know once he got into the operation center located in the only hangar on the American side of the Pakistani air base was where Ditka 03 needed to be, how much fuel they need to get there and return, how much they'd need to pass to the helicopters, and how long they'd have to be on station. Knowing what unit they would be refueling would also be useful, since the skill level of the helicopter pilots at the tricky task seemed to vary with the different units involved.

---

Ditka 03 Air Force MC-130P
"Combat Shadow" refueling aircraft
    Pilot—Maj. John Cline
    Copilot—Capt. Jason Wright
    Right Navigator—Maj. Don Tyler
    Left Navigator—Maj. George Akins
    Flight Engineer (FE)—M.Sgt. Jeff Doss
    Radio Operator—S.Sgt. Rodney Young
    Left Loadmaster—S.Sgt. Chris Langston
    Right Loadmaster—T.Sgt. Jeff Pohl

Chalk 1 Army MH-47E "Chinook" Helicopter
    Airborne Mission Commander—Lt. Col. John Buss
    Special Operating Forces Recon Team

Chalk 2 Army MH-47E "Chinook" Helicopter
    Special Operating Forces Recon Team
    160th SOAR Medic

Chalk 3 Army MH-47E "Chinook" Helicopter
    PJ Team Leader—S.Sgt. Chris Young
    PJ—T.Sgt. Keary Miller
    PJ—SrA Jason Cunningham
    Combat Controller (CCT)—T.Sgt. Gabe Brown
    Special Operating Forces Recon Team including SAS Medic

Ditka 04 Air Force MC-130P
"Combat Shadow" refueling aircraft

---

He also wanted to know the flight plan of the helos, in order to plot where they'd be coming from and when they might arrive. The veteran pilot didn't need the information engraved in tarmac; he expected it to change, often by the minute, but the more details he had, the more proactive he could be when changes started happening.

"In general, we live out on the tail of the dog," Cline acknowledges. "PJs and the guys that work ground are usually on the tip of the spear. When the ground plan changes, then it moves the helicopter plan, and then the helicopter plan changes and it finally works its way down to us, usually about half an hour after we're supposed to be where we're supposed to be. So we're always leaning forward, trying to get as much information as we can, because we know things are going to change."

Flying the Combat Shadow version of Lockheed's C-130 Hercules, although among the most challenging night low-level operations in military aviation, is not a glorious mission. But Cline is acutely aware that they're an important cog in the wheel, which means they can be a limiting factor on a mission. And that's something he never wants to be. Which is why no one was surprised when in a rush to get airborne after three hours on the ground, command and control still had not provided the helicopters' flight plan or the execution checklist for the mission.

The checklist assigns a brevity code to be used over the radios for every significant step of the mission. With the code, they can call their command and control and instead of saying, "Ditka 03. We've got our engines started," they can say, for example, "Ditka 03 bagel." If all the aircraft on a particular mission are using the same brevity code, then anyone with the checklist can track the progress of all the players involved. What this means when they're airborne is that his radio operator can determine—just by hearing these different code words—whether the helos are on time or falling behind, or if things are changing, or on rare occasions, that things are going just as they were planned. The buzzword for it all is SA—situational awareness. (Given that aircrews are made up of bright men and women who quite often have a lot of free time, it's no surprise there are stories of brevity code words being strung into lengthy sentences and transmitted to controllers at the Joint Search and Rescue Center as payback for what were perceived as repeated, annoying requests for information at critical times when pilots were on overload just executing the mission at hand.)

Cline also took off without his wingman. The second MC-130P assigned to the mission developed mechanical difficulties on startup, and without a lot of slip time available, Cline opted to get moving and let the other aircraft, which was essentially a backup refueler in the event something went wrong with Ditka 03, catch up. Later, when it became apparent that the repairs were going to take longer than expected, Cline asked control to reassign his wingman from the first mission of the day, who was now on his way back to Jbad. The reassignment approved, Cline got the other pilot on a secure frequency and briefed him about the mission details. On this particular night, the navigators and flight engineer had figured that if everything worked absolutely perfectly and went absolutely on time, one aircraft would have enough fuel to support the whole mission. Everyone knows the value of having a spare airplane on a mission; it means two extra hoses to put out in case something goes wrong. Considering that most of the 130s in the fleet are older than the pilots flying them, things regularly do.

The flight north to the rendezvous point was expected to take roughly ninety minutes for the MC-130P, which can fly high enough to go over the mountains at a speed of approximately three hundred mph. The MH-47E Chinook helicopters they were assigned to refuel can fly only half as fast, and fully loaded they're unable to fly over the peaks, which forces them to navigate through mountain passes.

Remember those problems in high school math? "If a train leaves Pittsburgh at nine A.M. traveling west at seventy mph, and a second train leaves

Chicago traveling east at ninety mph, and we want them to meet in Cleveland . . ." That was just algebra. In Operation Enduring Freedom, planners not only had to be mathematicians, they could benefit from a doctorate in alchemy as well. They had to factor into their computations the weather at different altitudes, geographic obstacles that prevent flying in a straight line, hostile-fire potential at various points en route, ornery machinery, and the personality quirks of mission commanders.

The three MH-47Es—the troops call them "47 Echoes"—were from the Army's 160th Special Operations Aviation Regiment (Airborne) based out of Fort Campbell, Kentucky. Known as the Night Stalkers, the 160th SOAR(A) is an elite special-operations aviation regiment in which every pilot is not only a volunteer, but jump qualified and combat medic qualified as well. The operation, they'd learned, was to infiltrate and exfiltrate a special-ops team on what had quickly developed as a high priority, militarily and politically significant reconnaissance mission. Were they assigned to kill a leader of one of the many rival factions in the area? Was it a snatch and grab mission? The participants aren't saying anything more than it was a big enough deal to cause other missions to be put on hold.

The team was made up of non-American, English-speaking special forces who, as one source put it, were "in the service of Her Majesty." British Special Air Service commandos? Australian SAS? Both were in country at the time as part of the coalition forces fighting with the United States in Operation Enduring Freedom. While their nationality remains unknown, what is very definite is that not one of them bore even a passing resemblance to John Wayne in *The Green Berets*. These special operators were wearing civilian clothing augmented with native scarves, and had apparently gone months without encountering a barber or a razor. Their intent was to blend in with the locals, and there was every reason to believe they were succeeding, since it required a very close examination to pick out the Afghan national accompanying them as a translator.

What they weren't succeeding at was getting to the rendezvous point on time. For reasons that were never made clear to Cline, the helos initially requested a delay of thirty minutes, then twice more pushed back the meeting time. Ultimately, Ditka 03 would have to loiter for an hour and forty-five minutes awaiting their arrival. Part of the delay was apparently caused by a decision to rearrange the mixture of troops assigned to each helicopter. When it all settled out, the helo designated Chalk 1 was carrying the airborne mission commander (AMC), Army Lt. Col. John Buss, riding in the cockpit seat behind the pilots, as well as a contingent of special operators and that Afghan interpreter. Chalk 2 carried special operators, while Chalk 3 was designated the CSAR bird, carrying a special tactics team consisting of three PJs and a combat controller, in addition to several more SAS types.

On combat missions, these helicopters fly with windows and ramp open to accommodate the machine guns, which means that their interiors are freezing cold. They're also flying blacked out, so it's dark inside. Perfect conditions for PJ team leader Chris Young to grab a nap, especially with several hours of flying till they reached their objective. After all, adapting to one's environment is something the Air Force teaches in the PJ pipeline. And if the thirty-one-year-old staff sergeant didn't learn it from the Air Force, he learned it in the Marine Corps Reserve, where he spent more than five years while attending and after being graduated from Texas A&M.

It was participating in several joint missions with Air Force PJs that showed him the error of his ways, and caused him to ask what he describes as a "lifestyle" question: "Do I want my wife living on Camp Pendleton," the desolate Marine Corps base north of San Diego, "or on an Air Force base?" So he made the switch to the USAF, and applied to join the PJs.

In July 1997 he completed the pipeline, donned the elite maroon beret, and moved to Moody AFB, where life was fairly routine until the terrorist attacks on New York and Washington. Then, it was only a matter of time before he knew that all the training was going to be put to use. In January, Chris and his wife, Rhonda, along with Senior Airman Jason Cunningham, twenty-six years old and barely half a year out of the PJ pipeline, and his wife, Theresa, and the other six PJs on the deployment got the "get your affairs in order" lecture from Major Savino. Then they got special attention from Chief M.Sgt. Donald Shelton, the unit's highest-ranking NCO and superintendent of all seventy or so assigned pararescuemen, a thirty-year veteran who parachuted in to help seize an airfield during the invasion of Panama. With Shelton's retirement imminent, he wasn't being deployed to OEF with his men, and it was tough to see them off. So tough that he didn't want to say good-bye at the Valdosta base, so he rode with them on the plane up to Baltimore, where he put them aboard the Rotator.

The end of the line for Young and Cunningham proved to be K-2, a former Soviet air base at Karshi-Khanabad, Uzbekistan, where a finger of the former Soviet Republic pushes into northern Afghanistan, several hundred miles northwest of Kabul, across the Hindu Kush mountain range. In addition to being covered with fine-textured dust that turns to ankle-deep, reddish brown soup following the slightest bit of precipitation, K-2 boasts low-level radiation where the former occupants are said to have buried the remnants of one or more nuclear reactors. Maps posted in the dining hall seem to indicate that the radiation is confined to one quadrant, an area thoughtfully placed off-limits to joggers. Since Defense Secretary Donald Rumsfeld personally visited K-2 to negotiate American rights to use what is now an Uzbek air base for OEF, presumably those who serve there will not glow in the dark should they snap a leg bone like a chemlight.

Upon arrival, Young was paired with a team leader from the 720th Special Tactics Squadron out of Hurlburt Field. For the first couple of weeks he was in-country, he served as assistant team leader, learning from the guy he was going to replace. They'd rotate between special-tactics assignments out of Bagram, where they'd be embedded with Army Rangers, Green Berets, or Navy SEALs as part of a QRF—Quick Reaction Force—and spending time back at Karshi-Khanabad manning the Rescue Coordination Center. Finally, the day came when he got what he describes as his "*hominus dominus*," the official blessing that he was good to go as a team leader. He didn't have to wait long for his first combat mission.

Only hours later, the QRF was given a classified mission flying aboard an MH-47E. Those familiar with the Vietnam War may confuse this special-ops version of the Chinook with the aircraft often seen flying over the jungle, a 105mm Howitzer dangling from the cargo hook beneath it, from whence came its too easy yet semiaffectionate nickname, the Shithook. While the exterior profile is much the same, a look under the hood will lead one to the immediate conclusion that this isn't your father's helicopter.

In addition to its aerial refueling capability, which didn't exist in Vietnam, this MH-47E has forward-looking infrared (FLIR) and terrain following/terrain avoidance radar which permits nap-of-the-earth and low-level flight operations in conditions of extremely poor visibility and adverse weather. The twin engines have been upgraded to produce four-thousand-shaft horsepower each, and the advanced avionics give the aircraft the capability of global communications.

One of the most exceptional features of the MH-47E is the construction of its fuel tanks, both internal and the external sponson tanks. They have a honeycomb shell construction and a vapor inerting system that almost eliminates the possibility of fires or explosions when struck by large, nonexploding projectiles. Testing also showed that the self-sealing, crashproof tanks could survive direct hits from .50-caliber machine-gun bullets. All in all, it's an aircraft the Army designed for precisely the sorts of special-ops missions it's carrying out in Operation Enduring Freedom.

Which brings us back to the mission at hand, inside a freezing cold MH-47E making its way in the company of two identical Chinooks through mountain passes, from Bagram toward a rendezvous with Ditka 03. In addition to Young and Cunningham, the third PJ on the team is a nine-year veteran, T.Sgt. Keary Miller, a soft-spoken northern California native and father of two, who'd left active duty and moved to Louisville in May 2001. There he joined the 123rd Special Tactics Squadron of the Kentucky Air National Guard to play a role in setting up the first special-tactics unit in the Guard. In October 2001 the unit was federalized, and with ten days' notice, Miller found himself on a plane headed for K-2, where he worked in the Rescue Coordination Center (RCC). Eventually he took over the CSAR alert teams and relocated to the airfield at Bagram, where the PJs set up shop in the tower building, just down the hall from the Army's 274th Forward Surgical Team. FSTs are a much smaller, more agile version of the old MASH units. They bring surgical and critical care down to the brigade level in order to stabilize critically wounded casualties who would otherwise not survive the trip to a rear-area combat support hospital.

The night of what turned into the infil-exfil mission, Miller wasn't even on alert, but at the last minute he joined the team, which included Young, Cunningham, and combat controller Gabe Brown. With combat rescue experience under enemy fire in Bosnia, the tech sergeant was definitely the veteran of the trio of PJs; nevertheless, Chris Young had previously been designated team leader on this flight, and there was no reason to change that.

While the helicopters are making their way toward the rendezvous point, Ditka 03's crew is killing time. In the cargo bay directly below and behind the cockpit, the radio operator, S.Sgt. Rodney Young, is jumping back and forth between two different sets of cryptological codes in the secure radios, trying to keep track of all the different mission players. Having a single crewmember responsible for handling communications with the world outside the aircraft allows the two pilots, two navigators, and the flight engineer in the cockpit to focus their attention solely on flying the plane over and through Afghanistan's unforgiving terrain. On this night, they're being given fits by the IDS, the Infrared Detection System camera (sometimes interchangeably referred to as FLIR) mounted on the nose of the aircraft. It has a normal field of view, and it has a zoom mode. Pilots usually rely on the normal view because it's basically a one-to-one ratio, the same as they're seeing through their night-vision goggles. Depending on atmospheric conditions, especially the amount of moisture in the air, on some nights the NVGs mounted on their helmets see better than the FLIR ball does; some nights the FLIR sees a lot better than the goggles, so using them both is a good cross-checking technique for attempting to identify terrain. Experience has taught them that on really dark nights like this one the FLIR ball is typically better. So they rely on it a lot. Unfortunately, as the helicopters are getting closer and they are getting ready to drop down and move into the critical refueling phase of their mission, it begins to malfunction. Uncommanded, it would go into zoom mode, making it impossible for the pilots to get any useful information off of it, and there seems to be nothing that Maj. Don Tyler, the right nav, can do to fix it.

As the cockpit crew is dealing with the FLIR problem, radio operator Young hears something disturbing on the AWACs frequency. The pilot of a reconnaissance aircraft flying over the general area the helicopters were headed to comes up on the freq pretty excited. He's just had a surface-to-air (SAM) missile almost hit his aircraft, causing him to dump all his decoy flares and half his chaff. What catches Rodney's attention is the tone of the pilot's voice. "The pucker factor was definitely up there." The pilot hadn't seen the launch; he didn't see the missile till it broke through the clouds coming up at him. When he settles down enough to rattle off the coordinates of the incident, Rodney relays them to the navigators, who plot them and discover that they are relatively close to the objective area where the infiltration was to take place.

Given their expectation that the target the recon team was going in to find would be highly defended, the SAM launch in that area makes sense. Just something else to keep in mind over the next couple of hours.

A few minutes later, the radio operator clicks in on the intercom and starts to speak. A big lightbulb had gone off above his head. "Y'know what? The helicopters aren't listening to the AWACs frequency. They didn't get that information about where this missile launch came from." Given the okay to pass it along, Young goes through another command and control network, jimmies his radios around, and relays the attack information directly to the approaching flight of helicopters.

The delay in the arrival of the helicopters does have one plus to it: Ditka 03's original wingman, Ditka 04, gets his maintenance problems straightened out, and launches toward the objective area. This allows Cline to release the aircraft he requested as a substitute backup, giving the mission a second tanker that has a full bag of fuel on board—certainly much more fuel than Ditka 03 has after spending ninety minutes killing time. Doing some onboard calculating, the lead pilot changes the mission plan slightly. Originally his aircraft was going to refuel all three helos before the infil and after the exfil. Now the plan will be for Ditka 03 to refuel the helicopters going in, climb up high and wait for the ground teams to be inserted and do their job, and, on the way out, 04 will take the lead and pump fuel for the exfil.

When the helicopters radio that they are approaching the refueling track, the two tankers drop down into a long, narrow valley. Even though they are more than ten thousand feet above sea level, they are below terrain on both sides. While this is a comfortable altitude for the fixed-wing aircraft to operate at, it's at the upper end of the helicopter's performance envelope for air refueling, and with the exception of the helicopter pilots themselves, no one is more aware of the dicey nature of the maneuver than the PJs aboard Chalk 3.

By their very nature, PJs dislike situations where others are in control of their fate. They recognize that for them to do their job, someone else has to fly the plane. And most have seen that the pilots who fly them, whether in fixed- or rotary-wing aircraft, excel at their craft. But trust and blind faith only go so far—and midair refueling is, for many of them, beyond the trust barrier. During training flights, it's not uncommon for the pararescuemen to ask pilots to drop them off before they begin practicing refueling. Keary Miller says, "It's kind of like if you [parachute] jump a lot, and all of a sudden you're doing a tandem, and you're the passenger. I'd rather jump and [have] me be in charge of the parachute and not somebody else. Air refueling is not one of my favorite things."

Sitting on some gear near the rear of the helicopter, his helmet disconnected from the aircraft's intercom system, Miller is unaware of where Chalk 3 is in the refueling process. PJ team leader Chris Young is still asleep on the floor of the helo, also not on comms. Jason Cunningham, meantime, is paying close attention to everything that's happening. This is his first mission in combat; it's precisely what he told the instructors at the PJ school he wanted to be doing. While some in his class were opting for mountain rescue duty in Alaska, and still others wanted to be assigned to bases that did a lot of civilian rescues at sea, Cunningham surprised everyone when he said he wanted CSAR. Now he is getting his wish.

At about three in the morning local time, the flight of 47 Echoes moves in behind Ditka 03 to begin the refueling procedure, a process that should take no more than fifteen minutes if everything goes as it should. Imagine a pas de deux between hippos—neither one is especially nimble, but that doesn't keep them from trying to perform the dance with some degree of dexterity. The tanker's job is to run the refueling track with as little deviation from the straight and narrow as possible. If they were refueling the more agile HH-60G Pave Hawk flown by Air Force CSAR units, the ballet would be much more graceful. But instead of a Baryshnikov, what's coming up behind them is a Pavarotti in toe shoes. An appropriate name for this particular ballet? How about "The Drogue Slayer"?

The reputation has been earned, in good measure, as a result of the way Boeing engineers designed the refueling probe mounted low on the right side of the 47E's nose. It's twenty feet long and fixed—that is, it doesn't lengthen and retract as the ones on the Pave Hawks do. What this means is that the rotor blades extend beyond the end of the probe. In order to plug in and refuel, the pilots must move the helo so that the rotors are actually over the refueling hose itself. At the end of the hose is a forty-two-inch-diameter, circular wire basket, covered with fabric, in the center of which is the coupling through which fuel flows when the probe is locked in. The device is called a paradrogue—drogue for short—and when the plane flies at refueling speed, the drogue fills with air, causing the hose to float behind the wing. The engineering theory that renders the Boeing design for the 47 Echo refueling probe acceptable is that the downdraft from the rotors will actually push the drogue down and away from a potentially disastrous interaction with the blades.

The theory passes the reality test with Chalk 1 and Chalk 2. The lumbering helos are able to simultaneously attach themselves to the hoses coming from pods under the left and right wings, get several thousand pounds of J-8 jet fuel each, and back out of the contact without event. On the right side of the plane, loadmaster Jeff Pohl is able to take a break. Chalk 3 is going to refuel off the left hose, typically the one used when a single helo is refueling because there's less turbulence coming off the 130's left wing than the right. It is loadmaster Chris Langston's job to flash the infrared light signals that tell the NVG-wearing pilots when they're cleared to the contact position.

He does his job well. Unfortunately, the pilots in Chalk 3 are having a bad night. Langston does a running play-by-play for the benefit of the cockpit crew, and the line that he uses most often is, "Swing and a miss." Chalk 3 would be cleared for contact, the 47 Echo would move in, and the guys in the back of Ditka 03 would feel the characteristic lift and push as the Chinook snuggled up to them. They'd make a stab at the drogue, miss, and have to back out and wait to try it all over again until flight engineer Jeff Doss could reset the hose. When the helo does manage to connect, he stays on for only a few seconds, then falls off.

Langston recalls this going on for a good twenty or twenty-five minutes, and conditions were not getting any better. "The further we went down the track, the worse the turbulence got, and the hose was bouncing around, and he was bouncing around." To try to minimize the hose movement the flight engineer tried weighting the hose down with fuel. No help. When he began to get concerned that Chalk 3 might really be desperate to get gas, he changed the release settings so that fuel began flowing the instant the probe made contact, rather than waiting until they had a solid lockup.

John Cline, who's the chief MC-130P pilot evaluator for the Air Force Special Operations Command and a former instructor at the MC-130P Schoolhouse at Kirtland AFB, New Mexico, and is known as an especially skilled and intuitive pilot, can empathize with the Chinook drivers. They're at high altitude, actually on occasion going above the limits the flight plan called for because the terrain is forcing them up, and the helo's controls are very mushy in the thin air. "We were going east to west, and the further west we got, the more mechanical turbulence we started to encounter. It wasn't gross," Cline says, but, "the guy was already having a little bit of a hard night; it definitely exacerbated his problems trying to get on the hose."

When pilots of air tankers are preparing for a mission, they need to take into account not only how much fuel they'll have to pass and when, but also where the refueling can be done. In a combat situation, they want to orient the refueling track so it takes the helicopters near their ultimate objective, but not so near that it wakes up the neighborhood. An ideal situation is to tank the helicopters on a track that ends at a point roughly twenty-five miles from where the helos are due to land and infiltrate the recon team. In this case, the track Ditka 03's crew had chosen was twice as long as what would normally be needed to give these three helicopters the amount of fuel they wanted. Depending on circumstances that include, among other things, what tank on the airplane the gas is coming out of and what tank on the helicopter it's going into, they can normally transfer 500 to 1,000 pounds of fuel per minute. Chalk 3 had asked for 4,600 pounds, just under 800 gallons.

Now, according to Cline, they're "down about five or six miles from the end of the track, he's on the hose, he's taking his fuel. He's only going to need to be on the hose for another two to five minutes. So I'm thinking, 'Hey, this is going to work perfect. We're going to hit the end of the track; this guy'll be done and we'll press on with the plan.'"

Some sort of unscrambled telepathy undoubtedly communicated that bit of optimistic thought to the demon of all things vital, Murphy. That would be the Murphy of Murphy's Law, which states, "If things can go wrong, they will, at the worst possible time," and its corollary, which asserts that "Murphy never rests." He may catnap, but it's always with one eye open for an opportunity to step in and really screw things up.

Major Cline remembers it this way: "We're down below this overcast now, and the guy falls off the hose right by the end of the track, and he's only got about half or two-thirds the amount of fuel he needs to do the mission. We didn't have all the information we typically have. I didn't have their flight plan; otherwise I'd have just pressed right on down there, whatever their next leg was on their flight plan. I would've just dragged 'em down that way."

In addition to lack of information, time is becoming a problem. "We've slipped all night long. Sunrise is approaching, and obviously we've got to do these missions all during the cloak of darkness. I think it was approaching three or three-fifteen in the morning. At that point, we had a limited window to get these guys in and get them out with the amount of darkness we had. So I was left with a choice: I could either just press on straight down this valley, which looked like some pretty bad weather. Could turn back around and head back east, which would be taking them away from their objective area, which [means that] every minute we fly east is two minutes that they've got to fly back west. So I just asked them where they needed to go."

The AMC in Chalk 1 responds with a heading of 210 degrees, a left sixty-degree turn, which makes sense to Ditka 03's crew because the objective area was about twenty-five miles south of where they were at that moment.

Cue Murphy, one more time.

Just as the AMC makes that call, Chalk 3 starts launching defensive flares, which light up the sky and wash out the image on everyone's night-vision goggles. For fifteen to thirty seconds, everyone is essentially blind. Caution dictates the instantaneous assumption that must be made is that they're under attack. Cline says, "The reason to launch flares is 'cause somebody's shot a missile at you. That definitely got our attention. We're now cruising a little bit beyond the end of the helicopter refueling track, trying to discern what that flare launch was all about. It takes—whatever it takes—half a mile, mile, [till someone] comes back to say, 'That was a false alarm, nobody shot at us.'"

In the back, Chris Langston guesses that Chalk 3 had their electronic countermeasures set to automatic, and something as benign as a fire on the terrain below triggered them, not an altogether unusual occurrence. It's just that given the frustrations of the last half hour, the timing couldn't have been worse. Score one more for Murphy, because now the choices get tougher. They can opt to pull in the hoses, leave the area, and set up to refuel in a different valley. Or they can press on with the refueling where they are. Cline and Lieutenant Colonel Buss confer by radio, and the decision is made to press on, and again Buss requests a heading of 210 degrees.

The Army commander describes routine midair refueling as a "high-adventure event," and a real-world mission "at ten thousand feet is much more high-adventure." He's certain that "the pilots were doing their best, but as with many things, the more you try, the harder you work at it, the more difficult it becomes. So I'm just going through this pilot's mind now. I'm sure he's trying to relax." Buss is convinced that his pilots will be able to stay on the hose long enough to get the gas they need. As a matter of fact, he sounds almost nonchalant discussing the difficulty Chalk 3 had been having. "It's a precision maneuver to connect with the refuel hose. You move up into what's called the 'refuel position,' and then it's a workout just staying on that hose under good conditions. Any little thing, any little bump or maneuver, or you get a little bit off cue, the basket just comes off the probe. Happens all the time."

Nonchalance aside, Buss does acknowledge what-iffing the situation. "It was going through my mind, 'What if he can't get his gas?' and I was thinking through contingencies if I had to send him down or have him land somewhere, if we could continue the mission. But I thought that the terrain was more favorable down the route further. I thought he'd get his gas, ultimately. So I wasn't too worried at this point."

Turning Ditka 03 in the direction of the insertion point for the recon team is a compromise to save time. The risk is that if the accidental flare drop didn't announce their presence to the bad guys, the noise they're generating might. A flying circus comprised of a pair of four-engine turbo-prop airplanes flying single-file, two hundred to five hundred feet apart, accompanied by three twin-rotor Chinooks in close formation, produces only slightly less racket than fifty thousand prepubescent girls at a Britney Spears concert—especially when they're flying relatively close to terrain that causes sound to echo side to side as well as up and down intersecting canyons.

With his NVGs once again working, it's easy for Cline, sitting in the left seat, to look left about sixty degrees and see what appears to be a nice valley almost precisely on the heading the helos were requesting.

As they're making the turn, they hear good news from Chalk 3. He needs to be on the hose for only another two to four minutes. Chris Langston again begins calling the play-by-play while signaling with infrared lights visible only through night-vision goggles. The signals clear the helicopter from the pre-contact position to move up and attempt to stab the end of their twenty-foot-long refueling probe into the center of the forty-two-inch-diameter paradrogue at the end of the hose trailing from the underwing-mounted pod.

"Strike one," calls Langston. In the cockpit, the FE resets the hose.

Moments later on the intercom, the crew hears from the left loadmaster again. "Swing and a miss. Strike two." The FE automatically resets the hose. And again the helicopter misses. And again. It is beginning to seem like watching a bad baseball game. You'd leave, but you can't get your car out of the parking lot until everyone in front of you leaves. For almost another twenty miles down the refueling track, the pilots of Chalk 3 keep whiffing.

In the cargo compartment, the radio operator has been scanning from the right forward window, and he does not like what he's seeing. Whether it's a function of depth perception through NVGs, or his relative lack of experience in this kind of terrain, he's convinced that if the aircraft moves even slightly to the right, the wing tip is going to impact the mountain, and he gets on the intercom to pass that warning to the cockpit. "The terrain is awful close out here. Don't go any further right."

He gets a little solace when both the pilot and co-pilot acknowledge him. "Okay, we won't come any further right. We're pressing on ahead."

Rodney Young has been "Radio" on 130s for only three years, but he grew up in an Air Force family—his dad is a retired chief master sergeant and his mom a master sergeant—and he joined up to fly. He'd wanted to be a loadmaster but there were no slots available when he was ready to enlist, so he opted for the radio job. He'd always been comfortable in airplanes. But now he can feel the nervousness in his stomach, and listening to the navs disagree about which way they should be heading is not improving the situation, because it underscores that they aren't where they thought they were or where they are supposed to be. "I know the terrain is rising and we're picking through to find the lowest altitude to get through, but it doesn't seem that anything is working for us. It doesn't seem like the mountains are moving [aside] fast enough for us to get into these gaps."

Rodney is watching his SCNS (self-contained navigation systems) panel, so he knows their altitude, heading, and airspeed. "And I'm hearing altitudes called off—this mountain is this height, this mountain is that height. Basically I know what height we're at and what height that mountain's at. We need to get a little bit higher."

It's not that he's uncomfortable with the fact that their flight plan has been changing, often by the second. Those plans are always altered by terrain. What's bothering him is that the right side navigator, Maj. Don Tyler, who's watching the moving map display and who is trying to coax the malfunctioning Infrared Detection System into providing some useful images, is telling the pilots to go in one direction, and the left nav, Maj. George Akins, who's keeping his eyes glued to the radar, is saying they should go in a different direction. And the FE is reminding them that they need to avoid the area where the missile had been fired at the reconnaissance plane as they were heading out. This is a crew that Rodney has flown with often; he was at the MC-130P Schoolhouse with Akins; he trusts them implicitly. But he also trusts his instincts, and his instincts are sending a message to his stomach: they're in trouble.

Up in the cockpit, the aircraft commander is flying the plane and trying to sort out what Rodney accurately described as conflicting information being presented by the navigators. Cline explains how it looked from the left seat. "We initially turned down a valley on the 210 heading the helos had requested. With Chalk 3 swinging and missing all the way through the eight- or nine-mile-long valley, we found ourselves slowly turning due south, onto a 180-degree heading. We could see that there was a Y in the terrain about five miles ahead of us. We had to go left or right into branches of the valley; climbing and going straight was not an option. At this point we are already over ten miles south of the original helicopter air refueling track and getting closer to the objective area and the area of the SAM launch. The right branch ran on about a 210 heading, which is the way the helos wanted to go, and it angled away from the objective area, whereas the left branch ran on about a 120 heading. I saw that we could have easily cleared the terrain to the left, but not wanting to get any closer to the objective area because of noise and the potential missile threat, I asked the navs specifically if the terrain on the right was going to 'box us in.' This is where Murphy took over once again. I did receive conflicting info from my navs, but it was mostly for good reason. George, the left nav, said there was terrain up over ten thousand feet in that direction (which was correct), and Don said no, that we weren't going to be boxed in, that there was terrain down to ninety-two hundred feet (we were at ninety-five hundred feet when I asked the question). Looking right, down the valley on the 210 heading, that is exactly what I thought I saw: terrain up over ten thousand on one side, and a nice cut in the terrain down to below our altitude on the other, so what the navs told me seemed to make perfect sense. I remember looking down the valley and not being concerned at all with what I saw.

Yep, we're going to go up here about five miles, turn right about twenty degrees through this—there was an arch of significantly higher terrain off to the left. It looked like the terrain was significantly lower off to the right about five miles ahead of us."

The conflicting info from the navs occurs because they are getting their information from different sources. Akins is getting his information manually off a paper 1:500,000 chart, and the pilots expect him to be able to identify only the highest terrain. They know he's trying to read contour lines on the paper chart in a darkened flight deck as they bounce along. Tyler, on the other hand, is using the GPS moving map display on a laptop computer. The software allows him to roll the cursor over any given point on the chart and it gives an exact elevation for that point. He had routinely used that feature to determine the exact heights of cuts in higher ridges they flew through on other missions.

Cline says, "Our bad luck was that Don was referring to terrain down the *left* valley. He was looking for the lowest terrain in general and I thought he was referring to terrain down the valley on the right. Knowing where each nav was getting his information from combined with the visual illusion to make these two pieces of seemingly conflicting info make perfect sense to me. Murphy strikes again."

The fact that they're still dragging a 47 Echo behind them is certainly complicating the task of flying the plane. During refueling, they can do only about 110 knots—126 mph—barely above what the manual says is stall speed. What's more, they're heavy with roughly 48,000 pounds of fuel in the wing tanks and the internal Benson tank, an auxiliary 1,800 gallon fuel reservoir that some tanker 130s carry inside the cargo bay. As a consequence, the controls are fairly sluggish. To top it off, the optimistic viewpoint Cline had several miles back about the helicopter needing only a few more minutes on the hose had faded like an aging starlet's looks. Things were, indeed, getting uglier.

From the left paratroop door where he'd been signaling the helo's pilots, Langston cuts in on the intercom. "He's coming in really hard. Holy shit, I hope he doesn't do *that* again!"

Not only is the pilot missing the drogue, he's lunging at it, getting ever more aggressive. Everyone on comms inside the tanker can tell by the rising tone of the normally calm loadmaster's voice that he's genuinely concerned. What he's watching the helo do after the latest miss is back up, and then do the exact same thing again.

Murphy was just biding his time.

The next time the helo lunges forward, Ditka 03 hits a bit of turbulence, popping the hose straight up into the end of the rotor blades. "He cut the hose!" Langston shouts.

The warning is directed at the flight engineer, Jeff Doss, who, if it's true, needs to immediately turn off the fuel supply. There's momentary confusion in the cockpit. Doss attempts to get the situation clarified: "Confirm he has *cut* the hose."

Langston responds, saying, "Hey, the hose is *not* cut. He just collapsed the drogue."

Doss recalls that there was some discussion back and forth, with the pilot asking Langston questions about what happened and what he was seeing. Finally, the FE interrupts in a rather loud voice, trying to drown everyone else out, "Confirm that the hose is in the pod."

And at that point he recalls Langston responding, "Yes, the hose is in the pod."

The difference between a cut hose and a collapsed paradrogue is important enough for the pilot to involve himself in the discussion. Cline explains: "It was a pretty important distinction from our point of view, emergency procedure–wise. The hydraulic system is active at that point, so it's only the drag that's on that parachute out there holding that basket up that keeps the hose out. Without the drag on that chute out there, the hose just shoots back into the pod; the hydraulics overcome the drag, and the hose wraps into the pod as fast as it can, which is the case if you just cut the parachute drogue material and it collapsed. As long as the big metal coupling is still on the end of the hose, it'll get inside the pod and hit the limit switches and shut the thing off. Kind of no harm, no foul. But obviously, if he's actually cut the whole thing off the aircraft, you've got a three-inch-diameter open fuel line thrashing around inside the pod, because there's nothing to stop it. It'll just go inside the pod and kind of start to bird-nest in there. You can have the pod up there whipping this open fuel line against hydraulics and electrics, and it's a pretty delicate control assembly up inside that pod. So again, in my mind at that point, the terrain wasn't my biggest concern. I saw what I saw, and I was really worried about what was going on inside the pod."

The flight engineer is equally concerned. He compares what could be happening inside the pod to a bait-casting reel run amok. "You've got some metal braided hose with fuel in it spinning around inside of a metal pod. You risk having what we call a 'wing off light.'" He explains, "That's an affectionate term for 'you're going to blow your wing off.' If it happens to spark out there, you've got a pod full of fuel. At that point there's an emergency procedure we follow that closes the refueling valve and takes power off the pod to keep the hose from spinning around inside."

Whether the drogue was merely collapsed and still attached to the hose, or cut clean off, the hose would have whipped back into the pod like spaghetti slurped from a spoon. The difference is whether gas is pouring onto the wing and spraying the fuselage, creating a high risk for fire, or whether the hose has merely been rendered unusable for continued refueling. In either event, the emergency procedure that the flight engineer is going to undertake is essentially the same: shut off the fuel flow and shut off the hydraulics to the pod under the left wing. And that's what Doss does. Without waiting to be told, he reaches with both hands for the electrical panel overhead, flips the appropriate switches, and turns the proper knobs. Glancing up almost directly above his head, Cline watches him do it.

Right about then, Doss comes on comms to remind the pilots that they still have a refueling hose deployed from the right wing. At this point, he doesn't believe anyone will really care, but since certain flight characteristics are altered when the hoses are out, reminding them is more or less a conditioned response. The FE actually considers cutting the hose free; he even has his right hand on the cage covering the switch that controls the guillotine inside the pod, but stops short. His thinking: There's still a helicopter out there that needs gas; with the left hose useless, cutting the right hose off would mean Ditka 03 would be unable to pass fuel.

Cline is still concerned with the possibility of damage to the left wing, and he calls Langston.

"Chris, look out on the wing; how's the wing look? How's the pod look?"

He hears what he hoped to hear. There's no metal hanging out, no torn-open panels. No fuel spray. No fire. Nothing to be concerned about. With a final glance upward to make absolutely certain that the FE has shut off the fuel and the hydraulics, he turns his attention back to flying the plane, asking the navs which way he should be heading.

One of the navs says, "Go to the right."

Cline responds, "I see it." What he sees, and the FE confirms, is a cut in the ridgeline the plane is headed toward. A few seconds elapse, and the left nav, who's got his eyes glued to the radar screen, says, "I'm not painting."

"Painting" means the radar sweep in front is clear. If the plane is higher than the peaks the radar is showing, they're "painting clear."

How could they, in a matter of seconds, go from having a gap to fly through, to having a rock wall of the Hindu Kush range in their face? Part of the answer rests with the corollary to Murphy's Law, "at the worst possible time." Only Murphy could have scripted the worst possible time to have the distraction of the hose strike occur. Here's what John Cline thinks happened:

"When I refocused my attention out front, the horizon line is a low-contrast ridge line. We had the big snow-filled bowl down this valley, and then that high overcast made for not a huge amount of contrast between where the mountains ended and the skies began. What I'd thought I saw, five miles previous, ended up being just kind of a crease in the ridgeline itself, not the actual dividing line between the sky and the mountains. Turns out the ridge was about two hundred or three hundred feet higher than that. The supposed open area to the right turned out to be just kind of a shadowing effect off of a big outcropping of rock, which was throwing a shadow up against a big open snowfield. So the out straight ahead to just climb over the thing—all of a sudden the terrain is a lot higher than what I had perceived just a couple miles before. And my out to go to the right—a mirage. It evaporated in front of our eyes. So at that point, what can you do?"

All the pilot can do now is throw the throttles forward in an attempt to get the airplane to climb. Cline is thinking, "Hey, we're going to scare the hell out of ourselves here," but they all believe they're going to make it over ridgeline. He's pulling the aircraft back, trying to will it to climb at the same time that he's pushed the throttles all the way forward. And he's remembering the simulator training at Kirtland, where pilots are put through stall situations so severe, so unrealistic, they do it believing that until they'd tried everything else in their bag of tricks, they'd never put an airplane into the kind of scenario where they pull and pull and pull on the yoke until the plane begins buffeting. Now, however, the trick bag was empty and Cline and copilot Jason Wright are reviewing what they learned not only on the sim, but also from reading dozens of C-130 accident reports. What pops up in their minds, in big, bold type: *The full power-on stall characteristics of a C-130, especially one that has pods out on the end of each wing, as does the MC-130P Combat Shadow, typically involve a wing roll that ends unpleasantly with the plane cartwheeling into the ground.*

The action that this message translates to, in Cline's words, is, "You gotta keep the wings level on this airplane." And what's going through his mind, knowing that they were going to be close to terrain, is, "Hey, we're not dead yet, we're not dead yet. Keep flying, keep flying."

So with his right hand, Cline has pushed the power all the way up on all four throttles, causing the propellers on the constant-speed engines to take the maximum bite possible of the cold, thin air. His left hand is instinctively pulling back on the yoke, actually flying the plane, applying trim with a little switch on the left-hand side that makes the control forces on the stick lighter as the airspeed changes. His feet are on the rudder pedals, just trying to "keep the ball centered," as they say, so the tail's not meandering right or left like a gimpy dog running down the street with its front and back legs out of alignment.

The copilot, meantime, is pretty much an observer of the process. It's not a time for conversation, and the only question Wright asks is if Cline wants him to reconfigure from 70 percent to 50 percent flaps.

What he asks is, "Do you want flaps fifty?"

What the pilot responds with is, "Close the bleeds."

It's directed at the engineer, who says, "They're already closed." The "bleeds" are valves that bleed hot air off the engines. It's used to keep the aircraft interior warm, and to run other systems on the aircraft. While keeping them open may make the temperature in the back more comfortable, it actually drains power from the engines, and protocol in OEF has been to fly their combat missions with the bleeds closed all the time. In contrast to the cargo compartment, which is freezing cold, the flight deck stays comfortably warm because of all the radiant heat energy coming off the avionics beneath the cockpit.

Once again, the copilot asks if he should reset the flaps to 50 percent. And once again, the pilot ignores the question.

The decision to leave the flaps set where they'd been is a judgment call. Cline has been running through his head everything he's ever been taught or learned from flying 130s, and nothing matches the situation they are currently in. The classic notion of trading speed for altitude won't work, because he needs both at the same time if they're going to fly out of the terrain trap they're in. If they reduced the flap setting to 50 percent, they might pick up some airspeed, but in all likelihood, the plane would lose lift and they'd sink a bit. When he'd pushed the power in and pulled the nose up, their speed dropped quickly from 115 to 100 knots, which is technically the plane's stall speed.

What he needs aerodynamically is the best angle of climb they can get, maximum vertical movement up for every mile they go forward. They've been taught maximum effort obstacle clearance speeds, but they're all based around takeoff configurations, particularly for short-field takeoffs. But the strategies all involve decelerating to the optimum speed that will allow them to climb quickly. They learn "escape maneuvers" to be used if, for example, they fly on a low-level mission into a box canyon at 250 knots. The protocol has them pulling the nose up, tracking the flaps to 50 percent, in order to catch the obstacle clearance speed that will give them the best angle for forward movement. That speed is 120 knots, and they're already well below that.

Cline says, "I didn't have the real estate to lower the nose and accelerate forward before pulling the nose back up to catch the obstacle clearance speed. I figured tracking the flaps to fifty, we were going to lose some lift. And if we lost at any lift at all, we were so critical that, y'know, that power-on stall is the biggest fear I had. So it was basically a gut decision, on the spot, to leave the flaps at seventy."

With the pilot flying the plane and keeping the wings level, copilot Jason Wright focuses his attention on the instruments, and then watches the horizon. Since the mountains are covered with snow, he has no depth perception and can't grasp how close they actually are to the terrain that's rising in front of them. But the fact that the horizon line is moving up tells him that either they're not climbing, or the mountain is rising faster than the airplane. The navigator who's watching the radar is seeing the same image, and from behind the pilot, George Akins says, "Climb!"

Cline's response to that command is fairly automatic: he pulls back on the yoke, putting the nose up. Wright notes that they immediately lost ten knots. And then the plane starts buffeting, an indication that it's about to stall, which is to say, stop flying and drop like a 130,000-pound rock. At his radio console in the back, Rodney Young hears the copilot say, "We're stalling. We're stalling," and he reacts. "That's the very moment that I was literally scared. I was cool and calm up to that point because I trusted my pilots and I trusted the navs that we were going to get out of it. That's when my heart went to the bottom of my shoes."

But John Cline hasn't given up yet. Again, he tries to bring the nose up between ten and twenty degrees—after all, it's not a fighter plane—pulling the aircraft back into heavy buffeting a couple of times—"trying to find that sweet spot," is the way he describes it. "I kind of pulled back into the heavy buffet, the plane would start to get real mushy, and I'd let off. I did that two or three times and found kind of the happy medium, y'know, right in the kind of light tickle where, hey, this is all this airplane's going to give us."

At that instant, just for a second, Maj. John Cline stops being the technician, or perhaps the artist, and gives in to a very human emotion. "As we came closer to the terrain, I just had a flash of just absolute white-hot anger at myself, swept over me for a couple of seconds, and then, y'know, the only airplane I've ever flown, I've prided myself on being able to do this stuff well. MAJCOM [major command] evaluator pilot, the chief evaluator pilot of the whole command for this airplane, and how in the hell did I get us in this situation? I never felt a flash of anger like that before, and just as quickly as it came, it went away. I was too busy to dwell on it. I just needed to keep flying this airplane."

His copilot, who has a lot of hours in the right-hand seat and admires Cline for his adroit handling of the 130, does not share whatever anger Cline is feeling toward himself. He sees the pilot's response to his warning that they're stalling is to let up on the stick pressure a little bit, and then milk it right there—they call it a "burble." It's where the plane is shaking because the wings are starting to lose lift—the definition of a stall—but the pilot is maxperforming the aircraft, which is something they learn on the simulator. "He had it max-perform and held it right there. It was perfect," remembers Wright. "There's nothing more you can do."

What he doesn't know is that they both feel they still have a chance. It is going to be close, but they believe they'll make it over the ridge.

One of the instruments crews rely on flying at low levels in mountainous terrain is the radar altimeter. It tells them their altitude AGL—above ground level—rather than the standard barometric altimeter that measures altitude above sea level, a rather meaningless bit of data when you're flying through canyons and valleys in the foothills of the Himalayas. Ditka 03's radar altimeter had an adjustable bug that the crew would set so that if they dropped below the set height above terrain, a warning light popped on. Their low-light level was set for 450 feet, and Cline's recollection is that it had already been on for about thirty seconds, and it was continuing to slowly count down.

The right nav, Don Tyler, doesn't need to look at the altimeter to know they are close to crashing. He can sense the cushion of air under the plane when the condition known as being in ground effect kicked in. He knew it happens at a height roughly equivalent to the aircraft's wingspan, in this case, 132 feet.

What the pilot sees out the window through his NVGs is a featureless white terrain covered with snow. On both sides there are big, craggy rocks, and he taps the rudders a bit just to keep the plane headed into the snow bowl. What he can't tell at all is whether they have a quarter mile, a half mile, or even a mile left. So he begins watching the radar altimeter needle count them down, lower and lower, the needle sweeping down slowly. It was obvious that they aren't headed for a vertical wall where they are just going to crash and all die. That isn't going to happen if he can stick with the game plan: "Don't let the airplane stall; do not let the wing drop down, 'cause once the wing drops, you cartwheel and you're done."

Behind him, a feeling of profound sadness accompanied by fear has overcome the left nav, George Akins. With no real tasks to occupy his mind, he's thinking about his wife and children as the recognition hits that this is what it's like to die.

And to Cline's right, copilot Jason Wright is thinking about his friend who was killed when a Marine C-130 crashed a month earlier after taking off from the same airfield they'd left earlier that night. What troubles him is that all of his friends had just gone through a really horrible time, and now they are going to go through it all over again. He especially focuses on his wife, Amanda, and how difficult it had been for her. And then he begins to dwell on what it is going to be like to die.

"About a million things flashed through my mind. I guess some people say that a million things can go through your head in a second, and it really did at that point. I think that's it, and the next thing I expected was the whole mountain just to come through me. I thought about what happened when my friend crashed, and I figured, Well, he probably never knew what hit him, 'cause the mountain hit him so hard. It just collapsed the whole airplane. So that's kind of what I expected to happen."

John Cline considers himself fortunate that he was occupied with flying Ditka 03. He didn't have time to think about his wife. He couldn't dwell on how he was the youngest of seven kids, and how he'd be leaving behind a really big, tight family. Cline pulled the airplane back in and out of heavy buffeting a couple of times. "I took a last scan of the instruments and I think the last thing I saw was eighty-five feet on the radar altimeter, and eighty knots of airspeed, which was incredible, considering how heavy we were. I had never, never flown an airplane down to that airspeed before. And the airplane was flying wings level."

Jason Wright's last recollection is glancing at the radar altimeter and seeing twenty-five feet. That was when he knew they weren't going to clear the ridgeline. "My heart kind of sank just enough to realize that, hey, we're not going to make it. And . . . and that's never been an option to me. I was thinking, 'We're always going to make it. We always make it.' "

On the right side of the plane, loadmaster Jeff Pohl is looking out the window and sees that the refueling hose, which Doss is in the process of reeling in, is hanging almost straight down. It dawns on him that the reason is that they don't have enough airspeed to keep the paradrogue inflated. Seconds later he sees the basket and the hose coupling strike the ground, sending out a shower of sparks as it rips away from the wing.

Forward of Pohl's position, Rodney Young hears the pilot say, "Oh, fuck!" Cline doesn't remember saying it, and no one else recalls hearing it. But Radio is used to monitoring four or more channels at a time and has good ears. As soon as he hears it, he grabs the window armrest with one hand and clutches an arm on his chair with the other.

And then they hit the mountain.

# CHAPTER 5

# "HOLY SHIT, DITKA JUST CRASHED"
## FEBRUARY 13, 2002

And then it was quiet.

One second Ditka 03 had four 4,900-horsepower turboprop engines screaming at full power, and the next second, nothing. Not a sound.

They'd gone from eighty knots on the airspeed indicator—ninety-two miles an hour—to zero in a distance of perhaps 150 feet, certainly no more than 200. To the cockpit crew it seemed as though they'd skidded into the hillside, nose up, all forward movement stopping in about twice the length of the airplane.

There's no raging fire, no roar of fuel tanks exploding, no chunks of hot metal flying through the air. The condition of the flight deck is pristine. There's not even a broken window.

Jason Wright remembers thinking, "We just stopped, and I was totally dumbfounded that we were still there." As in alive. Instinctively, he reaches out and throws the switches shutting down all four engines, then looks at John Cline and realizes the pilot is laughing at him. There are no engines that need shutting down; two of them have torn loose from the wings and hurled forward, burying themselves in the snow. The other two have just stopped, as if they know there is no need to continue a heroic effort to get over the ridgeline. Their mission has ended.

Ditka 03 in the snow as photographed by a Predator drone (*USAF photo*)

In the flight engineer's seat behind the pilots, Jeff Doss is dazed. He'd been wearing a lap belt but not the shoulder harness when the plane hit, causing him to jackknife forward, his helmet slamming into the back of the pilot's seat, then ricocheting into the center console. Like the others, he begins touching body parts to make certain they are still there. In his case they are, though somewhat the worse for wear. He wouldn't learn till weeks later that he had broken his sternum, had a cracked vertebra, and suffered a concussion that would affect his recall of the crash and what was to follow.

While the left navigator, Maj. George Akins, has come through unscathed, the right nav, Maj. Don Tyler, isn't so fortunate. He's the only one on the flight deck who wasn't strapped into his seat during the crash—in order to do his job he needed to be able to move back and forth to the window—and he's paying the price. He finds himself on the floor of the cockpit, down on one knee, cradling his left arm. To no one in particular, he screams, "Oh, fuck, I think I broke my arm!" After that announcement, he falls silent. What he'd done was dislocated his shoulder, popping the bone of his upper arm out of the socket by several inches, tearing an assortment of tendons and muscles from his shoulder blade and destroying the rotator cuff in the process.

In contrast to the flight deck, the rear of the plane does, indeed, look like it has been slammed into a mountainside, not surprising when the nose-up attitude of the crash is taken into consideration. From the inside, it's clear that the aircraft is in three distinct pieces: the section forward of the wing, the wing box (the structure that attaches the wings to the fuselage), and the fuselage and tail aft of the wing box.

The radio operator, S.Sgt. Rodney Young, who had been hanging on to handholds for dear life, finds himself hanging upside down, suspended from his lap belt. He'd put it on midway through the refueling process, and now is having difficulty getting out of it. Rodney is shocked at what he describes as the nonviolence of the impact: "I'm hearing a noise like a car crash. I thought we might have just scraped it and kept on flying." The absence of any engine noise doesn't sink in. What he does realize is that his radio console broke free of its mounts and hit him in the shoulder. Now his mind is up and running. He thinks, "Okay, I just got hit in the shoulder with something. I'm still alive. Wait for the airplane to stop."

All the way in the rear of the plane, the left loadmaster, Chris Langston, had been scanning out the window of the left paratroop door, leaning against a seat belt strap rigged as an improvised backrest, when he heard the copilot say that they were stalling. Two seconds later, they impacted.

"I remember hitting and everything just going black, and then going straight up in the air and then having that same strap clip me by the back of the legs and just kind of flip me around; I remember getting thrown backwards. At that point, it was over."

He'd actually done a complete back flip, landing in a crouch, the back of his ankles against his butt. What disorients him momentarily is that the top of the plane, where the interior lights are, is adjacent to his right temple. His feet are on the hinge of the cargo plane's huge rear ramp, which normally rises at an angle when closed. Now it is almost perfectly horizontal. It is a good five or ten seconds before he realizes that they've crashed. Oxygen is hissing and fuel is dripping everywhere.

The right loadmaster, T.Sgt. Jeff Pohl, isn't as lucky. He is pinned in the middle of the wreckage, against the Benson tank, facedown in jet fuel soaking into a cushion of packed snow that had been scooped up by the fuselage behind the wing box as it slid up the mountain. His right foot is at an ugly angle through the side of the aircraft, locked in place by sheet metal that has crunched around his ankle like a shirt collar a couple of sizes too small.

Pohl's injuries include a compound fracture of his right tibia, multiple fractures of his pelvis, a broken rib, fractured cervical and thoracic vertebrae, and head injuries that result in the permanent loss of his left peripheral vision. He has bruised the membranes that attach the intestines to the abdomen, ruptured his spleen, and has a scrotal hematoma. Of most concern is that he is bleeding internally, into his pelvic area.

How the *right* loadmaster ended up wedged against the aft edge of the Benson tank, which is mounted near the *left* wheel well, is a momentary mystery. What the crew soon discover is that the right side of the plane had crushed inward, violently shoving him left, mashing him to the cargo deck, and driving his right leg through the airplane's skin like an oversize rivet.

In the lead Army helicopter that had been in the left observation position behind Ditka 03, watching as Chalk 3 attempted to refuel, the pilot hit the intercom to Lt. Col. John Buss, the airborne mission commander for the entire operation. "Did you see that?"

Buss, of course, couldn't have missed the flash of light that marked the impact of the airplane with the mountain. It looked almost like a fire, but it didn't last. What they all registered on their NVGs were the sparks generated by the crash. Buss didn't believe anyone could have possibly survived what he thought had to have been a catastrophic impact. The immediate reaction was to have all three helicopters turn away from the terrain by doing a starburst maneuver and climb out of there. Then he instructed his pilots to circle back around and see if it would be possible to land near the crash site.

In Chalk 3, PJ team leader Chris Young, still wearing his NVGs, was on the floor relaxing when there was a sudden flash of light. He heard one of the crewmembers shouting, "Holy shit, Ditka just crashed!" In an instant he was on his feet, guys were handing him comm cords, and he was plugging in, trying to find out what's going on.

Back in the Ditka 03 cargo bay, Rodney Young is taking stock of his situation. The console knocked off his headset and wool watch cap when it slammed into his shoulder. No problem. He'll just get down on the floor and find them. What he can't figure out is why it's raining inside the aircraft.

"My face is cold and wet, so I'm asking, am I bleeding from my face? So I put my hand to my face and rub it off. Can't see anything; I've got black gloves on. Then I realized, whoa, that's gas spewing inside the airplane." The sound reminds him of a sprinkler system run amok, a loud, persistent, obnoxious sound that he can't place. Then it dawned: In addition to jet fuel raining down, there's liquid oxygen blowing on his face. The valve has broken on the tank that supplies the crew's emergency oxygen masks. Puddles of gas are already forming on the floor; the cargo area is being saturated with pure oxygen. A tiny spark is all it will take to turn a survival miracle into a front page disaster report about eight American deaths in the war on terrorism.

Rodney knows he's got to get out of the plane before that happens, but there's one small problem: he can't see a thing. The radio operator wears contact lenses, and, fearful that they'll get saturated with gas and he'll be temporarily blinded, he's got his eyes screwed shut. Even though the plane's emergency lights came on as soon as the triggering system detected an impact greater than 2.5 Gs, keeping his eyes closed is understandably making it difficult for him to crawl around on the floor looking for his wool cap, his survival vest, his GAU-5 rifle, and the bag with his crypto—the secret punch tapes he uses to program special scrambling codes into the radios. He doesn't want to evacuate the plane without the GAU—this is bad-guy land—and the 9mm pistol that was strapped to his leg doesn't represent adequate firepower. He's willing to exit without his cap and without his survival vest. He's well trained enough to realize that he *can't* leave without the crypto. This forces him to unscrunch his eyelids and peek just a little, thinking he might get lucky. Ultimately, he thinks, "Screw it," and opens his eyes wide to begin the search in earnest. Then he hears voices coming from up above, and realizes that people on the flight deck are alive.

Abandoning the search, he begins to make his way to the left side of the aircraft, where there's access to the flight deck.

All the way in the rear of the plane, loadmaster Chris Langston is slowly getting over the shock of realizing that they've crashed and he's still alive. His concern now is his partner, Jeff Pohl, and, getting no response when he calls his name, Langston begins searching for him. "I went maybe five feet and once I got closer to him, I could see him laying there. But he wasn't moving; he was just kind of laying there, not doing anything, not saying anything. I went up to him, and I touched him on his helmet. He started making some pretty painful moans, and I kind of shook him and said, 'Jeff, it's me. We can't stay here.' And he said, 'Okay, okay, I'm fine, I'm fine.' I said, 'You're sure?' and he's, like, 'Yeah,' and I remember him looking up at me, and there's a little blood trickle from his helmet. And I was, like, 'Well, it doesn't look real bad.' At that point, I said, 'Follow me; I'll dig around and try to find a way out of here.' As I turned around to walk away, he says, 'Hey, I can't move.' So I went back and I said, 'What's . . . ?' He said, 'My leg is stuck.' He was up against a snowbank, so I started digging through the snow. Probably a quarter of the way up the airplane was full of snow already, and even when I landed, I was standing in snow. At that point, I started digging around, and I saw where his leg was on the outside of the airplane. It wasn't mangled or anything, but I could tell it was stuck. But I knew there was no way I was just going to pull it out of there. I took one of those emergency exit lights, and I gave it to Jeff. I said, 'Jeff, hold on to this. I'm going to get help. I'll be back.' "

In the forward area of the cargo compartment, radio operator Rodney Young has reached the narrow stairwell leading to the crew entry door on the left and the ladder up to the cockpit on the right. Only he finds them blocked by a metal panel that's come down, leaving a circular opening big enough to stick his head through, but not, as he delicately puts it, his big butt.

Up above, copilot Jason Wright is shocked by the unexpected sound of Rodney's voice, desperately shouting from below, "Don't leave me; I'm trapped!"

"And that woke me up as to, oh, my gosh, what about the guys in the back? 'Cause you realize everybody up front was all right, but we're in a daze. So that was the first thing that made me think, hey, we gotta get everybody and get out of here."

Reacting to the sound of Rodney's voice coming from below, the pilot shouts, "Who's hurt? Anybody hurt? What about the loads?"

Rodney responds that he's okay, but he doesn't know about the two loadmasters, so they ask him to go check. As he heads toward the rear of the plane, he shouts back, "Make that hole bigger. I gotta get out of here." Actually, he uses the all-purpose, standard military adjective, adverb, and noun to underscore his desire that a clear way out be there when he returned.

Moving as far back in the fuselage as he can go, perhaps no more than twenty feet in what had been a ninety-nine-foot-long airplane, Rodney calls out the loadmasters' names and is gratified to get a response from Chris Langston. Realizing who's answering him, the radio operator shouts, "Hey, Chris, what's the situation?"

"We're both alive, one injured," comes the response.

Rodney acknowledges that he understands, and returns to tell the pilots that both loads are alive, but that he can't see them because everything back of the wing box is either crushed, twisted, or bent. Then he grabs the hunk of metal blocking his exit, and while shaking it realizes it is just a galley shelf that had collapsed from above. He quickly shoves it aside and scrambles up into the cockpit, discovering that navigator Don Tyler has managed to get to his feet and is turning off electrical equipment and trying to find a first-aid kit, all the while continuing to cradle his injured left arm. Meantime, the other navigator, Maj. George Akins, is already climbing the ladder that provided access to the circular escape hatch in the cockpit ceiling. Opening it, he pulls himself out of the plane and walks toward the wing while waving the mini Maglite that Tyler had given him, hoping to attract the attention of the helicopters. Next to pop out of the opening is the radio operator, carrying one of the powerful emergency lights that he'd removed from the cargo compartment. He begins walking down the spine of the broken plane, remembering the training they'd received in a survival class to wave a light back and forth rather than just pointing it skyward. They'd been told that if a light doesn't move, rescuers tend to assume that it's just a light on the aircraft, but if you move it from side to side, they'll definitely know there are survivors.

Even before they see lights waving on the ground, the airborne mission commander in Chalk 1 has ordered his pilot to circle back around to the crash site to see if they can land. The answer isn't an easy one. Chalk 1 is heavy, having taken on a full load of fuel from Ditka 03. Because the crash site is approximately 9,700 feet above sea level, it will require a significantly greater amount of power to set Chalk 1 down safely than would be needed at a lower altitude. Buss's pilots do some quick calculations and announce that it will be close, but their aircraft will be able to produce the needed out-of-ground effect power.

While it may seem counterintuitive that bringing a helicopter to a controlled landing may require as much, if not more, power than it does to take off, it is a fact that such is the case. A pilot bringing a helicopter in for an in-ground effect landing on a hard, smooth surface knows that when his altitude is equal or less than the diameter of his spinning rotor blades, he can actually *reduce* power. It all has to do with what is happening to the air that's being driven down by the rotors. But when a helicopter comes in for a landing on the sloping side of a mountain, the approach is not over a smooth, level surface; it requires enough power so the helicopter can hover out-of-ground effect, that is, with no bonus from the air compressing against the ground assisting in keeping the helo in the air.

An additional complication in landing near the crash site is the expectation of a full whiteout from the snow, reducing the pilot's visibility to less than zero, and making it exceedingly difficult to terminate the approach happily. That this is taking place at a high altitude is another complicating factor, since the capability of the MH-47E to produce lift is significantly reduced. Boeing says the service ceiling of this model Chinook is 10,150 feet, and the crew has already ripped open that envelope more than a few times on this mission. Finally, the heavier the helicopter, the more power will be needed to effect the landing, and Chalk 1 had recently taken on approximately seven thousand pounds of fuel.

There's not a lot of margin for error. If the power requirement for landing exceeds what's available, the rotors will start to droop and a crash-landing is the likely result. Making things even more complicated is the fact that the landing zone is snow-covered, and when a helicopter putting out about one-hundred-mile-per-hour winds lands in a snow-covered area it's usually engulfed in swirling snow, requiring the pilot to make the last ten feet of the landing with no visual reference to the ground.

With all this in mind, Lieutenant Colonel Buss has a brief conversation with his pilot as Chalk 1 executes a 360-degree turn to the left. "He said he thought we had enough power to land, so I go ahead and instruct him to land there, which he did. As we were on a short final to the aircraft location, I saw some flashlights coming from the wreckage, so I knew there were some survivors at this point, which was amazing to me."

They were also fortunate that the snow was fairly hard-packed and the landing wasn't made in a classic whiteout situation; the pilot had some visual reference all the way down to the ground as he put the Chinook down about one hundred yards downhill of the aircraft crash site, on a twenty-degree slope.

On Chalk 3, the PJ team leader is monitoring the radio and immediately picks up on the fact that there are survivors. Chris Young tells his colleagues to get ready to go in, then tells the pilot he needs to put them on the ground immediately. The pilot radios the AMC that the PJs are asking to be inserted. The AMC denies the request. Twice more, Chalk 3's pilot asks for permission to put the PJs in, and twice more Buss denies them permission to land, ordering them instead to go refuel first.

When the pilot passes that word to Young, the PJ team leader is in shock. For a second he can't believe what he's heard. Then he passes on the news to Keary Miller and Jason Cunningham, who are already jocking up to go in. "We are absolutely fuming about it. I mean, a bunch of type A personalities and in a blackened helicopter—and the thing is, I'm the only one that's on comm, so I at least have the situational awareness to hear all the conversations going back and forth, but I'm trying to brief my guys. And they're just, like, 'What?!'" Miller is so outraged he can't stand still. He goes storming up and back the length of the helicopter, screaming obscenities.

Young says they tried everything, including laying out the simple fact that Chalk 3 has more than enough fuel to put the PJs in the landing zone, and then go up to tank while the pararescuemen were treating patients. They get nowhere. The AMC's final answer is, "No. Hit the tanker. When you're done, come back down."

At that moment a few things are crystal-clear. Buss thought the crash unsurvivable, but he was wrong. Flashing lights say otherwise. Survivors mean there might be life-threatening injuries, or men trapped in the wreckage. Loadmaster Pohl qualifies on both counts. Buss knows nothing of that; yet he diverts Chalk 3 to an as-yet-unnecessary refueling effort, taking with it the very pararescuemen who were assigned to this mission to save trapped and/or injured personnel.

Lt. Col. John Buss, forty-one, is a West Point graduate, jump qualified, an aviation officer since 1983, which is when his Army career began. He served with the 101st Airborne Division, and since 1989 has worked his way up through the ranks, and through command and staff positions with the elite 160th SOAR (A), where he commanded the 2nd Battalion from 2000 to 2002, at its home base of Fort Campbell, Kentucky, and deployed to Operation Enduring Freedom in Afghanistan.

Hold a conversation with him and it's easy to infer that he's accustomed to being in control, comfortable making decisions under pressure and sticking with them. He's also accustomed to setting high standards for the pilots who serve under him—and two of them had just screwed up big-time, jeopardizing the entire mission with their inability to refuel under admittedly less than optimal conditions.

The reason the PJs are embedded with special ops units is to provide the highest level of combat search and rescue skill in the shortest amount of time. If ever a situation was created to make maximum use of their training, it was the crash of Ditka 03. It required the tools and the know-how to extract a victim from a crashed aircraft quickly, without causing further injury, and then providing medical treatment to stabilize the patient in order to keep him alive until they can get to a hospital.

Yet that entire rationale, which is the rationale for the existence of Air Force pararescue in the modern American military, was dismissed by Lieutenant Colonel Buss in favor of sending an aircraft to refuel whose pilots had just spent more than half an hour demonstrating an inability to adequately perform the task in that particular environment. Even more, those pilots had to believe that when they chopped the refueling hose, they set in motion a chain reaction that resulted in Ditka 03 slamming into a mountain a minute or two later. Certainly such knowledge would raise their stress level in an already stressful situation.

Finally, here was another potential lifesaving reason for putting Chalk 3 on the ground: Its rotor blades had just whacked something—whether it was the metal frame of the paradrogue, the hose, or the heavy metal fittings at the end of the hose, no one could say for certain. Caution dictates that if the opportunity exists to immediately land and check for damage, a prudent pilot would take advantage of it—and a prudent commander would expect no less.

Even though Buss acknowledges that Chalk 3 could have done as the PJs urged, since the helicopter had enough gas to land, none of these arguments held water for him. When questioned about the decision not to allow Chalk 3 to land and let the PJs do their job, he said, "That landing in there was difficult. And I was concerned about him [Chalk 3's pilot]. I really wanted him to settle down before he tried to make that landing in there." The irony is that the landing would have been easier for Chalk 3 than it was for Buss's own aircraft, which was several thousand pounds heavier, having taken on a full load of fuel.

Buss goes on: "the decision would've been different if I had had life-threatening injuries or folks pinned that needed the REDS kit immediately. But very quickly, I mean, almost immediately after we landed, we had folks [survivors] walking up to the aircraft on their own. I got reports of patients—the only guy we were concerned about was that eighth crewmember who was pinned but was coherent and did not appear to have any life-threatening injuries at that point."

He's referring to the right loadmaster, T.Sgt. Jeff Pohl, who at the time Buss sent the PJs away was pinned facedown in jet fuel–soaked snow, becoming hypothermic in the subzero temperature, bleeding internally, with one leg broken and jammed through the crushed side of the plane. It's important to note that to this point, Pohl had not been examined by anyone at all, much less anyone with medical training. And the REDS kit that contains the PJ version of the Jaws of Life and a special crash ax that can cut through a plane's skin that was available in the back of Chalk 3? Buss didn't think it was needed "immediately."

But back to the moments before Chalk 1 lands. Radio operator Rodney Young and navigator George Akins have used the rope from the cockpit escape hatch to lower themselves to the snow-covered ground. They're about to walk toward the back to find the loadmasters, when Rodney hears the flight engineer, Jeff Doss, saying, "I'm getting down, too."

Rodney's thinking, "Wait a minute. This isn't good. Me and George are together; that's cool, because we're together. The buddy system; look out for each other. Then the engineer's gonna get down by himself, so that's not good. So I made a decision. I said, George is going to go to where the loadmasters are. I need to go find the engineer so he doesn't wander off and fall down this mountain, 'cause it looked like the airplane was sitting on a ledge, and it could fall back down the hill at any minute."

In the back end of Ditka 03, Chris Langston has made his way to the aft escape hatch. He pulls it down and pops his head through the opening, while at the same time waving an emergency light in the air. He sees Akins standing on the wing, and says, "Jeff is stuck, but we need help getting him out of there." The loadmaster can hear a helicopter—probably Chalk 1, which landed moments earlier—and he can also pick out the sound of Ditka 04 overhead. Then he ducks back inside the fuselage and takes the escape rope that hangs next to the exit and tosses the free end back down toward where Pohl is trapped. The rope will make it easy for rescuers to locate him quickly.

At the same time near the front of the plane, Rodney waits for Doss to come down the rope, sees that he is wearing his survival vest, and thinks it makes sense for him to take Doss's survival radio and call the helicopters to let them know what they are dealing with. The radio is in two Ziploc bags to keep it dry. Doss is wearing gloves and trying to peel the outer Ziploc bag apart. So Rodney yells at him, "Dude, just tear it!" Doss rips the first bag, sees that there's a second bag and to Rodney's annoyance, tries to peel that one apart. Rodney yells again, "Tear that one, too. I mean, you gotta have your wits about you, c'mon!" What he didn't know at the time is that Doss had struck his head in the impact and had suffered a concussion that was affecting his judgment as well as his motor skills.

After several seconds Rodney gets the radio operating and begins calling, "Mayday, Mayday, Mayday, this is Ditka 03 with eight survivors; seven are ambulatory and one's trapped." (He didn't use the word *Mayday,* because that's used only if they're down in a friendly environment; instead he used the secret code word that meant they were down in enemy territory.) He makes the call, changes frequencies, and repeats the same message. He does this several times, never receiving a response.

Shortly after his last futile transmission, Chalk 1 lands about one hundred yards downhill from the wreckage, and the two men decide that they will start walking to the helicopter. The snow is up to their waist all the time, occasionally up to their armpits. They take two steps and sink, and every time that happens, Doss falls over to the side. Rodney stops, picks him up—Doss is six feet, 220 pounds, while Rodney is five-ten and 175—and says, "C'mon, let's go," and then they'd fall all over again. About halfway down, they meet one of the special-ops guys, who Rodney assumes is a PJ, and he yells at him, "Hey, we got eight survivors—seven are ambulatory; one's stuck." The two survivors continue down toward the helicopter, where they see another guy coming uphill. The same message is repeated: "We've got eight survivors—seven are ambulatory; one's stuck in the airplane."

By the time they make it to the ramp at the rear of the Chinook, both men are beat. Doss says it was the longest hundred yards of his life; he thought he was running a marathon, that he was never going to get to the helicopter, and once he got to it and discovered that the ramp was at roughly the height of his chest, he didn't think he'd ever get inside it. The radio operator solves that problem, using his last bit of strength to boost the FE onto the ramp. But then Rodney doesn't even have enough strength to pick up his leg. He's a smoker, and the thin air at ten thousand feet has just not delivered enough oxygen to support the strenuous effort it took to make it down to Chalk 1.

Finally, someone drags him into the plane, and the two of them settle onto the floor. There are only two or three men inside the big helicopter, but Rodney still needs to make sure his message has gotten through, so he tells the one nearest the cockpit to go tell the pilots that there are eight survivors, seven ambulatory. Then the two men wrap themselves in parkas and sleeping bags, and huddle together on the floor, trying to get warm.

While the radio operator seems to be dealing with their situation quite well, the flight engineer is having problems. "I'm cold, I'm cold," he'd say to Rodney. "What happened?" Rodney would respond, "Hey, dude, we crashed. We're in a helicopter." But that wasn't the end of it. "Three or four minutes later, he's like, 'What happened?' I'd tell him again. And this probably happened eight to ten times. 'What happened? I'm cold. My butt hurts. What happened? I'm cold. My butt hurts.' Y'know, a repetitive thing from him. I'm, like, 'Good Lord! Get it together!'"

Back at the crash site, everyone has finally gotten out of the forward part of the plane. Copilot Jason Wright comes out the cockpit escape hatch, and then realizes that navigator Don Tyler, with his busted-up shoulder, can't possibly climb the ladder and shimmy down the rope. He goes back inside where he finds the nav just standing there dazed, moaning in pain. Having spotted a gash in the fuselage just aft of the cockpit, Wright guides Tyler down the stairwell and maneuvers him over, under, and around wreckage, until finally they emerge from the plane. Then he begins walking the nav down to the waiting helicopter. Tyler remembers feeling helpless, or worthless, because he couldn't help anybody. While he had some injuries, including a knee that was cut and bleeding and a slice through his cheek, they were minor compared to the destruction his shoulder had suffered in the crash. Unfortunately, the two experience the same kind of travail as the others had on their walk to the helo. They take a few steps, and then fall through the snow. Wright is walking abreast of Tyler, who's clutching his injured left arm with his right hand. Every time the injured nav would fall, he'd reach out to grab him, but just being touched triggered a powerful pain that shot through Tyler's entire body. Finally he screams, "No! No! No, don't touch me!" and manages to make the rest of the downhill hike without help, even though it means that every time he falls through the snow, he has to dig himself out using just his right elbow.

When the pair gets to the helicopter ramp, crewmen inside motion Tyler to come around to the side door. They've finally figured out that after their ordeal, the Ditka 03 crewmembers don't have the strength to haul themselves aboard. Tyler indicates he's done walking, so one of the guys makes a stirrup by cupping his hands together. Tyler steps up into it with one foot, and they toss him up and onto the ramp, then prop him up against the inside wall next to Rodney Young, and cover him with sleeping bags.

At the crash site, aircraft commander John Cline is focusing on the one crewmember trapped in a plane that he knows still has the potential to blow up at any moment. Squeezing through a tear in the side of the fuselage, he moves around a corner of the Benson tank and joins Langston at the trapped loadmaster's side. A quick assessment convinces him that they'll need help with the extrication. He tells Langston to walk toward the helicopter and tell them what's needed. As Chris is doing so, he meets the copilot, who has returned to the crash site with one of the special forces troops.

"What's the situation?" asks the special operator.

Langston responds, "We're all alive; we got one guy that's stuck."

"How stuck?"

"He's stuck pretty good; we're going to need some help."

"Okay, go towards the helicopter and see the guy with the radio. Tell them to call that CSAR bird, and tell them to bring the REDS kit."

Langston is five feet, eight inches tall, standing in snow that's up to five feet deep—up to his armpits. Moving through it is a struggle, not a stroll. He estimates it took him ten minutes to get to the guy with the radio. On the way down he passes a string of special ops troops coming up hill who stop him and ask if he's okay. Langston's response is a mantra: "CSAR bird, REDS kit."

Every time an SOF soldier looks at him, he says, "CSAR bird, REDS kit." Finally he reaches the crewman with the radio near the back of the helicopter. "Hey, we need to call the CSAR bird with the REDS kit."

The crewman responds, "It's already on its way." But the simple fact is that it isn't. The CSAR helicopter—Chalk 3—carrying the three PJs who were the designated search and rescue team, is off in the distance somewhere, hoping that their pilots will have better luck refueling off Ditka 04 than they'd had off Ditka 03.

And there are no medics on the ground at all. None. Zip. Zilch. Nada. How can that be? According to PJ team leader Chris Young, the SOAR medic on this operation is aboard Chalk 2, which is the designated medevac bird on the mission, and Lieutenant Colonel Buss sent that helo back to its deployed base once he got permission to abort the infil mission. It never landed at the crash scene.

That leaves the question of just who made the evaluation Lieutenant Colonel Buss says he got from his ground troops indicating that none of the survivors had life-threatening injuries. Ignore for a moment that Buss opted to send the PJs on a chase for fuel even before his own helicopter landed, before the ground troops on his helicopter struggled the hundred yards uphill to the crash, and before his ground troops knew what was going on with Jeff Pohl inside the wreckage. Ignore all that for the moment, and just concentrate on this exchange when Buss was interviewed about the incident ten months after it happened:

"Once I got on the ground, I unbuckled from the jump seat and I was kind of in the cabin, kind of talking on the radio and moving around, mostly because I was freezing my ass off. I don't know how cold it was up there, but . . . at that point, we had a series of aircraft cycled through overhead, fast-movers overhead, providing us our combat air control over the top of us. I'm talking to all those folks; I'm talking to the big command and control aircraft above us, talking to the command post back in the rear. I'm constantly on the radio answering questions and requesting things and briefing people on stuff."

Buss clearly was a very busy man. However, had he let the CSAR team land, he would have had the opportunity to hand off almost all of the communications to the CCT, who is an integral part of the embedded special tactics team. T.Sgt. Gabe Brown had half a dozen different radios, from SATCOM to UHF, in his hundred-pound pack, and is uniquely trained to handle a cacophony of contacts with overhead aircraft and higher headquarters such as the Joint Search and Rescue Command at Prince Sultan Air Base, Saudi Arabia. But the CCT couldn't do any of that from the inside of a helicopter that was miles away, trying to get gas. And as long as Buss was preoccupied with radio traffic, he wasn't not focusing his attention on the actual rescue of the crash survivors.

Here's Buss again, explaining why he felt comfortable sending Chalk 3 for gas without first inserting the PJs: "I thought with the status of the patients, all ambulatory except one, and the one guy was coherent and didn't have life-threatening injuries—"

"But how did you know that?" he's asked.

"I got the report from the folks. The ground force was on board my aircraft, went over there and was talking to me on the radio, so they're sending me back reports ofnthe status of the patients. I thought the most important thing was to get my Chalk 3 some fuel, which he did, and then I brought him in to land. I don't know, time-wise, how much longer it took him to get there after us, but it was probably thirty minutes after we landed there."

He adds, "I wanted to get those guys [the PJs] in there, but we had medics on board my aircraft. And, as I said, there were no life-threatening injuries at that point, so I sent him to get his fuel, which he did successfully without further incident."

The consensus of the PJs and the Ditka 03 crew is that it took more than an hour before Chalk 3 was able to return and land. (Buss later said, "We were on the ground for over two hours doing this whole thing, so I kind of lost track of time.") In that time, was Buss certain that a medic who was on his aircraft was attending to Pohl, making informed assessments of his condition, and relaying those informed reports back to him? Not exactly.

Question: "So, just a Ranger medic is with the unit that's on your helicopter?"

Buss replies, "Right. I don't think it was a Ranger in this case, but I don't know who it was. But most of the ground forces we have, have medically trained personnel. And I think in this case they did have a medic."

He *thinks* they had a medic? He's being interviewed ten months after the crash, and he still doesn't know? One minute he says, "We had medics on board my aircraft"; the next he's saying, "I think . . . they did have a medic." Here are the facts: *If* they had a medic—it's *if* because the mission they were on is still classified and the Special Operations Command won't release information to the public about the makeup of the ground forces involved and precisely what they were doing—that medic didn't get close enough to lay hands on Jeff Pohl, to examine him, to check his breathing, take his blood pressure and pulse, to attempt to stop the external bleeding, to stabilize his broken pelvis before any attempt by his crewmembers to move him was made. Pohl says no medic examined him while he was trapped in the plane. And for the record, Don Tyler says he wasn't examined by any of the ground troops either, not at the crash site, not even when he managed to make it inside Buss's helicopter, where he sat moaning in excruciating pain from his mangled left shoulder.

Meantime, back inside Ditka 03's crushed tail section, a desperate effort is under way to keep the trapped loadmaster alive until competent rescue help can arrive. With the help of two of the SOF shooters, the pilot tries digging the snow out from under Pohl, then grabs anything he can find—sweatshirts, mats, cardboard—and stuffs it under Pohl to provide some insulation. "Jeff was amazing," recalls Cline. "He was stuck in there, busted up pretty bad, but he was cracking jokes and keeping us calm as we were trying to get him out of there."

When copilot Wright returns to the plane, Cline tells him to find the crash ax and anything else they might be able to use to pry Pohl out. He begins looking around in the dark, trying to find it, when Cline reaches up and hands him an emergency exit light. Wright says, "I'd forgotten they pull right off the wall and you can walk around with them. For some reason I didn't remember that, and when he handed it to me, I was, like, 'Duh, I knew that all along.'" He ends up finding the ax as well as a couple of other poles he thinks might be useful as pry bars. He also finds one of the litters they carry on the plane, and passes that back as well.

Copilot Wright remembers Pohl saying, "This is a Kodak moment; can you get to my camera?" Wright says, "I remember thinking that I couldn't do it, because if we didn't get him out or something happened to him, I couldn't explain to somebody that I was sitting there taking pictures rather than getting him out." (Someone else found the camera and snapped a picture, which didn't turn out.)

The likelihood of a bad outcome is staring everyone in the face. Two shooters inside the plane and one outside are hacking away at the metal with their commando knives as though their own lives depend on it. As good as those weapons might be in hand-to-hand combat, they aren't up to this task, and it's frustrating them to the point that one of them growls, "Where are they at with the REDS kit to get him out of here?" And another responds, "It should be here by now!" No one knew that the REDS kit and the PJs to operate it are miles away, refueling.

At the Joint Operation Center in Jacobabad, Pakistan, PJ T.Sgt. Ryan Schultz had been awakened as soon as controllers learned there was an MC-130P down. Schultz had been at Jbad a month earlier, when a Marine C-130 crashed with no survivors—that crew lived right next door to the PJs—and as he began getting his team ready to deploy, he thought this would be another body-recovery mission. When he learned there were survivors, but that the special-tactics team hadn't been inserted, he couldn't believe it. "I was flabber-gasted. It just blew my mind. If they had taken the PJs in first, they'd have had those guys off that mountain in less than thirty minutes. If they'd gone in with the REDS kit—all they needed was the ax out of there—ten seconds, the guy would've been out. All they needed was probably two inches to get his ankle out."

But the five men working desperately to get Jeff Pohl out couldn't get an inch, much less two. The crash ax on the 130 is similar to what civilian firemen use. With it, you can bash a hole in a bulkhead or wall, but it's hardly a precision instrument to be swinging in a confined place where a victim is trapped. In contrast, the PJs' ax has a sharp point at one end to poke a hole through aircraft aluminum; the other end of the extendable handle has what amounts to a giant lever-action can opener—sort of like the old military P-38 that GIs used for years to open C-ration cans.

Next they try to use a cargo strap to bend the metal. They're able to pass one end through a hole in the crushed bulkhead, then try simultaneously lifting the strap from outside and inside, but they have no leverage.

The shooter working on Pohl outside the aircraft had cut his boot off, then cut the leg on his flight suit. While they can't see bones protruding, everyone can see that the load's leg made a hard right turn at the shin, right where it poked through the wall.

Inside, Jeff is complaining to Cline that his hands and feet are cold. "I ended up stripping off all my survival gear and just laying it down around him and putting his hands inside my flight suit to keep his hands warm." But it is a stopgap measure, and everyone can sense it, including the trapped man.

The pilot wasn't optimistic. "It just ended up getting to the point where he was fading, he was starting to get glassy-eyed and said, 'Hey, you guys are really going to get me out of here, aren't you?'"

Apparently he recognized that they were trying to free him without hurting him any more, and it wasn't working. Jason Wright said, "We were pulling on him, we were doing like a one-two-three, and John had his head, I was in the middle, and the guy on the outside was kind of pushing the skin. Another guy was guiding it from inside. We'd go 'one-two-three, move,' and the guy on the outside is, like, 'Stop, stop, stop!' It looks like it's taking the meat off of his bone, like filleting the skin off his leg. And we said, 'What do we do?' And at that point exactly, Jeff was just, like, 'Just get . . . just pull, just get me out of here,' and that is all we needed."

The shooter outside scoops up handfuls of the hydraulic fluid that is soaking into the snow and slathers it up and down Pohl's injured leg while rescuers inside cut as much insulation as possible from around the aircraft structure where it has trapped Pohl's leg.

Then Cline says, "Let's go do it," and they pull harder, once, then again. Pohl recalls hearing "all the bones crunch at that point." They pop him free, but break his ankle in the process. Now it's a matter of keeping him alive till they can get him off the mountain.

# CHAPTER 6

# THE MOST RIGHTEOUS MISSION
## FEBRUARY 13, 2002

The special tactics team being bounced over and through the forbidding Hindu Kush mountains inside Chalk 3 still can't believe that the only guys with the training to save those eight lives, with the gear to save those lives, with the mission assignment to save those lives, haven't been allowed to get to the injured as quickly as possible. Didn't *M\*A\*S\*H* teach us the military helicopter was invented to facilitate fast treatment of the wounded? The only military acronym that fit this situation to a T was SNAFU (a World War II creation that means "Situation Normal, All Fucked Up).

However cold and uncomfortable they are as involuntary passengers on the helo's assigned mission to refuel before passing Go, collecting $200, or treating patients, they knew that the survivors are colder and more discomfited, especially the one trapped in the wreckage. They were well trained enough to know that he could have survivable injuries but succumb to hypothermia. The circumstances for it are ideal: a trauma victim, trapped and unable to move about to stay warm in a subzero environment, lying in contact with cold metal, clothes soaking wet from melting snow and fuel. Then comes the capper—if he had already become severely hypothermic and the other survivors or the SOF troops attempt to move him improperly, they could unwittingly trigger a fatal heart attack as cold blood from his extremities pours into his heart.

PJs Chris Young, Keary Miller, Jason Cunningham, and CCT Gabe Brown (*Courtesy of S.Sgt. Chris Young*)

Knowing that they're going to be put on the ground once Chalk 3 tanks up, the pararescuemen are running medical treatment checklists in their minds. Assuming all the survivors are breathing and any bleeding has been controlled, the biggest dangers are shock and hypothermia. Right behind those is the possibility that well-intentioned but untrained folks can do a lot of permanent damage transporting victims who might have fractured their skulls, necks, or backs.

That's why the Air Force spends, on average, a million bucks or more to train each of its PJs to be the most technically proficient members of the entire U.S. military in the conjoined skills of rescue and trauma care.

Maj. Brian Burlingame is chief of general surgery at Womack Army Medical Center at Fort Bragg, North Carolina, home base of many of the special-ops forces fighting in Operation Enduring Freedom. At the time of the Ditka 03 crash, the thirty-six-year-old West Point graduate was on duty at Bagram, Afghanistan, where he commanded the 274th Forward Surgical Team. This is one of the so-called FST units that have replaced MASH outfits in the modern Army. The doctor has worked with the entire array of "far-forward medics" in the U.S. armed services, including the three PJs aboard Chalk 3, Young, Miller, and Cunningham. He calls them "some of the best prepared medically" he's come in contact with.

"What makes the PJs special is that they have the medical ability, and they have the ability to get people out of bad places. I'm not an expert in the operational 'how to get a guy out of a burning aircraft' stuff that they do, or how to get a guy out from a flipped Humvee, or how to get a guy out of a firefight. They're good at it, and their peers respect them for that and think they're good at it. There are guys out there, organizationally—you're not going to hear this from a lot of people—that are better on an across-the-board spectrum of medical care. But they're not as good at going into bad places and pulling people out of there."

Chris Young wouldn't quarrel with that evaluation of their medical skills. He's quite clear in saying that PJ medical training is directed solely at trauma care. How do they keep a patient alive, with the best chance of recovery, for as long as it takes to get him to someone like Dr. Burlingame? In Operation Enduring Freedom, where distances are great and transportation difficult, that might mean twelve hours *after* they've extracted the casualty from the Humvee that struck a land mine. PJs don't do sick call in garrison; they don't generally go on long-range patrols with special operators nor take care of things like earaches or sprained ankles.

What they do is work day in and day out to maintain their bodies in peak condition so that when a Ditka 03 slams into a mountain, they're ready, willing, and able to get to, stabilize, and rescue the survivors.

PJ team leader Chris Young has no recollection of how many times the pilots tried to hit the refueling drogue this time before they managed to make it stick and top off their tanks. He's deep into monitoring radios, trying to get a mental picture of the crash site, trying to gather as much information as he can get and put it out to his teammates. Young knows that the instant they step off the helicopter and are no longer tied to its radios, CCT Gabe Brown will be his communication link to all of the air assets that are orbiting or en route to their location. Nothing in the area of responsibility takes precedence over a rescue mission; everyone wants a piece of the action, and they can all monitor SATCOM. Chris has to make certain that when that moment comes, the CCT knows what frequencies to dial up on his radios and what call signs to be listening for. Being able to simultaneously communicate with the wide variety of aircraft inbound to their position requires a unique kind of concentration; in this instance, they aren't under fire, but lives could hang in the balance.

One thing Brown knows for certain is that the skies above them probably have or are about to have more air traffic overhead than a slow-moving car chase on a Los Angeles freeway. He surmises correctly that the RCC is already repositioning fighter aircraft to provide cover, should it be needed, and additional tanker aircraft will be diverted from other operations so that those fighters won't have to travel too far to tank up and return.

Young had handpicked Jason Cunningham to join him for this overseas assignment. He'd been made aware that the young senior airman was coming through the pipeline and had kept tabs on him. Once Cunningham arrived at Moody, Young took him under his wing. He'd taught Jason a lot at Moody. They were both prior-service types—Jason from the Navy and Young from the Marine Corps. He liked the younger man's medical skills and admired his motivation. And he really liked the fact that Jason was a dedicated PJ; he wanted to do the mission. "The really bad part about our job," says the team leader, "is for us to do our job, harm has to happen to other people. I remember Jason saying before we came over, 'I don't want anything bad to happen, but I'm going to get a really good mission.'"

USAF aircraft down. Eight survivors. PJs on the scene—or almost there. Without a doubt it's a really good mission, and for Cunningham, this is to be the first real-world test of his pararescue skills, and he doesn't want to screw it up. He knows that Young's responsibility will be the big-picture stuff: coordinating rescue on the ground, assessing the threat from hostile forces, dealing with available air assets. That means he and Miller are going to have primary responsibility for treating and moving patients. The one thing he can do right now is to lighten his kit as much as possible, exiting the helicopter with only those things he'll really need. The first to go are the chicken plates in his body armor, the ceramic, dish-shaped pieces designed to stop bullets as well as shrapnel above waist level. With no apparent threat of hostile fire, that's twenty pounds he can do without. He debates about the ammunition for his M-4 rifle, and then decides to hang on to the minimum basic load that he's carrying. When he's finished, the pack he'll go out the door wearing weighs at least one hundred pounds.

Keary Miller has been in the Air Force for eleven years, all of it as a PJ, and risen to the rank of tech sergeant. He was under fire in Bosnia during a search for two French fighter pilots who'd gone down, but didn't make the pickup, which he says is a matter of luck—or being in the right place at the right time. "I've seen guys be on alert on a location for sixty, seventy days, and then the day after they rotate out, a mission goes. Or a guy fresh out of school will get a mission, and guys have been in fifteen years haven't done a mission. It doesn't have much to do with how great of a PJ you are, but more with timing and luck."

Like the others, he's trained for years to handle everything from fast water—he's based at Louisville, Kentucky, with the 123rd Special Tactics Squadron, which can be called out when the Ohio River floods—to the kind of mountainous terrain they're flying over. Miller, too, is concerned about the weight they'll be carrying, but opts to keep his body armor.

The pararescuemen are dressed in "full snivel gear." Young laughs: "Y'know, sniveling, whining, crying, 'It's cold!' Windstopper Gore-Tex, fleece, extreme-cold-weather boots, extreme-cold-weather gloves. The really bad part about our job is we spend a lot of time in the helicopter doing nothing. And so when you're sitting around doing nothing, flying around at over ten thousand feet at night, it's really cold. And you just sit there and shiver. So we try and dress for that." Finally, they get word from the pilot: They have the fuel they need; they're flying back to the crash site and are authorized to put the PJs on the ground.

Inside the wrecked plane, Pilot Cline, Copilot Wright, and the shooters are struggling with their next problem: how to get Jeff Pohl, who's no longer trapped, onto a litter and out of the plane. They realized from the outset that it would be impossible to bring a litter to his side, get him on it, and then carry him out. What that means is that Pohl is going to have to help extract himself. With a lot of coaching and encouragement, he manages to do it by crawling over and around the wreckage till, exhausted and racked with pain but fighting to remain conscious, he reaches a spot where they'll be able to get him onto the litter. That's when a blast of cold air sweeps through the wrecked fuselage, plastering everyone with driven snow. Chalk 3 is coming in for a landing and has flown directly overhead.

The helo's pilots begin to settle into a spot, decide it won't work, pull out, and opt for another a bit higher up the knoll. This one works, and an hour and four minutes from the time of the crash, the PJs are on the ground, about fifty to seventy-five yards uphill from the plane. It takes Young about two seconds to realize that evacuating the injured isn't going to be a walk in the park.

Wearing his medical rucksack and brimming with energy for his first combat rescue, Jason Cunningham steps off the helicopter first. Wile E. Coyote couldn't have done it any better. *Whoof!* He's up to his chest in almost five feet of snow. It gives Young the only laugh he's had in hours.

If it had been near Aspen in the Colorado Rockies, someone would've been charging big bucks to bring skiers to this pristine powder. But it's Afghanistan, and Cunningham knows there are men who need his help just yards away, and the thin crust atop the powder keeps breaking as he tries to use his arms to push himself out of it. Finally he figures the only way he's going to move is if he takes off the ruck and throws it down the hill. Then he's able to climb out of the hole, crawl across the snow to the ruck, and throw it again.

Keary Miller, meantime, has stepped off the ramp and into snow that comes up to his waist. He immediately sets out for the wreck, initially moving side by side with Young, and instantly feeling the effect of the thin air. "It's not normal; you're sucking wind two minutes into the mission. You're breathing cold air. And sweating." On the way downhill, he takes a fleeting moment to flip up his NVGs, the better to absorb the scene. Ditka 03 looks like a taxied 130 sitting in the snow. "There's some busting, obviously, a little snow over the nose, but the wings are pretty much intact." He remembers thinking that it was an amazing sight, but he couldn't give voice to the thought "because you're doing everything you can to get a breath. You're moving as fast as you can and you take one of those snap photos in the back of your mind while you're breaking the snow."

Despite the subzero temperatures and windchill, all three of the PJs are sweating profusely. The snivel gear, so essential when they're cooling their heels inside the helicopter, has become a nuisance and is quickly removed in favor of the Air Force–issue Gore-Tex parkas to block the wind. Headgear is a simple balaclava, but by the time they've moved a significant distance downhill, they've even pulled those down around their necks.

While the team leader stops short of the downed plane in order to establish a choke point—a place where he can keep track of the number of people going downhill and coming back up—Miller and Cunningham join the survivors inside the rear of the fuselage. Pilot Cline offers, "Obviously we're very happy to see those guys. They took control at that point. Jeff was busted up pretty bad. You've got to assume some sort of neck and spinal injuries and that kind of stuff. I was handling Jeff's head; they gave me all the commands, quickly give us the tutorial on how to move him. We had a stretcher from inside the aircraft, but we still had to get him out. It was very confined, very cramped."

And very noisy. Helicopters landing in bad-guy land keep their engines running in the event they need to make a hasty departure. With one 47 Echo downhill, and another uphill, the rescuers are getting hit with all that noise in stereo as they try to make themselves understood by the people whose help they need to get the loadmaster out of there without further injury.

Cline and the others move Pohl onto the stretcher and finally get the stretcher out of the aircraft into the snow. For a brief moment the pilot allows himself to think that they're home free. Then he actually begins to comprehend that the second helicopter has landed a couple hundred feet up the hill from their position, and he knows it has just begun. He compares it to being in a nightmare where you're being chased, but you can't run away.

The good news is that once they have their patient outside the plane the PJs can actually move with relative ease. In the cramped space where they found Pohl, they couldn't do more than a cursory assessment of his condition. Now Miller and Cunningham do the basic ABCs—checking to see that he's maintained an airway and stopped bleeding, and making sure his circulation is good.

Pohl quickly curls into a fetal position on the litter. It's one of the signs of hypothermia, and is to be expected. How bad off is he? Miller says, "I kind of thought he was critical, that he needed to get out of there. Not very alert, not really talking to us. Not really knowing what's going on. So there was some urgency to get this guy out of here."

It's at this point that Chris makes the decision to split up his team. He orders Cunningham and CCT Gabe Brown to head for Lieutenant Colonel Buss's helicopter and look after the five survivors who are already there, opting to keep the pilot and copilot close by, not only so they can help move the loadmaster up the hill, but because he surmises that while they've been so involved in the efforts to extract Pohl from the wreckage, the full impact of what's happened hasn't hit them yet. It's when they have time to sit down and do nothing but reflect on the disaster that they'll be in danger of lapsing into depression and shock. Besides, with five potential patients on the other bird, novice PJ Jason Cunningham already has his hands full.

If the trip *down* from the helicopter to the plane, breaking through the snow's crust and sinking waist-deep, had its comical elements, the trip back *up* the hill is nightmarish. Two shooters, the pilot and copilot, and both PJs begin a six-man litter-carry of the 175-pound loadmaster. Miller says, "It was literally, move a couple feet, take a couple breaths, move a couple feet."

Young knows the only way they can get it done is with "straight-up manpower. You're in the snow, and everybody, one-two-three, you lift it up, move it, and set it back down. And then you reposition and you just keep moving until you get him up into the helicopter."

For copilot Wright, the climb up the hill was the hardest climb of his life. "I felt like I was slowing people down at that point; I just couldn't breathe, and you're trying to move and you'd fall down, and the guy in front of you is falling down, the guy behind you, and then the litter would tilt and he'd start to slide off it or fall down the hill. You'd just reach in to grab him to hold him on there. Everybody was just kind of chugging and chugging, and after a while, we get to the point where we'd move five feet and stop, and then finally we got to the end of the climb, right at the helicopter, and it was just about four feet away from where we were sitting to getting him in the helicopter, and nobody could move, we were just so exhausted."

Pilot Cline remembers the ordeal this way: "It's five feet of snow uphill two hundred feet, and every second or third step two or three of us would break through up to our waist in snow and fall and drop the stretcher. We're moving him inches at a time, and it just seemed like forever. I think it took us over twenty minutes just to go the two hundred feet up to the helicopter, much less being under the rotor blast, freezing him. He's already freezing to death right in front of us, and we're underneath the rotors. Once we got inside the rotor disk and it was blowing some hot exhaust on us, it was a little better, but there was a while there where I just couldn't believe this was real. It was like living in a cartoon. Deliverance is a hundred feet away in that helicopter, and it was all we could do to move him six inches at a time, a foot at a time."

The PJ team leader doesn't actually know how long the uphill carry took.

He does know that he makes a point of staying in top physical condition, and this rescue whipped him. "I just remember that by the time we got there, I could barely breathe. Y'know, you're moving this guy and you're at that altitude and making all sorts of weird breathing noises. Everything else is frozen around you, but then you notice, 'Hey, I'm sweating. Wow. This is bad.' "

What may be a bad moment for Young is actually a victory for Ditka 03's pilot. "When we finally got in the helicopter, it was a rush. The weight of the world got off me, to see the guys in there. The PJs were just machines. I mean, that's the thing. This team was amazing."

While the two PJs and pilot Cline board the helicopter with the injured loadmaster, Wright realizes he has to go back down to the wrecked plane and retrieve the crypto bag and other classified items. "Standing there, I felt like I was dying, but I knew I had to go back. There was no way I couldn't go back."

As he starts the arduous downhill trek, Wright gets his first good look at the wrecked plane, sitting in the snow, and recalls thinking, like the teenager who borrows Dad's car and wrecks it, "Oh, man, are we in big trouble now."

"When I got down there, there were two guys coming around the plane with the stuff, and I grabbed it out of their hands to make sure they had the right stuff. I had put it outside when I came out earlier, 'cause I'd made several trips back and forth to get stuff that John was asking for. And I grabbed a couple other things."

Now he's got to climb back up the hill with the two shooters. But even though he knows the helicopter is waiting for him so they can take off, he has to beg for a moment's rest, shaking off one of the shooters who's trying to help him. "If he pulled on me," he later said, "I would just fall down, I was breathing so hard."

Inside Chalk 1, "Radio" Rodney Young's normally ebullient personality has officially become a casualty of war. After hearing flight engineer Jeff Doss say, "My back hurts. My butt hurts. What happened?" one time too many, he explodes. Doss thinks he remembers Radio saying, "Look, if you ask me this again, I'm gonna kill you." He's not sure, because he had gotten an extreme headache, which he now realizes was partially due to the concussion he'd suffered in the crash, but was also due to the fact that Rodney is soaked in fuel. Doss says, "It was like sitting next to a pile of gas-soaked rags."

Rodney would not quibble with that description. In fact, he'd likely blame his short temper on the fact that the jet fuel that sprayed him when the tank above his radio position ruptured has now soaked through his clothes to his skin. And it burns. The sensation starts in his legs, and, much to his chagrin, it is working its way up.

On the opposite side of the helo, Chris Langston is concerned that there is nothing he and George Akins can do for Don Tyler except snuggle up and try to keep him warm. Someone had tossed a sleeping bag over them, but they are still sitting directly on the cold metal deck. To make matters worse, Tyler can't remain sitting upright—he keeps sliding and falling over, which just sharpens the pain emanating from his shoulder. The cold he can cope with; he'd grown up in Michigan. But he's never experienced pain like this before.

Finally, close to ninety minutes after the crash occurred, Radio watches help arrive in the person of pararescueman Jason Cunningham. "He gets in the helicopter, he's got snow caked all over his pants, and he's lugging this big-ass backpack. And we're blocking his way. He's trying to lug this thing over us through the helicopter, so I kind of move my legs, make way for him."

No one asks what took him so long to get there, but the PJ offers a humorous explanation. "I just had to go from one side of the airplane to the other side of the airplane with this big one-hundred-fifty-pound pack. Whew! That's a long way to carry this pack."

He approachs Langston first. There must be something about meeting a guy for the first time who you know is there to save your ass, because Chris remembers the conversation verbatim. "When he looked at me, I said, 'I'm the least hurt,' so he went to each one of them, and he came back to me last, and he said, 'Hey, how's everything going?' I said, 'Everything's going great. I'm a little startled right now, but everything's going great.' He asked me where I was from, and when I told him, he said, 'Hey, my name's Senior Airman Jason Cunningham, PJ, United States Air Force.' I said, 'Hey, good to go.' He said, 'Are you sure you're all right?' I said, 'I'm fine. Not that I can feel or anything. I'm perfectly fine.' He said, 'Okay, just keep drinking water.' Then he went back to each one of the other guys."

Don Tyler also remembers Cunningham's arrival. "He was like a ray of sunshine in that dark night. He pretty much put his face right in my face, 'cause it was so noisy and screamed at me, 'Sir, I'm Airman Cunningham, and I'm your PJ.' He had a small chem light in his mouth as he was hovering over me. I remember just looking up and seeing that chem light in his mouth, and he was checking me for injuries. He hooked up an IV bag—and I was just begging for some painkiller. Finally he started giving me some morphine."

While waiting to see if Tyler will get some relief from the painkiller, Cunningham steps across the helicopter to see how flight engineer Jeff Doss is doing. Doss recalls, "He'd come up to me and asked me how I felt, and I remember telling him that my neck was sore, my back was sore, but the worst part was my tailbone was killing me.

"I remember distinctly him screaming at me, 'Don't move!' And at that point, I kind of froze and didn't do anything unless he told me to. He was very forceful. He got my attention."

Cunningham leaves for a moment, then returns with a backboard and straps Doss to it; then he goes back to check on Tyler. The morphine drip isn't making a perceptible difference in his pain. "He kept giving me morphine, morphine, morphine, and I was not getting any relief. I kept asking him, and he said something like, 'Sir, I can't give you any more. I've given you the limit.' I said, 'You're giving me fuckin' placebos!' And I thought it was kinda funny when I said it, and then he kinda grinned at me. I guess he wasn't, but I wasn't getting any relief."

During Cunningham's treatment of Tyler, the shooters who had gone down to help at the crash site board, and Chalk 1 lifts off.

By this time, Rodney has endured the fuel soaking into his skin long enough. "This stuff is burning, and it's burning up my thigh and inner thigh, and it's starting to get to the family jewels, and I start getting nervous. I know it's gasoline, and for some reason, the irritation is spreading. So then I look over at Cunningham, who seems to be just tidying up in his bag. I think he's done with Tyler, so I say, 'Hey, c'mere for a second. I got some gas all over me. It's starting to burn really bad down here. We gotta get this off.' So he cuts off my flight suit pant leg, rips up the inseam, and then he rips up the side of my torso and up my arm, so I got half a flight suit just hanging on me. And he gets some water or saline, and the cotton gauze pads, and he starts wiping it down. He gets close to the jewels and says, 'I think you can handle it from here.'"

Back in Chalk 3, the PJs are concerned that Jeff Pohl might not survive the two-hour flight back to the FST team at Bagram. They're kneeling on the floor in the back of a freezing cold helicopter doing roughly 150 mph thousands of feet up in the Hindu Kush mountains with the rear ramp and windows wide open. They've got a sleeping bag ready for Pohl, but it hasn't been warmed because they didn't leave anyone on board sitting in it. Somehow they've got to get him out of his soaking-wet clothing and into the bag without making things worse. So they begin cutting the injured man's clothes off of him, one appendage at a time, covering him up with a sleeping bag, then peeling back another section and cutting that off. What they discover is that while moving him up to the helicopter, they managed to pack snow between his body and his Gore-Tex jacket, effectively lowering his body temperature even more. So while some of them scoop the snow out and try and dry him off, the two PJs are activating MRE food-warming heater packs and packing them around the now barely conscious patient.

As Chris Young feared, hypothermia is a big problem. PJs are trained in measures to actively rewarm a patient—feeding him a high-sugar drink of hot water mixed with a packet of sugary, energy-producing Jell-O, or giving him massive amounts of warmed IV fluids. But an initial examination indicated that the victim's pelvis was unstable. Pushing fluids runs the risk of elevating his blood pressure, which can cause him to throw a blood clot and increase internal bleeding. And internal bleeding is one of the few things PJs can't do anything about. The only treatment for that, they kid, is bright lights and cold steel—surgery.

The helicopter ride highlighted another aspect of training that Air Force pararescuemen receive that other far-forward medics don't: providing high-level treatment inside a blacked-out, crowded aircraft that's often bouncing through the sky in what seems like three dimensions at once. One training exercise to prepare them for moments like this is to place a volunteer patient— "Airman, lie down on the litter; you just volunteered to be the victim"—in the bed of a pickup truck, and with his buddies bouncing the truck up and down to simulate a rough plane ride, the trainee has to start an IV in the volunteer's arm. And that's *routine* training.

Even as he's working on the loadmaster, Young is trying to keep tabs on the other two survivors they've brought on board, and just moments after they've lifted off, he sees a flash of panic race across the pilot's face. Cline has just recalled that he'd told the other five crewmembers to get on the first helicopter, but has never confirmed that they'd done so. Chris speaks to the aircraft commander, who makes a radio call. Within a minute or two he has the answer. "We got eight. Five on the other helicopter, you three here."

With that question resolved, Cline needs something to do. Every time he leans over and tries to talk to the injured loadmaster, he gets in the PJs' way and they have to push him aside. The problem is figuring out a way to keep the pilot involved in the process, but out of their way. Finally Keary Miller suggests he move down to Pohl's feet and see what he can do to warm them up. "I reached up underneath the sleeping bag and just kind of started rubbing Jeff's feet, and they were just frozen bricks. And at that point, y'know, the whole night I didn't experience any terror or horror or any real fear. For some reason, I don't know why your mind gloms onto certain things, but I was preoccupied with the idea that Jeff might be disfigured from this thing. That he might lose any fingers or toes terrified me. That was the thing that burned in my mind. 'My God, I do not want to be responsible for disfiguring someone.' "

So he starts blowing on the loadmaster's toes, a moment Chris Young hasn't forgotten. "I'm looking around, looking for the aircraft commander. And he's actually down at my patient's feet. He's got his head underneath the sleeping bag, blowing on his feet and rubbing on them." Young gets a quizzical look in his eyes. "It's really odd to see a major curled up around some enlisted dude's feet, blowing on 'em."

At that moment, no one has time to reflect on the fact that the patient whose life and limbs they're trying to save doesn't have to be in this predicament. But for the decision of Lieutenant Colonel Buss, they could have had him out of the wreckage in minutes, instead of his being trapped, bleeding and reaching the brink of a frozen death. Despite his West Point education, where he should have learned the importance of caring for one's troops, Lieutenant Colonel Buss never even bothered to walk fifteen feet back from the cockpit to the freezing cargo area of his own helicopter to offer encouragement to five guys who had just cheated death and were hurting. Perhaps he couldn't face men who needed medical attention knowing he's the one responsible for their having none for well over an hour?

Major Cline stayed beside Jeff Pohl for the duration of the flight to Bagram. "People were handing me those little pocket chemical warmers, so I started wrapping those around the toes on his broken leg, and trying to rub and rub and rub. And then I ended up touching his other foot, and it was just a frozen brick; that was supposedly his good foot. So then I started rubbing both feet.

"I guess it was almost a two-hour helicopter ride, and about halfway through the flight, Jeff started flexing both of his ankles, started moving both of his feet. A wave of relief came over me. I thought, 'Hey, the wiring is still there, it still works.' Once he started moving his feet around, moving his ankles around, I thought, 'Hey, y'know, maybe . . . It's all small shit from here on out. Jeff's okay, we didn't kill anybody.'

"About every ten minutes, I'd give this helpless glance up to the PJs. They were taking his vitals. I don't know what the procedure is, but obviously they were keeping the field hospital updated on his vital signs every ten minutes or so, radioing his blood pressure and everything. Every time, I was just begging

Jbad hangar interior during the early days, when all American special operation forces on the base were living and working there. *(USAF photo)*

Tent city on the base at Jbad. In the background is the hangar. In the foreground is a pallet of bottled water. CSAR crews in the tent city went through several pallets a day.

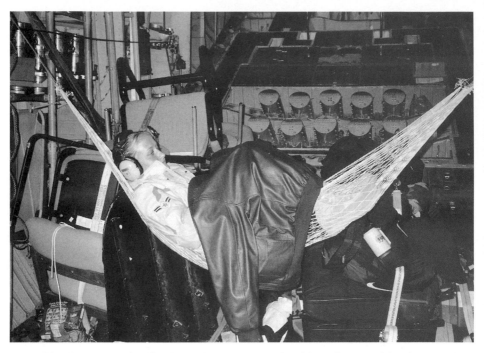

HC-130 loadmaster Sarah Jeffers knows how to get comfortable in the rear of the plane on the 9,000-mile flight from Valdosta, Georgia, to Pakistan.

Deluxe accommodations at the K-2 B&B in the HAS. Beats a dusty Army tent, complete with mice, any day.

The dining facility on the base at Jbad. "UGR" are rations that come in large, multi-serving trays.

PJs practicing snatch-and-grab rescues from an HH-60G at the end of the runway at Kandahar.

Not much room left in the rear of a Pave Hawk helicopter after the PJs have packed their gear aboard, including the Stokes litter strapped to the auxiliary fuel tank.

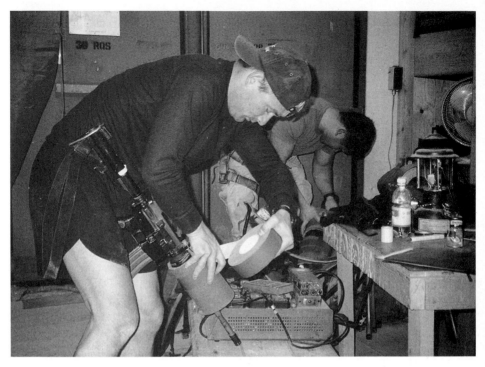

PJ Ben Harris prepares the scope on top of his rifle so that it will survive a HALO jump from an HC-130.

*Above:* S.Sgt. Caleb Ethridge cleans his M-4 GAU.

*Right:* PJ team leader Chris Young does some gear maintenance at the HQ of the 38th Rescue Squadron at Moody AFB, Georgia.

Inside the cockpit of a 71st Rescue Squadron HC-130 as the crew runs one of its checklists.

From left to right: PJs Terra Barrington, Rob Disney, Dan Killough and CRO Rob Taylor and author Michael Hirsh at the rear of an HC-130. The small canvas screen to the right is the privacy device for the "lavatory."

*Above:* Charlie, the cause of innumerable PJ near-riots, relaxing at Nellis AFB, where he currently resides with the 58th Rescue Squadron. *(Air Force photo by T.Sgt. Robert W. Valenca)*

*Above:* One of the 41st ERQS tents at K-2. The sign says it all.

*Left:* Elvis and CSAR patch.

*Above:* PJs with David Letterman, who visited with them at Kandahar just before Christmas. Which PJ wrote the line coming out of Chief Bob Holler's mouth is a closely guarded secret. From left to right: S.Sgt. Bill Hardin, S.Sgt. Ben Harris, T.Sgt. (Select) Soup Campbell, Chief M.Sgt. Bob Holler, David Letterman, SrA Ed Ha, SrA Tam Sirisak. *(Courtesy of T.Sgt. [Select] Justin "Soup" Campbell)*

*Right:* Don't mess with the Boyz 'N the HAS.

*Above:* Members of an American Special Forces A-team, along with SOF personnel, pose with Afghan warlord Hamid Karzai during their push toward Kandahar. The photo was taken shortly before a 2,000-pound JDAM bomb was mistakenly dropped on their position, killing three members of the team. To the right of Karzai is SOF battalion commander Lt. Col. David Fox, and next to Fox is A-team CO Capt. Jason Amerine. *(Photo courtesy of the U.S. Army Special Operations Command)*

*Left:* PJs Ryan Schultz and Pat Malone, who flew the JDAMned rescue mission.

*Above:* Ditka 03 crew before taking off. Standing (left to right): Maj. Don Tyler, M.Sgt. Jeff Doss, Maj. John Cline, T.Sgt. Jeff Pohl, Maj. George Akins. Kneeling (left to right): S.Sgt. Chris Langston, S.Sgt. Rodney Young, Capt. Jason Wright.

*Right:* Ditka 03 navigator Maj. Don Tyler smiles through the pain as he arrives at Fort Walton Beach, Florida, following a long trip from Germany. *(Courtesy of Maj. Don Tyler)*

Lt. Col. Lee dePalo, commander of the 41st Rescue Squadron, in front of the unit's K-2 HAS.

Senior M.Sgt. Bill Sine, who led the HALO jump to the minefield. The PJ team on the mission is on his computer screen.

Lt. Matt "Moose" McGuinness, the combat rescue officer who lobbied for his team to be allowed to make the jump to an injured Aussie SAS soldier in the middle of a minefield.

Maj. Terry Crabtree, 71st Rescue Squadron pilot, who, as aircraft commander, made the decision to permit the PJs to jump to the minefield.

*Left:* S.Sgt. Bill Hardin with a special pararescue crash ax with which the PJs could have freed the trapped Ditka 03 loadmaster in minutes.

*Below:* S.Sgt. Rob Disney, one of the Boyz 'n the HAS and lead guitarist of Jbad's number-one rock band, Camel Toes.

*Left:* PJ Terra Barrington, aka "Bob Vila" of *This Old HAS.* He painted the Rescue Angel on the front of their Jbad HAS.

*Below:* Senior M.Sgt. Dan Killough on a quad at Jbad with the unit's mascot, Charlie, named for the PJ icon that's been the cause of numerous near riots.

Members of the 41st ERQS sitting around the fire in Kandahar on Christmas night, 2002.

Combat controller T.Sgt Jim Hotaling in Afghanistan. *(USAF photo)*

CSAR HH-60G pilot 1st Lt. Thomas Cahill, awarded the Silver Star for heroism during Operation Anaconda and the DFC for saving his crew and helicopter following a crash in the Hindu Kush mountains. *(Air Force photo by T.Sgt. Robert W. Valenca)*

PJs from the 38th RQS and 106th RQW serve as pallbearers at the funeral of Pararescue M.Sgt. Mike Maltz. Senior M.Sgt. Bill Sine is second from left. *(USAF photo by Scott H. Spitzer)*

*Above:* Jason and Theresa Cunningham.
*(Courtesy of Theresa Cunningham)*

*Right:* SrA Jason Cunningham in Afghanistan,
three weeks before Operation Anaconda.
*(Courtesy of S.Sgt. Chris Young)*

Chief M.Sgt. Donald Shelton presents the U.S. flag from Jason Cunningham's casket to his wife,
Theresa. Maj. Vincent Savino brings a second flag to Cunningham's parents at Arlington
National Cemetery. *(USAF photo by T.Sgt. Mark D. Smith)*

for some feedback, and they'd give me the thumbs-up, hey, he's doing all right, he's alive, he's conscious, he's working. I tell you, aside from their technical expertise at trying to save somebody, they had a bedside manner that was exactly what I needed."

Copilot Jason Wright had never been in an MH47 before this flight. He recalls being a bit uncertain when he finally climbed aboard and walked to the front, where the PJs were already working on the loadmaster. Chris Young handed him a sleeping bag to cover up with, and an MRE heater to warm his hands. "I couldn't feel my hands at all. It was freezing. The first thing he said to me was, like, 'What branch are you?' and I said, 'Air Force,' and he said something like, 'The best damn branch' or something like that to me. Then introduced himself and he's, like, 'Hey, I'm Chris Young, a United States Air Force PJ.' I was so impressed at that point, because finally I knew someone else was in control of the situation and was going to take care of it, and I felt better about it, at least.

"It made me realize that he was going to take care of Jeff, and I could relax for a second. I hadn't been able to sit still for a second to realize what had happened. So it was weird, because I'd seen it in a movie before, and I'd thought, 'That's kind of corny that they'd say that to you,' but it was weird to me when it actually happened. I can't believe how much it calmed me down and made me feel better about what was going on, at least. He sat me down and got me in a sleeping bag, got me warmed up, and I was just like, 'This guy's the *man*. I've got nothing to worry about, 'cause he's going to take care of Jeff.'"

Part of Chris Young's bedside manner included keeping the pilot and copilot Cline from knowing just how bad off their loadmaster was. The truth? The PJs thought they were going to lose him. Chris Young says Pohl's level of consciousness kept fluctuating. "We were fighting hypothermia in him; I knew he had internal injuries; he could only be saved by a surgeon. It's not like he had a gunshot wound and I could stop the bleeding. He had internal injuries and there was nothing more we could do. At one point I went to the [special operations] team that was on board the aircraft and I asked them to pray for my patient. And one of the guys says, 'What's the matter?' And I said, 'Honestly, I think he'll die before we land.'"

Nevertheless, the two PJs and one SAS medic continue to do what they can for Pohl, while keeping an eye on the other two crash survivors. The conversation they had with the ambulatory survivors really has several purposes: to put them at ease, to assess their condition, and to make certain that once the stress of actually surviving the crash subsides, they haven't lapsed into depression or shock. Once Young has Cline involved in caring for the load-master, he turns to the copilot, who is just sitting there, staring into space. "In a crash like that . . . you can't let people dwell on what they just did. You have to give them something else to think about, something to keep their mind active. And so I told him, 'Hey, sir, I need your help over here.' And he said, 'Oh, oh, okay.' We wanted his help and he was eager to provide it. Once we got him into the fight, he was talking to my patient the whole time, making sure he's conscious. We kept asking him questions over and over again: 'Do you know where you are? Do you know what happened? Where did you go to high school? How long have you been in the Air Force?' Things like that, just so everybody has a part in the game."

Wright remembers being told, " 'Do not let him go to sleep. You gotta keep him awake; don't let him go to sleep at all.' So they were watching me when I was watching him. I would talk to him, and he would respond to my voice. I'd say, 'Jeff, open your eyes,' and talk to him about anything I could talk to him about. And they would be watching, 'cause if I looked down and his eyes were closed, I'd see a hand come in and tap him or shake him, even flick him on the cheek."

For more than two hours, including time for aerial refueling, the two PJs, the surviving pilot and copilot, and at least one special operator tend to Jeff Pohl. For Wright, the flight seems to take forever, and it is made even longer by the fact that they can all see that Jeff's condition appears to be worsening.

By the time they land at the American base at Bagram, the sun is coming up. Medical personnel back a Humvee up to the ramp at the rear of Chalk 3, and rush Pohl to the FST facility in the base of the control tower. At the same time, the five Ditka 03 crewmembers who are with PJ Jason Cunningham aboard Chalk 1 have also landed and are brought to the hospital. Maj. Brian Burlingame was in charge of the facility and remembered examining Pohl.

"The skinny on him is that he came in, he had critical injuries, and in the broad spectrum they were potentially life-threatening, but he was not going to die right now. He needed significant care. Pretty much everyone's hypothermic when they come in. He needed to be warmed, he needed fluid, he needed blood, he needed an orthopedic surgeon, and he needed a general surgeon to assess the rest of his wounds."

Burlingame had no idea what the PJs had gone through to get Pohl to his forward hospital in survivable condition. "It's tough, because I see the product they bring me, but I don't see what they had to go through to get it. Occasionally I hear stories about the environment, the conditions of, 'He was stuck beneath this thing; I had to use these devices to get him out.' For me, it's always just fascination that, 'Wow, how wonderful what you guys do.' And it's kind of the same thing when people come up to me and say, 'Oh, you guys, you do a great job, you do wonderful stuff,' and it's like, 'This is easy; this is no big deal.' And that's how they talk about their job, y'know. 'Oh, hey, you went in, you brought these eight guys out. You're phenomenal.' They're like, 'It's no big deal. We just did our job. It was not hard.' They're very matter-of-fact. The only thing they ever embellish on is the depth of the snow. I think it goes from, like, four inches to four feet over the course of a couple of discussions. But other than that, they're very humble as a group when it comes down to game time."

In the hospital, medics treat the cuts on Don Tyler's face and knee. Then they take him a couple of hundred yards to the British medical facility, where X-ray equipment is available. It's quickly determined that he has what one doc describes as "a horrible dislocation of his left shoulder," and will need to have it reduced immediately. Since they will need to take a postreduction X ray, there is no point dragging him back to the American OR for the procedure to, in layman's terms, put his upper arm bone back in the socket.

Don recalls being told, " 'We're going to put you to sleep with the gas and set your arm.' It was a beautiful thing—they had a pretty blond nurse with a British accent holding my hand as they put me to sleep."

The operation is performed under general anesthesia by an American orthopedic surgeon and nurse-anesthetist working side by side with a British surgeon in the Brit hospital.

At roughly the time the helicopter with the PJs lands at the crash site, word gets back to the 9th Special Operations Squadron at Hurlburt Field in the Florida panhandle that the crash had occurred.

The eleven-hour time difference made it just after six P.M. CST Monday evening. The squadron immediately attempted to notify the wives of the married crewmembers, but when they were unable to get through on the phone to tell Barbara Tyler about the accident—her daughter was on the computer tying up the line—they sent an Air Force captain out to the Tyler home with orders to pick her up and bring her back to the base, where she'd get briefed.

Unfortunately, when the uniformed Air Force officer pulled up in front of their home, Mrs. Tyler was several miles away, watching their son take his tae kwon do lesson, and their thirteen-year-old daughter was home alone. When the officer came to the door, she wouldn't let him in the house, but, recognizing the unit patch on his shoulder, she figured he was legitimate, so she kept the door locked, went into the kitchen and wrote down her mom's cell phone number, and handed it through the door to the officer.

The captain returned to his car and called Barbara. "Mrs. Tyler, there's been a problem with Major Tyler's plane."

"What kind of problem?"

"Well, I can't tell you that," he responded, adding, "but all I can tell you is, he's alive."

She immediately began trembling. Then she got a grip. "The first thing that went through my mind is, 'Okay, he's alive. My kids can't hear this unless they hear it from me.' The second thing was not to frighten them, because I didn't have enough information to give to my kids. I didn't want them to get the pieces of information that I was going to get; I wanted them to know in a calm way."

The captain wanted to know where she was; his orders were to pick her up and bring her to the base. But until she made arrangements for someone to watch the children, she wasn't going anywhere, so she refused to provide her location, telling him instead to call her back in five minutes. In that interval, Mrs. Tyler made arrangements for friends to take care of the kids. When the captain called back from his car parked in the Tylers' driveway, she said, "You're going to see a woman walk across the lawn and come into my house and take care of my daughter. Once that happens, then please come get me."

At about the same time as Barbara Tyler was being notified, the squadron was also trying to reach Jyl Cline, the wife of the pilot. She'd come home from her job as a budget analyst with a weapons contractor at Eglin Air Force Base, changed into sweats, and was on the treadmill saying the rosary when she noticed the phone ringing. Figuring whoever was calling would call back, she ignored it. Five minutes later it rang again, three times, and then the caller hung up. "Strange," she thought. It happened several more times, when suddenly, "Somebody was banging on the front door." Her two Labrador retrievers began barking, and the banging continued.

Now Jyl was scared. This had been going on for half an hour. She grabbed the phone and called her brother down the street, and as she did so, she looked through a window and saw a man in a green flight suit walking back toward her front door. She recognized the man as an officer in John's squadron. He said, "Jyl, let me in."

"I said no, and started crying," she recalls. "I remember saying, 'Something's happened, hasn't it?' and he said, 'Yes. Jyl, open the door. There's been a crash but John is alive.'"

She opened the door and let the officer in. He said, "There's been a crash. He's alive and he's in American hands. You need to come to the squadron for a briefing."

The timing of the notification of the families is extraordinary. The crash happened at three-thirty A.M. Afghan time, on February 13 (coincidentally, 0213 was the tail number of the Ditka 03 aircraft), which computes to four-thirty P.M. at Eglin Air Force Base on February 12. Officers from the 9th Special Operations Squadron were knocking on the door of the wives' homes by six P.M. local time, less than ninety minutes after the crash—and while the Ditka 03 crew was still on the mountainside. It's conceivable that at the moment Jyl Cline was being notified, her husband was still on his hands and knees inside the wreckage, trying to dig the injured loadmaster out.

Changing into the same black jeans and sweater she'd worn to work that day, Jyl rode to the base with her brother and sister-in-law for the briefing that was to begin at eight. "When I walked into the squadron, I was overwhelmed. I opened the door and there were green flight suits beyond the eye, and they were all staring at *me*. And I knew right then John was dead; I knew he was."

Only four of the crewmembers were married at the time of the crash, and only three of the wives were in the area that night. Eventually, Jyl Cline, Barbara Tyler, and Amy Akins, the wife of the other navigator, were all gathered in a private room for a briefing by the squadron commander. Jyl recalls the colonel saying, "There's been a crash as they were coming along a mountain ridge. We're unsure of the injuries, although we do know that there are some arm and back injuries. As we get more information, we'll keep you informed by the minute."

And then he said, "God shined on us tonight because he's going to bring eight heroes home." Jyl Cline promptly fell apart.

After a group prayer, the wives were told that their husbands would be home in two days.

By eleven-thirty Barbara Tyler was back home, where the unit's acting squadron commander called her with updates throughout the night. She also heard from the commander of the hospital at Hurlburt, who filled her in on Don's condition, even to the point of telling her what the X rays taken at the British hospital were showing.

What made the situation especially difficult for her to explain to the kids was that their dad shouldn't even have been on Ditka 03 when it slammed into the mountain. He should have been retired, a civilian, out of the Air Force. But he'd been caught in what the military calls "stop loss." It can cover everyone in the service, or be job specific. Don was a navigator; the Air Force was short of navs; ergo, the Tyler family's plans for Don to retire and build a new home not far away were put on indefinite hold.

During that first night, Barbara says she must have answered the phone forty times, but the one that came around two-forty-five was special. She picked up the phone to hear her husband say, "I'm okay. I'm coming home." No preliminaries, no "Hello," just, "I'm coming home."

Barbara recalls that his speech was "really, really bad, and his voice was very weak." She asked, "What's wrong with your speech? Did you hit your head?"

Don replied, "My mouth is dry. I'm coming home. I gotta go."

"That was it," she says. "The whole conversation took less than twenty seconds."

The unit called Jyl Cline every two hours through the night with updates on John's location and condition. They told her when he was en route to the FST team at Bagram, and when he arrived there; when he was on the way to K-2, and when he arrived there. The first call told her that they already knew John was capable of walking and appeared to have no serious injuries. At four-thirty in the morning her phone rang and it was John, on a radio patch from the hospital at Karshi-Khanabad, where they both had to say "over" at the end of each thought. "He was there with his crew and said he wanted to be with them because it was very therapeutic to stay together. His voice was elevated when he told me how happy he was to be alive. He said, 'Oh, my God, I don't believe we did this and walked away.' He was very upbeat, very positive."

Before John left on his deployment to Operation Enduring Freedom, Jyl had given him a scapular that had been carried by her father, a B-17 bomber pilot in World War II. He'd been shot down twice, and survived, and Jyl thought it might be a good omen for her husband to carry it. He agreed, and before each flight removed his wedding wing—all jewelry must be removed before flying—and would wrap it in the small piece of blessed cloth, and place it in the zippered pocket of his flight suit directly over his heart. In that first phone call, John told her, "I touched my heart, and I thought it saved your Dad's life, and it saved me."

Having injured servicemen call home as soon as they're able had developed almost into policy in Operation Enduring Freedom. The military had to do it in response to two separate and distinct problems created by the miracle of modern communications. One problem was described as "the CNN effect," even though it wasn't network-specific. Television coverage in the war zone was extensive—although not as omnipresent as it would be in Iraq—and almost as soon as reporters learned that Americans had been wounded or injured in a crash, the report would be broadcast. Even though they didn't announce names of the injured, nor their unit designation, loved ones back home would typically get a call from a friend saying that, for example, "a C-130 just crashed." Well, there are a lot of C-130s flying around OEF, but human nature being what it is, until it can be ruled out that it's not your significant other's plane, the possibility remains that it might be.

The other problem was the result of servicemen overseas having relatively easy access to the military's DSN telephone network and e-mail system. All it took was one man to call or e-mail back home to his wife or girlfriend, who would then get on the phone to other spouses in the unit, and before any official notification could be made, the spouse of the injured GI would get a well-intentioned call expressing concern, or worse, condolences.

That explains the Army field telephone being thrust into Don Tyler's hands as soon as the medics felt he was capable of conveying the notion that he had, indeed, survived the crash. It also explains the brevity of the call; he was on morphine and other painkillers and was in no condition to chat.

With their patients turned over to the FST unit, the three PJs, Chris Young, Keary Miller, and Jason Cunningham, raided the unit's supply room and restocked their med rucks. When they went back out to clean up the helicopters and prepare for the next mission, Jason took advantage of the lull to relive the events of the night with Chris, describing what symptoms each patient exhibited, and asking his mentor if he'd handled each one properly. As the senior PJ would have expected, Jason had performed flawlessly.

It was while they were cleaning up that Cunningham reminded Young that he had predicted they'd get a good mission. Young said, "Hey, this isn't how it always happens. It's the luck of the draw."

Exhausted from the activities of the previous night, Young had one more thing to do before he could get some sleep: attend the mission debriefing. In the Air Force, everyone who participates is encouraged to speak his or her mind, irrespective of rank or position. It's the time to call a spade a spade, sort it out, and learn from the experience. That's the Air Force. What Young discovered was that the Army doesn't play by the same rules. This debriefing in the command tent was being presided over by Lieutenant Colonel Buss, the mission commander whose judgment vis-à-vis the PJs was seriously in question.

At the end of the session, they typically go around the room, asking if anyone has any questions or anything they want to add. When they got to the

Special Tactics Team, Young rolled a verbal grenade onto the table. "Yes, sir, why did it take us an hour and four minutes to get down to the patients?"

At first Buss attempted to mollify the staff sergeant with his the-helicopter-needed-fuel explanation. Young wasn't buying it. "Sir, I was fighting hypothermia in my patient the entire time because of this hour and four minutes he was laying in this aircraft wreckage."

Buss sat there in front of the forty or so people in the tent and took a respectfully delivered tongue-lashing for a little bit. Finally, as one person recalls it, Buss said something like, "Sergeant Young, sit down and be quiet." It wasn't surprising that the lieutenant colonel appeared not to like having his judgment publicly questioned by an Air Force E-5, especially an E-5 who believed in his heart that he'd just watched interservice rivalry nearly kill his patient. Moments later, non-Army personnel in attendance were asked to leave the meeting, so the flight crews could do an "in-house debrief."

Young and other PJs in Operation Enduring Freedom knew that prior to the Ditka 03 mission, the Army special operations helicopter units were less than thrilled about being told by the joint command to carry Air Force PJs on their birds. Army officers contended that their own medics were quite capable of carrying out the CSAR mission. They had the training; they even had their own version of the REDS kit. The difference is that it's not their bread and butter.

Chris Young is realistic about the skills of pararescuemen. As self-assured as he and his colleagues are, they're not the type to overplay their hand. But if there's a lesson learned from the Ditka 03 mission, one that he wants the Army, Navy, Marines, and even the Coast Guard to understand, it's this: "If I had to go into a foreign land and treat the natives and all that, that's a Special Forces medic's job. They do that better than absolutely anybody. Nobody tries to say that they can do water missions better than the Navy SEALs. Our main thing is trauma, trauma care on airframes, especially helicopters, things like that, blacked out, and rescue is what we do better than anybody else. Why? That's our sole purpose in life."

Over the next few weeks as combat and accidents claimed American lives, Jason Cunningham found time to reflect on war, his role in it, and what could happen. He wrote a letter to be given to his wife, Theresa, if the worst should happen. In it, Jason apologized for not always being the best husband and for the hardships she would face if he died. It was not an atypical letter for a young man new to combat and seeing death close at hand for the first time to give to a buddy.

*I could not leave this earth without saying good-bye to you. I will miss you and the girls immensely,* wrote Cunningham. *You have always been the best wife. I want you to know I died a happy man, happy that I met you and happy that I have two wonderful girls.*

Chris Young, who is five years older than Jason, was much more circumspect about his situation when he talked with his wife on the phone after she'd seen reports of the Ditka crash on CNN. "She was pretty amped up about it, because she knows all the different airframes we fly on, and when I talked to her, she asked, 'Were you involved in a C-130 crash?' and I was, like, 'Uh . . .'

" 'I got two questions: Were you on it or were you the one who rescued it?' I said, 'We rescued it.' She said, 'Okay, that's fine.' "

Young has thought a lot about what he does—what they do, and why they continue to do it. "The main thing that I love most about being rescue versus being a Marine is that when you're in almost all the other services, what you do is the result of somebody's political will. 'This would look good,' or 'that would look good,' or, 'what if this? Give them this mission, or that mission.' And in rescue, we don't have to worry about that. We have without a doubt the most righteous mission in the entire military, because we don't have to worry about bad intel, going in and hitting the wrong target or anything like that, or having a bomb stray off course. When we go in, we're going to get an American or one of our allies, and that's it. It doesn't get any better than that. We're recovering our friends. That's what we live for."

Radio operator Rodney Young's slit-open flight suit has been replaced with a hospital gown so small he risks arrest for indecent exposure when he steps outside the FST unit. Neither modesty, nor the fact that he could freeze his ass off, keeps him from grabbing this opportunity to enjoy his first cigarette since leaving Jbad. And there is only a moment's hesitation when he discovers that the pack of Newports that had been in his fleece jacket have been marinated in jet fuel. This is combat, where you smoke 'em if you got 'em. No matter what they've been dipped in.

Loadmaster Chris Langston discovers that his smokes have also become a casualty of the crash. The pack he kept in his lower leg flight-suit pocket was bloodstained. He'd managed to nick his shin during the crash and it took three stitches to fix it properly. Chris is also getting used to being called "Ninja Boy," the nickname someone laid on him after learning about his perfect midair somersault during the crash.

Several hours after arriving at Bagram, the Ditka 03 crew is put aboard a medical evac Herc for the ninety-minute flight to Karshi-Khanabad. To stave off frostbite to vital parts, Rodney had managed to borrow jeans and a sweatshirt from another airman. A special in-flight medical team attended loadmaster Jeff Pohl, the only crewmember in critical condition. Navigator Don Tyler, his recently set shoulder still giving him off-the-scale pain, is doped up for the trip. Flight engineer Jeff Doss is still strapped to a backboard.

At K-2, more X rays of Tyler's shoulder are taken, and it's determined that he and Pohl will be sent by giant C-5 Galaxy jet to the principal U.S. military medical facility in Europe, Landstuhl Regional Medical Center, five kilometers from Ramstein Air Base, near Frankfurt, Germany. Aside from the fact that his pain isn't under control, all Tyler remembers of that six-hour trip is that he spent four hours of it trying to pee, which is a good trick when you're on your back, strapped to a gurney. He'd been told that a catheter with his name on it was standing by in case he couldn't. It was an effective motivator.

Meantime, the remaining six members of the crew are hospitalized for observation—and they get an overabundance of that, medical and otherwise, since they've taken on the mythic role of "the crew that crashed their plane into a mountain and walked away."

The day after they arrive is Ash Wednesday. Even though only a couple of the men are Catholic, it somehow is decided that they'll go to Mass en masse. So, wearing hospital gowns and slippers, they walk the quarter mile down muddy roads to the tent that serves as the chapel in the middle of the drab tent city that has been built over the past couple of months.

Back at the hospital, they have access to phones, computers, and food that is head and shoulders above the bulk tray rations being served at Jacobabad.

And they have a lot of time to sit together and contemplate what they'd been through. Pilot John Cline says they were six very happy guys. "We were giddy. I mean, we were looking around at each other, 'Can you believe that we just put an airplane into the side of a mountain, and we're all sitting here bullshitting about it?' And we skipped all the brooding. There was no terror, there was no horror, no depression. It was all just, 'Boy, we're really happy to be here. We've dodged a pretty big one.'" Now, confident that they're all okay and their two crewmates are in good hands, all they are waiting for is their release from the hospital, and a ride back home to Jacobabad.

Strange as it may seem, there is some apprehension about going back to their unit. Not because they are going to have to face a grueling safety board investigation into the cause of the crash, but because they don't know whether their fellow airmen will be looking askance at them.

They don't need to worry. It turns out that the plan had been to put them on a regular intratheater shuttle flight back to Jacobabad, but according to Jeff Doss, another crew in their unit made a big stink about that. "No, they're our guys; we're gonna go pick 'em up."

Doss says, "That was huge for our mental state, because you crash an airplane on a mountain and you wonder how you're going to be received back at your unit."

The unit in question is the 9th Special Operations Squadron (SOS). Elite among units at Eglin AFB, the 9th SOS is actually part of the 16th Special Operations Wing ten miles away at Hurlburt Field in the panhandle of Florida. Operating out of K-2 through November 2001, then out of Jbad thereafter, the 9th SOS personified the "Anytime, Anyplace" motto of the 16th Special Operations Wing. Cline says they were so reliable for helicopter air refueling that typically conservative Army planners abandoned their practice of always having a backup ground refueling site; it simply wasn't necessary. If the 9th said they would be there, they would be there. The 9th is famous among Air Force MH-53 crews for their ability to instantly adapt to changes on the ground. According to Ditka 03's pilot, quick action and innovative thinking by 9th crews averted disaster on several high-priority OEF missions. He says that in one case, a 9th crew appeared out of nowhere deep in enemy territory to refuel an MH-53 that had less than two minutes of fuel remaining.

Several complicated direct-action missions involved a quarter of the 9th SOS MC-130Ps conducting five in-flight refuelings of seven MH-53s over a nine- or ten-hour flight. The MC-130Ps would split into two two-ship elements for the "yo-yo"; while two were down low refueling helos, the other two would be up high taking on fuel from a KC-135, and then they'd swap positions three or four times during the flight. A single gallon of fuel could be passed from a KC-10 to a KC-135, then to an MC-130P, and finally to an MH-53 to be burned. The amount of contingency planning and "what if" scenarios required to execute such a complex aerial plan are mind-numbing, but the 9th never missed an air refueling control time.

And the 9th couldn't wait to welcome back the crewmembers of Ditka 03.

They are transported from the hospital at K-2 to the airfield, and as the Combat Shadow's ramp opens, they can see a huge American flag hanging in the plane's cargo bay. That's when the tears begin.

Three hours later, the plane comes in for a landing through the nighttime smoke and haze at Jbad. It taxis to the maintenance area at one end of the airfield, and as the ramp opens, the crew of Ditka 03 can see the entire maintenance unit standing at attention, another huge American flag next to the formation. What's more, the maintenance guys are wearing complete regulation uniforms, a feat that even the most zealous commander in a combat zone would be hard-pressed to make happen.

And as aircraft commander Maj. John Cline, copilot Capt. Jason Wright, navigator Maj. George Akins, flight engineer M.Sgt. Jeff Doss, loadmaster S.Sgt. Chris Langston, and radio operator S.Sgt. Rodney Young walk off the ramp, the entire assembled group snap a formal salute.

Then the party begins.

### The Badass Crew of 0213

By T.Sgt. Stacey A. Quarles
An engine mechanic for MC-130P Tail Number 0213
(Read to the crew at their welcome-home party)

Some heroes live
Some heroes die
Some heroes fly
In the Afghan skies
You are our heroes
For what you have done
You landed a plane
Where it couldn't be done
You have done the impossible
You make us proud to be a team
You are the badass crew
Of Zero Two One Three

\* \* \*

At the U.S. Army's Landstuhl Regional Medical Center, several thousand miles to the east, however, things are not as happy. Loadmaster Jeff Pohl is being well cared for, and plans are being made to transport him to Walter Reed Army Medical Center near Washington, D.C. What's happening with Maj. Don Tyler, however, is another story; it's why you should never assume you're out of the woods till you're out of the woods.

When Tyler arrived at Landstuhl, he was wearing a huge cervical collar because there was still concern that he might have a broken neck. Despite the fact that he was still in excruciating pain from the shoulder injury, it was his neck that became the focus of medical concern. Once they did a CAT scan and discovered that he had no cervical fracture, they removed the collar, arranged for him to once again call his wife, and within hours ordered him to leave the hospital.

At three in the morning, less than forty-eight hours after riding a plane into the side of a mountain and wearing only a hospital gown and paper flip-flops, doped up on painkillers that were not doing the job, United States Air Force Maj. Don Tyler is unceremoniously discharged from Landstuhl and told to check himself into billeting on the base. He manages to get a ride part of the way, but completes the journey on foot. It's raining and the temperature is in the mid-thirties. He has no clothes, no shoes, no money. His dog tags and wedding ring are missing. All he has left is an ID card and a credit card, without which he wouldn't be able to pay the twenty-four dollars a night the billeting facility charges.

At four A.M., after getting ordered back to his room from the tiny self-serve kitchen where he was trying to get a hot cup of coffee—the hospital gown didn't quite measure up to their dress code—he gets to bed. Three hours later he reports back to the hospital for more X rays. The doctors want to make sure the bone in his upper arm is in place. It is, and the next thing he knows he has a release in his one good hand telling him to fly home on a commercial aircraft. He is no longer Landstuhl's problem.

When Tyler first related this story, it sounded far-fetched. Landstuhl has long had a reputation in the public media as *the* place in Europe where the U.S. military brings its casualties. It's the largest American hospital outside the United States. It has approximately 110 physicians, 250 nurses, 900 enlisted personnel, and 550 civilian employees. Landstuhl has 162 beds, with an expansion capacity in excess of 310 beds. It's the only Army medical facility to house an Air Force Aeromedical Evacuation Unit.

Visit the hospital's Web site and you get a sense of its importance:

> LRMC has played a major role in many world events. Today, LRMC provides medical treatment to casualties injured during Operation Enduring Freedom in Afghanistan. LRMC treated the victims of the USS *Cole* bombing in October 2000. The hospital has also played an integral part in the repatriation of the three American soldiers who were taken prisoners of war in Yugoslavia in March 1999,

and treated American and Kenyan victims of the U.S. Embassy bombing in Nairobi in August 1998. In 1994, it served as the treatment point for hundreds of Bosnian refugees injured in the Sarajevo marketplace bombing, as well as treating victims of the 1988 Ramstein Air Show disaster, and the victims of the 1983 bombing of the U.S. Marine Corps Barracks in Beirut, Lebanon. During Operations Desert Shield and Storm in 1990/1991, more than 4,000 service members from that region were treated at the facility, and more than 800 U.S. military personnel deployed to Somalia were evacuated and treated here.

Is it conceivable that the drugs he'd been given for pain had addled Don Tyler's brain? Could he be making it all up? It's preposterous to think that a hospital whose very name is synonymous with the best medical care the U.S. military can offer would toss a seriously injured, hurting, drugged, virtually naked Air Force navigator out into the street on a cold winter night.

But that's what happened. And the individual who verified it is none other than Maj. Brian Burlingame, the surgeon who initially treated Don Tyler when the PJs brought him to the FST team at Bagram, and who is now chief of surgery at the Womack Army Medical Center at Ft. Bragg, North Carolina. Here's what Dr. Burlingame said when presented with Tyler's story:

"Well, first of all, I can tell you, I've heard that story about Germany over and over again. It makes me ill. You can put this in your book, and I can probably get spanked for it, but I don't care. In *Stars & Stripes*, they're always writing, 'Landstuhl did this—they rushed this patient from combat and had emergency surgery, something like three days after his injury,' which anyone who knows about medicine, is bullshit. They take all the credit. And our sick patients, yeah, they give great care to, but the guys that have been injured and aren't critical . . . Now, in his case, Tyler had a significant injury that was sort of glossed over. But time and time again, guys that were injured, they just discharge from the hospital and send them to housing."

When Ditka 03 slammed into the mountain, Don Tyler suffered what Burlingame described as an "inferior shoulder dislocation." The doctor says it's extremely rare, "and it causes a lot of damage.

"And when he came in, his pulse was gone, and he couldn't feel his fingers. Okay? He had what's called a neurovascular deficit. And relocating his shoulder, pulse comes back, neuropathy gets better, but it does nothing to treat the trauma that caused the injury. Basically, you do the reduction in order to get blood flow back to the fingers . . . again, our job [at the FST unit] is to get him fixed on life-threatening problems and get him out of there."

The surgeon's expectation is that when Tyler was seen at Landstuhl there would have been "a high index of concern for the exact injuries" he sustained to his shoulder, and that they "would have followed it up immediately with an MRI/CT scan. One or the other . . . I think that's what they would've done, as opposed to doing nothing and letting the guy go home."

Even more shocking than the treatment Don Tyler didn't receive at the hands of the vaunted Landstuhl medical team is the fact that Dr. Burlingame wasn't shocked to hear of it.

"It's a serious indictment on Landstuhl, and we've complained about it. I didn't realize how bad it was until after I got home and talked to guys that went through Landstuhl. And some guys said, 'Oh, I got great care there,' but then you hear other guys that maybe weren't ICU y'know, sick as shit, that had this exact same thing happen to them. And to me it was very distressing. I don't know the people up there, why it happened, what their thoughts were, but I'd certainly like to find out.

"We see our patients, and we think they do great, but we don't know how they do once they leave us. Interestingly enough, we get zero follow-up from Landstuhl. They won't return our phone calls. I mean, we're down at the front lines, making an effort to call back or e-mail back, and they wouldn't give us the time of day. The only time that we'd ever hear anything about our patients is when we'd call back, we'd e-mail back to Walter Reed. Our buddies are back at Reed, and they tell us what was going on with the guys. And that's only a fraction of all the folks that went out.

"Let me tell you, scary enough, he [Tyler] is one of many that that happened to, or I should say not 'one of many'; he's one of several that I know of that's happened to."

An athlete with a torn rotator cuff quickly learns that not only can't he throw a pitch, he can't tie his shoes, buckle his belt, zip his fly, put on a shirt, or perform any number of other tasks that he's used to doing with two hands. Don Tyler didn't just have a torn rotator cuff. He'd just about shredded every muscle and tendon from his left shoulder blade in back all the way around to his collarbone in front. It's an extremely painful injury, and the pain is made worse by any bumping or contact with the affected shoulder. That's why the notion of trying to get from Germany to Fort Walton Beach, Florida, on his own, is not a pleasant one.

His problems continue at Landstuhl, this time with the travel office. They want to see his orders. He doesn't have orders; the Air Force doesn't require them before they let you get carried onto a medevac flight from the combat zone. Not even for Army guys. When Tyler took off on his secret mission into Afghanistan aboard Ditka 03, he hadn't expected to be flying home at all in a few days, much less on a commercial flight.

After three hours of getting nowhere with the travel office, he finally manages to contact Capt. Chris Willard at his home unit in Florida. Within minutes Willard faxes orders and authorization for Landstuhl's travel office to issue a one-way commercial ticket home. They book him on a Delta Airlines flight from Frankfurt to Atlanta, connecting with a puddle jumper to Fort Walton Beach.

The next problem is finding something to wear on the flight home. Fortunately, his unit happens to have someone who accompanied him from K-2 to Landstuhl, and this individual is able to round up a pair of donated pants and a shirt that fits reasonably well. What he couldn't find for Don are shoes that fit, so he gives the major his own tennis shoes. They are at least one size too small, but after he'd suffered the consequences of hitting a mountainside, tight shoes barely nudge his annoyance meter.

Tyler spends some time on his last night at Landstuhl visting Jeff Pohl, who has not yet been shipped out to Walter Reed. Then he tries to get some sleep.

At four-thirty the next morning, Tyler boards the shuttle van for what he describes as a very bumpy, very painful ninety-minute ride to Frankfurt's huge international airport, where German security guards, in his words, "freaked out." He is practically a textbook case of fitting the profile of a terrorist: on a one-way ticket, the reservation made at the last minute, no luggage, and obviously on drugs. Finally, they let him board the Delta jet for a ten-and-a-half-hour flight to Atlanta, and as he settles carefully into his seat, he begins to think that the nightmare that had begun just a few days earlier is over.

He's wrong.

Don Tyler lands at Hartsfield International Airport and has to clear U.S. Customs and Immigration, plus airport security, in order to get into the concourse where the flights to Fort Walton Beach depart. Déjà vu strikes again. No luggage, no passport—just a military ID card—poorly dressed, wearing ill-fitting shoes that make him walk funny, unkempt, and the pain in his shoulder is keeping him from speaking up clearly when questioned by security personnel.

So on February 15, three days after slamming into a mountain on a mission to get the terrorists who attacked America, U.S. Air Force Maj. Don Tyler is profiled as a potential terrorist and shunted to the side for additional screening.

"Would you please remove your shoes?"

"Hey, look, I'm in serious pain. I was in an accident over in the war. I can't even bend over to take my shoes off."

They insist, "Take your shoes off."

"I can't. If I take them off, I won't be able to put them back on."

"If you don't take them off," says the officious security person, "you're not getting on your flight."

Somehow, he manages to endure the pain and get his shoes off, then gets them back on again, and makes his flight, and later that evening lands at Fort Walton Beach, where he is greeted by his wife Barbara, their two children, and members of his unit.

Throughout the welcome at the airport, Don was smiling through the pain. "When I returned home the adrenaline starts pumping and you're just so psyched to be with your family, nothing else matters. I was hurting, but there were also about forty people who had come there to greet me, so I tried to put on a good face." When he got off the plane, he wasn't wearing a wedding ring—it had disappeared after the crash. But his wife fixed that problem stat. "As soon as Barb greeted me at the airport, she slipped my 'real' wedding ring on my finger. When I deployed in December, she bought a twelve-dollar Wal-Mart special wedding ring, because we knew it would get lost or stolen. What a woman!"

Tyler spends the next five days in a reclining chair in his living room, enduring never-ending pain in his left shoulder. Finally Barbara is able to get him an appointment for an MRI at the Eglin Air Force Base Hospital, a test that should have been done at Landstuhl in order to determine precisely what was wrong.

The diagnosis based on the MRI is decipherable only by individuals with advanced degrees in anatomy, physiology, or orthopedic medicine. The medical mumbo-jumbo boils down to the following: complete, full-thickness tear of various tendons, partical tearing of various muscles, dislocation of the biceps tendon, and additional problems related to the shoulder blade and the upper arm bone. The good news? No fracture.

Surgery is performed on March 4, 2002, followed by ongoing exercise and physical therapy to recover range of motion that one orthopedic surgeon says he would never completely recover.

\* \* \*

Back in Afghanistan . . .

Within hours of the crew finally being evacuated off the mountainside, the order was given to destroy the plane. It wasn't until weeks later that Major Cline was able to watch the Predator surveillance video of the destruction. He says, "The first two-thousand-pound bomb hit 0213 dead center, where the wings connect to the fuselage, and right where the fuselage fuel tank (still full with eleven thousand pounds of fuel) was located. Huge fireball, pieces of aircraft flying all over the valley, but when the smoke cleared, the flight deck forward of the crew entrance door was still pristine. Not even a broken window.

"So another strike aircraft dropped two more two-thousand pounders on the flight deck section. Good enough, until the next day when 0213's emergency locator transmitter started going off, clogging up the emergency UHF frequency. The ELT is located high up in the aircraft's tail section. It had apparently separated and slid down the hill a ways after the first bomb hit. So a third airstrike had to be ordered to shut the ELT up.

"The plane truly had a tenacious heart."

The positive welcome home the Ditka 03 crew receives from their buddies is echoed by not only their own unit's leadership, but by commanders higher up. After a two-and-a-half-hour debriefing directly from the six uninjured crewmembers, the Joint Special Operations Air Component Commander (JSOAC/CC) decides they will all be returned to flight status immediately after their safety interviews are complete. Several Air Force fliers familiar with the situation say this is especially gutsy on his part, because the final conclusions from the formal safety investigation were many weeks away, and he would be severely second-guessed if any of Ditka 03's crewmembers, especially the aircraft commander, Maj. John Cline, were involved in even a minor incident or had any kind of mechanical malfunction requiring the normal cursory safety review.

It takes eleven days just to get the safety investigation board assembled and transported to the theater, after which they conduct six days of interviews and field work before heading back stateside to conduct their deliberations. Cline says that Col. Tommy Hull, an MH-53 helicopter pilot by trade, told him, "We send you folks out into some very tough environments to accomplish some very tough missions. Thank God you never gave up. You obviously did a lot of things right to be sitting here right now, and you're all way too valuable to just be sitting around while there are still missions to be done."

As a pilot, Hull understands the agony the crew is going through in the limbo of waiting to be allowed to fly again, and opts to put them back in the saddle rather than keep them grounded while the safety board evaluates their performance on the crash mission. Consequently, each crewmember is given his choice of whether to stay and fly more missions, or to go home and fly stateside missions. Flight engineer Jeff Doss and radio operator Rodney Young elect to return home immediately. Cline, navigator George Akins, and loadmaster Chris Langston all stay and fly several more combat missions before returning home. Copilot Jason Wright, who had joined the crew only three weeks before the crash, elects to complete his whole ninety-day rotation before returning home.

Don Tyler was finally allowed to retire from the Air Force, after one final insult: Neither he nor any of the other injured crewmen of Ditka 03 was awarded the Purple Heart. Despite the fact that the injuries occurred while they were flying through hostile enemy territory on a mission to insert a special-operating-forces reconnaissance team, they were told they didn't qualify for the medal because their injuries were not the *direct* result of enemy action.

# CHAPTER 7

# FREE-FALLING TO A MINEFIELD
## FEBRUARY 16, 2002

Air Force 2d Lt. Matthew Sean McGuinness is one of those guys with an irrepressible personality, certainly the life of the party when he was an enlisted PJ, a staff sergeant, and probably no different as a Penn State undergrad and national all-star rugby player. Now that he's a commissioned officer, and one of the first CROs to boot, he's trying hard to rein it in a bit. But he's made it through the PJ indoctrination course, followed by the training pipeline where they become experts at everything from HALO (high-altitude, low-opening) parachute jumps to scuba in order to make certain they can bring their high-level medical skills where they're needed. Guys like that don't repress easily. That probably accounts for his liking to tag-end the story of being the CRO for a history-making, combat rescue free-fall jump to a patient by saying, "I'm a Gemini and I like long walks on the beach." Bottom line: Matt "Moose" McGuinness is an easy guy to like—even with the David Letterman–like gap between his front teeth that an Army nurse at Kandahar has been fantasizing about ever since she met him.

He's completely dedicated to the twenty pararescuemen under his command. It's his job to make sure they're current in all their skill requirements. He's also their sponsor when they want things like advanced urban warfare training that's not in the budget, or better equipment, such as lightweight in-

The minefield jump team (left to right): S.Sgt. Jason Baird, T.Sgt. Richard Carroll, 2d Lt. Matt "Moose" McGuinness, Sr.M.Sgt. Bill Sine, and SrA Randal Wilkes, Jr. (*Courtesy of Bill Sine*)

terteam radios that not only improve combat efficiency but knock thirty pounds off their already overstuffed rucks. Before the Air Force opened up the PJ career field to officers, the people the PJs had to report to were flying officers, who weren't necessarily interested in going out on a limb to be their advocate. Now, with McGuinness, the brass knows that the guy making the pitch is a prior PJ; his pleas carry more weight, and as an added bonus, his prior experience had already earned him the respect of the men in his command. But don't ever forget that these are PJs, so all that respect doesn't stop them from employing the military's penchant for acronyms and teasing McGuinness about being a FAG—a "former action guy."

Matt came to the 38th Rescue Squadron at Moody AFB directly from Officer Training School. He spent ten months adjusting to his new role in life before being deployed with half a dozen PJs to Shahbaz Air Base at Jacobabad, Pakistan, where one cold mid-February day he drew the assignment as troop commander for the PJs on an HC-130 mission. This was new territory for McGuinness, who had always trained on rescue helicopters and, as an enlisted man, had been a PJ team leader on the HH-60G Pave Hawks. Now he was out of the dirt and supervising HC-130 transload missions, where combat casualty evacuation teams fly into hot areas, pick up patients, and take them to a more secure location, from which they can be transferred to a jet transport and taken to American hospitals in Germany, or stateside for a higher level of care.

Late on the afternoon of February 16, 2002, the on-alert PJ crew consisting of team leader Sr.M.Sgt. Bill Sine, assistant team leader T.Sgt. Richard Carroll, and SrA Randal Wilkes, augmented by McGuinness and S.Sgt. Jason Baird, draws a mission aboard King 22 ("King" is the stateside designation for an Air Force Rescue plane; it's being used here because the actual aircraft radio call signs are still being used in OEF). That particular HC-130 had been flown halfway around the world from Valdosta, Georgia, to Pakistan in four twelve-hour days by a crew commanded by Maj. Terry Crabtree, a nineteen-year Air Force veteran. Their mission is to move some personnel from the 66th Rescue Squadron, a helicopter unit out of Nellis AFB, Nevada, from Kandahar in Afghanistan, and take them up to K-2 at Karshi-Khanabad, Uzbekistan. Then they are to return to Kandahar, and back to their home base in Pakistan.

(Coincidentally, on this same night, crews from the 66th are ferrying a pair of HH-60G Pave Hawk helicopters from Bagram, northwest across the Hindu Kush mountains, to K-2. Two PJs are aboard each of the birds. When all the relocating is finished, there will be helicopter CSAR assets at K-2 to cover the northern half of Afghanistan, and helicopter assets remaining at Kandahar to cover the southern portion of the country.)

In airborne alert status, the HC-130 has a fully equipped PJ team on board, briefed for the mission with current radio codes and authentication data in case they should parachute in or otherwise end up on the ground, and one or more of them should become an evader.

The paratroop seats on the right-hand side of the cargo compartment from the wing area back to the paratroop door are flipped up to accommodate a row of metal chests containing PJ gear. And up forward, a steel container holds even more of the PJs' equipment, including a variety of parachutes. Most of that equipment stays on board the King aircraft. Before each launch, the PJs would back a truck up to the plane's ramp and load their personal gear, weapons, and medical rucks containing drugs that had to be kept under lock and key.

On this Saturday evening in February, King 22 is halfway into its mission, having just taken off from Kandahar with the passengers and equipment, when they begin hearing radio traffic about a convoy going out to an accident site. An Air Force CSAR crew hearing about an accident responds in much the same way a hungry lion does to a herd of wildebeest: They want a piece of the action, so their radio operator makes their presence known.

The response comes quickly. The Joint Search and Rescue Center (JSRC) at Prince Sultan Air Base, Saudi Arabia, asks them to return to Kandahar in preparation for a medevac transload. Crabtree turns the aircraft around to begin his approach back into Kandahar, and discovers that what had been blowing sand on their initial trip in is now a full-fledged sandstorm with visibility down to near zero. With no ground navigation aids available for use, King 22's navigator, twenty-eight-year-old 1st Lt. Brian Symon (pronounced Simone), computes a self-contained approach into the field, using the aircraft's high-tech radar and navigation instruments to vector them to a safe landing. The instant the plane comes to a halt on the ramp in front of the bullet and shell-pocked facade of Kandahar International Airport, the loadmasters begin dumping the helicopter personnel and the cargo bound for K-2. Their relocation up north can wait. The loads have to prep the rear of the plane for litters.

Still short on information, including how many casualties they should expect, when, and in what condition, the radio operator, S.Sgt. Kevin Rolle, begins asking questions. What he gets back are coordinates for an accident site, which he reports to the nav so it can be plotted on a map. The results are confusing.

"That can't be right," Symon says. "That's two hundred fifty miles away." As more information flows in, they realize the accident they are being asked to prep for is different from the one they've been hearing on the radios—one in which a vehicle has rolled over on an airfield with minor injuries.

Randy Wilkes recalls Bill Sine going up to the cockpit, then coming back and saying that the mission is not a transload; it's a guy who's a couple of hours away. "Then it was kind of like a light went on in his head. He says, 'Hey, we can get there and jump in on this guy before the helicopters can get there.' "

After takeoff, Sine runs up to the front of the plane to discuss the notion with the aircraft commander and the nav. What they determine after looking at maps is that the terrain where they're headed is benign, primarily flat desert on the western edge of Afghanistan, near the Iranian border. The only geographic feature of even minor concern is a nearby river.

Until this mission, most of their flying has been over and through the mountains, areas where terrain is arguably their biggest worry. That the PJs are, in the parlance of the Air Force, "leaning forward" to do the jump isn't surprising. Fortunately for them, the aircraft commander is also, in the words of the nav, "a leaning forward kind of guy." The upshot? When Sine gets back, he's all smiles—and all business. "We're jumping," he says.

Shortly after King 22 takes off, the 66th Rescue Squadron launches two of its HH-60G Pave Hawks helicopters from Kandahar, sending them to the same coordinates. The procedure is similar to contingency plans that had been used by the rescue units based at Incirlik Air Base, Turkey, guarding the northern no-fly zone over Iraq (Operation Northern Watch), and units based in Kuwait covering the southern zone (Operation Southern Watch). The rule of thumb is that if the HC-130 can get to the site a half hour or more ahead of the helicopters and drop PJs to the victims, it makes sense to do it, treat the casualties, and wait for the helicopters to come in and pick up both the victims and the PJs. In Afghanistan, the fixed-wing aircraft not only have the advantage of speed over the 60s—they can fly almost twice as fast as the helicopters—they can also fly above the mountains, whereas with the weight of personnel and fuel on board, the helicopters are limited to an altitude of about ten thousand feet. This slows them down, forcing them to fly through mountain valleys and passes, often in bad weather rather than over it, and sometimes in range of enemy artillery.

Staying in radio contact with the airborne mission commander orbiting in an AWACs plane, Rolle elicits more information about the situation that causes Crabtree to start rethinking his decision. They're going to arrive on scene right around sundown. But that's not the problem. What he's learned is that they'll be dropping PJs to an accident site immediately adjacent to a sizable minefield that's already claimed one victim. The veteran pilot knows that as the aircraft commander, he's responsible for everyone on the plane, including the PJs. If he lets them jump and something goes horribly wrong, it is his ass on the line, because he had the authority to say no.

Thus far in OEF there had been at least two previous opportunities where the notion of inserting PJs by parachute had been considered. In both cases, the senior officers involved rejected the option as being too dangerous. PJs in the rescue coordination centers arguing on behalf of the jump missions had the clear impression that the people in authority didn't know that precision free-fall jumping from an HC-130 was in the pararescue bag of tricks, something they regularly train to do.

There's an irony here that isn't lost on the PJs. Despite the allusion to "parachute" in the official "pararescueman" designation, and the acronym "PJ," which comes from their designation as "pararescue jumpers" in 1947, they still find themselves working for commanders who regularly use those names yet fail to acknowledge a PJ's ability to safely jump out of an aircraft and precision-fly his chute to within a few feet of a designated target.

Fortunately, Crabtree doesn't opt for the safe and easy way out and cancel the jump. Instead, he passes the sobering information about the minefield to Lieutenant McGuinness, the only one of the PJs still on headsets. Moose approaches Sine with the news. "Bill, fifty meters to the west of where you're jumping, there's an active minefield."

The lieutenant says Sine thought about it for a second. "You could see his mind working—and then it was, like, 'Okay.' Y'know what I mean? It was cool."

The ground unit turned out to be a five-man patrol of Australian SAS special operators accompanied by an American Air Force combat controller who had been on a recon mission in the desert of extreme western Afghanistan when, out of nowhere, there was a loud explosion. The patrol didn't know if they were getting mortared or possibly hit by friendly fire. The last thing any of them considered was an antitank mine—until they got a look at their Long Range Patrol Vehicle. But that took a minute or so. It was hard to judge time, because when the blast went off everything seemed to be happening in what combat vets describe as "slow time." People were crawling, looking for cover. There was a lot of ringing in their ears, like an annoying high-pitched tone that blocked normal communication. It felt like they just didn't know what to do, like life itself was on hold for one big pause. And then their training took over.

One of the SAS soldiers, thirty-three-year-old Sgt. Andrew Robert Russell of Perth, Western Australia, had suffered major injuries in the blast, including loss of a leg. Without aerial evacuation to a surgical hospital, there was no way he would make it. Even though several of the Australians had combat medical training equivalent to the American Army's 18-Delta medics, it was apparent to the CCT that Russell needed immediate medical attention at a level that could be provided only by pararescuemen.

In the CSAR Herc, Sine, Carroll, and Wilkes, with the help of Baird and McGuinness, and the loadmasters, T.Sgt. Charles Woods and S.Sgt. Bill Walker, begin to jock up for what the team leader has now decided will be a HALO jump. With a minefield adjacent to the target, they need as much control as possible on the drop, and Sine's twenty-seven years of experience tells him that a static line jump is wrong for the circumstances.

Even though PJs can jump with the round MC1-C chute from as low as five hundred feet, the disadvantage has to do with the technical capabilities of the parachute itself. A static line parachute has a very low forward drive, which means that if any significant wind comes up, the PJ is going to be blown off course and is less likely to land safely on target. On the other hand, the rectangular free-fall chute has roughly a twenty-knot forward drive; flown properly, it can cancel out a twenty-three-mph wind, and be flown to a precision landing. But you can't use it at five hundred feet because there won't be enough time for the jumper to pull the ripcord, settle under the canopy, get his bearings, and fly to the target. Although the free-fall chute requires a higher cloud ceiling and more altitude for the jump, the trade-off in maneuverability is worth it, especially when they're jumping near a minefield on an almost moonless night.

The PJs and the cockpit crew need to agree on a jump altitude that's high enough to give them the control they need, but not so high as to make calculating the effect of the wind on the jumpers a rigorous exercise. The concern is that while Crabtree, the aircraft commander, and Capt. James Woolsey, his copilot, have flown many such missions, Brian Symon is a newly minted navigator and has never done a nav-controlled free-fall jump, not even in training. If Symon blows it and puts the jumpers out past the calculated point, they may have no choice but to land in the minefield. Neither the maneuverability of their chutes nor their skill at flying them might be enough to allow them to make a 180-degree turn and fly into the wind, back to the drop zone.

While the PJs are figuring out the jump altitude, the airborne mission commander overhead in an E-8 J-STAR surveillance and attack targeting plane continues to relay information between the Aussies on the ground and the rescuers. On the one hand, Crabtree is being told that the Aussies definitely need the Americans' medical expertise to keep their man alive. On the other hand, he doesn't want to get any PJs killed trying to save the guy, and knowing they're near a minefield makes the drop iffy.

One obstacle gets removed when the Aussies relay that they can mark the drop zone with a flashing strobe light, but Crabtree needs more before his comfort level will be raised enough to let the guys jump.

"Can they mark the actual perimeter of the location of the minefield?" The question is relayed by the AMC. And the answer that comes back is the right one. "These guys were good," says the pilot. "Before we even asked them, they had already put red chemlights around the perimeter of the minefield as they knew it." Then he relays Sine's request, asking them to place the strobe marking the DZ at least fifty yards back up the road they had already traveled, the thinking being that if their vehicles had passed over the area, it was reasonable to assume the PJs could land there safely.

In the cargo bay, Sine and McGuinness confer on possible choices for a jump altitude. Then Sine chooses thirty-five hundred feet. He says, "We had talked about various altitudes if we had the opportunity to use the free-fall parachute, but when I actually had to think about it seriously, when I was actually confronted with it, I decided to go at the low altitude and use the RAMZ procedures, because that's something we do all the time, so it's familiar to everybody."

RAMZ is the acronym for Rigged Alternate Method Zodiacs, the inflatable rubber boat and thirty-five-horsepower engine that can be deployed by three PJs jumping with steerable chutes from the rear of an HC-130, dropping into the ocean near a ship that needs medical help, or to pick up survivors.

In addition to keeping the routine for this jump as familiar as possible, Sine has another concern about jumping from an altitude higher than three thousand five hundred feet at night. The higher you go, the more lights you're likely to see. While he expects to be jumping into the Afghan desert, where there should be no other lights, from the cockpit Major Crabtree is already surprised to see the lights of an Iranian city just across the border. The possibility is admittedly remote, but even a vehicle headlight could cause confusion for someone free-falling at two hundred feet per second.

One other factor goes into Sine's decision to drop from three thousand five hundred feet. "If anyone has a problem on the jump—their load shifts or they go into a spin or a tumble—they can ignore the five- or three-count and just pull right off, because they're not going to be that far off no matter what they do."

So it all comes down to the nav calculating the speed, direction, wind drift, and altitude correctly, and then taking maximum advantage of the clear conditions in order to spot the target strobe on the ground quickly, then calling the precise point at which the jumpers were to go out. Then it's a matter of the jumpers doing what they've trained to do, and preparing to counteract Murphy's Law, should it come into play.

That's why Sine begins briefing the "what-ifs." They've all been on parachute jumps where you don't land where you're supposed to. It could be a mistake by the navigator, or unexpected wind, or you're just in a bad situation and there's nothing you can do about it. Normally the worst that happens is you land off the drop zone. Occasionally it can mean a close call with power lines or other hazards. For this drop, the "other hazard" is a minefield. The other major "what-ifs" are, What happens if someone on the team gets hurt on landing, or they have a problem with their parachute and one man is lost? Is the priority finding the missing PJ, helping the injured one, or getting aid to the casualty who was blown up by the land mine?

Sine says they'd try to do it all simultaneously, using the Aussies on the ground who are more dialed into what's going on around them than the PJs. His concern is minimized by the fact that they each carry radios and signaling devices, and even though they deploy in teams, each man is trained to be self-reliant, even when hurt.

In Bill Sine's mind, free-fall jumping from the open ramp of an HC-130 in the dark of night to a flashing strobe light adjacent to a minefield three thousand five hundred feet below is a good time. It all has to do with conditioning, control, intelligence, and preplanning. Conditioning is definitely not an issue for Sine. At forty-four, he's in as good shape as he was when he became a PJ at age nineteen. It just takes him longer to stay that way now. (He does it with a five-mile run every other day; on his off days he swims fifteen hundred meters and visits the gym.)

As for intel, by the time they're ready to jump they know that there is no hostile threat in the area other than land mines; they know their victim's right leg has been blown off in the explosion. He has compound fractures of his lower left leg, a fractured femur, fractured arm, and fractured jaw, his face was cut badly by shrapnel, and he has shrapnel wounds all over his body with indications of internal damage.

The Aussies had splinted what they could. They'd stopped the bleeding as well as they could. They had a tourniquet above the amputation site. Their medic had tried to start an IV to get fluids into him, but had trouble finding a good vein amid all the puncture wounds. It had been two hours since the incident, and his blood pressure was very low.

With all that information, Sine is able to preplan what they'll do once they're on the ground, assigning specific tasks to Sergeant Carroll and Airman Wilkes. Now it is up to the navigator to put them on the drop zone. As for control, once the PJs leap out of the plane, it's all up to them.

While the loadmasters in the cargo bay have put on night-vision goggles for the drop, the pilots up front decide that since they're flying into the sunset, and the sun has just gone below the horizon, they can actually see better without NVGs. The plan is to put them on after they watch the PJs land, then hang around to refuel the two helicopters that are currently racing to the scene of the incident, and shepherd them back to Kandahar.

At six minutes out, the ramp is opened and Sine does a final check of everyone and their gear—parachutes on their backs, rucksacks right below the groin in front, and rifles on their left sides. Even though there's a full complement of Aussie SAS on the ground, the PJs are prepared to play an active role in their defense should the need arise. They've got the M-4 rifle, a 9mm pistol, and an assortment of knives and grenades, all of which has to be properly secured for a dive into the aircraft's 130-mph slipstream.

Before the ramp was opened, communication was difficult, as it always is in the back of a Herc. But now, the only way to be heard is to stick your mouth next to the other guy's ear and yell. The fact that everyone is wearing earplugs doesn't exactly help the situation. Wilkes says that Sine's instructions were pretty standard: whoever's lowest is the guy you follow in. You do what he does; turn where he turns. If all goes well, that guy will be Sine, picking out the pattern that they'll fly, determining whether or not they need to do S-turns to burn off altitude before they head for the flashing strobe. He reminds them that the landing is critical. Follow the leader all the way down. They don't want one PJ hooking around the target to the left and another going to the right. That leads to collisions, and over a minefield, a collision could get ugly very quickly.

There's a brief, rote discussion of what to do in the event of a malfunction of the main chute. In short, they're to cut away the main and deploy the reserve, which is also a steerable chute, exactly the same as the main. The only significant difference is that it comes out of the pack somewhat faster than the main because its pilot chute is nonporous—when it hits the air, it immediately inflates and yanks the reserve out of its pack.

While the PJs are getting their last-minute briefing, the two loadmasters are securing loose equipment, and, according to PJ Randy Wilkes, "They were looking at us like we were nuts." The loads had certainly watched PJs jump out of 130s before—HALO jumps off the ramp from as high as eighteen thousand feet, at night, with all preparations taking place in a blacked-out aircraft and everyone wearing night-vision goggles (until the actual jump, when the PJs take the goggles off). Or static line jumps out the side paratroop doors from as low as five hundred feet, daytime and nighttime. But to hurl yourself into space knowing that a slight miscalculation could put you in the middle of an uncharted minefield? Perhaps the loadmasters have a point.

At that moment, there is still some concern on Bill Sine's part that the JSRC is going to deny them permission to insert the PJs. It has happened on other missions when someone in the command structure comes down with a case of weak knees. The thinking is that if the jump goes well, no problem and "attaboys" all around. But if it goes badly, anyone who is perceived to have authorized it is subject to being second-guessed. So it's much easier to say no. Nevertheless, Major Crabtree chooses to go proactive. He has the radio operator confirm that the ground unit wants the PJs to jump. And then he simply tells the JSRC, "We're inserting the PJs." Case closed. By the time the powers that be at Prince Sultan Air Base can discuss it, Sine, Wilkes, and Carroll will be safely on the ground. Or so Crabtree hopes.

As the 130 comes into the area, the cockpit crew very quickly spots the flashing strobe. While there is some discussion of letting the PJs jump on that first pass over the area, it is decided to do a left-hand racetrack pattern and give the nav time to set up the drop properly. That's when Murphy arrives on scene and enforces his law: "If it can go wrong, it will." The nav's Self-Contained Navigation System fails. "At the worst possible time."

Now things will get interesting for the twenty-eight-year-old Symon, a former special ed teacher turned HC-130 Combat Search and Rescue navigator. Perhaps this is the right time to mention the confidence CSAR types have in their training and their ability to get the job done. A bit of CSAR humor makes the point. The Air Force is not anal about its crews wearing unofficial insignia on their flight suits. That explains the omnipresence of one of the more popular shoulder patches seen in the combat zone: a blue-and-yellow patch (or the DCU brown version, among other color combinations) featuring a silhouette of Elvis singing into a microphone, beneath which it says *CSAR*. And around the top and bottom, it reads, *If he's out there . . . we'll find him.*

Essentially, Lieutenant Symon says, "No SCNS, no problem. I'll do it the old-fashioned way." It's that "old-fashioned way" that long ago led to navigators being affectionately called "naviguessers" by their crewmates. Never mind that he's too young to have been there when the old-fashioned way was the only way.

A veteran navigator in the 71st Rescue Squadron, Capt. Steven Kline, says that making a navigator-controlled jump mission like this one work comes down to the aircrew, and the nav in particular, having a good working relationship with the jumpmaster and the PJs. "It goes to credibility, because if they know you and they've jumped out of your airplane before and they can say, 'Hey, I've never really had a bad drop with this guy,' they're more often than not going to trust you and go to your release point. . . . With the PJs and AFSOC as well, things are built on reputation and your skills, so you have to be good at what you do. It's when they don't trust you, when you don't know the other guy, that's where some of the issues start coming in." It's appropriate to note here that more than one Air Force navigator avows that the "rectal database" is quite often the source of definitive pronouncements. That's a polite way of saying that they pull it out of their ass.

Fortunately for all involved, even though he is young and without a lot of experience, Lieutenant Symon is confident that he can make this drop come out right, and the crew—including the PJs—know from past experience that he has his act together.

Here's the technical explanation of how Symon planned to put the PJs right on the drop zone. Note that "WAG" in navigatorese means "wild-ass guess," and that the PJs are jumping with parachutes that can counteract as much as twenty knots of wind.

"We had a right quartering headwind at about thirteen knots, pretty light, at three thousand feet. Every time they jump there are a couple of components. One is forward travel distance; how far forward the aircraft's velocity is going to push them before they stabilize. It's a good WAG to go at two hundred fifty to three hundred yards of forward throw. Every seven knots of wind at that altitude is going to give us two hundred yards of drift as well. So we had thirteen knots at three thousand feet; surface winds are calm, according to the Aussies on the ground. The minefields were all located south of their position. Our safety zone was to the northeast. I computed that they need to drop about five hundred to six hundred yards to the right, and about five hundred yards short. And that's what we went with."

Symon says on that first racetrack around, "I didn't feel comfortable; my nav systems weren't running. Usually you can back up your computations with your systems. With that failure, and using procedures I'd never used before, I called 'no drop.' I was nervous. The PJs are lean forward kind of guys. They'll jump out. You realize they'll do just about anything, so at times you have to reel them in a bit. I wanted to make sure I wasn't going to hurt them."

Crabtree recalls him saying, "I don't see the minefield; I don't see the drop zone. No drop!" If someone—anyone—calls a "no drop," it's never challenged, because at the moment it happens, only the person making the call knows why he's doing it. That's not to say that it didn't put Crabtree on edge. He knew the nav had never done a free-fall drop before. Nevertheless, he did pointedly tell his crew that they had to make this happen.

In the back of the plane, the three PJs on the ramp are surprised when the green light doesn't come on, especially since they can see the blinking strobe that the Aussies are using to mark the drop zone. One of the loads begins waving a clenched fist, the indication of "no drop." Sine turns back to Lieutenant McGuinness and mimes the question, *Why didn't we go?* He's concerned that someone has vetoed the jump. The lieutenant, who's still on headphones, asks a quick question, and then shouts that they're coming around for another shot at it.

In the cockpit, the flight engineer, Sr.M.Sgt. Art Millard, is trying his damnedest to get the SCNS back on-line, but Murphy prevails. It isn't coming back up. So the nav leaves his position behind the copilot and, as the veteran aircraft commander put it, "Symon basically got up in the window and kind of did it the old-fashioned way, using his years and years of experience—which was none."

Symon says that he tracked the strobe light through the pilot's left window, then "we tracked it, tracked it, tracked it, and called the green light," which the copilot flipped on, sending the PJs off the ramp.

However he manages to do it, the young navigator calls for the green light at precisely the perfect moment, and the three PJs go off the ramp with Lt.

Matt McGuinness proudly watching them go. He would have loved to have jumped with them, but realized early on that three guys on the ground for one casualty was adequate, especially with two Pave Hawks inbound to the site carrying four more PJs.

The moment of the drop is one he'll never forget.

"I thought it was the greatest. The night was black, inky black. I mean, it was phenomenal. They'd set up a big defensive perimeter on the ground and they had one overt strobe out there. It was blinking, and it looked like you were flying over a sea of blackness with hills on either side, and then there's—*bing!*—the light out there. It was awesome to be a part of it."

Maj. Terry Crabtree had a very different reaction to the jump. His moment of highest anxiety was the instant the three PJs left the aircraft, "because at that point I have no control over what happens next."

No matter how much Lt. Matt McGuinness lobbied to make sure his men had the opportunity to go, no matter how firmly Sine, Carroll, and Wilkes said they could jump to the target and avoid a minefield that had already blown one man's body to pieces, it was still on Crabtree. "If anything should happen, that's something I'd have to live with for the rest of my life.

"Obviously, for those guys probably, it's the other extreme, y'know? Now they're under canopy, *they're* in control. But until they land on the ground, we do an orbit, we watch 'em land; it's a bit nerve-racking."

Before the jump, Bill Sine was thinking of all the options, all the choices he had to make, and all the things that could go wrong. "Then once I had all my logic squared away, then it was making sure all our gear was good and that I didn't screw anything up, 'cause I'm running this whole thing, right?"

They were using the protocol for jumping with the RAMZ package, which they did all the time from three thousand five hundred feet. Technically, since they were not on static lines that automatically open their chutes, it was a HALO jump. On a true HALO jump, the navigator needs to use a special formula to calculate winds at various altitudes all the way down to three thousand five hundred feet, then do additional calculations for the final portion of the drop. That made this drop from three thousand five hundred feet a much easier proposition to deal with. Symon said it was more of "a hop 'n' pop than a HALO."

When the three PJs get the green light, they leave the ramp no more than a second apart. First goes Sine; he waits five seconds, then pulls his ripcord. Then Carroll. His is a three-second delay, and he pulls. Then Wilkes, who jumps and, the instant he's stabilized in the air, he pulls. Timing it this way keeps them grouped together, but out of one another's way. Then it's a matter of playing follow-the-leader all the way down to the ground.

Normally on a tactical jump, the PJs wouldn't be wearing lights. In training, they jump with enough light sticks to rival the Goodyear blimp on a game night. But given that there is almost no threat of hostile fire on this jump, McGuinness suggests that each of the jumpers should put on one blue chem-light. It wouldn't be visible from the ground, but they should help the jumpers keep track of each other. Sine feels the suggestion is a good one, so when they jump, each of the PJs is wearing a single blue chem-light tied to a loop on the back of his harness. While a blue light stick might not be much to key on, with no lights on the ground to destroy their night vision, it's good enough.

The first thing Bill Sine does once he's under canopy and pointed in the direction he needs to fly is look around for the other jumpers. "Boom, I saw two good canopies and saw their lights. It's crystal clear. I see my two guys behind me, and they don't have any problems. Then I concentrated on driving for the LZ."

An HC-130 doing a HALO drop moves at about two hundred feet per second. With less than a second delay as they exited, the jumpers are somewhere between one hundred and two hundred feet apart, and stacked at different altitudes.

While the cockpit crew continues to go through nerve-racking moments waiting to hear if the guys have landed safely, the jumpers are actually enjoying themselves. They left the plane at three thousand five hundred feet up, roughly a third of a mile short of the target, and a third of a mile to the right. Once they pop the canopy, they're going with the wind. Sine's initial reaction once his chute opens is that they jumped a bit too far away from the target, although he quickly changes that opinion when he realizes that, even if the nav was cheating a bit on the side of caution, they're going to be right on the money. His guess that the nav was cheating, he learns later, is accurate. Symon was intent on keeping them away from the minefield, so when he picked the jump point, his thinking was, "Worst scenario, they'd drop in two hundred meters short in that safety zone, and walk up."

The choice Bill Sine now has to make is whether they need to do some lazy S-turns to bleed off altitude, or if they're far enough away to just hold course almost all the way to the impact point, and at just the right moment hook around to land like an airplane, into the wind. What he quickly discovers is that the nav's seat-of-the-pants calculations were dead-on accurate. No S-turns are needed.

Randy Wilkes is enjoying the moment. He's managed to remove the foam earplugs that everyone riding on an HC-130 wears, and all he can hear is silence—and the wind rushing past. Looking down he can see the other two PJs, and beyond them the strobe, and "all the red chemlights marking where you didn't want to land." At this point in his brief Air Force career, the Georgia native had been a PJ for less than a year. He came to the PJ pipeline from the Reserves, where he repaired radar and communication gear on HC-130 aircraft. He'd never been much for outdoorsy stuff, and since he smoked, wasn't setting any records for being in great cardiovascular shape. But he had read about the PJs and was determined to become one. His ten weeks in the indoctrination course at Lackland AFB, Texas, turned into twenty, because the first time through he failed sit-ups in the seventh week—he was one short in the allotted time. But he had the one quality that veteran PJs say matters more than physical conditioning or strength: a will to make it through, to refuse to quit.

His time in the PJs was so short, Wilkes couldn't possibly understand his good fortune in getting this mission. He wasn't even supposed to be in Afghanistan. Four months earlier he'd broken several ribs in a training accident aboard a helicopter. The belt he was wearing around his waist didn't detach properly, slid up around his ribs, and cracked them. He was just getting back into shape when on a Thursday afternoon he was standing in Bill Sine's office at Moody and Sine asked him if he wanted to go. He said yes. Sine said, "Okay, you're going with me." By Monday morning they were on the Rotator out of Baltimore, and a week later he was bunking in a hardened aircraft shelter on the flight line at Jacobabad. Since then he'd flown several times, but no real rescue missions. And now he is part of the team parachuting to a casualty on what is, even for a twenty-seven-year veteran like Bill Sine, a mission of a lifetime.

Knowing that Wilkes and Carroll are having no problem with their chutes and staying right behind him, Sine begins to set up for his landing. "About halfway there I'm realizing, okay, this is going to work. We're going to be right on this thing." He flies past the strobe, makes a U-turn behind it, and spots the target again, going to what he considers "fifty percent brakes" on the toggles of his chute. At about two hundred feet up, he releases his equipment and allows the seventy-pound ruck to slide down so it's riding on his feet. That way there's no risk of it starting to pendulum, pulling him off his mark. When he sees he's about to hit the ground, a bit more than twenty feet up, he lets the ruck slide all the way off.

He lands precisely on target, hitting the desert scrub considerably harder than he'd expected to, and dropping into a PLF—a parachute landing fall. By the time he's back on his feet, Wilkes and Carroll are also safely on the ground. "That part of the mission had the most potential for screwups, for things happening that are out of my control. Anyone having a malfunction, getting hurt on landing—breaking an ankle or a leg, hitting a hole on landing, something like that. Once that was all done, I'm on to 'patient mode.'"

As they began to gather their parachutes, Aussies materialize around them. "Don't worry about that, mate. We'll take care of your parachutes."

Sine does a brief introduction that ends with, "Where's your bud?"

In King 22, the radio operator gets word that all three jumpers are down safely, and passes the good news on to the cockpit. That gets a quick sigh of relief, and it's on to the next problem for the navigator. "We got the helos coming in, and I'm worried about vectoring them, as well as trying to figure out how to get back to Kandahar. Plus we had to refuel the helos and make sure we had enough fuel to get back ourselves."

The Aussies lead the trio of PJs no more than fifty yards, to the side of a huge crater in the ground. The front of the demolished vehicle is still in the crater, and the injured man just a few feet away. Very quickly they learn his name is Andy, and his wife had just given birth to their first child five days earlier. Clearly they don't need the additional motivation, but the Aussies want them to know.

Sine had assigned Wilkes to take care of med-kit management and Carroll to actually assist him in treating the soldier. It's now more than two hours since the injury occurred, and things are not looking good. While the Aussie medic had a tourniquet on the stump, they learned that it had taken five to ten minutes to reach Andy after the explosion. Even though he was bleeding profusely, no one could ignore the possibility that there were additional mines buried in the area and just run to him without checking.

Thirty minutes before the PJs landed, their patient's blood pressure was only 70/40. Now Rich Carroll can't even get a blood pressure at all, even though he finds that Andy has a high pulse rate. The condition is called compensated shock, because the heart is beating faster as it tries to compensate for the lack of blood volume. Sine's prepared for the worst: He has one of the others keep an airway kit handy because he's expecting the man to crash at any second.

The first problem is to start a good IV. Easier said than done. The explosion had sent dozens of pieces of shrapnel into the victim, and finding a good, big vein where blood is flowing well is almost impossible. Doing it by dim flashlight doesn't make the task any simpler. So Sine does it by feel.

"When we tried to take a blood pressure, put the cuff on, we were having trouble getting a blood pressure. And I just had to leave it on, pumped up. So that's like the tourniquet you normally put on. And after a while, we were wiping his arm down and by then I could feel a little thing right there [in the crease of his right arm]. I could feel it, and got it right in there. Nailed that thing the first time. Good flow and just bombproof, perfect, not shaky, y'know?"

All the while they're working on him, the patient is semiconscious. Sine can hear him saying something like "My leg's hurt," and the friend who's at his head, talking to him, telling him, "That's just the pressure of the bandages, y'know, we're gonna get you out of here." What Sine would like to do is intubate the patient, to give him the best airway possible in an effort to oxygenate what little blood he has in him. But he knows that you can't intubate a conscious patient—it'll trigger a strong gag reflex that will just cause more problems.

They continue to work on the patient, plugging holes where they can, pushing fluid, administering drugs, but by the time the helicopters arrive, the situation isn't improving. The first one comes in, guided to a landing at precisely the same spot where the PJs had landed almost an hour earlier. Sine turns the patient over to the primary PJ on the Pave Hawk, T.Sgt. Patrick Harding, a friend of his with an even higher emergency medical technician rating. With the patient in critical condition, Sine doesn't want to lose time briefing the PJs on the HH-60G, so he tells Wilkes to climb aboard and continue working on Andy during the ride back to Kandahar. The second helo has come in right behind the first, giving Sine and Carroll just a few seconds to say good-bye to the Aussies, and board it for the ninety-minute-plus ride back to its base.

Almost as soon as the helicopters lift off, Andy crashes. Wilkes says, "His breathing went to crap, and he quit moaning and groaning and was just kind of laying there. You could tell he was hurting really bad. I think it might've been the movement, just moving him."

Very quickly the situation goes from bad to worse. Wilkes does what he can to help his patient breathe, but it is obvious that his respiratory rate is dropping. Harding is using a stethoscope, trying to find a pulse in the carotid artery on his neck, then in his arms, but can't find it. When his eyes are unresponsive to light, they begin performing CPR while continuing to force air into his lungs. About an hour into the ninety-minute flight, Andy dies. The PJs continue doing CPR all the way back to Kandahar, where they turn him over to the Army FST team that has an operating room in the airport's terminal building. But nothing can be done. His injuries were too great, he'd lost too much blood, and he was too far from a surgical hospital when his vehicle hit a mine. One of the surgeons tells Sine that if the injuries had happened right in front of his surgical tent, the man would still have had only a fifty/fifty chance of making it.

Two weeks later, Wilkes, Carroll and Sine appear before a medical board to debrief the case. The PJs have been arguing for months that they should be allowed to carry whole blood on their missions. They and the doctors know that just pushing fluids into an injured patient's circulatory system doesn't do anything to increase the oxygen-carrying capacity of his blood. If the patient is suffering from a critical loss of blood, only a transfusion of red blood cells can do that, and even though medics in past wars have been able to administer blood, it hadn't been okayed in Operation Enduring Freedom. Policies on the use of blood are reportedly as politicized in the military as they are in the civilian medical world, and the rules for processing and administration of blood since the onset of the AIDS crisis have only become more complicated. As a result of what they learned from this mission, that policy is changed. With strict guidelines in place, PJs are permitted to carry units of O-negative blood—the universal donor type—with them on subsequent missions.

One other medical advance did come out of this mission. Sine discussed with their flight surgeon the problem of being unable to intubate a semiconscious patient. As a result the doc taught the PJs a technique called "raid sequence intubation." It involves administering a combination of paralyzing drugs that shut off the gag reflex. The procedure itself has risks because they're basically paralyzing the patient for a little while, but in certain cases, such as the one they'd just handled, it might have allowed them to establish an airway *before* putting him aboard the helicopter. That would have meant that the PJs caring for Andy on the long flight back would not have had to perform CPR and intubate him in a pitch-black, cramped situation.

That said, Sine and his team don't beat themselves up over losing the patient. "When I analyze it," says the veteran PJ, "Everything went unbelievably smoothly. If I would've scripted this thing, I couldn't have done any better—except having the patient survive. But all phases, from insertion to recovery, it couldn't have gone any smoother.

"The Australians were real grateful that we'd made the attempt that we had, the U.S. with the 130 and the helicopters. We mounted a pretty major effort to try and help them out. And so they were real appreciative of it. We all wished the outcome had been different."

When he got back to their home base in Pakistan, Bill Sine sent his son Billy, who wants to be a PJ, an e-mail: "Check with so-and-so at work and he'll fill you in on my latest adventure."

Eight months after the jump mission, Randy Wilkes left the Air Force. "I want to have a family, and I want to be there. A lot of guys are gone when their kids are taking their first steps and saying their first words—this job keeps you going pretty good."

# EVIL IN THE VALLEY
## FEBRUARY 27–MARCH 2, 2002

Just call him "Hots." It's easier to remember that than how to pronounce H-O-T-A-L-I-N-G. (It's ho-*tal*-ing.) Of course the military isn't really concerned with how to pronounce his name. When they want him, they get on the radio and call for Jaguar 18—or whatever his current working call sign is. That's because T.Sgt. Jim Hotaling is a CCT who's specially qualified as a SOTAC with expertise in the kind of CAS that's needed in OEF by U.S. CENTCOM, which borrowed him from U.S. SOCOM, which found him in the USAF Reserve, which called him back to active duty as an IMA from his job as a Washington state trooper.

Need a translation? Okay, here goes.

Hots is a Combat Controller who not only can do airfield seizures and airfield surveys and run air traffic control, he's qualified in Special Operations Tactical Air Control, which means he's skilled at calling in close air support as needed in Operation Enduring Freedom, which is being run by the United States Central Command, which borrowed him from the United States Special Operations Command (both of which are joint service commands—Army, Navy, Air Force, Marines—headquartered at MacDill Air Force Base, in Tampa, Florida), which found him in the Air Force Reserve, which called him up as an Individual Mobilization Augmentee from his job as a Washington

Disputed territory. The Hindu Kush mountains in Afghanistan. (*Michael Hirsh*)

state trooper, making him the only enlisted CCT Reservist on active duty in the entire United States Air Force.

Hots is a veteran of Operations Desert Shield and Desert Storm, participated in humanitarian missions in Somalia, and in Operation Uphold Democracy in Haiti, as well as in other assignments that his military biography cloaks as "foreign internal defense training missions."

Jim married while on active duty in the Air Force; seven years ago he and his wife, Sue, had a son. When military life began to take a toll on family life, he got out of the Air Force and became a Washington state trooper, but stayed in the Reserves. September 2001 was a big month for the Hotalings. They learned that they were going to become parents for a second time, and they watched workers put the finishing touches on the dream house they'd built. Then terrorists attacked the United States, and the Air Force needed Jim back. The day they closed on the house was the day he put his uniform back on and kissed Sue good-bye. In a matter of weeks he was in Kandahar, Afghanistan, the only American assigned to a team of Aussie Special Air Service Regiment commandos sent into the desert on a reconnaissance mission.

While PJs are burdened with a rucksack full of medical gear, CCTs go on missions looking like field reps for Radio Shack. Not only do they have an assortment of radios that let them communicate directly with every type of aircraft being flown in OEF, they also carry SATCOM devices. There's more. Since the military has not yet developed an array of camouflaged solar panels that CCTs can wear atop their headgear, they also have to carry enough batteries to power each of their radios for the duration of the mission. On top of that, they're toting the standard weaponry and ammunition that special tactics troops need, plus water, rations and, if luck is with them, mission-appropriate clothing. Early in his tour in Afghanistan, Hots operated in deserts where the temperature topped eighty degrees Fahrenheit, and in mountains where it dropped to fifteen below. Missions often began at a base altitude of three thousand feet and topped out at eleven thousand feet. Getting there was not half the fun.

"We did a two-thousand-foot vertical ascent, and with that amount of weight, it's almost impossible to do. It took us two and a half days to climb that, and we were averaging about a hundred yards an hour. That's how slow we were moving.

"The entire time, you're just thinking to yourself, 'I can't believe I'm doing this.' But you put yourself in an out-of-body situation. You just have to put yourself in that mind frame that you're living for that one moment. You can't think about tomorrow, you can't think how much it sucks, you just gotta focus and do it."

If the physical task weren't enough, the fact that he was the only American on a recon team of Aussies added a little competition that he really didn't need at that moment. "You can't be the quitter out of the group. You can't be the American that quits in front of these other countries, 'cause they're the best of the best of their country. And here you are, the American, you've got to jock up and be right with them. So it was tough. Every step you think about just stopping. But you can't do that; you can't do it. It's the mental game that you play with yourself."

And he hasn't yet mentioned the people who tried to kill him.

Hots had been in country just two days, hardly enough time to figure out that you can't find a cold one, much less any kind of beer at all, on the growing U.S. air base at Kandahar, the onetime Taliban capital, when he was matched with the five-man SAS team and assigned a five-day reconnaissance mission on an enemy facility. His unit, with its six all-terrain vehicles, was inserted by helicopter, and then moved several kilometers toward their objective at the edge of a desert training camp. Roughly four hundred meters from where they were going to establish a covert observation post, they concealed the ATVs in a wadi—a dry creek bed in the desert—by putting them up against the embankment and covering them with dried vegetation. Then they moved on foot to a position that was elevated a good two hundred feet above the target, still about a third of a mile away, and settled in to watch.

Two days into the mission they were compromised by low-tech enemy assets: a shepherd walked right up to them. To say they were shocked understates the situation. The problem was only temporarily resolved when the one man on the team who spoke both Arabic and Farsi barked the order, "Get the flock out of here."

Predictably, the shepherd immediately went into the camp and notified Al Qaeda, which came after them in four-wheel-drive vehicles mounted with .50-caliber machine guns. Discretion being the better part of valor, Hotaling and his team immediately beat feet back to their all-terrain vehicles and started escape and evasion procedures. With the control faceplate for one of the radios on his back strapped to his left wrist, and earpieces in both ears—one SAT-COM and the other line-of-sight—he was able to communicate and drive the ATV at the same time. As soon as he radioed that they'd been compromised, he got a response from a Navy P-3 that happened to be in the area. The P-3, originally a submarine hunter, is part of an intelligence-gathering unit called "the Gray Knights" that has airborne video-surveillance capabilities. Almost immediately, the eyeballs overhead reported that the bad guys were closing in.

Staying and fighting was not an option. The team carried only small arms and a sniper rifle. Hots himself had his M-4 rifle and 9mm pistol—not nearly enough firepower to bring to bear against a horde of heavy machine guns. Luckily, the escape was happening in broad daylight, so not only was the plane overhead able to watch both the pursuers and the pursued, he was able to direct their escape.

Hots says, "He was literally telling us, 'Take a left now, take a right, now take a left. They're six hundred meters from you. Okay, they've stopped. Go this way, go that way.' So he actually directed our escape.

"If the enemy had gotten within small-arms range, I was obviously going to prosecute with fighter aircraft, but we were able to break contact with them through the use of the observation aircraft."

Getting out of the situation this way meant that the team was able to continue its mission by hiding in a different place and monitoring Al Qaeda activity for a few more days. Finally, they called in other allied forces that took what Hots euphemistically calls "direct action" while his team exfiltrated on helicopters with their ATVs.

While talking about that particular mission, Hotaling laughs when he notes that an off-the-shelf, handheld GPS device he purchased in an outdoor adventure store before leaving the States was what he used to determine their precise location so the observation aircraft could find them. It's not the only piece of civilian gear that he and other special tactics troops in OEF are using. Since his unit is based in the state of Washington and does a lot of extreme-cold-weather and mountain rescues, they went over with crates of civilian Gore-Tex parkas; fleece tops, pants, and hats; snowshoes; climbing gear; climbing boots; even technologically advanced socks; as well as multiple pairs of the cold-weather gloves of choice, Windstoppers by North Face. Long gone are the days when servicemen in combat are restricted to wearing what Uncle Sam issues, making inoperative the line that had long been a ready weapon in the verbal arsenal of grizzled Army sergeants: "Soldier, if Uncle Sam wanted you to have a [insert object of desire here—anything from beard to earmuffs to wife], he would have issued you one." In fact, special tactics and pararescue units routinely and legitimately use government funds to buy specialty items off the shelf in civilian stores or from catalogs, if they believe that doing so will benefit the mission.

For four months working out of Kandahar, Hotaling continued doing a variety of operations with special-ops teams from a number of coalition countries. They did strategic reconnaissance missions, direct-action missions, and sensitive-site exploitations, which he describes as "looking at caves or command and control facilities in an effort to exploit any information that was left behind." The missions might last a week, with a few days in between before he'd be sent out again.

One of those missions got named "the Walk of Death" after his team was assigned to locate and monitor a terrorist training facility. That mission required a climb straight up a cliff in order to get into an observation post without being detected by local villagers.

Some of them were carrying packs weighing up to 140 pounds. "It's not the X Games or anything like that, where you've got safeties and ropes and little helmets and things like this. It is do or die. It is a tough thing to do, but it's what you have to do in war." After getting into position, Hotaling was able to call in air strikes that destroyed what turned out to be the second largest Al Qaeda training camp in the country. On another mission they captured one of the top ten most wanted Taliban leaders.

"The most striking thing that I take out of working with coalition forces is that they care just as much as we did about what happened on 9/11, so that was very comforting. It wasn't like they're just here 'cause their country sent 'em, or it was just a nice show of cooperation. They cared. And they know it could've easily been in their country, or that it's eventually going to be in their country."

When there was a break in assignments, it was easy for Hotaling to hitch a ride to the larger American facility at Bagram, about five hundred miles to the northeast and just twenty-seven miles north of the Afghan capital, Kabul. Seven thousand Americans were managing to turn what had been a hotly contested former Soviet airfield into home. Sprinkled with land mines and unexploded ordnance by the Soviets, Bagram hardly qualified as an R&R destination, but for Hots, it was where the living was easy. "Bagram was hooked up for me. They had hot water. They had tons of food. Sometimes they had Cokes and Mountain Dews. They had a television. I lived under a roof. Man, it was easy livin'. So, when I went to Bagram, they used to laugh at me, because I would eat all their food, steal all their Coke, and watch movies from dawn to dusk and have a great time there."

Hotaling also was reunited at Bagram with a longtime friend, combat controller John Chapman, with whom he'd been stationed at Pope AFB, North Carolina, for five and a half years. Chappie had been on an overseas deployment when Hots got out of the active-duty Air Force, so the two hadn't seen each other for nearly six or seven years until they met up at Bagram.

"We were both fully bearded, with long hippie hair and just looking all crazy. It was a big reunion with him. Hugs and kisses and just a sloppy, teary reunion for a few hours."

And then it was back to Kandahar, where another coalition mission awaited, this one to a position near Takur Ghar mountain overlooking the Shah-e-Kot valley in eastern Afghanistan. Hots, carrying his usual 120-pound rucksack, and his Aussie SASR teammates were infiltrated onto a mountaintop for what was planned to be a five-day mission that the world would come to know as Operation Anaconda. From the beginning, he knew this one was going to be different.

The infiltration itself went fine, but the enemy knew that they and another observation team were there—somewhere. Al Qaeda forces tried to get Hotaling's team to expose themselves by walking mortar rounds through the area where they suspected his group was hiding.

"As the mortars bracketed our position—even if they landed close—it didn't matter, because they were looking for us to scurry and expose where we were at. We weren't going to do that; we weren't going to fall into that trap."

Enemy mortar shells falling within two hundred meters of their position weren't the only ordnance coming their way. They also had to worry about friendly fire. "We had various bombs that happened to either fall short, or some bombs—their ground proximity [fuses] would go off in the air as another bomb passed near it. So you had air bursts right over your head.

"I had the feeling it was just a matter of time before something might've happened. There were several times when the enemy basically came up [the mountain] on our positions. We had a sister OP that was approximately seven hundred meters from us. The enemy came up and the other observation post actually engaged in firefights at that point to where we were able to stay out of it."

They'd packed for a five-day mission. By day four they realized they were going to run out of food long before they could get off the mountaintop. A resupply airdrop was out of the question because it would expose their position. So they went into survival mode, rationing their food and making snow cones with flavored drink mix to ease the hunger pangs. When he ran out of battery power for the radios, someone from the nearby OP crawled to him in the middle of the night, delivering his own supply so Hots could keep calling in close air support.

As Hotaling tells the story of what turned out to be fourteen days on the mountain, there's no attempt at bravado. It's just what he and others like him have trained to do, and now they're being called upon to do it. Was there fear? Of course.

"You use it as a motivator. You work through fear. There's not much of a difference between a lot of what we do in training and in war. And so you learn to control that fear. You'd be a liar and fool if you said you weren't fearful every time you were in enemy territory. Obviously you are, but you just gotta work fast, use it to keep your senses well tuned."

Then Hotaling explains precisely what he means. "Each guy is obviously very different. But what I think is, the more fearful I am, the more I'm *not* in sensory overload, but my senses are completely tuned to what the job is and everything else disappears." Hots says some people, like himself, are able to "focus in," while others "focus out and get real berserky." For him, "when things really start going crazy, I end up being able to focus on the job and I'm able to communicate, whether it's to aircraft or to the commanders in the rear who need to know what's going on and what needs to happen."

He's also acutely aware that the mission is *his* mission. He's the CCT, the man with the radios who can reach out to combat controllers with units in the valley below, or by satellite to Central Command Headquarters in Tampa, or to an assortment of points, both moving and static, in between. The five special tactics men accompanying him have but one primary job—to protect Hotaling so he can stay on the radio. True, at least some of the others are trained to call in close air support, but the pilots dropping the bombs and firing miniguns or cannons at the enemy are Americans; there's a concern that even though the coalition forces he's with speak English, in the heat of combat their Aussie accent may not be understood by pilots. So it's Hotaling's job to stay on the radios.

For a covert mission like this one, "field sanitation" becomes a quaint notion in the military manual of the same name. "You go from your first few days to literally just putting it back in your MRE bags and things like that, to where you lay on the ground and you go in a bottle when you can't even stand up." Toward the end, when coalition forces controlled the area, they could actually go a little ways away and take care of business behind a bush. "That," says Hots, "was easy livin'."

"People don't realize that you come back from a situation like that, and I know this isn't a glamorous thing, but you're smelling like urine, smelling like crap, because a lot of times you literally have to do that in your pants. That's just the way it is. That's never in the movies. That's not Hollywood."

With temperatures ranging from a high of forty during the day to ten below at night, Hotaling worked for three days and three nights without rest, relying on his teammates to spot both targets and friendly forces. "They're calling out coordinates; he's checking them on the map; I double-check them; he double-checks me; I call it in and work the close air support. So it's a huge team effort. Maybe one or two are sleeping, and you just keep going in that rotation."

Both Hotaling's team, and another Aussie squad that included U.S. Air Force S.Sgt. Jessie Fleener as its CCT, were put in place in advance of what turned out to be the biggest battle of the war in Afghanistan, called Operation Anaconda after the snake that squeezes its prey till it suffocates. Anaconda was supposed to last no more than five days, but ended up running almost three weeks.

What they were trying to do was help keep the enemy from overrunning the American units that had become trapped on a ridge on the eastern side of the Shah-e-Kot valley, approximately two miles away and downslope from the position where Hots and his fellow observers were dug in. The trapped Ranger units were on Takur Ghar Mountain near Objective Ginger, a mountain pass that was a main supply route and an Al Qaeda stronghold that U.S. Army intelligence says had been built up over the last twenty years with caches of arms and ammunition.

Operation Anaconda began on March 2—it had been delayed two days because of inclement weather—when elements of the Army's 10th Mountain Division and 101st Airborne Division were airlifted into the Shah-e-Kot valley. The plan was to seal the Al Qaeda escape routes from the valley, and then slowly squeeze the Taliban fighters who were caught in the trap. Unfortunately, as every combat arms officer learns, sometimes painfully, the plan is not the mission and the map is not the terrain.

The Afghans who were supposed to block the west end of the valley were pushed back by mortar attacks. Their convoy was confused with Al Qaeda vehicles and mistakenly targeted by a Spectre gunship, killing an American, Special Forces CWO Stanley L. Harriman. Bad weather delayed the arrival of the 101st Airborne Division units that were supposed to block escape routes to the north. They were more than twelve hours late getting into position.

But what really confounded the American military planners was that the Taliban and Al Qaeda forces opted not to run, but to stay and fight. Lt. Col. David Gray, the chief of operations for all coalition forces participating in Anaconda, which included soldiers from Australia, Canada, Denmark, France, Germany, and Norway, said, "We looked at a combination of hit-and-run tactics, and the possibility they would stay and fight for a couple of days, and then exfiltrate the area. Then we looked at what we considered the most dangerous course of action, which was that the enemy would try to stay and fight American soldiers toe-to-toe. In this particular case, he decided to stay and fight."

According to an Associated Press analysis of Operation Anaconda based largely on information provided by Lieutenant Colonel Gray, within two hours of landing on the morning of March 2, American infantrymen had secured six of the seven mountain passes on the eastern ridgeline above the valley, often after brief but intense firefights. It was at the seventh pass, code-named Ginger Valley, where things didn't go nearly as planned.

In an intelligence failure reminiscent of Vietnam, helicopters dropped eighty-six soldiers from the 10th Mountain nearly on top of a large Al Qaeda position. They immediately took withering mortar and small-arms fire. Despite pounding by Apache attack helicopters—several of which were hit and forced from the fight—AC-130 Spectre gunships, and B-52 bombers, the enemy fighters continued to slam the Americans.

In an interview with the *Courier Mail* (Queensland, Australia) published on June 17, 2002, two Australian SASR veterans of Operation Anaconda said they protected themselves and the mounting number of casualties by digging foxholes with their bare hands and combat knives.

> "I was lying on my back in my hole looking up and the tracer fire was crisscrossing like the laser alarm systems you see in the bank vault of a movie," an SASR officer said.
>
> A 45-year-old father of two from Perth, SASR Warrant Officer Clint P [per SASR policy, the newspaper couldn't disclose his full name], said he knew he was in trouble soon after arriving by chopper. As he ran from the Chinook, the smoke of a rocket-propelled grenade [RPG] was trailing straight at him.

He stopped and as he instinctively threw up his left arm, he watched the grenade pass beneath it and hit the ground about 2m behind him. It didn't explode.

The time was 6.45am on Saturday, March 2, 2002, on the opening day of . . . the Operation Anaconda. "We hadn't moved 100 metres from the choppers when we started taking heavy fire from machine guns and RPGs. It was relentless," he said in an interview at the SASRs Perth headquarters. "There was no cover and 82 people were looking for some. We didn't understand what was out there."

"The strategy," according to the *Courier Mail* SASR sources, "during the opening phase of Operation Anaconda had been to block a large concentration of enemy fighters in the Shah-i-Kot Valley by massing troops at either end. Yet due to intelligence failures and the fog of war, unbeknown to the American planners hundreds of al-Qaeda fighters had anticipated a Coalition assault on the Shah-i-Kot and had fled into the mountains nearby. Consequently the enemy came to control positions within shooting distance of the landing zone selected for the American company.

The enemy was dug in above the snow line on the eastern ridge, yet thanks to the high angle of fire no one was hit during the opening salvos. The only available cover was a small depression, with a dry creek bed running through the depression. The two SASR men hit the ground and began digging in with their bare hands, with mortar rounds exploding around them. Things got worse when the SASR soldiers noticed a force of about 26 enemy fighters on the opposite ridge line. "We killed some of them but then started taking fire from that side as well," Warrant Officer P was quoted as saying. Air strikes were subsequently called in but the Apache helicopters were forced back after taking heavy volumes of fire. B-52 bombers later hammered the enemy positions, yet as Warrant Officer P continued, "Before the dust had settled they were out shooting at us again. They were even waving at us . . . it was a little disappointing." By the end of the afternoon the creek bed had been completely dug out to protect a large and growing number of wounded. "They were packed in like sardines. If a mortar had landed in there it would have been carnage."

At Kandahar, air crews from the 66th Expeditionary Rescue Squadron and PJs from the 38th ERQS were spending a lot of time in the Army tactical operations center listening to the war going on. The TOC was a tent filled with radios, computers, and classified Internet systems—but no live video from Predator drones—all of which seemed to be pumping out bad news.

Before lunch, they know that the company from the 10th Mountain has been ambushed. By late afternoon, the PJs learn that there are at least twelve casualties, and they get their first call. "You guys are Alert Five. You're going to escort an Apache Killer Spade 76 up to Texaco FARP."

A FARP is a forward arming and refueling point, a ground position where a Chinook with a rubber fuel bladder in the cargo compartment has been positioned to refuel helicopters close to the action. It's a more efficient way of giving them gas than midair refueling in this type of situation. Texaco FARP is just a "brown nothing" at approximately seven-thousand-feet elevation. There is a small village to the west, mountains to the east. With the Army pulling security, an Air Force combat controller directing traffic, and a couple of Chinook "fat cows" giving gas, the field has become nearly as crowded as New York's LaGuardia Airport on a Friday afternoon.

The local villagers, who probably haven't seen helicopters there since the Soviets pulled out of Afghanistan, are riding up on bicycles or in cars to watch the excitement. They are being told to go back to their homes by one of the Afghan interpreters brought in by the Americans, who is speaking to the villagers through a portable loudspeaker system.

As soon as the HH-60G helicopters arrive following a two-hour flight from Kandahar, they learn that the Apache they've guided up there is to replace one that has been shot up during the initial assault, and they watch as he loads up with Hellfire rockets and takes off for the battle. Then the combat search and rescue teams settle in to wait alongside Army medevac helos and special-ops Chinooks belonging to the QRF, the quick reaction force. The powers that be won't let them go in to evacuate the casualties. The word is that the battle raging fifteen minutes' flying time away is still too hot for rotary-winged aircraft, and the likelihood is that they won't be allowed to go in until after dark.

What that means to pararescueman Caleb Ethridge, a staff sergeant from Bakersfield, California, is that he's got time to eat an MRE, use the latrine, and put on clothing that's more appropriate to where they are and where they're going than where they've been. The temperature at the FARP is near zero, and after flying from Kandahar's three-thousand-foot elevation to their current seven thousand feet with the windows open, he's really cold—even when he puts on the high-tech polypropylene long johns and the fleece that's part of their kit.

Ethridge also works on the helos—identified by the call signs Gecko 11 and 12—with the other three PJs, T.Sgt. Patrick Harding, SrA Michael Flores, and S.Sgt. Bob Roberts, to prepare the cramped interiors for the upcoming mission. They dump extra rations and water, as well as the fast rope that is only needed to put guys onto the ground, not to pull them out. Anything that can not only give them more room in the back but also reduce their gross weight will be left behind.

Ethridge finds himself reflecting on how important it is to judiciously discard excess weight. He recalls how just two weeks earlier he got the lesson of a lifetime on the issue of weight limitations for HH-60Gs operating at high altitudes. He'd been aboard one of two Pave Hawks being ferried over the Hindu Kush mountains from Kandahar to Karshi-Khanabad. The 66th ERQS had received orders to pull out of their original base at Jacobabad and establish a second operating base up at K-2. Truth be told, "lesson of a lifetime" downplays what happened. The veteran gunner aboard the same helo, T.Sgt. Troy Durocher, says it's as close as he's ever come to dying on a helicopter.

The story is best told by the pilot of the Pave Hawk that was designated Gecko 17, for the mission that began on the morning of February 16. 1st Lt. Thomas J. Cahill, a twelve-year Army Black Hawk pilot who switched to the Air Force four years earlier to fly CSAR, took off in the morning as flight lead of the two HH-60Gs, Gecko 17 and 18, with another flight-lead qualified pilot, Capt. Ed Lengel, flying as his copilot. Ethridge and M.Sgt. Brian Oswald were the two PJs on board, and S.Sgt. Josh Fetters was the flight engineer. Their assignment was to take the two helos up the eastern side of Afghanistan, refuel at Bagram, and then go through the Hindu Kush mountains, aerial refuel north of the Kush, and continue on a northwest heading to K-2.

About an hour after they left Bagram, the remaining two Pave Hawks at Kandahar were tasked to pick up the Aussie SAS soldier that three PJs from the 38th were planning on parachuting to. Cahill was able to monitor the progress of that mission on the same SATCOM channel that his ship used to communicate with the Joint Search and Rescue Center in PSAB—Prince Sultan Air Base in Saudi Arabia.

It didn't take long till they had to put aside monitoring the other mission and just concentrate on keeping their aircraft flying. Cahill describes it this way: "We started getting into a bad snowstorm, and I was working my way up the mountain, and as you know, we're already power-limited. At about eleven thousand feet the digital electronic control fuel unit on my number one engine failed on me. And then we lost power to that engine."

At that moment, Cahill is convinced that they're going to die. "We're heavy, we've got six crewmembers, we're up at eleven thousand feet, and only five hundred feet above ground level. With two engines on the 60, that's pushing the limits. With one engine, what I was down to now, I just didn't think it was going to work out.

"Keep in mind that we're up in the Hindus. There's nobody to talk to. The only radio that we had was the SATCOM, but concurrently on the SATCOM that other mission was going on, so the last thing that I was going to do was get on the radio at the last second and try to spit something out when I knew they had some stuff going on. Besides, from the time we lost the power till when we hit the ground only took four seconds. So there was really no time to get anything out."

He was also acutely aware of the fact that they were in hostile territory. On the way up they'd overflown at least nine enemy emplacements, equipped with anything from rifles to 23mm guns to RPGs, but weren't fired upon, probably because by the time the Taliban forces saw the helicopters and manned their weapons, the helos were already over the ridgeline and out of sight.

At the last second, as they were falling through the sky, Cahill spotted a little patch of snow on the side of the mountain. "I just figured, well, I'll continue to try to fly the helicopter and see if we can work something out."

His ace in the hole was sitting next to him, in the left seat. Ed Lengel was also a flight lead, an experienced pilot. The only reason he was flying as copilot was that he needed to catch a ride up to K-2. Cahill says it's what Lengel did that saved them. "He reached up into the center console above his head and grabbed the throttle for the number one engine and basically did a manual override called a 'DEC lockout.' He took the throttle and pulled it down, and went full forward with it to give it all the gas that he possibly could.

"He did it instinctively, and that's what somebody with a lot of experience will do. The standard setup, a flight lead with a newer copilot, that guy's probably not going to do that unless the other pilot directs him to do it. But seeing how everything happened so fast when it failed, and it started falling so quickly, nobody had a chance to say anything."

Even if they had, they might not have been understood because the low-rotor-speed horn had gone off. It's a loud, constant klaxon that they can't make go away, except by increasing rotor rpm. And that clearly wasn't possible.

"Ed reached up and bypassed the throttle, and we had just enough power before I impacted the snow to clear a giant boulder that was in our way. First, if we hadn't had just that one little quick boost of power, we probably would've hit the boulder. And then, second, I was able to somehow get the helicopter to impact that one area of snow, 'cause everywhere else was pretty much just rock, glacier face."

It might seem that a critical moment like the crash would be indelibly and realistically emblazoned in Cahill's memory, but both he and Lengel have discussed what they recall seeing. It's surprisingly similar—and surreal. Cahill says, "Just prior to crashing, what I have in my head is that it was almost like daytime. I don't know if that has anything to do with the adrenaline of a crash sequence or what, but that one piece of both our memories is that it was quite bright out at the time. After we hit the side of the hill and realized that the aircraft was still at least semiflyable, at that point is when it pretty much got pitch-black."

They impacted the side of the mountain at about a thirty-degree angle, nose up. And that was when the fun began. What apparently saved the helicopter from being busted apart on impact was a fifteen-foot-deep snow pack. That, however, didn't stop the rotor blade tips from flexing down hard, and chopping off a good portion of all four tips on contact. Cahill had a moment to register surprise that the rotors were still moving, and that they weren't on fire. Literally, just a moment.

Because the helicopter immediately began sliding backward, and only four feet behind them was a vertical cliff with a two-thousand-foot drop, straight down. The HH-60G has wheels, not skids, and the brakes on those wheels were not holding in the ice and snow they'd landed on. Looking out the gunner's window in the left rear of the plane, Troy Durocher hit his intercom switch and shouted, "Power, power, power. We're sliding back."

Durocher remembers hearing Cahill acknowledge with an "Okay," but the brakes didn't do any good. They continued sliding. "I tell him, 'Stop back!' so he pretty much tried flying it on the ground, but we didn't have the power to take off. Now we're about two and a half feet in front of this two-thousand-foot drop-off. The stab's just hanging over it right now and the wheel is about two and a half feet in front of the drop."

Durocher is thirty-seven years old and he's been in the service since he was eighteen. He's seen combat in 1993 in Northern Iraq, and he's spent time flying in a special-operations squadron. But on this night, he says, "the pucker factor hit a thousand and one percent. This was the scariest night I've ever had in a helicopter. It was probably the closest I've come to dying."

When Cahill heard his gunner calling for power, there was only thing he could do: "pull in a lot of power and put a lot of forward cyclic, which pretty much put the rotor system into the snow. By the time we finally stopped, the guys in the back told us that the tail rotor system and the stabilator had just cleared two giant rocks that were behind us by maybe two or three inches on each side. And that we had about another foot before the tail would've gone right over the cliff."

He had about two seconds to marvel at the fact that they were all still alive. Then he had to figure out their next move. "I was debating what to do. I didn't know if I should shut the helicopter down or . . . Keep in mind, we're sitting here about ten thousand, five hundred feet and it's snowing. We're up in the middle of nowhere. There's no way anybody could possibly get to us. My other aircraft was circling about a mile away, but did not know what our status was, 'cause at this point we didn't have radio contact with them anymore. I also knew there was no way they could pick any of us up. And I knew the second I would've shut that aircraft down, the rotor system would've started to hang a little more and would have hit the rocks. At that point, the rotor system would have come off the aircraft.

"So I just told everyone, 'Look, we're gonna try to get this helicopter up this mountain here."

Thinking about the event months later, he recalls that the last thing that came out of his mouth before they impacted—not over the intercom, but to himself—was, "I'm sorry, Cheyane." Cheyane is Cahill's daughter, and that day was her fourth birthday. He had actually been happy about making the flight up to K-2 because he'd have telephone access there and would be able to call Cheyane.

"The last thing that went through my mind, as we were getting ready to hit the side of the hill, I thought, 'This is going to be a terrible thing for my daughter to always think that her dad died on her birthday.'"

But they'd survived the crash, so rather than being preoccupied with the immediate possibility that he was going to die, he put his mind back in gear and began working on how they were going to live. Cahill told Lengel to do the calculations on the helicopter's computer. The answers weren't encouraging. At that moment they didn't even have the power to hover just one foot above the ground.

The only solution was to lighten the load, and the easiest way to do that was by dumping fuel. That presented a number of problems. First, they had to defeat a switch that prevents fuel from being dumped while the HH-60G is sitting on the ground. It's a little switch on the right-hand side of the under-carriage that automatically clicks into the off position when the helo settles in for a landing. Informing the crew of his plan, the pilot also advised the guys in the back that one of them might have to lean out the door, reach down, and press the button to override it in order to allow the dump control switch in the cockpit to work.

Luck was with them, however. Because they were pulling enough power to keep the helo from sliding back off the cliff, they had enough weight off the wheels that the switch was no longer depressed. In essence, they fooled the device into thinking the helicopter was flying.

That was the good news. The bad news was that they were now confronted with the consequences of that action. Cahill says, "Keep in mind that no one's ever done this, at least to my knowledge, no HH-60G crewmember's ever dumped gas while their helicopter's been running on the ground. When we're dumping gas it comes out of the left side of the helicopter, just aft of the transition area, where the tail boom starts. And it flows out at a fairly good rate. And we're starting to smell the fumes and one of the backenders got concerned about a fire breaking out."

The concerned "backender" was Durocher. "I said, 'Sir, if there's a fire, meet off the nose and we'll break out the hot dogs and marshmallows.' Brian Oswald was the PJ on my side. And he and I look at each other like this." Durocher pops his eyes wide open, lifts his eyebrows, and his jaw drops. It's a "We've never been here before" look. He says, "I can't believe we lived through that landing, and then we can't take off, we're in the fuel."

When Gecko 17 hit the side of the mountain, they had roughly twenty-nine hundred pounds of gas on board, not quite five hundred gallons. They calculated that they had to get down to around one thousand pounds in order to have enough power for a two-foot hover. That would allow them to hover high enough to turn the ship around and fly it off the mountain. It meant dumping three hundred gallons of gas, while just sitting there knowing that jet fuel was gushing out of the helicopter in close proximity to hot exhaust from the jet engines.

Cahill remembers his briefing to the crew: " 'Look, if a fire does break out, what we're going to do is, everybody just hop out of the helicopter on the right-hand side, jump into the snow.' I wanted everybody out except me. Then what I was going to do is just let the helicopter drift backwards, off the side of the hill, 'cause there was a vertical cliff there. And it may sound good now, maybe magnanimous, but at the time all I was thinking was, 'I want to try and save as many people as possible.' "

That action would have been a suicide move for the thirty-three-year-old pilot that would have left his wife of sixteen years, Roxane, to raise their three children, Ryan, Doss, and Cheyane, alone. "If I just pulled a little bit more power and brought the cyclic backwards, 'cause I had it almost full forward— about four or five inches forward—if I would've just come back with it, I could have just easily let it slide off the side of the mountain. At that point, I just figured we'd only lose one helicopter and one guy, rather than the other five guys."

On the first try, they dumped five hundred pounds of gas, then stopped the outflow of fuel and tried to hover. Durocher was watching out the left side and as soon as the helo lifted, he saw the tail swinging toward the ridgeline. He hit the intercom and said, "Stop the tail left and put it back down." They still didn't have enough power to get off the ground. Once more, the pilots dumped another five hundred pounds of fuel. Still not enough.

Cahill remembers telling Troy Durocher, "Dude, I need you to get everything out of this helicopter you possibly can." He responded by throwing a few cases of MREs, water bottles, some ammunition for the miniguns, and some odds and ends out the door. The problem was, there wasn't much to toss out. They weren't on a tactical mission, loaded for battle. It was just supposed to be a nice nighttime ride over the Kush, getting a pair of 60s from K-1 to K-2.

Watching as best he could from the right front seat, Cahill had the feeling that what was going overboard wasn't going to be enough to get them off the hill. He said, "All right, before you throw anything else out, let me dump the rest of this gas." He was thinking that if that didn't work, he'd begin dumping guns and would tell the PJs to dump all their gear out. Clearly he knew that every pound mattered.

It was about that time when the PJs suggested that they'd be willing to get off and hike down the mountain by themselves. Ethridge was actually nonchalant about the suggestion. He'd climbed to the 14,494-foot peak of Mount Whitney in Northern California several times. Cahill remembers looking at the pararescuemen, contemplating the notion that they were willing to get off a helicopter and walk down the mountain, not even knowing where they were. He said, "Dude, that's really strange." Ethridge responded, "Yeah, but that's okay. We can do that."

"I don't know if the guys in their heads actually realized how far from anybody friendly we were. When I assessed everything," Cahill says, "I realized that if we had to go into a survival situation, we would have been in a bad position. We really would've." But in the back of his mind at the time, he thought, "Brian is one of those guys where if I would have told him, 'We're gonna shut down. It's your job to lead us down the side of the hill,' he would have done that."

Also weighing on Cahill's mind at that moment was what was happening with the other ship, Gecko 18, that he presumed was circling somewhere close by. He knew that asking them to land in order to evacuate his crew was out of the question. There was no way they'd be able to lift off with an additional six guys on board. The best they could do was note their position and get a radio call off via SATCOM. But his real worry was that his own crash landing could turn out to be a death knell for the other crew, as well. "My concern is that the other aircraft doesn't have a superexperienced crew. I'm a little bit worried about what's going to happen to them, 'cause I knew if we would've bit it in the side of that hill, or not made it off, now those guys are sitting there. And the weather's moving in, getting worse and worse."

There was still one more option that might get them all off the mountain. If he could turn the helicopter ninety degrees, they might be able to quite literally fly it off the hill. Problem was, he couldn't do the standard maneuver to turn a 60 around—a pedal turn. That's bringing the helo to a one-foot hover, then turning with the pedal controls. The problem was the boulders the tail had wedged itself between.

The trick that finally worked was hopping the helo forward three or four times in order to get it to a spot about forty feet off the nose that was flat enough for him to do a two-foot hover and do a pedal turn to the right ninety degrees until he could actually see a good flight path off the side of the hill.

Next step was to do precisely what the Knife 04 crew had done after rescuing the downed crew and having trouble taking off due to limited power at high altitude. In that case, they could get a rolling start and build up steam by flying a foot or two off the ground for half a mile. On the side of the mountain, Cahill and Lengel didn't have half a mile, but thought they had enough room to get a running start to where effective translational lift (ETL) would kick in. Cahill says, "As long as I could do that, fly it off the side of the hill staying at one or two feet until I got past ETL, I thought I'd have enough power to continue flying."

What he's basically saying is that he and Lengel had enough experience and confidence to believe that once they got over the edge of the cliff, they were going to be able to fly away, as opposed to dropping like a rock. They still have the problem with the engine that went bad, so for this trick to work, the copilot would have to keep his hand on the overhead throttle, moving it forward and back as necessary for the remainder of the flight in order to bypass the DEC lockout and make power adjustments every time the pilot moved the collective to go up or down.

While the maneuver they were about to attempt was dicey, the backenders had flown with Cahill enough that they believed he knew what he was doing. Finally the moment came. He clicked the intercom switch and said, "Hey, I'm gonna go ahead. We're gonna go for it."

With his hands on the controls and his heart in his mouth, Lt. Thomas Cahill flew Gecko 17 off the hill—directly into complete blizzard conditions with no visibility whatsoever.

Within seconds they were able to make radio contact with his wingman, and he told them their plan. The flight up to K-2 would be abandoned. He said, "Look, we're obviously not going to make it over these mountains. We're just going to fly reverse routing on the same path that we came in on, and we're going to recover back into Bagram airfield."

Each of the two helicopters has an ELMO, an Electronic Layered Map Overlay, that drops a dot on the computerized map display at five-second intervals, indicating the position of the helicopter. They'd gone down in a very narrow canyon about fifteen miles northwest of Bagram. What he was telling the pilots in Gecko 18 to do was to precede them, and fly back where they came from by connecting the dots. Even though that course would put them over the antiaircraft emplacements they'd overflown on the way north, it didn't concern Cahill. "Because at this point, it was complete blizzard conditions. Freezing. I really wasn't too worried about those guys; I was more worried about keeping this helicopter flying."

And he was going to have to fly it behind the less experienced pilots in

Gecko 18. "My wingman was just ahead of me when we flew off the hill, and the gorge that we were in was too narrow to do a lead change. So I directed him to get on his moving map and just fly us by reverse routing, back out of the mountains."

If they'd been in weather that gave them decent visibility on the other helicopter, the plan would have been relatively easy to execute. And if the queen had balls, she'd be the king. Decent visibility for the flight back, unfortunately, was just going to be a dream. The viz got so bad, they quickly lost sight of each other. That called for refining the plan.

The map display updates every few seconds by dropping a flashing dot on the map marking their current position. As the craft moves, the dot stops flashing but remains in place, and the next one flashes. While following the dots would keep them on course, it wouldn't keep them from colliding with each other. Cahill's order was, "Start calling your airspeed out to me [on the FM interplane radio channel]. I will hold the same airspeed and also hold our point-three Tacan separation." The Tacan is a device that sends a signal from one helicopter to the other that tells them the distance between the two helos, although it doesn't indicate whether the accompanying helo is left or right, in front of or behind them.

"We were holding anywhere between seventy and eighty knots, and as a turn would come up, they would tell us, 'In three seconds, seventy-degree turn to the right' or 'forty-degree turn to the left.' And they would count it down, 'three, two, one, turn.'"

If the tactic sounds familiar, it may be because the submarine commander used the exact same method in *The Hunt for Red October*.

Cahill continued explaining how they made it work flying blind in the Hindu Kush. "As soon as he would turn, I would wait about three seconds, and then I would start my turn. That's how we kept separation. It didn't work out one hundred percent of the time."

That last comment is ultrasubtle understatement of the type common to people who do this sort of thing for a living. Cahill explains what it "not working one hundred percent of the time" really means, "Once lead got disoriented a little bit and didn't realize he started zeroing his airspeed out, I could tell we were getting close to him, just because our Tacan was counting down toward zero. And then I could start to see the glow of his tail rotor light; it became this giant halo. So we made an immediate left turn, a three-hundred-and-sixty-degree left turn, and what we didn't realize as we made that turn was that we were actually flying over a large peak that was coming up from the bottom of the canyon. And about a hundred and eighty degrees through the turn, we just missed impacting terrain by about two or three feet.

"That was the one time of night where Troy Durocher's voice inflection changed considerably, 'cause it came right out his side of the helicopter."

Durocher recalls the event vividly. "Initially it started off as rain, went to snow and cloud—we were inside the cloud of snow. Gecko 18 slowed down and almost fell out of the sky. What happened is they flew into a zero-zero condition where they could not see anything, and they kind of slowed, slowed, slowed back trying to fly, thinking, 'Hey, maybe I just need to slow down. I'm going through this stuff too fast.' Well, when they did that, we don't have the power to maintain flight, so we were going to do a three-sixty turn coming behind them. While they're doing this, they don't have the power, either, to maintain flight, and they started falling out of the sky, and their flight engineer tells them, 'Nose it over, nose it over!' And we hear this on the radio: 'I'm nosin' it over and goin' for it.'"

When Gecko 18's pilot unintentionally zeroed out his airspeed, it pitched the nose of the helicopter up. The pilot got disoriented, and the ship started falling back on its tail. Then they went to about fifty degrees nose-low, gained airspeed back, and then leveled the aircraft out. Disaster had been very close. They were only about fifty feet above the valley floor when they recovered.

Durocher didn't have much time to ponder the other helicopter's maneuver, because his bird was having its own problems. "As we get into the beginning of our three-sixty turn, we get hit by some wind, and it's weird. Six months, maybe eight months prior to this flight, I had a dream that we had crash-landed on the face of a mountain. And it just popped into my head at this time, as we were making this turn, that this is the exact same moment in my dream. And I just knew we weren't going to make it, and I started screaming, 'Power! Power! Power! Power!' And no kidding, there's a mountain that we didn't see in front of us, and we ended up clearing it. Our altitude warning system was set at fifty feet, and she went off four times before we came across and she stopped talking."

The "she" is the female voice used by the device to get a pilot's attention. She says, "Low altitude, low altitude, low altitude." The lowest altitude Cahill told the crew he read on the radar altimeter was ten feet. That's measured from the belly of the helicopter, which has an entire undercarriage hanging from it; they actually had cleared the mountain by only six or seven feet.

Cahill recalls that Durocher yelled for him to climb, but they didn't have the power to do that. "Looking through my chin bubble"—that's the clear plastic windshield in front of his feet, figuratively on the chin of the helo— "it's black, and then all of a sudden I see terrain just a couple of feet below us, passing us by. Let's just say that it probably brought my blood pressure up a couple of points."

Durocher remembers that they continued flying through snow showers for another thirty minutes—Cahill thinks it was only ten minutes. "Everyone was so focused, it was amazing," says the gunner. "You're only hearing out of every guy what you need to hear. 'Clearance on the right, clearance on the left. I got good viz up in front.' It's clicking right on. The bird in front of us is saying, 'Okay, we got an eighty-degree turn to the right here in a minute.' And they did it, and all of a sudden it's just rainy and they're out of the mountains, over open terrain just north of·Bagram."

"There was a little town there, at the base of the hill," says Cahill. "I could start to make out some lights of an old village, and the visibility and the ceiling greatly improved. It was still snowing and raining, but at least we had about a thousand-foot clearance to the clouds, and I could see more than five miles out.

"I gotta tell you, from the time we impacted to that point is about forty-five minutes. That's the first time in the night where I knew, I thought, 'Well, okay, we're gonna make it now.' Because the whole time flying back out of the mountains, it was touch and go. I thought, 'Really, I don't know if we're gonna make it outside these mountains, but we'll just keep trying.'"

A few minutes later they landed at Bagram and shut down the engines. Cahill says it was an indelible moment. "It's funny, because I remember when we landed, complete silence in the crew. I'll never forget Caleb. Caleb Ethridge walked around the side of the helicopter, came up to me, and just gives me a hug and says nothing. Then looks at me and goes, 'Dude, I've never been so scared in a helicopter in my life.' And then he said, 'Thanks.'"

When they checked the helicopter, the only damage they could find was to the rotor caps, which were badly chewed up. Cahill knew that in the HH-60G, "when you start losing pieces of your rotor system, an imbalance starts, and then usually it leads to losing everything. For some reason that night, even though we have four rotor caps chewed up, I'm telling you, I did not feel anything in the flight control system. And I don't know if that's because I didn't feel it, or I didn't care about it, y'know what I mean? Because I just wanted to get home. I just wanted to get wheels down somewhere that had food and a place to sleep."

It took three days before he was able to call Cheyane and wish her a be-lated happy birthday.

When gunner Troy Durocher finally had a chance to talk with his wife, Lisa, he didn't lay the story out minute by minute. He says, "I tell her that I'm the best at what I do, so don't worry. And she believes me." He laughs heartily. "Silly her!"

# RECON BY CASUALTY
## MARCH 2–4, 2002

Throughout his high school days in Bakersfield, California, Caleb Ethridge dreamed of joining the military to travel the world for four years, then get out. He also knew that with his good grades, he could get into the Air Force, avoiding the fate of his buddies who were being scooped up by the Marine Corps recruiters.

When he was a junior in high school, he went digging through the closet in the office of the local Air Force recruiter who had been touting his becoming a cop (there are more security police in the Air Force than any other occupational specialty) or a linguist. That was where he found the literature about pararescue, and he was hooked. "That's it. I want to do that."

After graduation, he gave college a shot, but he didn't like the lifestyle. So he hooked up with a buddy who was also interested in pararescue, and before they were inducted, the two of them got themselves into shape. Using a pamphlet they'd found describing the physical requirements to get out of the indoctrination course, they ran mile after mile and worked themselves up to swimming three thousand meters freestyle in decent time.

It wasn't that Ethridge had been out of shape, just that he was realistic about what it would take to become a PJ. In high school he was a star athlete, lettering in both football and wrestling. It was at a physical exam for football

American soldiers on alert in the freezing cold of the Shah-e-Kot valley during Operation Anaconda (*U.S. Army photo by Specialist David Marck, Jr.*)

that the doctor told him he'd probably overdone it lifting weights in eighth and ninth grade and stunted his growth. That was when Ethridge began to figure out why he hadn't grown taller than five-ten, while both his father and younger brother are six-two.

As things turned out, not getting any bigger than five-ten, 185 pounds, didn't hurt him in the struggle to become a PJ. "You have little guys, and then you have these huge guys, but for the most part, most special operators are all about medium build, medium height, five-ten, six feet, like hockey-player size, and I think that's because they have a combination of both speed and power. They can get up and run long distances; they can pick up something heavy. They're right in the middle, because if you're all huge and muscular, you can't run twenty miles to get away from bad guys. Eventually you run out of bullets and you gotta run, you gotta get away. And then there's the little guys—those guys are studs. The smallest guy on our team can rock-climb like you wouldn't believe. One-arm pull-ups. Just amazing."

What it takes to make it out of the ten-week PJ indoctrination course at Lackland Air Force Base, Texas, is not only endurance and power, but the ability to manage stress, and the tenacity not to quit. Over the years, the pararescue school faculty has devised various forms of underwater torture designed to sort out the candidates who can handle stress from those who can't.

It all begins with a basic supposition: Can there be anything more stressful than knowing you're running out of oxygen? Caleb Ethridge went through it in 1997, and remembers it like it was yesterday.

"We had to tie knots underwater, and the instructors said, 'You either tie 'em right, or you've got to go back down and do them again.' They usually brought you back up and smoked you, so you pretty much want to stay down there and finish it. You block out of your mind that you're underwater, you've been swimming for two hours and are totally exhausted, and you've got to hold your breath down at twelve feet and tie all these stupid knots—a bowline, a girth hitch and a square knot.

"Well, I got to the square knot and I tied a granny knot, right over right, right over right. I knew it was wrong, so I untied it, and then I tied right over right, right over right again. I just kept on tying it. I'm on the bottom of the pool, and I passed out. Everyone else is up, done. They ended up going down and pulling me up by my shirt. I knew that I was holding my breath and it's unnatural and it's hurting and it sucks, but I gotta finish this. I have to do this so I don't have to do it again, when it would suck even more."

And what's a wanna-be PJ who doesn't make it do in that situation?

Ethridge also remembers seeing that—and it wasn't pretty. "This guy was six-two, just looked like somebody in the movies who was already in. He looked like he's a PJ or a SEAL. But doing his underwaters, he ended up crapping in the pool, he was so stressed out. He came up. He couldn't do it. And he freaked out. They ended up taking him to the shower room. He's yelling, 'I can't fuckin' do it! I'm fucked up in the head!' and on and on. And I thought, 'If anybody can make it, this guy can make it.' So you're seeing these guys cry and crap in the pool. You doubt yourself, like, 'Shit, how am I gonna make it?' But you do."

One of his fellow PJs, twenty-five-year-old S.Sgt. Robert Disney from De-catur, Illinois, survived an HH-60G helicopter crash on takeoff into a full brownout. His team leader was S.Sgt. Matthew White. Not unexpectedly, Disney remembers the crash and its aftermath as though it happened in slow motion—yesterday. "My teammate called the other helicopter to let them know that there were survivors. The incident's forever etched in my mind. The special forces guys showed up, and there was mass confusion. I can still see Matt standing up on top of the helicopter and saying over the buzz of conversation, 'Everybody listen up! Everybody shut up! Here's the situation. We've got a helicopter that just crashed. We got six people inside, everybody's okay but they need to get checked out medically. We've got classified documents, and we've got weapons on the inside that need to come out. And we need to get a security perimeter set up. Now, let's make it happen.' And Matt standing on top of that helicopter, saying that, doing that, taking command of the situation, it's something I'll never, ever forget."

They just did what they had to do, when they had to do it, and afterward, Disney connected it with the water torture at indoc.

"The point of it isn't to see how well you can hold your breath. What better way to test your reaction to stress than to take away your oxygen supply? Under stress, your heart rate increases, which increases your oxygen demand, so they put you underwater and see if you can control it. It doesn't matter how well you can swim, how well you can run, and how well you can do push-ups or sit-ups. It's how you react to stress, and that's why the pool is the place where people lose it, and that's why the people who graduate that school end up being the pararescuemen of today, because they are able to handle the kinds of stresses that are put on them in combat. They can keep their heart rate down, their head together, and get the job done."

The success of Air Force Combat Search and Rescue lies in the selection of the right people for the job, and training them so they can do it under circumstances that would make many folks lose more than just their concentration in the pool. While the PJs are unique, credit certainly has to be given to the pilots—male and female—and backenders who get them where they need to be.

The crews have their own unique sense of humor, which is clearly in evidence outside the rows of dusty brown tents they occupy a half mile from the flight line at K-2. Under an American flag flying from the top of one is a hand-lettered sign that proudly announces:

CSAR
Downed behind enemy lines?
Ran outta gas?
Any Time . . . Any Place
You fuck up!
We pick up!

The man in charge of those CSAR helicopter crews sitting at Texaco FARP on the day Operation Anaconda began was Lt. Col. Lee dePalo, a sixteen-year Air Force veteran who spent ten years flying special operations helicopters before coming to CSAR and ultimately taking command of elements from the 66th Rescue Squadron at Nellis AFB, Nevada, that were sent to Operation Enduring Freedom. DePalo is convinced his men are well trained, skillful, and smart, which is why he can walk past their hootch on Air Force Hill in Kandahar and smile at the sign on the door that says:

## WE'RE SO SECRET
## WE DON'T EVEN KNOW
## WHAT WE'RE DOING

The unit commander is respected by his aircrews for a number of reasons, not the least of which is the way he keeps his calm, even with ten or eleven things hitting him at once. Lt. Thomas Cahill, who flies for dePalo and was flight lead for the mission that crashed in the Kush, says his boss "gives you the personal authority to do the right thing on a mission where, unfortunately, in the day and age we live in now, most commanders don't give pilots very much leeway on what they can do. And he does. He basically says, 'Dude, as soon as you go out the door and you're on this mission, it's completely your call, anything you do. Unless you do something gross, I'm not going to challenge that call that you made. Do you put PJs in? Do you not? Whatever you decide to do, man, that's your call.' He knows that he's trained the flight lead to a certain level, and that's what's expected of them."

Cahill adds, with no conscious sense of drama, "Definitely a guy who I'd probably follow into the pit of hell, that's for sure. And not even question it."

DePalo may not describe the location his men were going to fly into on the first night of Operation Anaconda as the pit of hell, but he knew it was going to be ugly. "What they were going to do is as close to the edge as anything I've ever been involved in," says dePalo. "Some aspects to that mission, particularly on night one, were unknown. The threat. We knew the threat was bad, but we didn't know what it would be like in the pitch-black night. We didn't know how much the enemy had been degraded at that point. The enemy held the high ground, and it had proved to be very tough. Nobody completely understood what kind of threat we'd encounter going in there."

The aircrews on their upcoming adventure include Capt. Ed Lengel as flight lead of the two-ship mission and pilot of Gecko 11. Capt. John Gallick is the copilot. The flight engineer on his bird is Josh Fetters, with T.Sgt. Troy Durocher as the gunner, and the PJs are S.Sgts. Yandall Goodwin and Michael Ames. The other helicopter is Gecko 12 with pilot John Mangan and copilot Phil Swenson; PJs are Caleb Ethridge and Brian Oswald. A shortage of gunners leads the unit to put two flight engineers on board to handle the miniguns on both sides. S.Sgts. Greg Sisko and Ted Mirich draw these assignments.

Before they even arrive at Texaco, Durocher has been monitoring the SATCOM radio transmissions from "Deliverance," the code name for the JSRC. "It's strange, 'cause we could hear them talking as we're flying up there, we can hear the guy on the ground saying, 'We need to get our guys out of here. We've been getting mortared all day long.' The guy he's calling for close air support says, 'Okay, dude, we're sending somebody on the way.' But they sent in some Apaches, from what I understand, and they got shot up and had to limp out. They didn't feel it was comfortable for us to go in. We sat there at the FARP, waiting for it to cool down enough for us to be able to go in there."

For several hours, the two crews go back and forth several times from a five-minute alert posture to, "Stand down. We're going to wait till it cools off." Finally, according to Durocher, "We got the word that it's not going to get any cooler than it is right now. The Apaches got shot out of there, and they weren't going to be able to provide support for us. So they said, 'You're cleared in.' It was up to us whether we went in or not."

That puts it on the shoulders of the flight lead to weigh the risks. Simply put, he has to ask the question, "Are we going to make it out of there alive? Or is this a one-way mission to try to save somebody?" If it is, they can't go in. But there's a reason they call it *Combat* Search and Rescue. The gunner says, "You weigh your risks and say, 'Okay, the threat is huge, yes, but we've got ways to deal with that.' We've got the minigun, and it's nighttime, so we had the cover of darkness. We fly low, so it's hard to find us at night. As a crew, we decided we were going to go in there. We wanted to get those guys out of there."

Does that mean it's a discussion and vote among six guys—two pilots, two PJs, a gunner, and an FE? "Not really. It is and it isn't," says Durocher. "It's kind of strange how helicopter crews function. The AC says, 'What do you guys think?' and everybody usually goes 'yea' or 'nay,' and it's usually a consensus. The AC is the ultimate decision maker. If everybody goes 'yea' and the AC says, 'Yeah, I was thinking the same thing,' you all go. I haven't been in a situation yet where one person said, 'I don't think so.' It just gives everybody the warm fuzzy that, 'Hey, y'know what? I volunteered to do this. I raised my hand and said I'm gonna go do this.' It's more a formality that we do with each other."

What if someone on the crew had serious misgivings? "If somebody really believed that they weren't going to make it out of there alive, or it was a one-way mission, they'd say, 'Hey, y'know what? What if we waited, or we do this?' I've taught this to all my young gunners: Don't come up with a problem. Don't say, 'We can't do it because of this.' Come up with a solution. 'This is a problem, but this is how we're gonna fix it.' Don't tell me we can't do it; tell me how we can do it."

The decision to finally do something rather than sit around freezing their collective butts off energizes everyone. Durocher observes that "as soon as the mission's going, for some reason you're not cold anymore. You've got so much going on in your mind. Your adrenaline is rollin'."

The plan, as Ethridge relates it, is to have Gecko 11 and 12 go in and pick up the worst of the 10th Mountain Division casualties, no more than three per helicopter. There is an Air Force TACP—a tactical air controller—with the ground forces, and they know he is setting up a landing zone for them. They also expect that the infantry medics would have triaged the casualties. Beyond that they don't know what to expect. "We just knew we're going in to get the worst guys, and get out. And it was still hot. They were fighting all throughout the day, and they fought well into the night."

They've been unable to directly monitor radio transmissions from the unit. Only later would it be reported that most of the unit's radios didn't work in the tough terrain, and commanders had to use runners to carry messages from one squad to another. The helicopter crews were getting their information from their own command, and from the Joint Search and Rescue Center.

At nine thirty P.M. local time, about a half hour after dark, the two helicopters take off from the FARP, flying west-southwest to the ridgeline above Ginger Valley. They fly past snowcapped mountains, trying to stay no more than two hundred feet above terrain, finding their way up through the valleys by following certain landmarks such as dry creeks and identifiable ridgelines. Ethridge says, "We kept going for quite a ways, but it started getting darker and darker and darker and darker. It wasn't really dark when we left; it was dark, but not that dark. But there was really no illum that night."

Unlike operations flown by Air Force Special Operations Command helicopters, where planning for a mission can take hours or even days, the CSAR crews, both fixed- and rotary-wing, don't hesitate to launch a mission and do the planning en route. Sometimes that's the only way to save lives. Lieutenant Colonel dePalo says it goes with their mission. "A lot of times we don't know everything about where a survivor is ahead of time, and we have to do that in the air. In this case, we got a lot of good information being fed in from the ground guys through the JSRC back to the helicopters saying, 'Okay, this is what you should see as you're coming in,' and they gave them certain terrain features, a direction to come in that the ground parties had recommended. And those sorts of issues were fed to us in the air, and the crewmembers have to process that, update navigation systems, and make sure everybody on board understands the mission. And then they go from there."

Scanning from the left side of Gecko 11, Durocher works hard to match what he's heard on their five primary radios with what he's seeing out the window, and to interpret it into useful information to feed the pilots. His main job is to monitor SATCOM transmissions, which is how they'll hear from Deliverance, and if there's anything that's really pertinent, he has to make sure the pilots hear it. With everything they have to do keep the helicopter in the air, it's easy to miss a critical message. "It's things like, 'Okay, they're attacking this town out to my ten o'clock. This is where they're going to be attacking in about another thirty minutes, so we gotta be out of this area.' There's a lot of things going through your mind as we're going up there, besides the objective of the mission. We have to get there first."

In the extreme darkness of the mountainous areas, it is easy to see the attacks taking place. Durocher recalls, "There are bright flashes of light, kind of like *Star Wars* lasers going back and forth. On NVGs, it's really a light show.

That's all it is. Of course that's the standoff portion of it, but once you get in—once you're *in* the light show—it's no longer as enjoyable."

Part of the concern is that there are so many different command and control chains that communication between them is rarely perfect; more often it's spotty, untimely, or nonexistent. It's very easy for ground forces to call for air support, and for the air support to be coordinated without concern for other assets that might be coming into or passing through the area. And then there's the possibility that even with perfect communications, mistakes can happen. The B-52 pilots who dropped the two-thousand-pound JDAM that fell two klicks short and landed on the special forces unit with Hamid Karzai did what they were told to do. One report says that the pilots were mistakenly given as a target the map coordinates where the SOF troops were, rather than where the intended target was located.

With thirteen years' experience doing what he's doing, Durocher knows things can go horribly wrong. "They were supposed to drop some pretty large-sized bombs, some JDAMs in the vicinity, and as much technology that goes into the JDAM, you still have that in the back of your mind that sometimes that technology just doesn't work out. You don't want to be on the receiving end of a JDAM gone wrong. So making sure we were staying clear of that JDAM going in was a priority."

When the big bomb goes in, the helicopters are still about four miles away. "It was a huge light show. It smoked! There was a big, bright, long-lasting flash that went quite a ways in the air. You could only kind of hear it. There's so much noise, with the radios and the helicopter, and trying to talk on the intercom, it's very faint, almost like someone politely knocking on the door."

With all the distractions from the basic job of flying the helicopter, the HH-60G crews need a system to make sure nothing gets by them. It helps that most of the time they're "hard-crewed." The same pilots, flight engineer, and gunner not only fly together, they live together in the same tent; it works that way whether they're at Jacobabad, Kandahar, or Karshi-Khanabad. The back-enders get to know the idiosyncrasies of the pilots to the point that they can tell whether it's the AC or the copilot on the controls just by the way the ship is being handled. Hard-crewing also allows them to use their own shorthand when they communicate with each other in the air, and leaves little room for tasks falling through the cracks. Everyone knows what they're supposed to do, where they're supposed to be looking, and when. Durocher says, "My job is to scan to the left; FE's scanning to the right and checking the systems, making sure we got good fuels, got enough fuel to do the job, enough power to do the job. And then the copilot is usually heads down, watching our map displays and following us on the map and trying to make sure we're following the right course. And then the pilot—actually whoever is on the controls—is pure on the controls, scanning forward and making sure that we stay safe. When we're on a flight lead, like this mission, there's a little bit more for them to do. But those guys are experienced; they've been doing this for quite a while."

Within twenty minutes after taking off from Texaco, the two helos have reached their insertion point and are ordered to hold, to wait. For a while they are just circling, burning holes in the sky. Finally they get the call to go in.

What they see as they fly into Ginger Valley are the mountains looming behind the landing zone, mountains that they know are filled with Al Qaeda soldiers who have no shortage of ammunition, and who have had hours to target the LZ. About a half mile from the objective, they begin to see heavy tracer fire. Through it all, they're trying to locate the flashing infrared strobe, visible only through NVGs, that would show them where the ground team they need to locate is positioned. Durocher is scanning when he realizes the strobe is going to be less than useful for finding their LZ. "When we get into this valley, there's probably fifty strobes going on. And then the enemy also had some strobes, so you couldn't tell who was good and who was bad, 'cause rounds are going both ways and strobes are everywhere." And if the enemy has IR strobes, they also have night-vision goggles that enable them to see the American infrared strobes, which are invisible to the naked eye, and don't even need to be worn outside the uniform. Just turning them on in a pocket reveals their location to anyone with NVGs.

This is the moment this crew realizes through firsthand experience that the Al Qaeda or Taliban forces they are fighting are not some ragtag bunch of guerrillas. Afghanistan is not Vietnam; the enemy is not the Viet Cong, forced to make hand grenades out of discarded Coke cans. The enemy here is well equipped, well commanded, and well trained. The only shortcoming that seemed to be regularly reported by American forces was that while the Al Qaeda fighters had plenty of ammunition, their marksmanship skills were often—but not always—lacking.

Seeing the strobes causes significant angst for Durocher, who sits behind the GAU-2 minigun that fires at a rate of up to six thousand rounds per minute. It's obvious that the American force is under fire, but from the helicopter, there is no surefire way of sorting out the good guys from the bad.

"That's when I elected not to fire," he says. "We weren't getting engaged, and I don't want a fratricide," which is the term du jour replacing *friendly fire.*

"That's my number one goal. I'm not going to kill anybody who doesn't need killing. There was nobody to shoot at, 'cause they're shooting at each other and pretty much leaving us alone."

The lead helicopter pilot, flying his ship slow and low, goes straight in, hops over a slope, and prepares to land behind it. The landing is sketchy, minimum power, certainly not enough to hold a steady hover that will let them really pick their spot.

Just as they are about to settle in, the pilots realize that they'll be pointing in a direction that offers no escape if they come under fire. As a result, they opt to make a U-turn before coming to a hover and beginning to settle. The second ship, with PJs Ethridge and Oswald on board, comes in and prepares to land, but at the last second the pilot realizes that the two birds would be nose-to-nose, a less than ideal situation considering the nearby threat.

Ethridge says his pilot tried to hover and turn around, but it wasn't working. "We're not getting too much power. We're just *bup-bup-bup-bup,* drooping the rotors. We're having a hard time hovering, and kind of sliding left. It felt like we were going to just fall out of the sky. Even though we weren't very high—about twenty feet—it still felt like we could, any minute, just kind of—whoa!

"Finally we turn around so we're facing out. As we're coming around, there's an explosion about fifty meters—or fifty feet, I'm not really sure—but it hits. I didn't see it, but I heard it. It's right in front of lead and kind of spooks him a little bit."

A couple of RPGs landed about fifty feet off the tail of Gecko 11. Durocher says, "You don't see it coming at you, but you see the big flash, the light-show effect again. You see a quick fire, and then you see the explosion. We didn't even know those guys were there, 'cause it came from a different spot than the normal fire. We'd seen the two groups that are firing at each other, and while we're on the approach, out of nowhere comes these two RPGs and some small machine-gun fire, and then the mortars that were up on the hill firing down on the guys trained their sights on us. They got off a couple rounds before the AC-130 Spectre gunship took out the mortar position."

Neither helicopter has actually landed at that point, and the incoming rounds cause the pilots to think twice about committing. Complicating the situation is that they can see infantrymen heading their way with casualties, and the blast from their rotors is knocking them to the ground. Ethridge is on the right side of the helicopter behind the flight engineer, with the door wide open. "The blast kind of spooks everyone. We weren't really sure what it was. We're just asking, 'Oooooh, what was that?' But everyone's still focused."

What happens next is something he was not prepared for. "It's like *Night of the Living Dead* in a way. It looked like an exercise, how we moulage patients—rip their clothes off, make 'em bloody and all that stuff for training. I just see three wounded soldiers and other soldiers who are not injured helping them up, up the hill up to me, as I get out. Then I look behind them, and I see red tracers just shooting up, shooting down. I can't see the guys who are firing 'cause it's so dark in the valley, but I can see tracers going like crazy up the mountain, coming down from the mountain. They're just constantly firing on each other, 'cause all the Al Qaeda and Taliban had the high ground. And they were just pinned down, shooting up. And Al Qaeda was just lobbing mortars and RPGs and whatever." Clearly it's a scene that has stuck with Ethridge, even though it was not the first time he'd been under fire.

Pararescuemen carry an assortment of weapons on missions, and are fully prepared to engage the enemy in order to defend their patients. In addition to the standard 9mm sidearm—which a lot of the guys dislike because it doesn't have the close-in knockdown power of the old .45—Ethridge has chosen the GAU-5, a version of the M-4 rifle, which is a cut-down, special-ops version of the M-16—other PJs carry the GAU that not only fires the small 5.56 round, but has the M-203 grenade launcher underslung beneath the barrel. Preference even extends to choice of ammo for the grenade launcher, with high-explosive, white phosphorous, and tear gas rounds all in the arsenal.

When the PJ hops off his helicopter to start dealing with the wounded, his rifle is slung at his side where he can grab it and, if necessary, begin shooting with the weapon at his hip. It's equipped with an infrared device mounted on top of the barrel that sends out a beam visible through his NVGs. All he has to do is point and shoot; the bullets hit what the beam hits. Unfortunately, the system doesn't work as well if the shooter has to fire uphill, which is the situation the entire infantry company finds itself in.

Ethridge is also wearing his LBE, the load bearing vest carrying ammo and supplies he may need to reach quickly; and under that he's wearing the standard body armor with chicken plates in front and back. And there are plenty of bullets coming down from the mountain. The Al Qaeda fighters have been shooting constantly since the troops were infiltrated more than twelve hours earlier, and they show no signs of running short on ammunition. As anticipated by Ethridge, and as predicted by the senior sergeants who supervised his selection as a PJ five years earlier, Ethridge acknowledged the existence of the enemy fire, but didn't let it bother him. "I just kind of put it out of my mind. I'm here to pick up these guys. Yeah, I see tracers; they're firing. But even if they were to start shooting at me, I can't see what I'd be shooting at." He really doesn't finish the thought. He knew that his job was to take care of patients. That's what he did.

Inside Gecko 11, gunner Durocher has watched his two PJs run about twenty meters to check with the medical guys on the ground. "It was still dark out," he recalls, and then emphasizes it. "As dark as the inside of a black cat." Realizing that there is no point in remaining at his position on the left side of the cabin when all the action is on the right, Durocher moves over in order to help load patients. "I'm pumped. I'm pumped hard. The only problem is everything's on the right-hand side now, 'cause of the way we came in there, and I can't shoot at anybody." It's a frustrating moment because all he can do is sit and watch red tracers impact the ground all around the helicopter. Eventually he helps load four patients, one who is critical in a Stokes litter, another in a standard field litter, and two who are ambulatory, one of whom is sitting behind his gunner position. When they are all packed in, both PJs are kneeling in the center of the cabin, facing outward and caring for their patients.

Looking at the casualties, especially the walking wounded, Durocher sees men who are in the same state of mind as those taken aboard Gecko 12. "There's dismay on their faces. They just can't believe it happened to them. I don't believe anybody goes into combat with any misconception that they're not going to get killed, but I don't think anybody ever thinks they're gonna get hit, y'know what I mean? It's like you think, 'Y'know what? I'm not coming out of this alive, but I'm okay with that.' Or they think they're not going to get hurt at all. Once you get hit, it's like, 'Holy shit, I can't believe that happened.'"

On the other helo, the PJs are able to determine that all the patients are stable, with only a couple in bad shape. They have picked up one soldier who has a core temperature of ninety-three degrees and is very hypothermic, with a couple of gunshot wounds to boot. Caleb says, "The other guys were going to live, regardless. We were just getting them out, getting them out of the way, getting them back to safety so a lucky BB doesn't kill them, or a mortar land on top of them."

What surprised Ethridge when he had a chance to think about it was not the way he reacted to the gunshot wounds—PJs do their practical medical training riding ambulances in America's inner cities, places like Prince

Georges County, Maryland; Washington, D.C.; Brooklyn, New York; New Orleans, St. Louis, and Virginia Beach. They've seen more gunshot wounds, more trauma on those tours than they're likely to see in a year riding HH-60Gs in Afghanistan. What Caleb reacted to was the way the soldiers looked after being under heavy fire for more than a dozen hours.

"The first guy I put in had a bullet wound to his left shoulder and to his right thigh. Looked pretty bad. He was lucky; it missed major vessels. But it was freezing cold, and you could tell he was hurting. He was done yelling. You could tell he was just too exhausted to yell or talk or anything. Just eyes glazed over. And they all . . . their skin looked just pale—I felt bad; they were really cold. They'd been out there for a while and nobody was able to get to them. They walked up to us all ragged, with no weapons, maybe an LBE, flak vest on still. But they were done fighting. They're out of it. And you can tell. The guy, blood down his lip, or he fell and there's blood running down his nose. He looked like he just got the crap smacked out of him, like he got jumped and then he got shot twice."

The casualties have been out in the cold so long, it's too much of a struggle to even talk. "They're not trying to say, 'Hey, thanks.' They're not saying, 'Get me outta here!' They're just relieved. I've been really cold before, like that, and all you can think about is getting warm again. You just concentrate on being warm. And you're not really thinking about anything else. You're just quiet."

Ethridge's team leader on this mission is Brian Oswald, an ex–Army Special Forces Green Beret who crossed over into pararescue. While Caleb is loading three casualties, Oswald has gotten out the other side, run around to the front of the helo, and is helping move more of the wounded. At one point several rounds slam into the ground near his feet, and he turns and fires up toward the mountain. Caleb says, "He wasn't hitting anything—probably—but he returned fire up there. And then he walked down and came over to me. I already had three patients in the helicopter, and I shouted, 'I think this is about it.' I had the one guy with the gunshot to the shoulder and thigh, and the other guys had shrapnel wounds and gunshot wounds to their feet, so they couldn't walk. And then Brian goes, 'I need a litter. We got a litter patient we need to carry.' "

Two things go through Ethridge's mind. First, with three patients, a gunner, a flight engineer and two PJs, they don't have room for a litter patient, especially not on the Stokes litter, which is the standard wire basket they use to hoist patients on a cable when necessary. Second, while the folding Israeli litter they carry takes up less space, when bullets are flying, he's not inclined to take time on the ground to put it together.

"It was about a hundred, hundred-fifty meters down into the valley, where a lot of the Army guys were sitting in groups. Brian and I are running from the helicopter in the open. It's down a slight slope to the valley, scree, like rocks and some shrubs. Really nothing out there. We get to the 10th Mountain guy Brian wanted the litter for, and the guy is riddled with shrapnel from the mortar. I guess it landed pretty close to him, up and down his legs, so he can't even move. Well, he can move his arms, but it's painful to move his legs. He'd been laying there ever since he got hit. His buddies are around him, hearing a boom here, a boom there, and he's screaming in pain."

Ethridge has followed Oswald down the hill to the wounded soldier, carrying his rifle with a round in the chamber, and the 40mm grenade launcher attached. When he gets there, Oswald is kneeling next to the patient and he reaches up to grab Ethridge's weapon, thinking it's the litter. "I had to yell in his ear that there's no time for a litter. We already got three guys in the back. So we'll just drag him. His spine isn't compromised.

"I'd always talked about that," says Ethridge. "If a guy just has a gunshot wound to the thigh, and if I'm gonna go out there in a hail of bullets, I'm just gonna pick him up, fire, and carry and run. All that medical stuff goes out the window. Under the circumstances, it's better to get him and let's go."

And that's what the two PJs did under fire. "I got to the patient's left shoulder, and we pretty much picked him up and carried him. Two Army guys got to the feet and were gonna carry his legs. He's yelling all the way. We're walking kind of weird. I slung my rifle, and we're walking up the hill, kind of tripping and falling, and drop him a couple times. Not hard—he's already real close to the ground and he hits, and he shouts, 'Ahhhh!' It's, like, 'All right, sorry,' but they're still shooting behind us."

The amazing thing is that they weren't hit, and neither was the helicopter. Ethridge says, "It seems like we got this force field around our helicopter. It was kind of amazing."

Both PJs have kept their flight helmets on and remained in radio contact with the helicopters throughout the ordeal, just in case they are called back to make a quick exit. Each time Ethridge comes back to the helicopter, he gets questioned by the flight engineer, usually about what's taking them so long. Helicopters tend to be bullet and RPG magnets; while running up and down hills may expose the PJs to enemy fire, sitting and waiting for them in a very large target is definitely unnerving.

After loading the mortar casualty, they pick up one more 10th Mountain soldier carrying an M-249 SAW—a light machine gun, officially a "squad automatic weapon." The man has a gunshot wound to the foot and can't walk. With him on board, they now have five patients and four crewmembers in the back end, making the rear of the Pave Hawk look a lot like a circus clown car just before entering the big top.

They have one patient behind the flight engineer on the right side of the helo toward the front of the compartment; another is squeezed in behind the gunner on the left side. Oswald crams himself in behind that patient, his butt against the door. Two more are seated on the floor, and the man with shrapnel wounds down his legs stands, his back toward the auxiliary fuel tanks. That leaves no room for Ethridge to get in, much less sit.

"That's when Brian and I talked to the aircrew, 'cause three more patients had moved up. We're saying, 'We can stay on the ground and help out with any other casualties,' but the aircrew was saying, 'Nope, tell 'em to wait.' There were Chinooks that were going to come in and pick them up.

"But I was sitting there with the door open, and one of the three, he looked like a young guy, nineteen or twenty, started climbing on the nets of the aux tanks. It's like he was thinking, 'Help is here, so I'm going home.' While I was talking to the pilot, he's crawling up into the helicopter. I grabbed him and pulled him down and out of the helicopter.

"He looked heartbroken when I told him he had to stay. 'No, you guys gotta stay here. We'll come back, or the Chinook's gonna land.' He gave me this look like I'd just signed his death warrant or something. He was done. He'd got shot up and was exhausted, and here's the rescue that's come to get him, and they're too full.

"I ended up getting in. I had to move the legs of the guys with the shrapnel wounds just to get my feet in, and then I closed the door right behind me. My butt's against the door. I'm standing straight up, and I got all this gear on. And all I can think of is getting shot in the ass on the way out. It was a forty-minute flight back to Bagram, and anytime I moved my feet or anything, the guy with the shrapnel is moaning.

"I couldn't move; neither could Brian. We were packed in there like sardines in a can. And I just checked their level of consciousness; it was pretty much all I could do. I knew they were going to make it. I just wanted to make sure if anyone crashes, I can push the guys who aren't dying out of the way and start working on him. But I checked—they only wanted to go to sleep; they were so exhausted."

The crews of both helicopters know that lifting off from the LZ is going to be its own little adventure. The lead ship was ready to go while Ethridge was still figuring out how to take his ass with him on the return flight, so rather than wait, Ed Lengel opts to get airborne and out of range of a potentially lucky RPG. Durocher remembers that "the takeoff is sketchy. We get about a five-foot hover, a ground-effect hover, and then just run forward, flying down this ridgeline and barely take off outta there. We were really close on power.

"You feel the helicopter take off, and you can feel a good, steady five-foot hover, four-foot—or whatever you've got. And then it's like the Little Engine That Could from that point on. You ease it forward and ease it forward, and you'll drop down a little bit 'cause you're losing that ground effect. And the faster and faster you get, the more and more lift you provide. As soon as you feel the grab in your butt, it's like, 'Okay, we're gonna actually take off,' and you know you're okay.

"We cleared a couple big-sized rocks, got on out of there. And then pulled up into an overhead to provide firepower for the guys on the ground. But the AC-130 gunship was handling that pretty well, and I didn't think my minigun would help out very much."

Gecko 11 goes up about seven hundred feet above the LZ, and then begins flying a circle.

Gecko 12's pilots also planned to try to get a rolling start to give the rotors a chance to do their job. Ethridge recalls, "You could hear the engines just whining, tweaking every bit of energy possible to get out of there. The HH-60Gs are already way overgrossed; it's scary. And then we're at eighty-five hundred feet, picking up five people, which is not really what we're designed to do. We're always trying to pick up one pilot or two pilots who eject. And the whole time in Afghanistan we're picking up SOF personnel and 10th Mountain soldiers. There weren't any pilots ejecting."

In addition to coping with excess weight and as a result not being nearly as nimble as they can be at sea level, they have to worry about enemy fire on liftoff. It was confirmed by one of the Australian SAS after the helos had already gotten to Bagram that a couple of RPGs had been fired at them, including one while they were still in the LZ.

All the way back to Bagram, Ethridge and Oswald continue checking everyone's consciousness level, "just waking them up to ask, 'You all right, you good?' and hearing 'Yeah, I'm okay,'" and other unprintable responses reflecting their annoyance at being awakened.

On the way back, the PJs pass medical information to the pilots, who radio it to the FST team at Bagram. The big concern on the ground is whether they're coming in with anyone who is critical and needs immediate surgery. In this case, the report is that two of the patients have serious but not life-threatening injuries.

As a result of discussions that took place in the weeks following the death of the Australian SAS soldier whose vehicle had hit a mine, the PJs were able to carry whole blood—O-negative and O-positive—on their missions, and they have done so on this one. Fortunately it isn't needed, because there is no room to administer it. Ethridge says, "The helicopter's not the greatest place to do treatment. We'd rather sit down on the ground where no one's shooting at us, let the helicopter go away, and then we can treat. Because then you can hear and use all your senses and treat properly. The helicopter yanking and banking, flying low, you can't hear anything and it's hard to see anything."

What if one of their patients had started to crash?

"We'd make room, tell the helicopter to just go faster; do what we can if the guy starts going into cardiac arrest from trauma."

The flight to Bagram is, fortunately, uneventful. Offloading the patients is not difficult. A number of Special Forces types come out to help, along with several of the pararescuemen assigned to special-tactics units. The PJs aboard the other helicopter have put the hypothermia patient in their Stokes litter, and while they are waiting for someone to bring the litter back out to the helicopters, Ethridge attempts to figure out whether his back will ever be the same again. He recalls, "I had body armor, vest—I had about fifty pounds on up there, just no ruck and no combat load. I had a lot of weight on top. And my back was—oooh!—I could barely move. Every time I'd start to put my chest forward, I could feel it. My back was shot."

He doesn't get much time to work the kinks out; they get orders by radio to refuel at Bagram and head directly back to where they started the mission, Texaco FARP. Moments after getting the order, a PJ comes racing back out to the helicopter on one of the quad all-terrain vehicles that's part of their basic equipment. It turns out it is Jason Cunningham, who is still on loan to a special-tactics squadron following the Ditka 03 mission. Cunningham drops off the Stokes litter with the PJs in the other helo, waves at Caleb and Brian, and peels away on the tarmac, holding the quad on two wheels as he drives by.

On the flight back to Texaco, still wearing a bloodstained uniform in a bloody helicopter, Ethridge has time to reflect on what he's just been through. "My back was hurting; I was tired. We flew a long time and I was just exhausted. I was thinking, 'Dang, I can't imagine doing this over and over again like the guys in Vietnam did.' I started getting my first taste of how it would be if it were just all-out war. I knew what was going on was big. I knew it'd been a long time since something like that had happened. But I was just doing my job.

"I remembered when I first came into the Air Force, and an older guy at Lackland said to me, 'Y'know, PJs have a cool job and do a lot of stuff. But when it comes to combat, they're like small-town cops who never get to pull out their pistol and use it. Like Mayberry cops.' He was saying that PJs help out civilians and do this and that, but they don't ever get to shoot gangbangers or ever actually do anything. When I was at Nellis, and had all those deployments to the northern and southern no-fly zones in Turkey and Kuwait, I felt, 'Shoot, I'm just a Mayberry cop. I've got all these weapons, but . . . ' And that's kind of the way it was for the PJs in the eighties, too. They didn't see any real action— the raid on Panama and that was pretty much it."

Now, at last, the PJs were doing more than civilian rescues at sea and on mountains in Alaska. They were in heavy combat, and for the most part taking it in stride. Pushed a bit, Caleb Ethridge reflects on their training and their emotional makeup. "They're weeding you out during the indoc course and se-lecting you to make sure that when you're out there and things are going on . . ." He pauses to think for a second. "Maybe it's like a dumb pill they give. Maybe they figure out you're not too bright. That's the reason that PJs do it, too. Y'know, jump out of planes, all this stuff, go into a firefight and just ig-nore what's going on. Duh-duh-duh. They help the guy, and they don't look and go, 'Dude, this is pretty jacked up.' They need guys that have a screw loose, y'know? Guys who're willing to go into this high-sea ocean and pick up some-one they don't even know."

More than one CSAR pilot didn't hesitate to say that PJs are crazy, which, in all fairness, brings to mind the old saw about the pot calling the kettle black. Certainly Ethridge doesn't think they're nuts. "I don't know. A lot of us are itching to do stuff and help people, and we're always hanging around, waiting. I don't feel crazy. None of the guys do. We just do things that other people think are crazy." And they do them for roughly three thousand dollars a month, about the same as paramedics in most large American cities earn.

Crazy or not, the men of the 10th Mountain Division, based at Fort Drum, New York, were thankful the PJs and Air Force CSAR crews were around. The battle on that hill between Al Qaeda forces and the company of eighty-six men from Charlie Company, 1st Battalion, 87th Infantry, raged for eighteen hours. They took twenty-eight casualties—a third of the force—before helicopters were sent in at midnight to withdraw the Americans and the Aussie special forces.

The Aussie SAS troops were especially candid in their comments about the failure of the American commanders in Bagram to properly plan and support the mission. Interviewed by the Queensland, Australia, *Courier Mail*, Warrant Officer P and SAS Signaler Jock W said they believe that if they had not been evacuated at midnight, the entire force would have been wiped out the next day. There was no question in their minds that without the support of the AC-130 Spectre gunships, they would never have survived to be evacuated. The obvious problem is that the Spectres fly only at night, and the ground force endured constant enemy fire throughout the day, until the sun set and it was safe for the Americans to send in the low-flying gunships.

While the Aussies claim that heavy casualties were inflicted on the enemy in this opening battle of Anaconda, they were clearly annoyed that "coalition intelligence miscalculated badly in selecting a landing zone on a flat, open plateau, within range of the enemy who controlled the high ground." They also insist there were problems relying on American air power before the insertion of the 10th Mountain Division company. In the *Courier Mail* interview with the SAS troops, the claim was made that during the initial phase of Operation Anaconda, American aircraft "dropped just ten percent of the bombs allocated to reduce enemy positions prior to the company assault, whilst those bombs that were dropped seemingly had little effect."

Finally, being unaffected by the U.S. SOCOM's restrictions on discussing Operation Anaconda with the media, the Aussies expressed considerable annoyance that "just a few hours before the company was inserted they were told that enemy numbers might be higher than expected, with estimated enemy strength jumping from one hundred to five hundred, and even then they turned out to be more. Indeed some estimates assert that as many as one thousand Al Qaeda and Taliban fighters dug in to fight in the Shah-e-Kot."

Remarkably—or perhaps not so, considering that the U.S. military and its civilian leadership has a tradition that dates back to Vietnam of trying to convince outsiders that defeat is really victory by another name—Army Lt. Col. David Gray, chief of operations for all coalition forces participating in Operation Anaconda, told the Associated Press that this aspect of the battle was an intelligence coup. "While it was very scary and fierce for the men, it helped us back here realize where the enemy was concentrated. . . . We found the enemy the first day."

Perhaps it was out of respect to the men who were in it, their families back home, and the Air Force CSAR crews who risked their lives to bring out the casualties that Gray didn't call it "recon by casualty." That kind of extrapolation of the combat doctrine of "reconnaissance by fire"—meaning they send in infantrymen to blast the hell out of an area to see if anyone shoots back—might have been too straightforward.

Perhaps, too, if Lieutenant Colonel Gray had any combat experience at all, he would have had the fortitude to call a screwup a screwup, as the battle-hardened Aussies had no difficulty doing. But Gray's Army résumé indicates that the closest he's come to combat was serving as a brigade S3 (operations officer) with the 25th Infantry Division at Schofield Barracks, Hawaii, a location where there's been no intense enemy contact since December 7, 1941. He has, however, earned a Ph.D. from Ohio State University and served as an assistant professor in the Department of History at the U.S. Military Academy at West Point.

Gray's comment to the press begs several questions: Did the command at Bagram have enough quality intelligence to launch Anaconda? What was the command doing with the intelligence reports they'd received from coalition observation posts? Aussie SAS with American Air Force combat controllers Jim Hotaling, Jessie Fleener, and other CCTs were positioned to observe enemy troop movements in the valley, and special-operations teams with Navy SEALs who had been sent into the Shah-e-Kot valley well before Anaconda began were also gathering intelligence. For Lieutenant Colonel Gray to say that putting a company of the 10th Mountain Division on the low ground directly below enemy guns was a legitimate way to find out where the enemy was hiding reveals a callous disregard for the lives of American fighting forces. What he should have said is, "Sorry, we fucked up."

To those outside the military it provides an inkling that even with the many aerial surveillance tools, such as the unmanned Predator, that were supposed to help revolutionize the way war is fought, the generals still needed to rely on ground troops going nose-to-nose with the enemy to really find out what was going on. And this battle was just the opening chapter in Operation Anaconda.

# KIA
## MARCH 4, 2002

When he arrived at Bagram before the Ditka 03 mission, SrA Jason Cunningham was suffering the normal anxieties of a young man about to face the ultimate test of his manhood. But the twenty-six-year-old PJ's apprehension was less about how he'd perform under fire than whether his training in trauma care had prepared him well enough to do the job when the surgeons could be hours away and a soldier's life might be in his hands and his alone. It wasn't long after he moved into the spartan accommodations the PJs had commandeered in the base of the airfield tower that he wandered down the hall and began hanging out with the FST team.

The surgeon in charge was Maj. Brian Burlingame, and he likened Jason to the kid brother who hangs around making a pest of himself when your friends are over. "He just wanted to hang around all the time, like any little brother. He just won't leave. Eventually your friends start liking him, and he becomes part of the group. That's the way he was. He hung around and became part of the group."

The doctor got to know Jason very well, on both a personal and professional level. "His motives were absolutely pure, and his desire to take care of wounded guys was pure. It wasn't because he wanted to be a guy with a bunch of medals on his chest or have others say great things about him for a long

Predator unmanned aerial vehicle armed with a Hellfire missile (*U.S. Air Force photo*)

time. He just wanted to do that job, 'cause he felt strongly about it. I can't say that about every single doctor I meet, every single nurse I meet, every single PJ I meet. In that regard, I don't want to say 'unique,' but certainly a cut above in terms of his motivation and his desires and his purity. The smartest PJ I've ever seen? No. The most technically proficient one? No. But I found him to be the most ready to do whatever it takes to take care of somebody. By 'whatever it takes,' I mean, both putting himself in danger and then, before getting to that point, finding out his knowledge deficits and correcting them. And then finding where he had ability to improve and what was out there new and high-speed that he could put in his aid bag."

The fact that Cunningham suddenly found himself part of a special-tactics team assigned to the Special Operations Command QRF at Bagram was unusual. Coming out of the PJ school, he was assigned to the 38th Rescue Squadron at Moody AFB, Georgia. That's an Air Combat Command unit in the Big Blue Air Force. Blue has always been concerned about having its own CSAR capability to go in and snatch downed fighter pilots from the enemy's grasp. It's a mission that certainly proved itself in Vietnam.

But when the Special Operations Command was created in 1987 to boost the morale and effectiveness of U.S. special forces, the Air Force began funneling more support to AFSOC, the service's own Air Force Special Operations Command, creating special-tactics teams with their own aircraft and mission.

Some in the Air Force will say, off the record, that elements of AFSOC have "gone native," meaning they've begun thinking of themselves as no longer part of the Big Blue Air Force, but their own branch of service. They think their mission is more important, more au courant, more difficult, and, of course, more secret than Big Blue's. One example: AFSOC crews flying MC-130 aircraft and helicopters over Afghanistan are told not to provide media interviewers with their full names, ostensibly because the enemy might track down their families, but aircrews flying 130s and helos in ACC CSAR units over precisely the same territory are allowed to fully identify themselves.

The AFSOC public affairs officer, Maj. Karen Finn, actually said that ACC and Air National Guard PJs could not possibly qualify to do the same missions to which AFSOC pararescuemen are assigned. That, of course, begs the question, what was Jason Cunningham doing with the QRF at Bagram? The answer is quite simple. Even though AFSOC seems to collectively disassociate itself from the regular Air Force, it still needs Blue to create PJs and CCTs; it doesn't have its own pipeline. And because Blue won't lower its standards, and only recently got an influx of cash to begin advertising for pararescue recruits, it hasn't been able to mint PJs fast enough to meet the demand. So in the early months of Operation Enduring Freedom, AFSOC discovered that it was rapidly burning out its own PJs, and issued a call for help. They brought in Reservists from the 123rd Special Tactics Squadron at Louisville, which was where Keary Miller and Pat Malone came from. They also borrowed PJs from ACC units, among them the 38th Rescue Squadron, which was how Cunningham found himself in Bagram hanging out in the FST operating room, learning the latest techniques that he could adapt to delivering trauma care to the far-forward injured soldier.

Dr. Burlingame says, "Some guys ask for knowledge because they want you to see how smart they are. Some guys ask for knowledge because they want to see if *you're* a smart guy, because they have to depend on you. So it's like a test. Jason asked about knowledge for the sake of having it and for the sake of using it to improve his ability to take care of soldiers."

Working out of Bagram, Jason Cunningham, his PJ teammate Keary Miller, and combat controller Gabe Brown were now a special-tactics team "embedded" CSAR, riding Army Chinooks belonging to the 160th SOAR(A) Night Stalkers. But Cunningham, Miller, and Brown were Air Force—and not the Air Force guys who habitually trained with and had gotten to know the Rangers. The Rangers had mission rehearsals with *their* PJs and CCTs on how to offload a Chinook *their* way, how to conduct CSAR *their* way. They knew each other's faces and names. They trusted *their* Air Force guys. But not the Air Force.

No one in combat trusts an institution. Not even when ordered to. American fighting units in Vietnam were most often less than thrilled to find themselves on joint operations with their South Vietnamese counterparts. And the distrust isn't necessarily of *another* country's forces. Consider that when the Army's 101st Airborne Division arrived in Afghanistan, they flew a platoon of troopers to Khowst in order to take control of the airfield. When the platoon landed, one of their Chinooks rolled in the LZ and several people were hurt. As soon as that happened, an order came down through the task force controlling the Army Rangers that none of their soldiers was to set foot on 101st aircraft, no matter what. They didn't trust the 101st pilots to do the job.

The problem also exists at the so-called "coalition forces" level as well. Canadian ground forces are not likely to be thrilled to hear that close air support will be coming from U.S. Air Force jets, not after one of their units was mistaken for enemy troops firing on American jets, and bombed, resulting in the loss of four lives. In the opening battles of Operation Anaconda, the tough Australian SAS soldiers who were married up with U.S. units precisely because they knew how to fight and survive in that kind of terrain and weather were hardly enamored of U.S. Army planners. These were the same Army planners who put them on the ground at an Al Qaeda ambush point precisely where Russian units were obliterated by mujahideen fighters a little over a decade earlier.

What it comes down to is that while the paperwork and the press releases may have called Anaconda a "joint" operation, that's a top-down description, not bottom-up. In combat, bottom-up is all that counts.

It's one thing for Special Operations Command to tout the joint nature of its operations; it's another to have the guys actually doing the missions believe in it. In the case of Operation Enduring Freedom, it seems clear that SOCOM, CENTCOM, and the Department of Defense have done a much better job of selling the concept externally than internally. Even in Bagram, the headquarters of the commander of *regular* Army units on the ground, Maj. Gen. Franklin L. "Buster" Hagenbeck, who was responsible for planning Operation Anaconda, wasn't colocated with the headquarters of Air Force Brig. Gen. Gregory Trebon, who was commander of special-ops troops including the Army Ranger units, the Navy SEAL reconnaissance teams, and the observation posts manned by Australian coalition forces and American combat controllers. A liaison officer who reported to Trebon sat near Hagenbeck. Since Trebon has refused requests for interviews, there's no way of knowing whether he deigned to have a representative of the Army general in his command post.

What this separation of powers meant is that Trebon didn't hear Army communications from the battle, and Hagenbeck didn't hear special operators, and he certainly didn't hear radio communication from the Chinook helicopters that were being targeted by Al Qaeda.

The lack of interservice or even intraservice trust influenced and undermined the decisions made about CSAR as well, with the attitude of some units being, "Those are our own guys; we'll go in and get them out." One source, speaking not-for-attribution a year after Anaconda, says, "Command and control of CSAR was messed up from the get-go, and I don't know if it's fixed yet." Even a command like the Joint Search and Rescue Center at Prince Sultan Air Base, Saudi Arabia, may be "joint" down to a certain level, but then things fall apart, because generally units just don't want to get involved with—read "trust"—other units.

Consider the Air Combat Command CSAR units flying HC-130s out of Jacobabad and K-2, and HH-60G Pave Hawk helicopters out of K-2 and Kandahar. These units take orders from the JSRC, who tells them when to launch, where to go, and often tries to tell them what they can do when they get there. But if the unit whose troops need rescuing doesn't bring the JSRC into the loop, the best-trained Combat Search and Rescue people in the American military will just burn holes in the sky or camp at a FARP. Given the parallel systems of command and control, it's very easy for a ground unit *not* to talk to an Air Force rescue unit, even when the ground unit has an Air Force TACP or CCT with it. That's because those guys aren't talking to rescue. They're either talking to the people overhead in AWACS or J-STAR aircraft who control air support assets already in the air, or directly to the pilots flying the planes that will deliver bombs and bullets to keep bad guys at bay.

On March 3, 2002, the second day of Operation Anaconda, General Hagenbeck regrouped and repositioned his forces, most often on higher ground, to more effectively continue the fight with Al Qaeda who were presumed not to have fled the area. While the infantry was being moved about, the bombing campaign was accelerated, including the first-time use of a two-thousand-pound thermobaric bomb that was designed to pulverize the interior of caves and tunnels that were too deep for the occupants to be affected by conventional bombs. (While acknowledging the use of the controversial new munition, which some say violates international warfare treaties, the American command did not indicate whether the bomb had hit its target.)

That night, another pair of 66th Rescue Squadron Pave Hawk helicopters flying out of Texaco FARP made a spectacular pickup of three injured American soldiers, coming in under fire from mortars and machine guns. The mission would earn the flight lead, Lieutenant Thomas Cahill, a Silver Star, and his crewmembers the Distinguished Flying Cross. The PJs on that mission were T.Sgt. Patrick Harding and SrA Michael Flores flying with Cahill, and S.Sgts. Caleb Ethridge and Bob Roberts flying with Capt. Jeremy Turner.

Early on the morning of Monday, March 4, a Chinook carrying a SEAL recon team was ordered to put the special-forces unit onto Takur Ghar mountain. The plan was to do the infiltration under cover of darkness, with enough time to allow them to climb to the summit unobserved. In Bagram, General Hagenbeck explained that "it was a dominating piece of terrain, and if we had observation up there, it gave us a three-hundred-and-sixty-degree look across several trails as well as Shah-e-Kot."

Is it conceivable that no one believed that the well-equipped Al Qaeda forces had the same thought about that "dominating piece of terrain"—only sooner? Did no one on the general staff study the history of the valley before committing American forces? Did the general really believe that bull and bluster could beat the enemy? This was an enemy that had already proved itself not to be your garden-variety towelheads, to use the vernacular that got tossed around after 9/11 that made it easier to demonize them, as had nasty nicknames like gooks, slopes, dinks, zipperheads, japs, nips, and krauts in earlier conflicts.

Hadn't American commanders already learned at the battle of Tora Bora that they could pulverize enemy strongholds with a Heinz-57 variety of bombs, and somehow the enemy was prepared for the worst, and could survive it? It's not as though Afghan fighters hadn't had a couple of centuries to prepare the caves and shelters, updating them in recent years with concrete reinforcements. Is it not a clue to the resolve of a foe when you learn he is willing to haul tons of concrete up those mountainsides, not to mention thousands upon thousands of rounds of ammunition for rifles and heavy machine guns, plus RPGs, hand grenades, and other weapons of modern warfare? Was there not a lesson to be learned from the tunnels of Cu Chi in another war?

The *Los Angeles Times* interviewed the former CIA station chief in Pakistan, Milt Bearden, who said that the entire area where Anaconda played out was always the last redoubt for the local warlords. "When all else failed, guys would fall back there." He added, "The Soviets took more casualties in this valley than in any setting since World War Two. It really is the home-field advantage drawn out to some exponential degree. There's not a square kilometer that hasn't been used for an ambush of somebody."

Maybe General Hagenbeck didn't read that CIA analysis. Maybe he thought he knew the territory. Maybe he even knew something that Alexander the Great didn't know in 327 B.C. Or the British in the mid-1800s. Or the Soviet Union in 1987, when they lost 250 men in a single day of fighting against mujahideen, equipped, coincidentally by the CIA. If he did, it wasn't passed along to his ground commander, Col. Frank Wiercinski, who told his forces they had two missions in Anaconda: "To defeat an enemy. And to never leave a fallen comrade."

Right or wrong, it's that last mantra that has sewn the seeds of tragedy and pain for families of warriors who went back to get their fallen comrades in conflicts ranging from world wars to street-corner battles. Some pararescuemen say they couldn't do their job without knowing that what happened in Somalia wouldn't happen to them. They're referring to the scenes of a dead

American pilot being dragged through the streets of Mogadishu. Others acknowledge their obligation, yet state that they wouldn't want their comrades to die merely to retrieve their body. It's a sensitive issue to broach with people whose full-time job is combat search and rescue. But it's apparent when the subject is raised that many of them have pondered it quietly, alone.

About the same time that the Chinook carrying the SEAL team was moving toward Takur Ghar, the PJs and aircrew from the 66th were in the middle of a crew swap. Caleb Ethridge had spent about twelve hours at Kandahar, trying to get the kinks in his back worked out, and then trying to get some sleep. He was more successful with his back, which got tended to by an orthopedic surgeon in the unit, than he was getting some rest. Aircrews sleep by day and work by night, and in theory, when they're in "crew rest," they're not supposed to be disturbed. That theory doesn't restrict the hundreds of others in the area whose job it is to build the infrastructure that would make the place livable. So between hammering, drilling, and sawing, Ethridge didn't get as much sleep as he wanted, but he claimed to be rested and ready to fly.

At four in the morning, a pair of HH-60Gs left Kandahar and headed in the direction of Texaco FARP. More than an hour later, they were near the city of Gardez, when they were ordered to circle for a while, rather than proceed to Texaco and land. What they didn't know at the time was that disaster had struck the SEAL mission.

The original plan had been to insert the SEAL team at night at a so-called "offset" location, then let them move up to the top of the mountain and establish a concealed observation post before the sun came up. Unfortunately, the helicopters assigned to the mission had maintenance problems, and a scheduled B-52 bomb drop forced them to delay even longer. They reached a decision point where the mission either had to be aborted completely, or they had to find a new LZ much closer to their objective. The choice the SEALs made was to proceed with a landing right on top of the ridge, assuring they could get the observation post in place before the sun came up.

While not the biggest helicopter flown by the American forces, the MH-47E Chinook, with its fifty-two-foot-long body under tandem three-bladed rotors, each just under thirty feet long, is, like most helicopter models, especially vulnerable to ground fire during power-limited landings and takeoffs at high altitude. One well-placed RPG, long established as the antiaircraft weapon of choice for third-world fighters like Al Qaeda, can knock a Chinook out of the air.

The Army's tactic for offsetting that vulnerability is to have the side-door gunners sweep areas adjacent to the landing zone with heavy fire as the aircraft comes in. That's hardly an ideal solution to the problem, but it's better than nothing. However, when the helicopter is on a special-ops mission to clandestinely insert an observation team, announcing their arrival with even more noise than that created by the engines is not part of the plan. So they're left armed with nothing more than intelligence reports that should contain reliable information about the threat level where they're going.

Razor 3, the Chinook carrying the seven-man SEAL team plus an Air Force CCT, left Gardez close to dawn, accompanied by a second aircraft, Razor 4, that had a different mission down the valley. The two ships were to accomplish their tasks, then join up and fly back to base. It had been expected that at some point prior to the infiltration mission, an AC-130 Spectre gunship would survey the area to make certain it was clear. As the pilot of Razor 3 later said, "With a recon mission like this, you don't want to land where the enemy is."

One observation that's been made by the troops who were on the ground during Anaconda is that the terrain is so difficult, and the choices therefore so limited, that it's relatively easy to pick out the few spots that can serve as a landing zone for helicopters. The mujahideen did it when they were fighting the Soviets, often putting mines in the landing zone and setting ambush positions around them.

When Razor 3 came in to the small saddle at the top of Takur Ghar, the SEAL team prepared to exit off the rear ramp. At the head of the line was Navy Petty Officer 1st Class Neil C. Roberts. As the helo settled in, the crew spotted a heavy machine gun about fifty yards to the front, but it appeared to be unmanned. In Afghanistan, where mountain ridges are littered with abandoned weaponry, the presence of the gun caused only marginal concern.

Just as the SEALs were about to pour off the ramp, machine-gun fire erupted from several directions, followed by an RPG that came in from the left, penetrated the cargo area, and exploded. According to a version of the story reported in the *Washington Post*, which was allowed exclusive access to the participants in Operation Anaconda even after CENTCOM issued a ban on media interviews, the right rear crew chief shouted over the intercom, "We're taking fire! Go! Go! Go!" The pilot applied full throttle, but the RPG had short-circuited the aircraft's electrical power and damaged its hydraulic system at the same time that the gunfire had punctured oil lines and wires.

The big Chinook wobbled and jerked as it lifted off, and as it did, Roberts went flying off the back ramp.

One of the other crew chiefs tried to grab him, but lost his balance on the oil-slickened ramp and slipped over the edge, dangling by his safety harness and tether. Fortunately the other crew chief was able to haul him back onto the ramp. But Roberts wasn't on a tether, and he fell the ten or twelve feet to the snow-covered ground below.

According to the report in the *Post*, "The pilot, thinking an engine was out, sent the chopper into a dive, hoping to gain airspeed. Quickly realizing both engines were working, he leveled the chopper and tried to climb.

" 'The thing was shaking like an out-of-balance washing machine,' he recalled. 'There were holes in the rotor blades, and the hydraulics were doing some funny things.' "

Told that Roberts had fallen out, the pilot tried to turn back. But with no hydraulic fluid, the controls locked up. One of the crew chiefs grabbed the hand pump and started pumping quarts of hydraulic fluid back into the system. His action brought the controls back, allowing the pilot to level out. But with his aircraft severely damaged, there was no way they could go back and try to pick up the fallen SEAL. Razor 3 limped out of the area, desperately looking for a safe place to land in the valley below. With its radio out, they couldn't contact Razor 4, which was already waiting at the rendezvous point. Razor 3 finally landed at the north end of the valley, about four miles from the ridge top. Within minutes they got word that Razor 4 was on the way to pick them up. When it arrived more than half an hour later, the two teams discussed returning to the mountaintop to rescue Roberts, but with both aircrews on board, the ship would be too heavy to reach the ridge. Leaving the extra aircrew on the ground wasn't an option; they were already receiving reports of enemy forces half a mile away heading toward them. The only viable option was to return to Gardez. There they dropped off the excess personnel and, with the original SEAL team and Air Force T.Sgt. John A. Chapman, their combat controller, on board, they headed back to the ridge top to find their teammate.

A short distance away, burning holes in the sky near Gardez, the pair of CSAR birds continued to circle. It was apparent from their radio contacts with Deliverance, the JSRC, that something had happened, but no one had yet told them what, and they certainly hadn't been put on alert to go in to try to find Roberts. Ethridge says that the way the communications system is set up, they never get their information directly from a primary source. "Because we worked with JSRC out in Saudi Arabia, we get this big loop. We're not talking directly to the commanders in Bagram. So there's a lull in the time it takes information to get to us. So we're circling, circling, trying to figure out what the hell's going on. It turns out we were only about three miles away from all that stuff happening."

They were so out of the loop that while the HH-60Gs were circling, they watched a pair of Chinooks—one of them obviously shot up and crippled— flying past them and land. Caleb Ethridge says, "They flew right by us, but we didn't have their freqs; we couldn't talk to them." The CSAR crews were able to watch the recon team and crew board Razor 4, and take off in the direction of Gardez.

Finally, about an hour before sunrise, both HH-60G Pave Hawks headed back to Texaco to gas up. It was already apparent that even though they were close to the action, the command wasn't going to let them in. "They just kept saying 'Stand by, stand by.' They don't really know, either, what's going on.

"I just remember being so tired, still tired. It's freezing in the back—the windows have to be open. So we're just cold, and wanting to sleep. You're looking out, and you're trying to scan and look for any gunfire or shooting at you, but can't. I was wondering if I'm feeling this tired, how're the pilots feeling? They're flying this thing."

Once at the FARP, all they could do was sit, wait, and pick up reports from one of the combat controllers who was monitoring what was going on. Later, they traded a case of MREs to the Army troops assigned to guard the perimeter for temporary use of a portable radio that would let them listen in to the action being reported on the SATCOM frequency.

About ninety minutes later, three Task Force 11 Chinooks landed, with about twenty-five special-ops types aboard each one. It was a joint operation mixing supersecret Air Force 24th STS operators, including PJs, with SEALs and other SOF teams. PJ Ethridge recalls that they immediately attempted to take charge, saying, "Everybody works for us!" That would have included the Apache gunships, the CSAR birds, and anyone else who might be able to offer some help.

Meantime, back at command headquarters at Bagram, a desperate effort was going on to put surveillance aircraft over Takur Ghar in an attempt to see what might have happened to Roberts. First on the scene was an AC-130 gunship that reported seeing what the crew believed to be the SEAL surrounded by four to six enemy fighters. The assumption at the time was that he had activated his infrared strobe shortly after surviving the fall from the helicopter, because the Spectre crew could see it though their NVGs. Within minutes, however, a Predator drone arrived and beamed a video picture back to Bagram—and to CENTCOM headquarters in Tampa—and the strobe was no longer visible.

Whether the Predator ever showed Roberts on the ground is questionable. The imagery was fuzzy and subject to interpretation. What they would learn forensically after his mutilated body was recovered was that he'd been shot at close range after attempting to engage the enemy with his SAW.

What is not known, either because the records of radio transmissions don't exist or they've been sealed, is how much information about Roberts's condition—if any at all—was relayed to Razor 4 as it flew back to the area where he'd been lost. And because they didn't know if he was alive and hiding in the area, the gunners did not lay down suppressing fire for fear of hitting him as the big helicopter came in to land.

The plan was to put the helo down just long enough to let the SEAL team off, then retreat from the area. Al Qaeda had other ideas. About forty feet above the ground, according to the *Post*, the pilot saw the flash of a machine-gun muzzle off the nose of the aircraft. "I thought, 'Oh, this is going to hurt.' And then the second thought was, 'How do I get myself into this?' But we had to go. We had to put these guys in."

Gunfire began hitting the aircraft, "pinging and popping through" in the words of one crew chief. In Bagram, Hagenbeck says he could watch Razor 4 land and the SEALs and Chapman rush off toward the enemy positions. He had little view of the enemy fighters on the television screen displaying live video from the orbiting Predator. They were apparently hidden under trees, dug into trenches, and obscured by shadows. Once again, low tech trumps high tech.

According to the Special Operations Command review of the action, Chapman saw two enemy fighters in a fortified position under a tree. He and a nearby SEAL opened fire. Then the Americans began taking fire from another bunker position about twenty yards away. That's when a burst of gunfire hit Chapman, killing him.

As the firefight continued, two of the SEALs were wounded by enemy gunfire and grenades, forcing a decision to disengage, and as they moved off the mountain peak, one of the SEALs contacted the orbiting AC-130 gunship and requested covering fire.

In Bagram, the QRF was awakened shortly after word got back that

Roberts had fallen off the helicopter. The commander of the Rangers jocking up for what would be his troops' first combat of the war was Capt. Nathan Self, a twenty-five-year-old West Point grad, husband, and father of a five-month-old baby. His team was part of the 1st Ranger Battalion, 75th Ranger Regiment, out of Hunter Army Airfield near Savannah, Georgia. Self had a reputation for training his men hard and long, wanting them to be ready for any mission they might get assigned. Now he and the unit's noncoms knew that all that training was about to pay off.

Their initial orders were to board a pair of MH-47E Chinooks that were sitting cold on the airfield, but even as they were racing from their tents to the tarmac, the orders were switched. Two other Chinooks had recently landed and were still spooled up. By switching to those birds, they could save ten or fifteen minutes. Dashing to these aircraft, Self was surprised to find a special-tactics team already on board. PJ team leader Keary Miller, PJ Jason Cunningham, and CCT Gabe Brown had just returned from a mission and had yet to remove their considerable gear from the helo. The problem for the Ranger was that he didn't know these guys, and despite the fact that they must have known their business or they wouldn't have been on the bird in the first place, he had no desire to go into combat with complete strangers.

Self was already upset that the STS team his unit habitually trained with was already flying support for another task force mission, and that theater CSAR had assigned an available team to fly with him. About ten minutes before they were due to launch, his regular STS team showed up, having completed whatever mission they'd been on. Gratified, Self prepared to integrate them into his unit. That was when he discovered Miller's team already on his bird, equipment strapped in, ready to fly.

The urgency of the mission left no time for pleasantries. Self made it clear that he had his own STS, ordered them off, and turned to deal with other matters. A few minutes later, when the pilots pulled power and the two-ship mission took off, the captain discovered, to his considerable consternation, that Keary Miller and his team were flying with them. Apparently the two STS team leaders had discussed the situation and decided, all things being equal, that since Miller's team had their gear already on board and in place, they should take the mission.

The problem was, as far as Self was concerned, all things were not equal. And it was more than lack of trust or lack of confidence in guys they didn't know. The theater CSAR teams didn't work with the Rangers; they didn't know how the assault teams were organized, didn't know their procedures for exiting a Chinook under fire, didn't know what to do once they did get off the aircraft, which way to go—left or right, front or back. These are the tactics, techniques, and procedures, the TT&P, that teams like the one Self commands drill and drill and drill until they can do them in their sleep. Each man learns not only his role, but the roles of his comrades, so that if one of them goes down, someone can immediately step in and keep the unit functioning.

Self wanted the STS team he was familiar with. Instead he got a unit he didn't know, with a radio operator who didn't know the Rangers' command and control structure, didn't know to whom he needed to be talking on the radio, didn't know the proper frequencies, and didn't know the call signs of the SEAL observation teams that were working the area they were flying into. None of this speaks to Gabe Brown's skills or abilities as a combat controller; it was just one more example of a communications snafu that could cost lives.

Fortunately the situation, so far as communication was concerned, appeared not to be without a built-in solution. One of the men attached to Self's team was Air Force S.Sgt. Kevin Vance, an enlisted terminal attack controller. His bag of tricks included radios to direct close air support from fast movers and attack helicopters and artillery, which in Anaconda was limited to nothing with a bigger kick or longer reach than mortars carried by the infantry. The military command had decided that in the interest of being fleet of foot—or rotor—they wouldn't utilize artillery pieces. It was a decision that the troops on the ground, under fire, would come to question. Before Vance was assigned to Self's platoon, he'd completed TACP training, Ranger School, air assault school, basic and HALO jump school, and pathfinder school. Once in country, he'd trained with Self's platoon and knew the drill, the command and control structure, and all the radio nets. Self wanted two radio operators on his team; in the event one was hit, he'd still have someone available to call in close air support. And if neither man was hit, the plan, in effect, gave the platoon leader an extra rifleman.

Realizing there was nothing he could do about the STS situation, Self did a quick assessment of who was on the aircraft. There were a total of twenty-one people—eight aircrew, three STS, and ten members of the Ranger team, with all but the aircrew sitting on the floor of the aircraft.

For the special-tactics team that had been together on the Ditka 03 mission, this one was palpably different. The Ditka crash was not the result of hostile fire. At that moment they were on their way into an area where one helicopter just like the one they were on had been shot out of the air, and another had been crippled and managed to limp away. Already at least one man—an airman just like they were—had been shot and killed, and no one knew how the battle had gone while they were flying out from Bagram.

At a few minutes before six in the morning, local time, according to a sworn affidavit by Vance, the men on the helicopter were told "a military member was on the ground in a hostile area in Afghanistan after falling out of a helicopter." Their orders were to link up with the SEALs on the ground, and extract them along with the man who had fallen. Beyond that, they knew nothing. The Department of Defense review of the battle of Takur Ghar says "the QRF was unaware that a squad of Al Qaeda fighters, who by this time had already killed two Americans, were poised and expecting their arrival." As in Somalia, even the enemy apparently knew that U.S. military policy was to leave no man behind, and they were sophisticated enough to prepare to exploit it.

Self told the *Post*, "You have this dilemma: Hold guys on the ground longer so they know exactly what they're going to do, or push them ahead so we can affect the situation sooner. A quick reaction force is never going to know everything that's going on. If they did, then they wouldn't be quick."

Commanders at Bagram say they tried to notify the Rangers that the SEALs had retreated from the ridge top and to direct the helicopters to another landing zone farther down the mountain. Due to intermittently functioning aircraft communications equipment, the Rangers and aircrew never received the instructions, nor were attempts by HQ to "provide situational awareness to the QRF commander on board Razor 1" successful, stated the *Post*.

"As a consequence, the Rangers went forward believing that the SEALs were still located on top of Takur Ghar, and proceeded to the same location where both Razors 3 and 4 had taken enemy fire."

At about ten after six, Vance noticed they were flying in circles around the mountaintop. Through one of the windows he had identified the same terrain features twice, and could also see that the sun was just beginning to crest the mountains to the east of the LZ. As the pilots put the Chinook into a hover preparatory to settling into the LZ, they were hit with a rocket-propelled grenade. Sparks flew from the right side of the aircraft and it started to shake violently. Aborting the landing was out of the question; the pilots had their hands full trying to have it land wheels-down. The helicopter, according to Vance, "seemed to just fall out of the sky about fifteen feet to the ground." Photos released by the DoD show the helicopter on the ground, nose pointing up the hill toward the main enemy bunkers where Air Force combat controller John Chapman had been killed.

The RPG had taken out the right engine at the same time that small-arms fire peppered the Chinook from three directions in a classic landing zone denial ambush. The closest enemy shooters were no more than ten meters away; the farthest about fifty or sixty meters out.

Between the time the RPG hit and when they struck the ground Vance remembers nothing other than "it was a blur." Sgt. Philip J. Svitak got off a one-second burst from his minigun before being struck and killed by an enemy bullet. The other forward gunner, David, also returned fire and was almost immediately hit in the right leg, breaking one of the bones. Everyone in the cargo area of the aircraft was slammed to the floor upon impact, but apparently no one was injured as a result.

At the same time, bullets were slamming into the cockpit as well. A round shattered the leg of one of the pilots, Chief Warrant Officer Chuck, and another round or piece of shrapnel almost severed the left wrist of the other pilot, CWO Greg Calvert. Chuck opened his emergency side door and slipped onto the snow. Calvert staggered from the cockpit toward the rear ramp, holding his wrist as it spurted blood.

Within a few more seconds, another two or three RPGs hit the helicopter, one of them starting a fire as machine-gun bullets turned the Chinook's insulation into confetti. Someone in the rear passed a fire extinguisher to the 160th SOAR(A) medic, Sergeant First Class Cory, and through the blood dripping from a cut on his forehead, he was able to see enough to put out the blaze. Cory later told Bradley Graham of the *Washington Post* that in fifteen years in the service, which included combat in Panama in 1989 and the Persian Gulf in 1991, he had never seen fire so intense.

Soldiers and aircrew in situations like this describe a downed bird as "a bullet magnet," and their first job after surviving the initial impact and attack is to get out and get cover. Normally the Ranger team has a prescribed order for exiting the helo, but in this case, all that mattered was to get out. As they attempted to do that, Sp. Marc Anderson, thirty, was shot and killed while at the top of the ramp. By the time Captain Self, who had been forward in the helicopter, got to the ramp, two more Rangers had been killed. They were twenty-one-year-old PFC Matt Commons, and twenty-two-year-old Sgt. Brad Crose.

Vance, the radio operator, had difficulty unsnapping his safety line, so his exit from the helicopter was delayed by about fifteen seconds. "I knew we had three killed in action [KIA], which left seven of our team, three of whom were injured. I had shrapnel in the arm, but did not notice it until later. My platoon leader had shrapnel in his leg, a pretty good chunk, and another team member had shrapnel in his lower left calf and was moving slowly." Vance notes that his team knew how to fight and operate on the ground, but the Army aircrew didn't have the same training.

With three of the Ranger shooters dead and a heavily dug-in enemy attempting to destroy them with withering fire, Vance made a decision: He would concentrate on shooting with his M-4 rifle, abandoning his duties as a radio operator for the moment. The platoon leader's initial concern that CCT Gabe Brown didn't know their radio frequencies and command structure was about to come home to roost. The enemy had confounded Self's backup plan to use Vance as his RTO. The good news was that Vance trained with the Rangers and knew how to maneuver and fight with them.

Vance says, "I exited the aircraft and threw my rucksack off but kept it within twenty meters from me. I figured out which way we were being engaged from and I sought cover behind a cutout in the rock face. It was just big enough for four team members to kneel behind it. We set up a perimeter. Two other members were back to my right and three members to my left. I was closest to the enemy. There were two enemies about fifty meters north of us near a tree. There was one enemy behind me and to the right, already dead. There were some more enemies to the south coming out. Then we started to engage them."

Vance's personal plan was to keep firing with his rifle, and then seek assistance for close air support (CAS) on the PRC117F radio that was still in his rucksack. At one point he turned around and yelled at combat controller Gabe Brown to begin working on communications, but saw that Brown was already on his own radio. "I decided that I needed to be on the line fighting. If I had been on the radio, then the combat controller would have been sitting there doing nothing because he doesn't have the assault training."

Vance told Brown that his rucksack had a radio in it, and had a member of the aircrew drag the rucksack over to the CCT. The problem with having Brown do the job was his lack of familiarity with communicating *for* a Ranger unit, rather than operating independently, as CCTs routinely do from observation posts overlooking combat situations. Brown didn't know the Ranger team's call signs or the call signs of some of the assets that were flying overhead. He also didn't know the call signs of assets such as SEAL observation posts that were collecting intel for the Ranger task force. Communicating with CCT Jim Hotaling wasn't an issue, but Hotaling and the Aussies he was with were at least two klicks away, and didn't have a visual on the fight that was raging.

While it might seem to be a simple matter for one radio operator to tell another what the correct frequencies and code names were, with a gun battle raging and Vance taking the place of one of the three dead Rangers, it didn't happen right away. It took Brown nearly twenty minutes from the time of the crash to get in touch with headquarters and request air support. With the communications confusion, the only way he could contact the Ranger command and control people at Bagram was to have his messages relayed through the air command net.

When all the various accounts of the battle are stitched together, there are some pieces that just don't seem to fit. And since the U.S. Special Operations Command has put discussion of Operation Anaconda with the media by any of the participants off-limits, serious questions remain.

One example: The *Washington Post* reported that while Razor 1 was crash-landing, military commanders in Bagram, including Major General Hagenbeck, were watching the action live on a video feed from a Predator drone. "It was gut-wrenching," the *Post* quotes Hagenbeck as saying. "We saw the helicopter getting shot as it was just setting down. We saw the shots being fired. And it was unbelievable the Rangers were even able to get off that and kill the enemy without suffering greater losses."

Although Hagenbeck was the commanding general of the 10th Mountain Division and the senior U.S. commander with responsibility for planning and running Operation Anaconda, he didn't control the Rangers. Under a plan that appears to have its origin in the doctrine of "Divide and maybe conquer," Air Force Brig. Gen. Gregory Trebon had that responsibility. That's presumably why Hagenbeck told the *Post*, "Literally, we were spectators watching. We did not know what the SEAL rescue squad on the ground had been reporting. I still don't know to this day what they reported to the commander here and what was transmitted to the Rangers on board the helicopter—whether they said 'there's no other way to get here,' or if they said we can suppress enemy fire, or if they said we're going to lose some guys but it's the only way to do it. We were just looking at a screen without any audio to it."

For all the good watching the much-touted and highly secret Predator feed did, one can infer from Hagenbeck's confession of ignorance weeks after the battle that Trebon wasn't going out of his way to help him interpret what they were seeing on the television monitor, much less putting their heads together to figure out what they could cooperatively do to help Captain Self and his beleaguered platoon.

Why didn't an Air Force general immediately order fast movers over the battle and let *them* try to establish contact with the radio operators on the ground, and by their very presence compel the enemy to keep their heads down? Such an approach may have saved lives. Indeed, in the sworn affidavit given at Bagram three weeks later, TACP Kevin Vance says, "Every time the plane showed up and you could hear them, we weren't being shot at. Just having the planes nearby kept the enemy away." (He was referring to the planes that eventually showed up once radio contact was established.) What was General Trebon proactively doing to try to save the lives of the guys who were still deep in the shit? We don't know, because Trebon refuses to answer any questions related to Anaconda, including whether or not interservice rivalry had struck again, this time actually costing American lives.

Up north, at the U.S. base at Karshi-Khanabad, PJ team leader Chris Young had been awakened with the terse announcement, "The QRF's been shot down." Young knew that some of his buddies were likely to have been out with the quick reaction force, and when he arrived at the operations center tent, his fears were realized.

"The worst thing about SATCOM is you know for a fact you can pick up that handset and talk straight to the guy at the other end. You're hearing this happening," Young says. "You're hearing your friend's call signs come up on the radio, and you want to call them and tell them, 'Hey, dude. I'm here. I'm going to get you as much help as I can,' but you know you can't do that, 'cause then you're just tying up the net."

Back on Takur Ghar, the survivors of Razor 1 continued to fight for their lives, while inside the carcass of the Chinook, the two pararescuemen and the aircrew medic were treating the wounded. The pilot, Chuck, had been pulled from the outside of the cockpit, around the back of the helicopter, and was doing all right with a bullet through his leg. The copilot, who'd had his left hand almost shot off, seemed to be okay for the moment, but there was concern that he'd lost a lot of blood, even though a tourniquet now seemed to have the bleeding under control. The third casualty, flight engineer David, with the bullet wound that had apparently broken his leg, also seemed to be doing okay. Even though their patients were stabilized, the medics were concerned that a combination of shock and cold could cause any one of them to crash, and they discussed the need to get the casualties evacuated as soon as possible.

Outside in the snow, Captain Self was hearing the pleas from the casualties, the medics, and the flight crew to do whatever it took to get them off that mountain. Without a doubt, it was a lot of pressure on a twenty-five-year-old who found himself in charge and under fire for the first time in his life. They'd been exchanging small-arms fire from the moment the helicopter slammed into the ground, and while none of his men nor any of the helicopter crew had been hit since the initial seconds of the battle, it was clear they'd need help to keep the enemy at bay. But at that point, the CCT still didn't have contact with jets that could provide them with close air support.

And then the Al Qaeda forces upped the ante. They began firing mortars at the Rangers. The first one hit thirty meters off the nose of the downed helicopter. That put it at the twelve-o'clock position up the hill from them, just to the left of what they'd soon discover was a manned enemy bunker hidden next to and beneath trees. The next volley landed to their rear, a couple hundred meters behind them. It quickly became apparent to Captain Self that the enemy had their position bracketed, and they were going to start walking the mortars in on them. The two PJs and the aircrew medic, who had moved the casualties out of the helicopter because it was an easy target, now carried the wounded back inside the Chinook in an attempt to protect them from shrapnel.

That was about the time that Self decided they needed to assault the hilltop to improve their position. With only six men capable of actually skirmishing—and some of *them* already wounded—doing the Ranger thing and going on the offensive seemed like a Hail Mary play. But he decided to chance it. Four of them, Sergeants Vance and Raymond DePouli, his squad leader, Sgt. Joshua Walker, and Self attempted an uphill assault with covering fire provided by a fifth Ranger on a machine gun while one of the aircrew worked as his assistant gunner.

Rifles at their shoulders, they moved up the hill firing: two or three shots, then peer over the top of the sights trying to acquire a fresh target; fire another two or three shots and do it all over again. On the left, Sergeant Walker was firing his M-203 grenade launcher, trying to reload as they moved uphill. On the right, Sergeant DePouli had a grenade ready to toss as he blazed away with his rifle. They advanced in a classic fire-team wedge, spread out, shooting. Vance and Self held the center positions. They had gotten about halfway up— about twenty-five meters from the enemy—when Self noticed that rather than charging into an enemy concealed behind natural rocks or trees, they were actually attempting to attack a well dug-in, fortified position. Four wounded soldiers climbing uphill in knee-deep snow were no match for the Al Qaeda fighters, and despite Hollywood depictions where the good guys always seem to manage to make it up the hill, dropping grenades into the bunkers and blowing the enemy to kingdom come, Self did a reality check. When he recognized that the risk of losing everyone on the assault was a very real possibility, common sense prevailed, and the captain yelled, "Bunker! Bunker! Bunker! Get back."

It was shortly after they'd backed off from the assault attempt that Gabe Brown established a radio link with the SEAL team that Self's platoon had come in to rescue. That was the first word they had that the SEALs were no longer on the ridge top. Brown relayed to Self that with two wounded, the SEALs were holed up for the duration until someone came in to pull them out.

Moments after he reached the SEALs, Brown also got through to air controllers and requested air support. They gave him additional frequencies, and presumably the right codes, so he'd be able to talk directly with incoming jet fighters. It was about twenty minutes after the crash when he was finally able to shout, "We have F-15s inbound on station."

The first thing the Rangers wanted the jets to do was take out the bunker above them. Not wanting to fall victim to a bomb gone astray, Brown asked for strafing passes first, from the jets' 20mm cannon. The first passes from the F-15s didn't silence the bunker, so more fire was brought to bear from a pair of F-16s that had been 180 miles away over north-central Afghanistan when they got the call. They, too, emptied their guns, but the Al Qaeda fighters hunkered down and came back up firing.

That's when the decision was made to use five-hundred-pound laser-guided glide bombs. One of the radio operators would talk directly to the pilots, identifying the targets visually, and passing along the captain's initials if the target was "danger close." When the flier was certain he knew what he was supposed to hit, the radioman would turn back to Captain Self. "Sir, they're ready to drop it. Are you ready?" Receiving an affirmative answer, the pilot would be told, "You're cleared hot." That's a brevity code term meaning it's okay to drop ordnance. Moments later the pilot would respond, "Bombs are away."

The first bomb dropped down the hill behind the bunker. The next struck nearer to the ridge crest but still behind the bunker. The blast, which was definitely in the "danger close" zone, showered the Rangers with debris, but it still didn't knock out the bunker. The third bomb also struck on the reverse slope—over the crest of the saddle top—while the fourth and fifth five-hundred-pounders slammed right into the top of the hill. Each time one of the jets came in on a bomb pass, the noise was deafening. Anyone who's heard a low pass at an air show can imagine what it was like.

But the sound of the laser-guided bombs themselves was like nothing the men on the ground had ever imagined, certainly nothing like the World War II movies where a stick of bombs falling from a Flying Fortress generate the classic descending whistling noise. These bombs sounded like they had their own jet engines. While the noise alone kept the Al Qaeda in their holes, none of the bombs took out the bunker.

That's when Self had one of the radio operators ask if the Predator circling high overhead was armed. Both the Air Force and the CIA had modified the surveillance aircraft to launch Hellfire missiles, which were originally designed as antitank weapons to be fired from low-flying helicopters. Both organizations had Predators flying in Afghanistan. One of them—an informed guess says it was the CIA—gave Self's radio operator the answer he was hoping for: The unmanned aerial vehicle that was feeding live video of the battle back to Bagram and lazing targets for the CAS was also carrying the missiles. He asked that one be targeted on the bunker. Vance initially objected; they were well within the danger zone for a blast from the Hellfire. But necessity being a mother, the TACP relented and called for the shot, first asking Self to once again provide his initials for the controller to indicate he knew that the possibility of a friendly-fire incident was not remote.

The missile scored a direct hit, knocking out the bunker and, it appeared, everyone in it.

# CHAPTER 11

# "WE WEREN'T GETTING SHOT AT THAT BAD" MARCH 4, 2002

As soon as the Hellfire took out the bunker, the three medics began moving the casualties back out of the downed helicopter to what they thought was a protected spot behind it. Given where they knew the enemy was located, it offered more protection than being inside the hulk, whose sides had been breached by RPGs as well as machine-gun and rifle fire. Once again they let Self know that the sooner they could evacuate the wounded, the better. Hypothermia was a risk for everyone on the hill, but the casualties who had lost a significant amount of blood were at greater risk. What the surviving aircrew members were already thinking, but not yet verbalizing, was that special-ops headquarters would probably not be willing to send in a helicopter during daylight hours, and nightfall was still about eight hours away. The nickname for their unit, the 160th Special Operations Aviation Unit (Airborne) is the Nightstalkers. Their helicopters are painted black, to help them disappear in an inky black sky. One doesn't need to have the photographic eye of Ansel Adams to imagine how an MH-47E would look from the ground against a bright blue sky or silhouetted on a ground-hugging approach against snow-covered ridgelines.

There was no question in Captain Self's mind that if they were to survive until evacuation was possible, they needed help. What made their situation

Jason Cunningham at his pararescue school graduation ceremony (*Courtesy of Jackie Cunningham*)

desperate was that the captain could see enemy forces maneuvering to their rear; the observation posts manned by combat controllers Hotaling and Fleener with the Aussie SAS were reporting by radio that Al Qaeda reinforcements were attempting to move into the area; and intel sources monitoring enemy radio transmissions were telling him that the Al Qaeda commanders were hungry for a total and complete victory.

The only help Self knew he could count on was from the remainder of his platoon that had been aboard Razor 2, and was now slowly making its way up the mountain. The men were hampered by the weight they were carrying—a minimum of eighty pounds per man; by the forty- to seventy-degree slope of the terrain that was covered in places by up to three feet of snow; by the clothing they were wearing, which wasn't ideal for the task at hand—some had on standard-issue suede desert boots, which, despite having a Gore-Tex lining, soaked up water from the snowpack; by the thin mountain air; and last but certainly not least, by enemy mortar fire that, luckily, was sporadic and poorly aimed.

According to the official DoD summary of the battle, the other half of Self's QRF, ten Rangers and a Navy SEAL, were deposited at an "offset" location on the ground that was some eight hundred meters east and more than two thousand feet below the mountaintop.

What the official report fails to mention is that Razor 2, carrying the rest of Self's platoon, had flown to Gardez, the town that was being used as a staging area for the American offensive. According to the account in the *Post*, "'At one point, I had a crew chief by the collar,' said Staff Sergeant Arin Canon, the ranking Ranger on Razor 2. 'I'm screaming at him that regardless of what happened, the first bird only had ten guys on it. That's the bare minimum package. If something happened to them, they need us. We complete the package.'"

The account continues, "'Then word came in that the chopper carrying Chalk 1 had gone down. Within 30 to 60 minutes—accounts vary—Chalk 2 was back in the air and heading toward the ridge top.

"The first challenge was finding a place to set down. 'It's the side of a mountain, so there are not a whole lot of places to land,' said Ray, who piloted the chopper. 'You basically hunt and peck around.'

"At about 8:30 A.M., the crew found a space just big enough to get all the wheels on the ground. The aircrew had advised the Rangers that Self's group would be straight ahead of them, about 250 to 300 yards away. After they got off, the Rangers learned that Chalk 1 was actually about 2,000 feet up the mountain, at an altitude of 10,200 feet. The plan had changed, but no one told the Rangers."

The climb up the mountain was excruciatingly slow for the climbers, who at times got down on their hands and knees because it was the only way to make progress, and even slower for Self and the crash survivors. Finally the platoon leader ordered the reinforcements to start dropping some of their gear, in particular the heavy back plates in their body armor. Even with their load lightened, it still took them between two and three hours to reach the downed helicopter.

By ten-thirty in the morning, both the crash survivors and the reinforcements were completely exhausted, but still had to defeat the enemy controlling the top of the hill, which was barely fifty yards from their position. Gabe Brown called in one final air strike—a five-hundred-pound bomb that hit just over the backside of the hilltop. Vance says, "It hit at an angle where it blew everything back over the top of us so it was raining debris and metal pieces down around us. That was the only point where we were really concerned with our safety from friendly bombs."

At least one of the pilots was not nearly as sanguine about the safety of the men on the ground. Whichever radio operator he was listening to—Self had ordered both Vance and Brown to use the latter's call sign, Slick 01, to avoid confusion that might result in controllers thinking that two different locations were seeking CAS—the call often included the words *danger close*. The pilot recalled he'd been told that at one point the enemy was "two helicopter lengths," about one hundred feet, from the Rangers' position.

It's possible that the training Vance had received to call in CAS had given him some sort of circumstantial immunity to fear of friendly fire, but the Ranger captain clearly had not received that inoculation. When he had a moment to himself, Self reflected on how many times he'd provided his initials to authorize calling in close air support. He knew it had to be done, but also knew that what they were asking the pilots to do was crazy. The possibility of headlines screaming about friendly-fire casualties was haunting. Nevertheless, even though the word *insane* kept coming to mind, it played out as the right thing to do in that situation.

After that last bomb struck behind the hilltop bunkers, the Rangers stormed the snow-covered hill, rifles at their shoulders, pausing only to throw grenades when they were within range. Throughout the assault, two machine gunners laid down suppressing fire that was surprisingly effective in keeping the Al Qaeda forces from attempting to repel the charge. During the entire fifteen-minute assault, they encountered almost no return fire, although once they reached the top of the hill they discovered additional bunkers on the reverse slope and attacked them, dispatching several more enemy fighters.

It was while he was moving his men up the hill that Self began to sense that the shrapnel wound in his right thigh was going to cause mobility problems as the day wore on. At first he had paid little attention to the wound, probably because it hadn't bled through the multiple layers of clothing he was wearing, and he was able to keep it numb by burying his thigh in the snow. That worked for a while, but eventually the muscle seized up, causing him difficulty in walking.

Once Self was in control on top of the hill, a search turned up several other enemy bodies scattered about, probably killed by the air strikes. They also found the bodies of Navy SEAL Neil Roberts, and of combat controller John Chapman.

After roughly five hours on the mountain, the captain was finally able to move his command post, with radio operator Vance and combat controller Brown, to the top of the hill. And he gave the order to have the able-bodied men begin the arduous task of carrying the casualties from their relatively exposed position near the helicopter to the relative cover of high ground, where extraction would be easier when helicopters were finally sent in to get them. While it was difficult enough for individuals to make it up the hill, moving the wounded from the casualty collection point to the commanding ground was nightmarish. The enemy had never stopped dropping an occasional mortar round near the helicopter, which meant that the four or six relatively healthy bodies who were carrying the wounded to the top were continually exposed to the possibility that a lucky shot would bring them down. And once they made the fifty- or sixty-meter climb, they were spent, and had to take two or three minutes to catch their breath before they could even consider making another round-trip.

At the casualty collection point behind the downed Chinook, the pilot with the injured hand was taking a turn for the worse. The aircrew medic told the *Post*, "I hesitate to say he was close to dying. But he had a definite change in his level of consciousness. He was starting to speak to me as if he was going to die."

Because the details of what happened next are crucial to telling the story of Air Force pararescuemen in the war on terrorism, now is the time to explain why, unlike other operations reported on in *None Braver*, the chapters dealing with Operation Anaconda include quotes from two lengthy articles by reporter Bradley Graham that appeared in the *Washington Post*. SOCOM and AFSOC didn't want the author of this book to have access to the soldiers, sailors, and airmen who did their best under terrible circumstances and worse high-ranking leadership, so they used the power of command to muzzle them in the apparent hope that the author would be satisfied with the previously published reports as well as sanitized military puff pieces that alleged the success of Anaconda.

Repeated requests to interview participants were denied, and almost every time the reason given was that generals higher up the food chain didn't want the people interviewed. Finally the request reached the desk of the newly appointed public affairs officer for CENTCOM and General Franks, Air Force Col. Ray Shepherd. He acknowledged that a ban on interviews about an operation almost a year old didn't make sense, and offered to pursue it. Weeks later he came back with a response:

*Sir,*

*After having discussed this issue with all the units and commands involved, we regrettably can not honor your request. While the individuals involved are welcome to speak as private citizens, I have been informed, most do not wish to be interviewed any further about their actions during Operation Anaconda. I am honoring their desires and will not pursue any further interview request.*

*However, if there is some information I can provide you from our historian's office or some other available information that might help you in your writing, please let me know.*

*Ray Shepherd, Colonel, USAF*
*Director of Public Affairs*

Seizing on the notion that Shepherd, who speaks for General Franks, said that the individuals involved were welcome to speak as private citizens, this author pursued the request again with AFSOC and with the public affairs officer for the 75th Ranger Regiment, citing Shepherd's e-mail. The response came back from both organizations that according to Army Col. Bill Darley, the PAO for the Special Operations Command, Anaconda was off-limits for media interviews. The fact that interviews were granted to some media and denied to others is a clear violation of long-standing Department of Defense policy prohibiting exclusive interviews with military personnel—what's available to one is supposed to be available to all.

A parallel inquiry through another channel attempted to find the reason for the prohibition. The not-for-attribution response was that immediately after the debacle with the shoot-down of the Razor helicopters, an article appeared in *Newsweek* that used the actual Razor call signs for the helicopters involved. Since that call sign was still being used to identify MH-47E Chinook special-ops helicopters, revealing it—and publishing it—violated communication security. One general, perhaps the commanding general of SOCOM—but that's only an educated guess—was so irate at the breach of basic COMSEC, that he ordered that no further interviews were to be allowed with Anaconda participants.

Apparently, before the ban, the *Post* had received a promise from a general officer that its reporter Bradley Graham could interview those involved in Anaconda. Even though the ban had been promulgated, the general kept his word, and Graham was allowed to conduct the interviews. In addition to the *Post* articles, the leaking of the Vance affidavit, which SOCOM's Colonel Darley authenticated, and off-the-record interviews with military officials were crucial to filling the holes in the official Department of Defense "Executive Summary of the Battle of Takur Ghar," a document riddled with inaccuracies and excuses, not to mention its omissions.

The *Post* article picks up the story of the battle on Takur Ghar mountain, with a description of what turned out to be an enemy counter-attack that began about ten minutes after the Rangers had taken the hill and Captain Self had begun moving his command post to the top.

> But just as he said that, three or four enemy fighters on a knoll to the south, 300 to 400 yards behind the chopper, opened fire.
>
> Machine-gun fire and rocket-propelled grenades started ripping into the casualty collection area. Bullets also ricocheted around the feet of Rangers and aircrew members carrying the first of the casualties up the hill—David, the flight engineer, who had been shot in the leg.

The group dropped the litter and ran for cover, leaving David on his back on the hillside. Stebner, one of the carriers, twice dashed out to try to drag David behind some rocks, only to abandon him again. "I stayed out there a good 15, 20 minutes, just watching stuff go over us," David said.

The third time, Stebner reached David and pulled him out of harm's way.

Down behind the chopper, Cory and an Air Force pararescueman, Senior Airman Jason Cunningham, had just inserted a fresh IV into Greg when they came under fire. Their position left them exposed.

"We realized we were just going to have to sit there and shoot it out with them," Cory said. "Neither Jason nor I were going to leave."

One rocket-propelled grenade came straight at them and zoomed over their heads, exploding above the helicopter. One bullet struck about three feet in front of Cory, kicking snow over him.

"We were shooting back and forth," Cory said. "And I can remember getting down, thinking, 'I have only two magazines left—something has to happen here pretty soon.'"

That's when he and Cunningham were hit.

"I had turned over on my stomach and crawled up a hill about five feet, thinking this might do something," Cory said. "I turned back on my back to shoot, and it was just shortly after that that Jason and I got shot at the same time. We were sitting no more than five or six feet apart."

Two bullets hit Cory in the abdomen, but the impact was cushioned by his ammunition pouch and belt buckle.

"It took me a little while to get up enough courage to check myself out," he said. "As a medic, you realize that a penetrating wound to the abdomen can be absolutely the worst thing. So I reached my hand down there and tried to see how much blood there was. I pulled my hand back initially and it was wet with water. That was a very reassuring sign." The water was from his punctured canteen.

Cunningham was in worse shape: He was hit in the pelvic area and bleeding profusely. Although still lucid, he was in considerable pain.

There appeared to be no question that the enemy was targeting the casualties, but because the enemy was firing uphill, from well below the downed helicopter, the rounds were coming all the way to the top of the hill, past the helicopter. An RPG whizzed up past Self's head and blew up, and bullets were smacking into trees and rocks. Everyone was kept down by this effective grazing fire.

The counterattack had been expected, since the Rangers could see the enemy maneuvering toward positions where they might have clear shots at the twenty-seven Americans still alive. What was most important, however, was that when Razor 1 was shot down, the enemy was firing from positions as close as ten meters from the helicopter. Now, through effective use of the limited firepower they had, plus close air support that had forced the Al Qaeda soldiers back, they were an estimated four hundred meters away and having difficulty getting closer.

Intelligence sources able to monitor Al Qaeda radio transmissions clearly heard commanders issuing instructions on how their soldiers should maneuver to get closer, specifically warning them not to bunch up into large targets, staying in groups of four or five and trying to attack from several different locations simultaneously, or in sequence. At one point, American intel picked up one of the enemy requesting that a video camera be brought to their position so the battle could be recorded.

What the Rangers were able to observe were Al Qaeda forces moving on a small ridgeline that paralleled the one they were on, at a lower elevation and to their rear. The enemy forces were clover-leafing—they'd come up, crest the ridgeline, and four or five individuals would fire RPGs and a machine gun at them. Then they'd go back down the slope, where they were protected from return fire, traverse the slope, and come up in another location and fire on the hilltop again.

The most effective means of interdicting that technique was to drop bombs on the side of the slope the enemy was attempting to exploit. As before, whenever planes flew into the area close enough to be heard, the enemy stayed down and stopped firing. Realizing this, Vance and Brown kept cycling bombers through the area, ultimately, with the help of combat controllers Hotaling and Fleener, dropping thousand-pounders from B-52 and B-1 bombers.

The bullets that found their way beneath the ceramic plates in Jason Cunningham's protective vest had done maximum damage. The entry wounds were on the side of his lower back. One, it was reported later, fractured his pelvis, while another pierced the iliac artery, the vessel that carries oxygenated blood from the abdominal aorta to the legs and feet. The two medical personnel who were unhurt, PJ Keary Miller and the Ranger medic who had climbed the mountain with the recently arrived reinforcements, immediately knew that Cunningham's wounds were life-threatening, and that short of getting him to the nearest surgical hospital, there was little they could do but try to keep him as comfortable and as warm as possible.

In the preceding hours, Jason had worked with Cory to move the wounded from the inside of the helicopter to one collection point, then to another, putting the welfare of his patients ahead of his own. Even after he was hit and unable to move about because of the pelvic injury, the uninjured medics say Cunningham made sure that he passed on to them whatever information he had that could aid them in treating his patients.

There was a certain sad irony that Cunningham had been one of the PJs who lobbied military medical authorities after the minefield jump mission to allow the pararescuemen to carry units of red blood cells into the field, the better to treat patients who'd lost considerable blood, because now one of the blood packs was being given to him, and the other went to the other wounded medic.

It was readily apparent to Captain Self that several of the casualties might not survive if evacuation was delayed another seven or eight hours, until after dark. In his affidavit, radio operator Vance says, "Controller asked me if the pickup zone was cold and how many guys we were going to lose if we waited to be exfiltrated [until after nightfall]. I asked the medic, 'If we hang out here, how many guys are going to die?' The medic said at least two, maybe three. I reported to Controller, 'It is a cold PZ and we are going to lose three if we wait.' Just as I said it was a cold PZ, we were shot at."

The three that the Ranger medic thought might die were Cunningham, Cory, and Greg Calvert, the pilot whose hand had nearly been shot off seconds after the crash-landing.

After the battle they'd been through just to stay alive, the occasional rifle shots that Al Qaeda forces fired at them were of little concern and no consequence. So long as the enemy didn't get reinforcements, or bring in a skilled sniper, Self's concern was more about convincing his headquarters that it would be safe to come in during daylight hours and evacuate at least the wounded, than it was about being overrun by the enemy.

Once Self no longer needed Vance as a rifleman, the two radio operators had worked out a relationship between themselves and the captain that seemed to be effective. Vance stayed in contact with observation posts in the area, and when word came that Al Qaeda forces were moving in their general direction, he'd have Brown direct close air support to suppress the potential threat. At least that's the way it's described in the Vance affidavit.

After the Vance affidavit was leaked, sources in the combat controller community claimed that the threat from enemy forces in the area was greater than Vance realized. What makes it difficult to sort out the truth is that there is a long-standing tension—some would say animosity—between the CCT community and the TACPs. And those who have asked why Captain Self's request to bring in a medevac helicopter was ignored—among them Jason Cunningham's parents—have never been given the satisfaction of a detailed answer. When told that the parents wanted to know, AFSOC's public affairs officer, Maj. Karen Finn, said, "I hope you're not going to be the one to tell them." She then went on to insist that Captain Self and TACP Vance were wrong in claiming that the LZ could be made "cold" for a safe extraction of the critically wounded. Her claim was that they "didn't have the big picture."

Military sources with whom Finn's claim was discussed say, in no uncertain terms, that her statement is "an insult to the integrity of a highly qualified Ranger officer whose actions on Takur Ghar earned him a Silver Star, a Bronze Star, the Purple Heart, and an invitation from the President to attend the State of the Union address."

The fact is that Finn wasn't there. Her comments, and her pushing the credibility-challenged DoD "Executive Summary on the Battle of Takur Ghar," smack of the worst sort of flackery. The notion that Finn's assertions should be accepted and the standing of two people who were in the thick of the battle written off is offensive.

If she wanted to press her case on behalf of SOCOM and AFSOC, she needed to make available for interviews the combat controllers who were in and around Takur Ghar mountain during Operation Anaconda, among them Jim Hotaling and Jessie Fleener. That Finn would be biased in favor of what she implied was the combat controllers' point of view on the decision not to bring in an evac helicopter during daylight isn't surprising. AFSOC "owns" the combat controllers, and one would expect her to take their side in a dispute with an Army Ranger officer and an Air Force TACP attached to the Ranger unit.

Fleener was contacted shortly after he was graduated from Officer Training School and preparing to move on to training as a combat rescue officer, and he was willing to discuss Operation Anaconda if Finn granted permission. Jim Hotaling had been on a cross-country tour during which he gave several unclassified speeches that included details of his role in Operation Anaconda. Both were easily reachable by phone. In theory, both were in position during the battle to have a different, if not bigger picture of what was happening nearby while Jason Cunningham lay bleeding out. Yet neither was made available for interviews for this book by Finn.

Finn's assertions aside, Captain Self did, indeed, have other eyes watching the potential enemy threat in the area. Nearby Aussie SAS patrols were looking out for attempts by Al Qaeda to move on Self's platoon. Several SEAL observation posts were in contact with the Rangers. And while the action was taking place, even Hotaling, who had been atop a ridge about two miles south of Takur Ghar for more than a week, said that despite intel reports that some seventy enemy soldiers were heading toward the downed Americans, he never saw anything more than small groups of men trying to get into the area. When he saw them, he bombed them. None got closer than three-quarters of a mile to Self's platoon. TACP Vance confirmed that the reported seventy enemy soldiers never appeared.

Headquarters had also relayed to Self intel that they were picking up on intercepts of enemy radio transmissions that seemed to indicate an attempt on the part of the Taliban or Al Qaeda to marshal a force of 250 fighters for yet another counterattack. But as with the reports of a force of seventy moving into the area, the 250 never materialized.

It wasn't difficult for the men on the hill to surmise what was going on at headquarters. They were thinking, "We've already had three helicopters shot up in the same location. It's a bad location. Even though the captain thinks it's cold, he may not have complete situational awareness. And the consequences of bringing another helicopter in there—if it doesn't make it out—is that helo's crew is now added to the twenty-seven men who need to be pulled off the mountain. Even more, the small LZ would now be cluttered with the wreckage of two helicopters and useless, and those guys are going to have to hike hundreds of meters to find another suitable pickup zone."

Nevertheless, Captain Self believed that with the availability of close air support, as they'd been using it all morning and into the afternoon, the landing zone they were on was safe for an evac mission to get in and get out, and ordered Vance to continue pressing the point with the controllers at headquarters. The official radio logs indicate that the Rangers had made "adamant" calls for medevac with the suggestion that a bird could get in to take out the three critical cases, meaning the helicopter would be on the ground for no more than two minutes.

At one point the Ranger medic himself was put on the radio to convey the specific nature of the casualties, followed by "Six Actual," the platoon leader who reiterated that if they didn't send in the helicopter, they were going to lose two or three more men. The response was as cold as the temperature on the top of the ten-thousand-foot-high mountain: "We understand the nature of your casualties, and the consequences of not sending a medevac."

Up at K-2, while waiting for a plane to Bagram, Chris Young was listening to the SATCOM channel when he heard Anaconda headquarters radio back to the Ranger team that "there would be no attempt to pick them up until nightfall."

Military experts who have examined the situation the Rangers were in say that what the brass in Bagram didn't seem to understand was that the tactical situation on the ground had dramatically changed since Razor 1 was shot down. At the point Self was getting insistent about bringing in a helicopter to evac the critical casualties in daylight, all the enemy fighters who did the shooting from close in were dead. The problem was that the platoon leader hadn't been able to make it clear on the radio that they were no longer dealing with enemy shooters ten to thirty meters away; the enemy was three hundred to more than a thousand meters out. Would it be a gamble to bring a helicopter in? Yes, but it also had been a gamble to bring in the CSAR birds under fire on the nights the 10th Mountain Division needed help extracting the wounded. Long after the mission had ended, in after-action reports and the inevitable "lessons learned" documents, it's mentioned that headquarters may have chosen to ignore Self's declaration that the LZ was cold because, simultaneous with those radio calls, the platoon was asking for bomb drops on nearby ridges and valleys. What the leadership watching their live Predator feeds in the comfort of a warm building at Bagram couldn't seem to understand was that the bomb drops were preventive in nature, not evidence that the platoon was under enemy attack.

Everyone on the hill was aware that Cunningham would not survive if they did not get him out of there before dark. The Ranger medic who was caring for him declared his condition to be "urgent surgical." He knew there was nothing he could do to stop the internal bleeding, and he knew that of all the people on the mountain that day, Jason Cunningham was one who clearly understood that fact.

Vance continued to maintain his position that the landing zone could have been kept cold enough to permit an evac helicopter to come in. And Self had doped out the situation and determined that a Chinook could be directed to land on the reverse slope, away from where the enemy had launched their counterattack, completely concealing the body of the aircraft, with only its rotors visible from the enemy-held ridgeline four hundred meters away.

None of the men trapped on the mountain knew that less than fifteen minutes' flying time away, a pair of Air Force HH-60G Pave Hawks were waiting at the Texaco FARP for orders to go in and get the casualties out. Had they known, they could have told Bagram that considering the significantly smaller size of the 60, one could land and be totally hidden behind the ridge—not even the rotors would be visible to the Al Qaeda forces.

They could have even provided instructions for the route the CSAR birds should fly in order to make the pickup. Vance detailed it in his affidavit. "I gave Controller the approach heading, the land heading, and the departure heading. There was a zero-nine-zero approach heading, a two-thirty-five land heading, and a two-seventy departure heading." This wasn't guesswork; it wasn't a question of whether wishing would make it so.

What *is* left to guess is whether the special-ops commanders, including Brigadier General Trebon, himself an Air Force general, knew that the CSAR birds were ready, willing, and able to attempt the rescue. In a phone call to Brig. Gen. John H. Folkerts, the CG of the 347th Rescue Wing at Moody Air Force Base, to tell him that one of his men had been hit, Trebon indicated that the area had been too hot to bring in a medevac helicopter during daylight hours. Folkerts says Trebon never mentioned the availability of Air Force HH-60G CSAR birds with Folkert's own PJs aboard that had been sitting just fifteen minutes away at Texaco FARP.

At one point earlier in the day, Trebon apparently had more grandiose plans for a rescue mission. That was what all the activity that PJ Caleb Ethridge had observed at Texaco was about.

Ethridge says the SEALs took charge of the situation, spread out a map of the area, and started coordinating what everyone would do. At about noon, the special-ops leaders came over to check out the Pave Hawks in order to determine how many people they could carry. "We were going to go in with these three Chinooks full of bad guys, and our two helicopters, and then two Apaches, so it was going to be a seven-ship that was going to go in.

"It was like *Apocalypse Now*, 'Flight of the Valkyries,' that was playing in my head when we were getting ready to go," says Ethridge, who then hums the unforgettable melody, "Da-da-da-da-DUN-DUN . . ." and was thinking, "this is going to be way worse than a couple nights ago. This is going to be daytime. This is not good."

The PJs had heard through the grapevine that a PJ had been shot, but dismissed it, assuming that the wound was minimal. Ethridge says, "We knew there were a couple of the guys who were killed right off the bat; we found out they were killed instantly, and we're just, like, 'Dang, something's going on bad.' "

Ethridge surmises that the special-ops force that came in to Texaco had been given the leeway to plan a rescue mission and then execute it. He describes it as, "You guys get yourself squared away and make a plan and go."

Finally the order was given to launch the rescue mission. The seven helicopters spooled up and took off, but they didn't get very far. "We just took off," says Ethridge, "and then we all turned around. The command in Bagram said, 'No, no one's sending anybody else.' They weren't going to send anybody in till it got dark again. Or until fighting ceased. So we kept getting ready to go, but then we wouldn't."

Ethridge was conflicted. When he got word that a PJ had been shot, the potential mission suddenly became personal. "We're going to go get our own guys; they're a little closer to us than regular Army. It was, just, Wow! Our own guys are getting shot up. But we really didn't know what was going on. We weren't going to second-guess our leadership. They're saying 'It's too hot,' and we're thinking, 'Well, we went in last night and it wasn't that hot. I mean, we weren't getting shot at that bad, y'know?' "

What was disturbing to some of the men who were able to monitor SAT-COM was that it appeared that the Rangers trapped on Takur Ghar mountain were being conned into believing that a rescue mission—at least one to evacuate the critical casualties—was still being planned, when they knew that the 160th Chinook pilots at Texaco FARP, who had been on duty for more than twenty hours, were told to get some sleep, that no one was flying in until after dark.

One of the difficulties of being in the military is that it's very difficult to question the decisions of those who outrank you. And when an officer reaches that magical point in his career where someone pins a star on his collar, it's even more difficult for those not similarly exalted to question an order. So no one in uniform is going to publicly question Brigadier General Trebon's decision on March 4, 2002, while pararescueman Jason Cunningham was bleeding out on top of a mountain in Afghanistan. And Trebon himself has apparently decided it's beneath him to respond to questions from civilian journalists on the matter. He's got his career to think about.

What would be the consequences to the career of an officer who, knowing that three helicopters had been shot up in a specific area earlier in the day, sent in a rescue helicopter, and it got shot down?

A forthright answer came from a career military officer whose decision to remain anonymous makes a lot of sense, given the system. "It's always easier to be safe. It's safer to be safe. Maybe that's what happened."

At around five P.M., the weather on the ridge where the Ranger team and aircrew were hunkered down turned colder, and the wind picked up. The only good news was that the sun was hidden behind nearby mountains, which meant that nightfall was little more than an hour away, but trying to keep the wounded warm and their spirits up was becoming more difficult.

At age twenty-five, Texas-born Capt. Nathan Self was among the youngest of the twenty-seven American survivors on the hill. The oldest, one of the aircrew members, was approaching forty. It fell to Self, as part of his command responsibility, to plan and implement a tactical approach to keeping them all alive until they could be evacuated. But he also had to counteract the natural tendency of men who are facing hours of cold, hunger, pain, and threatened attack by a potentially overwhelming force to lapse into self-pity, hopelessness, and certainly grief for the friends they'd already lost, and this he did by projecting self-confidence in his ability to do the job, even when doubts may have entered his mind.

Self quietly gave in to a bit of introspection, recalling Psalm 121, which he first heard while on a road march at West Point, and had just read again the night before this mission at a Bible study group on the base at Bagram.

> I lift up my eyes to the hills—
> where does my help come from?
> My help comes from the Lord,
> the Maker of heaven and earth.
>
> He will not let your foot slip—
> He who watches over you will not slumber;
> indeed, He who watches over Israel
> will neither slumber nor sleep.

The Lord watches over you—
the Lord is your shade at your right hand;
the sun will not harm you by day,
nor the moon by night.

The Lord will keep you from all harm—
He will watch over your life;
the Lord will watch over your coming and going
both now and forever more.

Shortly after six P.M., just as it was turning dark, Jason Cunningham's condition worsened. With PJ Keary Miller assisting, the Ranger medic began doing CPR, but it was to no avail. In his affidavit, Vance says, "I was watching our medic . . . as he was working on the PJ. I saw him doing CPR and I knew it was bad. I then saw the medic stand up, look over at me, and start walking to me. That is when I got on the radio to Controller and told him we now have seven KIA."

Cunningham had lived for roughly six hours after being wounded. His death was the result of internal bleeding that could likely have been stopped by surgeons waiting at Bagram, about an hour away.

Just about two hours later, a pair of Chinooks accompanied by Apache gunships lifted off from Texaco FARP, and at eight-fifteen P.M., the first one began lifting Self's platoon, the aircrew, and the wounded off the ridge. The second Chinook evacuated the bodies of the seven Americans who died during the battle of Takur Ghar. Yet another helicopter picked up the SEALs, whose abortive attempt to establish an observation post in the middle of enemy-held territory was what triggered the fifteen-hour fight.

By the time the helicopters arrived at Bagram Air Base, Chris Young was already waiting on the tarmac with several other PJs, and with the doctors from the FST team. Chris knew that a PJ had been shot, but didn't know that he'd died. And he had no idea which PJ had been hit. "With standard triage of patients, the worst come in first, and then it trickles down, until finally the last to come in are the dead. When the birds landed, it sounds bad, but we were looking at the patients—yeah, you're looking at his injuries—but you're looking at his face, too, to see, 'all right, is this my guy?' So we brought them in, transferred them into the emergency room, and I'm thinking, 'Okay, cool, the worst patients just came in, and one of our guys wasn't there. Things are looking good so far.'

"As we were going back out to the flight line to meet the next helicopter is when I ran into Keary Miller, and the fact that he was walking, straight up, no bandages, still had his weapon, that showed me, 'Okay, Jason was the one who got hit.' And I went up to him, and the first words out of his mouth were, 'We lost Jason.' And the world comes crashing down around you.

"I gathered up all the special-tactics guys, and I said, 'Hey, look, I just talked to Keary. We lost Jason. Everybody else needs us here right now. We'll deal with that later.' "

Then he went to find Dr. Brian Burlingame, the commander of the FST team who had befriended Jason, and gave him the news. The doctor described his reaction as perhaps the most unprofessional moment of his life. For a moment he allowed himself to react like a friend; then it was back to treating the injured. Later Burlingame had to go into the morgue tent and examine each of the fatalities. They'd been placed in body bags by the PJs who brought them off the helicopters. The doctor recalled the moment he was confronted with the reality of Jason Cunningham's death. "When I finally did see him, it was very devastating. It's like losing a friend. We've always lost friends in our lifetime, car accident, cancer, and illness. But Jason was a little different, just because of his nature: young, happy guy doing his job, and excited about doing his job, and died in the conduct of doing his job in a selfless manner. He had been in my area three, four hours a day, every day for weeks, and for me, he was as much a part of my unit as any of my other guys were.

"Jason's death was overwhelming; however, within seconds, there were other things going on. And it sounds almost contrived, but it was almost like turning on and off a switch. If I thought about him for just one second, it was hard. But I could then literally turn my head and engage in another action and be fine.

"I've never felt anything before or since like that, where you're emotionally involved for a minute with one particular thing and then have that not weigh on you. Maybe it's because other things were going on that were so important that I knew that I needed to be that way. But it was after everyone was taken care of, and Keary was back, and some other folks were back; then you start thinking about it, talking about it."

Dr. Burlingame continued, "The way you deal with it is saying, 'The kid did a good job; this is what he lived to do, which is to take care of wounded soldiers.' And he did it using his training and he did it well. His whole family can rest assured that he didn't die in vain; he died saving someone's life."

Then he said something that combat surgeons have known forever: "There's one fact in war. Young men die no matter what we do."

For PJ Pat Harding, the pain of that night was excruciating. Not only had he lost a fellow pararescueman, but combat controller John Chapman, who had been killed early in the fighting, had been Harding's team leader in the early stages of training, and the two were close. Caleb Ethridge was helping with the casualties. "You could see in Pat's face, you could just see tears, and he had a little bit of anger, sadness—and just pissed. He was just torn up seeing his friend's body."

Chris Young was trying to focus on the job, trying to keep the PJ team functioning through their grief. He recalls, "The hardest part for me was the fact that I've never lost anybody on my team before like that. I've had one guy get seriously injured, but I've never had one die in combat, let alone from an injury that just happened to hit him where his armor didn't protect. You try to think, 'All right, he was shot. Where was he shot? He was shot in the back. Well, did he have his body armor on? Yes. Did he have the plates in his body armor? Yes. Well, then how the hell did he die? Because it went in underneath his body armor, right below the bottom of it.'"

Then Young begins thinking about the message he had monitored on SATCOM, the one that said no attempt would be made to evac the wounded until after dark.

"When it's our job to treat the injured—'Save Life and Aid the Injured,' as the creed goes—and you're treating one of your friends, that brings it into a whole new realm of, 'Well, we need a helicopter.' 'Well, it's too hot.' 'I don't care if it's too hot. Get a helicopter in there.'

"I understand the decision-making process of the higher-ups. I don't like it. A lot of things happened over there that we don't like, but you have to understand it."

Does he understand the notion of sacrificing more lives to recover the body of a dead American, which was how the tragic day started?

"The easiest thing to say is, 'If I'm the one that's dead, no, I don't want you to recover me.' On the flip side of the coin, 'If you're dead, I'm going to do anything I can to recover you.' Just because that's the bond that we have with each other.

"If I'd been out there, I would not have even hesitated. We lost a dude; we have to go back and get him. The way that I understand it, they didn't know one way or the other. If there's even a question, you have to go back. And then it becomes, 'Is he dead-dead? Does he have injuries incompatible with life? Or is he just severely injured?' You don't know that. Unless you make the effort, you'll never know. As a leader, that's something that'll eat you up.

"I learned a long time ago, the best thing you can do is the right thing to do. The next best thing you can do is the wrong thing to do. And the worst thing you can do is nothing."

The loss of Jason Cunningham was devastating to another PJ, twenty-five-year-old SrA Adrian Durham. The two had started the indoctrination course together, had suffered injuries and been set back together, and ultimately graduated together. They'd had a long time to get to know each other very well, and to ponder the meaning of their lives. For him, Jason's death was crushing. "It's like he was my brother. Jason was, like, more to me than my brothers were. I spent day in and day out with him. We lived with each other as roommates, worked with each other for three years. You see the same people everywhere you go; you get tired of them, but you go away from them and then you miss them. You can't wait to get back 'cause they're your family. And I lost Jason, it hurt more than anything else. I've had family members who've died and never shed a tear, and I couldn't stop crying when Jason died. It was one of the most hurtful experiences in my life. The only thing that's comforting me was that he didn't die needlessly. He didn't die in some worthless training accident. He died doing the job.

"And then you're kind of jealous, in a way, because he got to go up there, he had the option to go out and do it. I didn't get that chance. You're thinking, 'When's it going to be my turn?' The only terrible thing about that is that he had two beautiful daughters, and they'll never see him again, and a wife who'll never see him again. That's the worst part about it."

Lt. Col. Patrick Pihana, the commander of the 23rd Special Tactics Squadron to which Jason had been attached, was still coping with the fact that he was the one who had sent him into combat. "Yes, you know you're in command of troops that you've just sent into combat, and you get past the 'I just talked to Jason at dinner the night before.' But probably what impacted me the hardest was the night he died. Here I stood knowing what had happened. I knew that we'd lost one of our nation's children, and there was a family at home that didn't know yet, a wife and children and mom and dad and brothers and sisters and aunts and uncles and the whole network of people. I knew there was going to be bad news that was going to come to them, and it breaks your heart. At the same time, you're trying to carry on the battle, recovering people you still have out there, and continuing on with the next mission."

Given his position as head of a special-operations unit, Pihana has had to cope with the death of one of his men in the past, and is realistic enough to know he'll be dealing with a similar situation again. To bear that burden requires a coping strategy. "My philosophy on it has been based on four things: First, a faith. I have a firm belief in God. Then family and friends. I come from a family that's supported me and, obviously, a family in the Air Force and friends that support us here. And then our flag, our country. So the three Fs, or four if you will, that if I had to prepare myself for this, everything I do kind of stems from the support I get from those three or four areas right there. Yes, it's always a possibility it could happen. We train our best and do our best to make sure it doesn't happen, but if it does, we take care of those who are still left behind, and then we carry on as best we can."

A couple of days later, a memorial service was held at Bagram for the seven men who were killed during the battle on Takur Ghar mountain. The sky was cloudy, but the sun was breaking through in places, accenting the mountains surrounding the base that were still snowcapped. It was a beautiful early spring day that belied the sadness of those who were gathered to mourn. Against a background of continuing air operations, a chaplain offered prayers, an honor guard fired a twenty-one-gun salute, and a close friend of each of the men killed in action stood in front of the mourners and offered remembrances of their friend. Speaking for Jason was his team leader and mentor, Chris Young.

"I talked about how he was an annoying little shit, y'know, about how he crossed over from the Navy, and me being a former Marine, we kind of bonded and joked and things like that. I wanted the guys to know how eager he was to train and to learn, and I know that he failed his first medical class at Bragg, and he got set back to the next one. Well, in between those classes, he was supposed to be doing cleanup chores and things like that. But what he ended up doing was skipping out of his chores and going to listen in on other medical lectures so that he could be a better medic. And then I tasked him with writing a patrol order over the weekend, and it got to the point where he was calling the house so much that my wife would just look at the caller ID and she'd say, 'Chris, it's Jason. You get it this time.' Y'know, so we joked about that. I told them that one of the formal schools I'd been to, the instructor told us, 'Do good; don't suck.' And that's what I told Jason before I left Afghanistan to go back up to K-2.

"After the service, Captain Self came up to me and he said, 'Y'know, Chris, three of my guys are alive because your boy did it right up there.' And when that happened, the only thing I could think of was, 'Well, if I can't bring Jason home, then the memory that he was doing it right, right up till the end, is the best thing that we could ask for.' "

# CHAPTER 12

# "I REGRET TO INFORM YOU . . ."
## MARCH 5, 2002

Shortly after 9/11, Theresa Cunningham heard the rock group Five for Fighting sing "Superman," and the lyric "I can't stand to fly. I'm not that naive, I'm just out to find the better part of me" immediately reminded her of Jason. She bought the CD and would play it for him often. "It was who he was. He wanted to do great things, but he didn't want to be glorified for it; he just wanted to do it."

When she met Jason, they were both in the Navy, in Italy. Theresa was twenty-three, Jason was twenty, and though she had never even thought about getting married, the day they met she knew she wanted to be friends with him forever. They got married, had baby Kyla, and got divorced. The trouble was, as she now puts it, "We were both thirteen." But they never gave up on the friendship, and a couple years later they remarried, and then had their second daughter, Hannah.

By this time they were both out of the Navy, and Jason was on track to become a pararescueman. He'd considered joining the SEALs, but decided he'd rather be in the business of saving lives rather than taking them. Unlike many of the PJs who were aching to get into Operation Enduring Freedom, Jason wasn't enthusiastic about leaving Theresa and the girls for Afghanistan; she

PJ Keary Miller comforts Theresa Cunningham following the formal presentation to her of Jason's Air Force Cross (Posthumous) at a ceremony attended by four thousand at Kirtland Air Force Base. (*Michael Hirsh*)

says he was actually upset because there were more medical training classes he wanted to take before he put himself in a combat situation. Once there, however, his calls home and the e-mails he sent her were nothing but enthusiastic.

When Cunningham got his first combat save on the Ditka 03 mission, he called home about thirty times. Theresa, an Air Force ROTC cadet at Valdosta State University, had class all day, and missed the calls. "He kept calling and calling. He was obviously living on the line to get to use the phone. And then he got hold of me, a little past midnight on the fourteenth, on Valentine's Day, and he began to tell me the story and we got cut off. Just heard a click, and then he called me back later, saying, 'I guess I can't talk about it.' I could hear it in his voice. He was dancing. And he said, 'Watch the news! Watch the news! I can't tell you what's going on, so watch the news and I'll tell you about it as soon as I get home.'" She still has one of his phone calls on her answering machine.

Like any man who goes off to war leaving a family behind, Jason Cunningham wanted to comfort Theresa, assuring her that he was safe, that he was being careful. His e-mails were short and to the point. *Safe as usual* was a typical message. "I think he was trying to reassure me, and I knew that as much as he was an adrenaline junkie, he really wanted to be careful. He wanted to make sure that he was the most prepared guy there; he wasn't taking any chances with his life."

Even so, when Jason's mom, Jackie Cunningham, called from New Mexico to tell her that the news was reporting a helicopter down in Afghanistan, she got concerned. She'd come home from school to grab lunch, and the phone rang as she was dashing out the door. Theresa doesn't know what caused her to pick it up. "I never answer the phone when I'm home on my break, 'cause I just want to eat. But I picked it up and it was his mother."

Jackie Cunningham recalls the conversation vividly. She'd heard a report on the radio and there was no one for her to call for more information except Theresa. "I don't want to alarm you, but have you heard from Jason? 'Cause there's a helicopter that went down on a rescue mission."

Their mother/daughter-in-law relationship had never been very close, and her initial reaction was annoyance. "I don't know. I haven't heard anything. Don't worry." Promising to call if she did hear something, she hung up, and immediately turned on the TV. "They said there were two helicopters down, and that was all they said."

Theresa remembers being extremely frustrated. With an emphatic "Shit!" to no one in particular, she picked up the phone and called the 38th Rescue

Squadron at Moody. " 'What's going on? There's a helicopter down. Is Jason okay?' "

"They said, 'We haven't heard anything about it; don't worry about it.' I said, 'Fine, whatever.' So I went to school and I came home, and then I was just glued to the TV. There was a helicopter down. They said there were seven people dead. And I thought, 'There's no way. There's too many people. There's a million people in the military and there's hundreds of thousands of people out there. There's no way.'

"But I was still worried, so I called up again and talked to Terry." Maj. Terry Johnson was the Director of Operations of the 38th. "He said, 'I haven't heard anything, and no news is good news, Theresa. We haven't heard anything.' "

A bit later she went to the home of Stephanie and Craig Clark. Craig, another PJ in the unit, did a search for the story on the Internet, then tried to calm her fears by saying that PJs didn't fly in Chinook helicopters. It didn't work. She said, "You're wrong, Craig. It's a joint mission out there. They're on any kind of helicopter." Theresa returned home around eight o'clock. An hour and a half later, figuring that if something was wrong she would have heard, she went to bed feeling totally confident that Jason wasn't involved.

At five-thirty the next morning, her alarm went off. She took a shower and began to get ready for school. The girls would sleep until seven o'clock. She did not turn on the television.

At about six-thirty, there was a knock on the door. "Jason had sent me an e-mail and it said he might be home sooner than we thought. And he's come home before, unexpectedly. So when there was a knock on the door, at first I thought, 'Oh, God, it's one of those creepy neighbors.' And then I thought, 'Oh, he's home.' So I ran to the door.

"It was a bunch of people in uniform. And I thought, 'He's hurt; they're going to take me to him.' And I guess I was expecting them to say, 'Get dressed. We're leaving.'

"I think I knew the situation. There's no other reason those people would be coming in at six o'clock in the morning. And when they came in, a part of me knew."

General Folkerts followed protocol. "Are you Theresa Cunningham?"

Theresa, standing there in a robe, her dark hair still wet from the shower, didn't respond. Major Savino looked at her, and then answered for her. "Yes." And then they came in.

Somehow she found herself seated on the couch, with General Folkerts sitting on the coffee table facing her. "I regret—"

It was all she heard. Theresa doesn't know what he said after that. She has no recollection of any of it. The room went into soft focus; sounds blended together into a background buzz. "I remember people, like voices in the background, kind of talking to each other and not to me. And I think somebody said, 'Somebody's coming over, Theresa,' and then people just started coming over and over and over."

The babies, ages four and two, woke up to the sounds of commotion in the living room. Theresa heard the girls, and went to them. "I sat with them and I just hugged them. I didn't say . . . I was kind of . . . I still feel like I'm in shock. At the time I felt like, 'I don't know what's going on,' and then I think I was hysterical because later I heard things that I did and they don't sound normal. I don't remember them, so I think I must have just been out in space somewhere."

Half an hour after that knock on the door, Theresa pulled herself together enough to make three phone calls: to her parents in Southern California, to school, and to Jason's parents in Gallup, New Mexico.

It was five in the morning when the phone rang in the home of Jackie and Red Cunningham. Jason's mom was already awake. She'd found it difficult to sleep, even though Theresa had phoned the previous evening and said that no news was good news. But Red was still asleep, and the phone startled him. "I just jumped straight out of bed. I knew when I heard the phone ring. I knew what happened."

Red dressed, and then drove his GMC pickup truck to the Conoco propane facility where he worked as a welder and crane operator. Rather than going inside, he asked the first person he saw to get his friend and coworker Greg Peterson to come out to the parking lot. Just the day before, Red had spoken to Greg about his fears for Jason. He'd told him that a helicopter like the one Jason was flying on had gone down, but they hadn't heard anything.

"I came out there and he was leaning against his truck," Peterson said. "I could tell he'd been cryin'. Red said, 'Them bastards got him.' I said, 'What?'

"He said, 'They got him. They killed him.' We just hugged, stood there for five or ten minutes. He was crying. I just stayed there and held him for quite a while. That's the only time I seen him cry the whole day. The rest of the day he was just quiet and reserved, which is not Red."

On the drive home from the Conoco facility, as Red turned the corner onto their street, he saw three Air Force people at a neighbor's house. He remembered Jason had always told them, "Don't believe anything till they pull up there in that blue car."

"But they were at the wrong house, so I still had that flicker of hope. And then, what seemed like an hour later, they got their addresses straightened out and they showed up at our house."

All Red Cunningham remembers is that it was three people from Kirtland Air Force Base, home of the pararescue school, near Albuquerque, and that one of them was a woman and another was a chaplain. "They hand you a piece of paper, and it's got this written out on it. I don't remember—I was in shock at the time. I wanted to know what the hell happened."

The piece of paper—not letterhead—didn't provide any answers. It read:

*5 March 2002*

*Dear Mr. and Mrs. Lawrence D. Cunningham,*

*On behalf of the Chief of Staff, United States Air Force, I regret to inform you of the untimely death of your son, Senior Airman Jason D. Cunningham. He died on 4 March 2002, as the result of injuries he received in combat. While further details are unavailable at this time, you will receive a letter from your son's commander, which will provide additional circumstances. If the Air Force can further assist you, please contact the Air Force Personnel Center, Casualty Service Branch, at 1-800-433-0048. Again, on behalf of the Chief of Staff, please accept the Air Force's deepest condolences.*

*Signed: MICHAEL C. MCMAHAN, Major General, USAF*

*DELIVERED BY:*
*KEVIN GARDNER, Major, USAF*
*Kirtland Air Force Base, New Mexico 87117*

The words that echoed through Red Cunningham's mind that morning were what his son had told him when his four years' enlistment in the Navy was up. Jason had already passed the physical tests to become a Navy SEAL, but told his dad, "That's just not what I really want to do. I want to save people."

Red says, "Those were his exact words. 'I want to save people.' Not go out and search out, destroy, or capture or whatever. 'I want to go out and save people.' And he told me at that time, 'I'd like to become a pararescueman someday.'"

Jason came home from the Navy, spent some time in Gallup, hunting elk with his dad in the nearby mountains where the PJs in school at Kirtland AFB actually trained. He was trying to come to some conclusions about his life, and once he did, he explained them to his father. "He decided to get in the Air Force, try to get in the PJ program. He had me pretty well educated into what they did and how dangerous their job could be."

Red also knew that the attrition rate for wanna-be PJs was incredibly high, higher than SEALs, higher than Green Berets. One time he asked Jason, "What if you don't make it?"

"And he had no answer to that, because he was going to make it, one way or the other. He would go all-out; that's just typical for him, through his whole life. 'What if you don't or if you can't?' doesn't enter into the equation."

And the credo, "That Others May Live"?

"He had a heart-to-heart with me to make sure I understood what that meant. He knew what that meant."

That didn't mean that there wasn't an ache inside a father's heart, knowing the path his son had chosen was a difficult and dangerous one. "You got to come to a point where there's no more arguing about it, there's no more trying to convince them. You just have to accept it, and then pat them on the back and tell 'em, 'Do the best you can do.' From that point on, I've got to deal with the 'you might die' part of it. I always emphasized, 'just don't take any unnecessary chances just to become a . . .'" Red Cunningham's voice breaks. He never does say the word *hero*.

"I always told him, 'You're just like John Wayne in the twenty-first century.' That attitude. I was surprised he didn't rip his shirt off and there's a big S tattooed on his chest, the way his attitude was. He was going to do what he started to do, regardless. And that's the way he was."

The Air Force notification team wasn't able to give the Cunninghams any information about what had happened or where. What Red remembers being told was, "You have two hours to notify anyone you want to tell, and then it will be released to the media."

What's that supposed to mean to a pipe welder living in Gallup, New Mexico, population twenty-one thousand, about 140 miles west of Albuquerque, a town that doesn't even have its own broadcast television station? "It'll be released to the media in two hours." Yeah? So what?

"So what?" got answered in midafternoon, when there was a knock on the door of their modest one-story home. Greg Peterson, who had stopped by to see if there was any way he could help, answered the door. He recalls it was a woman who identified herself as a reporter for the Associated Press. She wanted to talk to Jason's parents. Peterson asked her to wait, and went back to relay the request. At the time Red was on his way to the Albuquerque airport to pick up their elder son, Chris, who was coming in from Seattle. Jackie had no interest in talking, and that was what Peterson told the AP reporter. He remembers her saying, "Well, you know, all the press knows and they're on the way." He didn't know. She elaborated: "Everybody from Albuquerque is comin' this way. There's people from Phoenix, and other areas from all over the state."

Reiterating that Jason's mom had no desire to talk at that time, Peterson sent the woman away. But when he got back into the house, he warned Jackie about what was to come, and said he was going to ask the Gallup police to send some men over to "be there and help control this mess when it came." Peterson, who was a former Odessa, Texas, cop and spoke the language, didn't have any trouble getting their help. He asked them to set up a perimeter that would keep the media from tramping through the Cunninghams' front yard and banging on the door.

Meanwhile, fifteen hundred miles to east, in his home near Hurlburt Air Force Base, Florida, Maj. Don Tyler was in a reclining chair watching the news on television. He was recovering from surgery that had been performed the day before on the shoulder he'd mangled three weeks earlier in the crash of Ditka 03. Suddenly he called for his wife, Barbara, who came running back into the room to see what was wrong. What she saw were tears streaming down her husband's face. "Something terrible has happened," he said. Barbara had known about the American casualties when they were reported the day before, but the men hadn't been identified. That was when Don told her that one of the dead was Jason Cunningham, and he thought Jason had been the PJ who had taken care of him after the crash.

Out west, it didn't take long for the media horde to arrive. TV crews from the Albuquerque ABC, CBS, and NBC affiliates set up near the house, as did the Fox station from Farmington, New Mexico. At its peak, Peterson counted eight or nine video cameras, four or five still photographers, and reporters from newspapers and radio stations in the surrounding area; roughly forty media people in front of the house.

What everyone wanted besides the photo op was a statement from Jason's parents; interviewing neighbors who really didn't know the family well wasn't adding much to their stories. But what could Red Cunningham say that would be meaningful at that moment? How many ways can the father of a young man just killed in combat say, "I don't have any details"? Should he be required to tell the world how he feels at that moment? Did they really need video of him being reduced to tears to make their viewers understand that the parents of a soldier killed defending his country are hurting?

Could an assignment editor ever contemplate being in the position Red and Jackie were in that afternoon? Would that contemplation lead to compassion, and a decision *not* to send a reporter out to ask, however politely, "How do you feel?" while divining that something journalistically important had been captured on videotape when tears poured from Red Cunningham's eyes.

It's not that the local news shouldn't make a big deal about a homegrown airman killed in combat. They should. It's their responsibility to headline it so that citizens are reminded in very real terms of the human consequences that go with a political decision to fight a war. But descending in a horde on his parents' home within hours of their learning that their boy was dead is neither productive nor respectful. An informed assignment editor would know that the pararescue school is only minutes away, on the military side of the Albuquerque airport, at Kirtland Air Force Base. There were people there who knew Jason, who'd trained Jason, who could explain what a pararescueman does, and why a young man with a wife and two children might seek an assignment that requires him to live by the credo "That Others May Live." Jason was the first PJ to die in combat since Vietnam. You'd think the instructors at the schoolhouse, or current PJ trainees might have something consequential to say about the nature of their commitment, about the impact of losing one of their own, about flag and country. Surely that would be more meaningful than reducing a father to tears on camera.

But the horde wanted the parents, and Red and Jackie decided that they'd try to write a statement that Red would read for the cameras. With the help of a woman that Jackie had once worked for at a local radio station, they wrote the statement. Peterson says that friends tried to make it clear that they didn't have to do it, but the parents felt they owed it to Jason's memory. So the media was told they could set up their microphones inside the picket fence bordering the front yard, set the cameras outside the fence so that they'd be a good twenty feet from Red when he came out, and wait. That made everyone happy except the Fox affiliate crew, who moaned that their newscast went on an hour before everyone else's and they needed the statement to be made sooner. Peterson explained that they'd have to take no for an answer.

Sometime around nine o'clock, Red Cunningham came out of the house and read the family's statement. Not surprisingly, he began to break down as he read. His friend Greg Peterson said that was the first time Red cried since they were together in the parking lot early in the morning. Peterson says that to their credit, the media people were respectful.

In addition to their having to deal with the media blocking the street in front of their house, the Cunninghams' phone had been ringing off the hook all day long with calls from newspapers, radio stations, and other media from all over the country, all taking advantage of the fact that until that awful day, Red and Jackie never saw the need for an unlisted phone number. Peterson tried telling Jackie that she didn't have to answer the phone and talk to everyone who called. That it could be done later. He even suggested unplugging the phone. But he says, "She was afraid not to answer because it might be someone in the family she needed to talk to. Then she'd get on the phone, and you know how they are, before you know it they'd have her going, and she's bawlin' her eyes out, she's an emotional wreck, and she has to sit down and talk to these people on the phone, and this had been going on all day and all night long."

Around ten P.M., everyone who'd been in front of their house had packed up and gone—except for one car. In it was a field producer for CBS's *The Early Show*. With her was an acquaintance of the Cunninghams', the local radio station executive who had been trying for hours to convince the parents to go to Albuquerque in the middle of the night in order to appear live on CBS with host Bryant Gumbel. Thus far she'd been unsuccessful, especially with Peterson and Chris and Lori, Jason's brother and sister, lobbying their parents hard not to put themselves through that ordeal. Peterson had been especially clear, saying, "You guys do not need to be haulin' across the country in the middle of the night."

So a compromise was reached. The network was going to send a satellite truck from Albuquerque so the interview could be conducted live, inside the home. Shortly thereafter, the family was told that the New Mexico–based truck had been sent elsewhere. Instead, arrangements had been made to bring in another broadcast truck from Phoenix, 330 miles away, which could arrive in time to set up and do the interview between five and six in the morning.

But Peterson still wasn't comfortable, especially when he saw the two women in the car, waiting, hours before the Phoenix truck was due to arrive. When he walked over to the car, they assured him that everything was fine, the truck was on its way, and he had nothing to worry about. Maybe it was that he still had some of his cop instinct in his blood, but he wasn't convinced. He said, "You guys do not try again to talk them into going to Albuquerque. I don't care how bad they think they need to talk on the TV, they do not need to do that now. They are going through so much hell, they do not need to go to Albuquerque tonight. They're tired; they're emotionally beat up. You guys just need to leave them alone until this truck comes; you'll do the thing inside, hopefully short and sweet, and then move on."

His warning was not oblique. "I made them promise that they're not going to bother them, not going to try and talk them into going to Albuquerque. I specifically went over that with them, and not in a roundabout way, and they promised me that this was not going to happen. They said, 'Everything's fine, we're not going to bother them anymore.'" His last words to the producer were, "They are at a vulnerable state right now and they're not thinking straight, and I don't want anybody railroading them."

Apparently, the only words she heard were *vulnerable* and *not thinking straight.*

Shortly after Peterson left, the Cunninghams were told that the Phoenix truck was not going to be coming, and that they had to go to Albuquerque. The network was even going to provide a limousine. Jackie wanted no part of it; she desperately needed rest. But Red, who recognized after the fact that he'd been manipulated and coerced, that his grief had been exploited, agreed. "It shouldn't have happened," he said on the one-year anniversary of Jason's death. "But while it was happening, I was thinking that I wanted the country to know the sacrifice that Jason had made." So at one in the morning, he and Jason's sister, Lori, were picked up and driven to a studio in Albuquerque, where from New York, Jane Clayson conducted a very brief interview with Red and the parents of one of the other soldiers who had been killed. They didn't get back home until ten in the morning. Red Cunningham had been awake for thirty straight hours.

Late the previous afternoon, the manager of Conoco's Gallup facility had heard from Red's boss, Chuck White, that the media circus was out of hand and that the Cunninghams could use some professional help. He contacted the company's director of public affairs for the Western United States, a former Associated Press writer named John Bennitt. He spoke with Jackie from his office in Denver, and then, at about the same time that Red had been driving to

Albuquerque to pick up Jason's brother Chris, Bennitt began working the phones. He called people he knew at the TV stations and newspapers in the area, telling them in no uncertain terms to call off the dogs, adding that if they wanted to talk with the Cunninghams, they could go through him. Unfortunately, there was little he could do about what was already happening at the home except contact the Gallup PD and reinforce Greg Peterson's request for a police presence there.

It had been suggested to Theresa by the commandant of the pararescue school that the famous national cemetery overlooking the nation's capital would be the appropriate place to bury the first PJ killed in combat since April 6, 1972, when T.Sgt. Al Avery and Sgt. Bill Pearson died during an attempt to rescue a downed aircrew in Vietnam, and she'd reluctantly accepted the idea. The problem this created for Jason's parents was that there was no provision for the Air Force to pay for or provide transportation for the entire immediate family. Immediately after notification of a death, the next of kin receives a check for six thousand dollars from the Air Force to cover those kinds of costs. But the parents of a married serviceman are not considered his beneficiary or legal next of kin, and as a result receive no financial aid. The widow's immediate concern was getting her own parents and family from their home in California to Valdosta, and then to Arlington. She says they spent more than eight thousand dollars on plane tickets—and that was taking advantage of so-called "bereavement fares" where they existed.

When this problem was communicated to Conoco's district manager in Gallup, Mike Johnson, he got in touch with Bennitt, and it was quickly agreed that with all the hassles in post-9/11 air travel, it would be better if they provided one of the company's aircraft to fly the family to the funeral.

Bennitt wouldn't meet the Cunninghams in person until a few days later, when he picked them up at the Gallup airport on a Gulfstream G-4 jet, to fly Jackie and Red, their daughter and son, as well as their respective spouses, to Washington for Jason's funeral at Arlington National Cemetery. In an era where corporations regularly get reamed for not doing the right thing, it's worth mentioning that Conoco also picked up the entire cost of the family's trip, including hotel and meals, and kept John Bennitt with them through the ordeal to serve as liaison with the Air Force and try to keep things as smooth as possible.

What Jason's parents had discovered in their long day with the media, his widow was also going to learn in the upcoming week. That is, Jason was no longer theirs alone. "Everyone wanted a piece of him," said Theresa, her voice revealing an anger that still smolders. Clearly she saw no merit in the presumption that, in death, Jason belonged not just to her and her girls, but also to the country. Jason was not a public figure, not an assassinated president, and Theresa did not naturally come to the role of Jackie Kennedy in a pink pillbox hat. Feeling like that, getting through all of the public ceremonies was going to be a painful ordeal.

The fact that there had been long-standing tension between Theresa and the elder Cunninghams also made this time more difficult, and things would get worse, not better, over the next few months. The military has its protocol for dealing with the death of a serviceman or -woman, and clearly the support system is structured to aid only the legal "next of kin." In Jason's case, "next of kin" were his wife and daughters. But Jackie Cunningham is very clear when she says the system actually abuses the parents of a young man, disenfranchising them at a critical family moment. She says, "They confuse 'beneficiary' with 'next of kin.' Jason was my son for twenty-six years."

It's easy to respond that he had been a husband and father, that clearly the son had moved on, and no matter what relationship he'd had with his parents growing up, the parents needed to let go. But there are millions of parents who have discovered that letting go isn't easy. Fortunately, most of them are granted adequate time to let the transition happen naturally, albeit slowly. The Cunninghams weren't that lucky, and that would serve only to make reconciliation more difficult, if not impossible. Whether it meant that they'd not only lost their son, but their granddaughters as well, only time would tell.

The days between learning about Jason's death and his funeral were going to be especially difficult for Theresa Cunningham. They were like an unnaturally long intermission between acts of a tragic play.

Through tears she recalled her four-year-old daughter Kyla's reaction the first night. "She told my friend Tanya that she wanted to get me flowers because I was sad, and it wasn't until everybody left, and all that was left was me and the girls, that I put Hannah to bed and I talked to Kyla. And I said, 'Do you know what happened to your daddy?' And she said, 'Yes.' I said, 'What do you know?' And she said, 'He's dead.' And I said, 'Do you know what that means?' And she said, 'No,' and I said, 'It means that he's not going to come home again.'"

There's no way to recall that moment, or hear about it, without being reduced to tears. After a pause, she says, "That evening when I was alone with my daughters was the last that I was alone for a long time."

On March 12, 2002, eight days after Jason Cunningham bled to death on a remote hilltop in Afghanistan, the ritual that attends the burial of an American military hero began at Arlington National Cemetery. With his fellow PJs standing guard in the chapel, one night of visitation was held for the family, and a second night for the military.

Theresa was having an understandably difficult time coping with expressions of condolence that, while sincere, didn't convey sentiments that she thought were helpful. Perhaps her response was a reflection of how tough the wife of a pararescueman has to be in order to cope with the life the military asks them to lead.

"Jason wasn't *not* careful. He was careful. So when he died and a few of the guys were saying, 'Oh, if I had been there . . . ,' that was very upsetting for me. It was probably one of the more upsetting things, and I don't know why they felt the need to say that. I understand that they were saying, 'I would have . . . ' But I do not believe there's anything anyone could've done, as far as making him safer. Yes, they could've brought him home." She pauses, thinking. "I don't think anyone could've been more prepared. I think that he was definitely not taking chances."

One thing that Theresa realized at Arlington is that the spotlight was on her, and wouldn't be off until long after the interment scheduled on their third day there was over. How she wished that his death had not been the cause for public memorialization. "There's a part of me that wishes that this hadn't been the way he died, because I would've liked to have had some privacy. Everybody's kind of watching you, and you're thinking, 'I just want to sit, I just want to climb in the casket and lay there.' And you can't act like a maniac. You've got two kids and everybody staring at you. So Arlington was a blur. It was people making strange statements, people fighting over position—it was obnoxious."

When she's reminded that those sorts of things happen every day, at ordinary civilian funerals, she responds, "Yes, I understand that. But a lot of people wanted to be aligned with Jason's memory, because this was their one chance to be on the news."

On an average day, twenty-three funerals are conducted at Arlington National Cemetery, most of them not attended by members of Congress, the Air Force chief of staff, the national news media, and a pair of Air Force HH-60G CSAR helicopters. When VIPS are expected, ordinary folks often have to wait—even if the ordinary folks happen to be the family of the deceased. The delay in this case was about fifty minutes, with the family waiting it out in a parked limousine.

When it was communicated to Theresa that some of the bigwigs wanted to speak with her before the ceremony, she was not happy. As she relates it, "So we've been sitting out here, Jason's casket is sitting here in the sun for an hour because you people . . . I mean, if it's Jason's day, why is this about you?" And the response from the minions was, "Okay, we'll be ready to have our interview with you in fifteen minutes."

The assumption was that she'd agree to it. Wrong woman. Wrong place. "I said, 'No. If they want to talk, they can talk afterwards.' And we left. That's when we started moving. I just thought it was very disrespectful to Jason and to us."

The graveside service was quick—Theresa describes it as a blur—less than a quarter hour, very formal, no singing or extended remarks. She may not even have heard Air Force chaplain Martin McGuill say, "If we take his life as an example of selflessness, then we are called by Jesus to love more than we are loved and to forgive more than we are forgiven." The ceremony concluded with a flyover by the helicopters, a twenty-one-gun salute, "Taps," and presentation of the flag that had covered his casket to his widow, and another flag to his mom.

In attendance were more than fifty Air Force pararescuemen, and, with his arm still in a sling and in considerable pain, Maj. Don Tyler, the first patient Jason had treated in combat, specially invited to the ceremony by his widow.

Before she returned to the limousine, a sobbing Theresa Cunningham, holding tight to their two daughters, gently touched the gleaming silver casket.

Ten days later, at a memorial service held near her parents' home in Camarillo, California, Theresa spoke to those who'd come to pay respects at St. Mary Magdalene Church, and read aloud from the letter Jason had given to Chris Young after the Ditka 03 mission, asking that it be delivered to Theresa in the event he didn't make it.

*I could not leave this earth without saying good-bye to you. I will miss you and the girls immensely. I want you to know I died a happy man, happy that I met you and happy that I have two wonderful girls.*

Theresa added, "Even in the face of danger, he was still thinking about us. I keep looking for a reason why. Why? We were really happy. We had two children. Was this his time? Was it his destiny? We don't know."

On September 13, 2002, in a hangar at Kirtland Air Force Base, New Mexico, home of the pararescue school, Air Force chief of staff Gen. John Jumper awarded the Air Force Cross (Posthumous) to SrA Jason Cunningham. The presentation was made to his widow and parents in front of more than four thousand who attended the solemn ceremony.

In presenting the Air Force's highest award for heroism, General Jumper lauded Cunningham as an American hero with supreme dedication to his job and family. "Jason did not get a second chance, but he gave a second chance to others."

The presentation marked only the second time since the close of the Vietnam War that the Air Force has presented its highest award for heroism. The other post-Vietnam AFC was awarded to T.Sgt. Tim Wilkinson, also a PJ, for heroic actions during the battle of Mogadishu.

> Please don't stand and weep
> Those men I had to save
> Not just because of courage
> Or because I'm brave
>
> Not because of orders
> Or because it was my dream
> I did it for my brothers
> I did it for the team
>
> So please don't weep for me
> For all I had to give
> I did it for a reason
> "So that others may live"

> —Jared Marquis
> Jason's brother-in-law

# WHERE ARE THEY NOW?

War is nothing if not fluid. Nothing stands still. Change happens every day, often throughout the day. When I finished the reporting phase for *None Braver* and returned home from Operation Enduring Freedom to write, the people I'd left behind continued to do their job. Some who go to war are lucky enough to rotate home, returning to family and friends, no worse for wear physically, although—whether or not they'll acknowledge it—surely changed by the experience. Others come home broken, and have to begin the long process of healing with the help of doctors, nurses, physical therapists, as well as those who love them. Still others came home, and because those who do what they do are in short supply, took barely more than enough time to resupply, and were sent off to a new war.

I remain touched by those who spoke with me while their hearts were still raw and bleeding as though they'd been ripped from their breasts and scraped and bumped down a gravel road. That is the pain that comes from the loss of a son, a husband, a brother in war. It's a pain that doesn't heal as quickly as a broken bone or a bullet wound. This wound cannot be seen on an X ray; it is deeper, impossible to see, more difficult to treat.

Except, perhaps, for the superdevout, when a son or daughter, or husband or father, or brother or sister is taken from them, there is no consolation to be

Lucky to be alive, PJ Rob Disney receives an emotional welcome from one of his PJ buddies after being released from Walter Reed Army Medical Center. (*Courtesy of Barbara Disney*)

found in the all-too-often glibly spoken belief that "he's in a better place." If you tell that to a five-year-old little girl or boy who will never be hugged again by Mommy or Daddy, you're fooling yourself, and you're certainly not comforting the child. Perhaps as they grow older they'll find some solace in the knowledge that their mom or dad died for our country, performing the most righteous mission of all, so that others may live. But in a better place? No. You won't find a mom or dad in their forties or fifties, or a child of five, or a teenager of fifteen, who will buy into that trope. Their loved one, taken too soon, belongs with them, but that will never be. And they've had to get on with life.

Two months after Jason Cunningham was buried at Arlington National Cemetery, his commanding officer at Bagram, Lt. Col. Patrick Pihana, found himself seated at his computer contemplating the fact that it was Mother's Day, a holiday that forevermore would cause Jackie Cunningham's heart to ache. He'd long ago done the expected military thing, written the letter of regret to the grieving parents, but as he sat at his desk, he was moved to write once again.

> *Dear Mrs. Cunningham,*
>
> *I'm sitting at my computer at work on Mother's Day, and struggle to tell you how deeply sorry I am for our loss—especially on this special day. I say ours, because Jason belonged to a tremendous group of people all over the country, including myself, that he touched during his wonderful life.*
>
> *Although I had never met Jason before, I ate chow with him the night of his last mission. We stood in an extremely long line waiting for our food, and we had some time to talk. Jason, like his colleagues in Pararescue, was a professional, brave young man. What struck me most was how easy it was to talk to him. He reminded me very much of my own younger brother. He was intense when we talked about his job, yet had a ready smile and a great sense of humor. You could also tell Jason was a born leader, and someone who made things happen. I always hoped if I ever fell wounded in battle, I would look up and see a PJ over me, someone just like Jason. Fortunately for the survivors of that battle, Jason was there.*
>
> *Your son was very special; you already know that. Unfortunately, not everyone in our great country will know of Jason's sacrifice, or how*

*he upheld the highest ideals of our great nation. Although I am fortu-
nate to say I have been in the presence of one of our great military heroes, I would do anything to bring him back.*

*My words will be lost to history. But having a deep faith in God, I
know Jason's presence here was a direct gift from God, and everything
he accomplished will live forever in our hearts.*

*May God bless you on this special day.*

*Lt. Col. Patrick P. Pihana*
*Commander, 23rd Special Tactics Squadron*

Months after Jason's death, Jackie and Red Cunningham were still struggling with both the emotional and financial burden the tragedy had wrought.
For months Jackie was unable to work. Initially Red's employer, Conoco Oil,
picked up the cost of counseling for the family. But as things happen these
days with big corporations, Conoco merged with Texaco, expenses had to be
cut, and the Cunninghams were told they'd have to cover the copayment out
of their already diminished income. At the same time, they were out-of-pocket
in order to attend the Air Force Cross ceremony at Kirtland AFB, as well as
several other ceremonies honoring Jason's memory. How could they *not* go?

Recall that had not Conoco jumped in to provide a plane to take their
family to Arlington and to cover the costs of hotel and meals in a high-cost,
expense-account location, attending the funeral of their youngest son would
have been an overwhelming financial burden. While the Air Force would have
eventually reimbursed them for their own travel, the cost of flying Jason's
brother and sister and their respective spouses would not have been picked up
by the military. As it stood, Jason's grandparents were unable to afford the trip,
and there was no more room on the Conoco jet.

The financial burden on the Cunningham family is not unique to relatives of servicemen and -women who die for their country. Little more than a
year after Brig. Gen. John H. Folkerts had to personally notify Theresa Cunningham of her husband's death, he was faced once more with the onerous
task. An HH-60G helicopter from the Moody-based 41st Rescue Squadron
crashed in Afghanistan, killing all six on board. The helicopter had been on
the most righteous of missions, flying with another HH-60 to medevac two
small, seriously injured Afghan children, when it went down in bad weather.

A memorial service was scheduled for all six crewmembers at Moody Air
Force Base near Valdosta, Georgia. Again, the Air Force could help reimburse

the costs of transportation for next of kin, but as General Folkerts said in an interview after the service, "One family had eleven people that needed to fly from Michigan to Valdosta. We have to draw the line somewhere." He's not being unsympathetic; just realistic.

But what if the solution existed outside the government? Here's how the problem could be solved: All the airlines that received bailout money in grants or loan guarantees, and all the airlines that accept government contracts to fly troops or cargo should be required as a condition of receiving those grants, loans or contracts, to fly *at no cost* the close relatives of those killed in combat or who have died as a result of combat wounds or injuries, to any funeral, official memorial service, or posthumous medal award ceremony. "Close relatives" does not limit it to legal next-of-kin or beneficiaries. It means what it says. If the funeral, memorial service or medal ceremony is held at or near a military base, housing accommodations should also be made available at no cost to close relatives.

Consider Operation Iraqi Freedom. There were fewer than two hundred coalition deaths as a result of that war. If each of those who died for their country had ten people who needed tickets, the airlines would have had to provide two thousand seats. Given the load factors on airplanes since 9/11, that would hardly be a burden—even on financially strapped carriers. Besides, they owe it to the country. This is an idea that should receive bipartisan support in the Congress. All it requires is for some of the lawmakers who have served in our military to take the lead.

In late winter at Moody Air Force Base, Brigadier General Folkerts had insisted that his squadron commanders in the 347th Rescue Wing role-play a mass casualty scenario. Reluctantly, they humored the boss and went through the exercise.

Less than three weeks later, the flags at Moody were lowered to half-staff. Thirty Lowndes County Sheriff's Department cruisers, their blue lights flashing, formed cordons outside both of Moody's gates, demonstrating the solidarity of the people of greater Valdosta with the Air Force community mourning its loss. And inside the largest hangar on the base, close to two thousand people had come to pay their respects to the aircrew of Komodo 11, Lt. Col. John Stein, Capt. (Select) Tamara Archuleta, S.Sgt. Jason Hicks and S.Sgt. John Teal, as well as pararescuemen M.Sgt. Mike Maltz and SrA Jason Plite. Once each of them had been eulogized by a colleague, and the formal service ended with the playing of "Taps," an informal ritual began. Hundreds of people lined up to walk silently and alone to a makeshift shrine at the front of the hangar, behind which stood a large portrait of each of the deceased, and upon which were symbols of their profession—an aircrew helmet, a maroon PJ beret. On the table, or in baskets in front of it, the mourners left a gift. Women most often placed a single white rose in the basket, while those in uniform or wearing flight suits would remove one of their unit patches, or in the case of the PJs, the metal "flash" from their berets, and leave it front of their buddies' photos. The procession to the front of the hangar lasted nearly an hour.

Later that evening, more than a hundred men and women—aircrew, PJs, wives, friends, even groupies—showed up at the home shared by PJs Soup Campbell and Ben Harris for a traditional PJ wake. The invitation said, *Come send off our fallen brothers! Celebrate their lives PJ style tonight after the memorial service! So bring great stories and your drinking boots!*

Jews sit *shiva*, a seven-day mourning period that begins after the burial. Catholics have somber wakes before a burial and feast afterward. Mourning rituals have evolved to suit the ethos and needs of the particular group involved. In the case of the pararescuemen and the CSAR aircrews, the wake following the official memorial service was not a time for tears, but for the kind of laughter that hides the pain. There would be time for tears in the days ahead, when many of those in attendance would be called upon to serve as pallbearers at the funerals of their colleagues.

Soup Campbell called the ritual toasting a "PJ roast." And while some, like helicopter pilot Maj. Chas Tachney, were respectful as he raised a bottle of bourbon and toasted the flying skill and demanding standards of Lieutenant Colonel Stein, others told stories that ranged from ribald to riotous. SrA Jason Plite was remembered as a chick magnet, able to walk off with women who had already committed to spending an evening with one of his fellow PJs. M.Sgt. Mike Maltz, who had a reputation as a workout fanatic who often finished his sessions in the gym by pummeling the heavy bag, then knocking it off its moorings and sending it flying, was lionized as the scourge of PJ trainees. One younger pararescueman told the story of going to breakfast at four in the morning with several other trainees. They were not supposed to be talking as they walked from dormitory to the dining hall, but often did. One morning, as they were chattering away, they heard a strange noise. A rope came flying off the roof of the building they were passing, and Maltzy came rappeling down, shouting that he'd caught them talking, and ordering them to drop and start pumping out push-ups. Earlier, someone had shown a video of Maltz doing an inspection of dormitory rooms, finding things unsatisfactory, and throwing everything in the room including the mattress out the window to the ground below. At the end of every bit of testimony, the bottle would be raised, a healthy swig taken, and the assembled crowd shouted a lusty, "Hooyah!"

Among those at the roast was Sr.M.Sgt. Bill Sine, who'd won the Distinguished Flying Cross for his jump mission to the minefield in Afghanistan. In early 2003, Sine put in the paperwork for retirement, ending a twenty-eight-year career as a pararescueman.

A number of the pararescuemen who had served in Operation Enduring Freedom, as well as elements of the 71st Rescue Squadron (HC-130) and 41st and 66th Rescue Squadrons (HH-60G), were reassigned to bases in the Middle East in support of Operation Iraqi Freedom. By the day Saddam's statue in Baghdad was toppled, Air Combat Command PJs had been credited with "emergency exfils" of compromised ground teams, saving fourteen soldiers; they'd rescued two Navy pilots who ejected over the Iraqi desert after the engine on their F-14 Tomcat strike fighter failed; and they'd done two severe casualty evacuations. ACC PJs flew numerous other missions which, at this writing, they're not permitted to discuss.

Pararescuemen belonging to the supersecret 24th Special Tactics Squadron out of Pope Air Base, North Carolina, were part of the special operations force that rescued Army POW Jessica Lynch from an Iraqi hospital.

As the one-year anniversary of the death of Jason Cunningham approached, Barbara Tyler, wife of Maj. Don Tyler, wrote a letter to Jason's mom.

*Dear Jackie,*

*It has been nearly a year since Jason passed and I just wanted you to know that he is still in our prayers and thoughts daily. Our family remembers him and continues to be grateful to him. We also remember you, his girls, Theresa, and his siblings. We think of your loss and we pray for all of you.*

*Don has finally retired from active duty. He continues his physical therapy. Although his shoulder will never fully recover we are happy he was able to retire and begin a new phase of his life.*

*It's important that you know our children will always remember what Jason did for their dad on that cold mountainside. They will pass that on to their children. Jason's life has affected them and he will be remembered for many years to come.*

*We are deeply grateful to all of you.*

*Barbara*

I asked Barbara Tyler to tell me how life had changed for her family in the year since Don was injured in the Ditka 03 crash in Afghanistan. This is what she had to say:

*Dear Mike,*

*Don retired from the Air Force on 1 Dec 2002. We celebrated his retirement at Disney Orlando as a family. First his injury, the quality of his life has been greatly limited by this injury. I have known Don my entire life and never do I remember him not being a "jock." He has always jogged (almost daily), played sports like golf, tennis, basketball. He no longer golfs (a big passion of his); he can't throw the ball up to serve in tennis. He has constant stiffness and pain in his shoulder and occasional pain in his knee. This has impacted his enjoyment in life greatly. It's very difficult for me to watch him struggle; a few weeks ago I saw him try to trim a limb off a tree and he just kept struggling because it was over his head. Watching things like that makes me so sad; it's painful to watch him do his therapy and work so hard to do things that were once very easy for him. I'm heartbroken to see him struggle and to know that his pleasures in life are now difficult and painful. There isn't much I wouldn't give to see him free of pain and discomfort and able to enjoy the pleasures of his life, like golfing.*

*As for our family, yes, you do "get over" something like this. It's a long time of healing. We all miss how things used to be. Even something as simple as a hug is now different for all of us. Time will hopefully help us all heal and have full acceptance of Don's limitations. On the upside, we often remember just how blessed we are to have Don here with us. A few weeks ago the Lotto was $50 million and my daughter and I were talking about it. I told her I would buy a ticket or two, but I said to her "We already had our Lotto; I think you only get one in your lifetime." She agreed. It's still pretty emotional for all of us. Don has just completed a year of physical therapy. Through sheer determination he has gone further than it was ever expected, but he was deeply disappointed that he didn't recover more use of his arm.*

*We didn't celebrate the anniversary of the crash. We were home as a family. Earlier in the day I stopped to see George's wife. The minute she saw me she began to cry. I was concerned about her because George is back in the theater again. I was quite unnerved on that day. A year earlier I was as tough as nails. I had two kids looking to me to show them I wasn't afraid and that everything would be okay. I also had to set the "tone" with our extended family and friends. Then when Don came home I stayed very strong because he needed someone to carry the ball. I didn't really let myself become emotional about all of this until the fall of 2002. So on the anniversary I was angry, sad, grateful, and blessed. All those emotions at the same time. I would be lying if I said we are only grateful and blessed; however, I hang on to those the most. We thought of Jason as we do every day, and said a prayer of thanks to him. Don, on the other hand, was probably more concerned with my reaction to that day; for him, as he said, "I live with that accident every day. I don't need a calendar to remind me."*

*Today Don is working with a defense contractor. We have secured a builder and we should be breaking ground on our new home within days. The children continue to grow and are well. Life does not stop. We still have tae kwon do, track, riding lessons, work, school, church, homework. Life goes on; it's just different. It's also lived with more gratitude, more love, and a dash of sadness.*

*Barbara*

*   *   *

*Rob's been shot.*

That was the subject of an e-mail one night in mid-April. My heart sank. Rob is Air Force pararescueman Rob Disney, a twenty-five-year-old staff sergeant I'd gotten to know during late-night cigar-smoking sessions outside the HAS at Jacobabad, Pakistan. I'd stayed in touch with Rob, and at his request had called his parents, Barbara and Bob Disney, in Bethany, Illinois, when I returned home from the war zone. The e-mail was from his mother. She had some details; I dug up others.

Rob and two other PJs, along with an American special-ops team, had been aboard a Russian-built troop-transport helicopter flying in the tribal area of southern Pakistan, somewhere between Jbad and the Afghan border. An Australian news report said they were on a mission to survey gas pipelines.

Rob says they were going out to do some "land navigation and GPS training." The area is one to which thousands of Taliban are thought to have fled from Afghanistan. Desolate though it may be, it's a refuge for Al Qaeda and Taliban because the Pakistanis won't permit American troops to cross their border from Afghanistan in pursuit.

The helicopter was flying with the rear clamshell doors removed. Disney was sitting on the ramp, tied in with his three-foot-long cowstail tether, as they came in to land. About fifty feet above the ground he heard a pop that sounded like a flare being discharged. He turned around and looked into the cabin and saw that everybody's eyes "were really big." Apparently, they'd flown right into an ambush.

"Everybody on board was looking at me, and I yelled, 'Hey!' and I grabbed my weapon and I put it on my shoulder and charged it. And while I was looking at them, I got hit." The AK-47 round entered the back of his neck and knocked his sunglasses off as it came out his face, to the right and below his right eye. At almost the same time, a second bullet shattered the forearm of PJ Craig Fitzgerald, who had been seated to Disney's right, lodging in his chest. Another round slammed into the body armor of the American flight engineer, bounced off, and lodged in his arm.

Shouting, "I'm hit," and bleeding like a stuck pig from a wound that had left cheekbone, nerves, and muscle tissue exposed, Disney jammed the stock of his rifle against the gash to establish a cheek-weld so he could begin returning fire, and dropped to the floor of the helicopter because he expected it to crash—he'd already been in one helicopter crash and knew that getting onto the floor would minimize the chance that he'd be thrown around upon impact.

Experiencing a rapid amount of blood loss, he began to feel funny, and he thought to himself, "So this is what it feels like to die." When he recognized that the crash hadn't happened and the helicopter was gaining altitude, he put his weapon on safe, flung it aside, and began stripping off his combat gear so he could check himself out. That's when he saw his right leg covered in blood, yet it didn't dawn on him that it was his own. He was certain that someone else had taken a round.

"I did a head-to-toe on myself and I found my own open wound. I pressed my hand to it, and at that moment Ross [PJ Ross Funches, a former Army Ranger] came to me and I told him I'd been shot in the face—I didn't realize I'd been shot in the neck.

"He said, 'You're not that bad, Diz, you're not that bad.' He grabbed a Ker-lex bandage out of my ruck and put it on my face and I continued to hold pressure on it." Funches went back to continue treating Fitzgerald and the flight engineer, while Disney, obviously agitated, moved from seat to floor and back again, trying to find a comfortable position. Finally, he ended up on the floor, his legs elevated to prevent shock. Funches started an IV, and a lieutenant colonel on board held the IV while giving Diz sips of water from his Camelbak. "Water was all I wanted in the whole world." During the half hour flight back to Jacobabad, Funches administered two units of blood to Fitzgerald.

At some point during the flight, Disney decided that he wasn't going to die. Lying on the floor, he momentarily closed his eyes, and recalls that Funches looked over at him, saw his eyes closed, and screamed, "DIZ!"

"I looked at Ross, saw blood all over his face, and yelled, 'I'm fine. It's okay.' He said, "Don't fuckin' do that. I love you, man.' He was awesome. He triaged, treated, packaged ready-to-go three patients with what looked like critical injuries in thirty minutes' time."

As soon as the helicopter landed, Funches ran off and began shouting for people to come help. Two people got Rob to his feet and he was able to walk off, aware of his surroundings enough to actually snap a salute to the shocked base commander. As they put Rob in a Humvee, he told the waiting flight surgeon that he needed morphine, blood, and antibiotics, "And I need it now!" (You've probably figured out if you've read this far that PJs have control issues.)

All three casualties were medevacked to Al Uedid Air Base, Qatar, where the pararescuemen based there for Operation Iraqi Freedom immediately swarmed them. One of the first doctors to see them was told that the casualties were PJs, and he leaned over Disney, took a look, and then turned to the medical team and shouted, "Hey, everybody, listen up. This is high-priced real estate. Let's take good care of 'em." Disney says, "I needed to hear that."

The first phone call that Rob's folks received from Lt. Col. Vinnie Savino, the commander of the 38th Rescue Squadron, marked the beginning of three days of agony for them. While Savino kept in touch to tell them when Rob was moved to Qatar, and from there to Landstuhl Regional Medical Center in Germany, specific information on the damage to his face and his prognosis wasn't available. And the promised phone call from Rob himself didn't come as quickly as they'd hoped.

But at three-thirty in the morning the day after Easter Sunday, the phone rang in the Disney home. It was Rob calling from Landstuhl with what only a

PJ could describe as "good news." The bullet had missed his spinal column by little more than a centimeter. Surgeons had to make a two-and-one-half-inch incision from his ear lobe to his eye, and another of similar length on the front of his neck to look for internal damage. Miraculously, aside from fractured cartilage in his outer ear canal, the bullet hit nothing but soft tissue. Doctors said that bruised facial nerves were causing his face to droop, but they expected that to clear up as the swelling subsided. Disney and Fitzgerald were ultimately medevacked to the States, with Rob going to Walter Reed Army Medical Center and Craig to a military hospital near San Antonio.

Barb Disney said, "I am so very relieved. It is truly a miracle, of that I have no doubt. We were prepared to expect the very worst, with horrific damage to his face, and very long recovery time. A multitude of prayers were answered."

Aside from splitting headaches and pain when he chews, Disney told his parents in the call from Landstuhl that he was fine, adding that the psychiatrist who examined him didn't believe him. She claimed his coping skills were abnormal, that he needed to seek professional counseling when he got home. Apparently, most folks who take a bullet to the head in an ambush—a bullet that missed killing them by mere inches—don't walk around saying it's no big deal. It's a good bet the shrink had never dealt with PJs before.

# In Memoriam

~

Dedicated to the memory of those who have
died in Operation Enduring Freedom,
*"So That Others May Live"*

**Pararescuemen**
M.Sgt. Michael Maltz
M.Sgt. William L. McDaniel II
S.Sgt. Juan Ridout
SrA Jason Cunningham
SrA Jason Plite

**CSAR HH-60G "Komodo 11" Aircrew**
Lt. Col. John Stein
Capt. (Select) Tamara Archuleta
S.Sgt. Jason Hicks
S.Sgt. John Teal

**Combat Controller**
T.Sgt. John A. Chapman

# INDEX